EDUCATION, RELIGION AND DIVERSITY

The challenge of diversity is central to education in modern liberal democratic states. Religious education is often the point where difference becomes most acute, but is also believed to be the most likely curriculum subject in which resolutions to the challenge could be found.

Education, Religion and Diversity identifies and explores the commitments and convictions that have guided post-confessional religious education and concludes controversially that the subject as currently theorised and practised is incapable either of challenging religious intolerance or of developing respectful relationships between people from different communities and groups within society.

It is argued that despite the rhetoric of success, which those involved with religious education are obliged to rehearse in order to perpetuate its status in the curriculum and to ensure political support, a fundamentally new model of religious education is required to meet the challenge of diversity to education and to society. A new framework for religious education is developed which offers the potential for the subject to make a genuine contribution to the creation of a responsible, respectful society.

Education, Religion and Diversity is a wide-ranging, provocative exploration of religious education in modern liberal democracies. It is essential reading for those concerned with the role of religion in education and for religious and theological educators who want to think critically about the aims and character of religious education.

L. Philip Barnes is Reader in Religious and Theological Education at King's College London, UK.

EDUCATION, RELIGION AND DIVERSITY

Developing a new model of
religious education

L. Philip Barnes

Routledge
Taylor & Francis Group

LONDON AND NEW YORK

First published 2014
by Routledge
2 Park Square, Milton Park, Abingdon, Oxon OX14 4RN

and by Routledge
711 Third Avenue, New York, NY 10017

Routledge is an imprint of the Taylor & Francis Group, an informa business

© 2014 L. P. Barnes

British Library Cataloguing in Publication Data
A catalogue record for this book is available from the British Library

Library of Congress Cataloging in Publication Data
Barnes, Phillip (L. Philip)
Education, religion and diversity : developing a new model of religious
education / L. Philip Barnes.
    pages cm
1. Religious education.   2. Religious education—Great Britain.   I. Title.
BV1471.3.B37 2014
200.71—dc23

2013035420

ISBN: 978–0–415–74158–3 (hbk)
ISBN: 978–0–415–74159–0 (pbk)
ISBN: 978–1–315–81522–0 (ebk)

Typeset in Bembo
by RefineCatch Limited, Bungay, Suffolk

CONTENTS

PREFACE

This book brings together and gives final form to ideas expressed in articles and papers over the last six years or so. Much of the material has been shared at conferences and presented in talks and lectures to various university audiences, chiefly in Australia, Germany, the United States of America, and in the United Kingdom and Ireland. I am particularly grateful to Professor Ulrich Schwab for the invitation to join him in delivering a lecture series on the implications of religious diversity for religious education at the University of Munich in 2003, which acted as a stimulus to clarify my position and to reflect on British educational responses to increasing moral and religious diversity in society. More recently, I am grateful to Professor Bernd Schröder for his invitation to contribute a public lecture on 'Religious Education in England' to a series entitled *Religionsunterricht wohin? Konflikte – Modelle – Perspektiven* and for the opportunity to engage with students in seminars at the University of Göttingen, in June 2013.

Three colleagues at King's College London deserve special mention: Reverend Professor Alister McGrath and Professor Chris Winch, who in their professional capacities facilitated my research and writing in various ways; and Professor Andrew Wright, with whom I have discussed many of the ideas expressed here in the context of our work together (along with Professor McGrath) within the Centre for Theology, Religion and Culture at King's.

At a personal level I wish to express my thanks and love to my wife, Sandra, who has supported me and been my faithful companion over thirty years of marriage. The joy of research and writing would be greatly diminished without the knowledge that more social pleasures await. I am also grateful for the support of our children, Andrew, Rachel and Christopher. Finally, I wish to thank my mother, who has lived long and has seen her encouragement of my education and studies at last bearing some modest fruit.

INTRODUCTION

The commonly recited narrative of modern British religious education, at least among professional religious educators (as in Bates 1992; O'Grady 2005), is of confessionalism (in the form of Christian religious nurture) giving way to neutrality, commitment to professionalism, and indoctrination to education. It is a tale of progress and the triumph of reason over unreason. Tradition records how 'closed' religious education came to be replaced by 'open' religious education, and how sectarian attitudes were superseded by enlightened ones. According to its supporters, British religious education advances on a trajectory of increasing reasonableness and successfulness, constrained only by a shortage of funds that prevents the full and speedy translation of its aims and commitments into reality. This is the view endorsed by the Religious Education Council of England and Wales, which in March 2007 petitioned the government for £60 million to implement and develop existing policies (see RE Council 2007: 12–14). In truth, as a number of writers have pointed out (Copley 2005; Thompson 2004), the story is more controversial, contested, convoluted and ideological, resulting in educational losses as well as educational gains.

There is mounting evidence that British religious education has not been particularly successful in either engaging the interest of pupils or preparing them to live respectfully and responsibly amidst moral and religious diversity. It is this second issue that poses the greatest challenge to contemporary educators, and to religious educators in particular. Diversity in Britain, as in most countries of Western Europe, is growing. Continuing immigration, social policies and appeals to human rights that protect and accentuate individual choice over established traditions and social customs, reasonably high levels of disposable income that enlarge the range of lifestyles choices that are accessible to individuals, and the decline of religion as an instrument of social and moral conformity have all contributed to an increase in moral and religious diversity. Yet it has become increasingly clear that current, inherited ways of conceptualising the nature and practice of religious education are limited in their application and incapable of meeting the challenge posed. Commitments and methodologies that served British religious education well during the 1970s in effecting a shift from confessional Christian education in state maintained schools to non-confessional education are revealing themselves to be ill-equipped to develop the kind of skills and virtues that are necessary to prepare pupils for life in a democratic society that is characterised not only by religious and moral diversity but also by a propensity for distrust and segregation between communities.

That rich vein of intellectual thought that gave impetus to non-confessional religious education has been exhausted. Much religious education in Britain remains in thrall to assumptions, beliefs and practices that are incapable of furthering liberal educational aims and contributing to the common good, yet nervous of any development that challenges earlier oppositions. Religious education is also unacknowledging of its role in segregating communities by pursuing a form of education that fails to meet the needs of minority religious communities, while simultaneously misrepresenting their religious commitments; thus tacitly encouraging them to build and manage their own schools and implement their own forms of religious education. In the ten years to 2013, eleven Muslim schools, three Sikh, one Hindu, one Greek Orthodox and one Seventh Day Adventist have been granted public funding (Bolton and Gillie 2009). Outside the maintained sector, there are over 950 religious independent schools (40 per cent of all independent schools); four-fifths of these are Christian and one-eighth Muslim, again figures that have grown significantly in the first decade of the twenty-first century. The existence of these schools constitutes visible evidence that state ('community') schools that are by intention and statute meant to be inclusive of community diversity are perceived by some parents as hostile to pupils with 'orthodox' religious convictions; and religious education is part of the problem.

The aim of this book is both to review the current theoretical models that underwrite teaching and learning in modern British religion and to introduce a new model, which while incorporating the strengths of former models is better equipped to meet the needs of society and of pupils. Ambitiously, a positive attempt is made to give coherent form to a new, integrated set of beliefs, pedagogical commitments, assumptions and values that will direct the practice of religious education and enable it to fulfil its educational potential. A new framework is required to structure, justify and direct this practice in Britain.

The virtues of a new, more self-critical approach to religious education in schools, however, can only be appreciated if we are familiar with the inadequacies of the old and its inherent limitations, and recognise the potential of the new to succeed where the old has failed. This means that much of our discussion will focus on exploring the commitments and the inherent weaknesses of religious education in Britain and on identifying their historical origins. Current ways of theorising and conceptualising religious education are deeply entrenched. The remark (paraphrasing the words of George Santayana) that those who do not remember their past are condemned to repeat their mistakes has a clear application to the field of religious education. For some religious educators the historical narrative of modern religious education is one of unbridled success and rational progress, a perception that gives little encouragement to retrospective reflection; for others, the historical narrative is a simple recitation of events, debates and personalities, each event completely explicable in terms of its immediate cause. Both approaches are insufficiently critical, neither is attentive to the influence of historically extended and deeper intellectual movements or to the assumptions, beliefs and values that have shaped and continue to shape contemporary theory and practice.

Part of the inspiration for the development of a critical account of religious education is to show the fruitfulness of an interpretation that interacts seriously with the intellectual and social context in which religious education is set, for it is only when this wider context of religious education is appreciated that particular debates and individual contributions can be properly understood and assessed. To use a geographical analogy: the intention is not to move along the surface explaining each particular topographical phenomenon in turn, but rather to explain surface topography in terms of wider, more fundamental geological processes operating above and below the earth's surface. The present landscape is fully explicable only in terms of historically extended tectonic and geo-morphological processes whose influence on the surface is not always obvious. Similarly, the present 'landscape' of religious education is fully explicable only in terms of wider and deeper intellectual and social movements that have exerted their influence over time (albeit much less extended than in the case of geological processes). Acquaintance with the underlying principles of change and development provides the key to explaining 'surface' phenomena and potentially opens the door to a more critical and discerning reading of the landscape.

It follows from this that no attempt is made to provide a comprehensive account of evolving events and debates in religious education; such accounts are available elsewhere (see Copley 2008; Barnes 2012). Instead influences and patterns are identified and then traced back to more fundamental assumptions and value commitments. The perspective pursued here is critical, interpretive and genealogical/archaeological, concerned chiefly with ideas and beliefs; historical only in the sense that ideas and influences are traced through their historical succession. The modern history of religious education is pursued for its deeper meaning, its unstated assumptions, and its underlying configurations of thought that guide the institutional practice of religious education in schools. Moreover, the focus falls on the ideas and beliefs that relate to the issue of diversity. Ideas, policies and influences that have little or no bearing on the matter of diversity and how religious education engages with and responds to diversity will for the most part be overlooked. Attention is given to the ways in which different theories conceptualise diversity, privilege some methodologies over others, and condition what goes on in classrooms – though the extent to which classroom practice faithfully reflects particular theoretical commitments and stances is an empirical matter and not one considered here (but one which I, along with others, have considered elsewhere, see Conroy *et al.* 2013). It may be acknowledged that theory is sometimes inadequately translated into practice, or inconsistently applied, or much less influential in classrooms than one might have anticipated from attention to scholarly and academic discussions. In addition, classroom practices and methodologies do not always follow deductively from theoretical commitments. The reality of the classroom confounds much of our philosophising. Acknowledging this does not detract from the reality and priority of beliefs and theoretical commitments over classroom practice in religious education or from the fruitfulness of the largely theoretical perspective that is pursued here in relation to the issue of assessing the contribution of religious education in Britain to challenging religious intolerance and effecting better relationships between different communities.

Education is necessarily contextual, for it is conditioned by its national setting – a distinctive political history, a particular legislative framework, contrasting political and social groupings, and so on. Religious education is no exception to this, and to the list of factors that influence education can be added others that apply more particularly to religious education: the demographics of *religious* change, the historical role of religious involvement in education and different patterns of secularisation, for example. One cannot talk about religious education in the abstract but only about particular forms of religious education, and these forms differ greatly from country to country. This initially suggests that an analysis of the nature of religious education in one jurisdiction, which if it is to be convincing must be fine-grained and detailed, will be largely irrelevant to other national contexts. This is not the case, however, with Britain, for a number of reasons.

First, in the last fifty years British religious educators have been widely influential internationally, particularly in the English speaking world (e.g. Australia, New Zealand and the United States of America) but also in such countries as Turkey and Russia. The writings of Ninian Smart, Michael Grimmitt, John Hull, Robert Jackson and Andrew Wright are well known and discussed internationally. Their ideas have inspired curriculum policy and practice in numerous countries. More recently, closer co-operation between the countries of the European Union has seen British religious educators taking the lead in initiating joint curriculum projects and in bringing their ideas to European audiences (see Jackson 2011 and 2012). Second, and closely related to the previous point, the English language has increasingly become the language of international communication, thus the writings of British religious educators are widely accessible and influential in a way denied to those who do not write in English. Third, a growing commitment to human rights and to legislation that embodies appeals to rights means that a common framework has been provided for European and international co-operation and agreement across a range of issues, including education and religious education: the 'Toledo Guiding Principles on

Teaching about Religions and Beliefs in Public Schools' (ODIHR 2007) is the fruit of one such European initiative. Finally, whatever differences obtain between national education systems, they are increasingly subject to the same social influences and forces: secularisation, urbanisation, the impact of globalisation and global capitalism, the privatising of religion, individualisation, and of course multiculturalism and its associated moral and religious diversity.

Accommodating diversity through developing strategies to challenge intolerance and to effect positive relationships between different communities is one of the biggest challenges facing education systems and educational institutions in different countries. There is much to be learned at an international level from a careful consideration of the response and initiatives of British religious educators to the challenge of increasing diversity in society and how to build respectful relationships between individuals and between communities. In fact the next chapter gives careful consideration to (and raises objections to) the not uncommon refrain of British religious educators that British religious education provides a model for other countries to emulate.

Thomas Kuhn, paradigms and revolutions

It is commonplace for scientists to speak of different models or paradigms, by which they mean different sets of assumptions and commitments (epistemic and otherwise) that interpret and explain nature and account for scientific progress – as one model gives way to another. Much of the inspiration for this way of thinking about the nature of science is indebted to Thomas Kuhn's *The Structure of Scientific Revolutions* (1970). In it Kuhn described the process of scientific achievement in terms of the transition from one conceptual paradigm or model to another. As the title of the book indicates, Kuhn was interested in what he called 'scientific revolutions'; that is, the process by which one set of scientific ideas is replaced by a radically different (new) set of scientific ideas. Examples in science are the Copernican revolution in astronomy; the Einsteinian revolution in physics that replaced Newtonian mechanics with quantum mechanics; and the Darwinian revolution in biology. Each of these revolutions led to a fundamental change in the existing scientific world view: one set of (determining) beliefs gave way to another. In the second edition of his book, and largely in response to critics who alleged that he used the term too promiscuously (see Masterman 1970: 61), Kuhn stated that a paradigm consists of 'a network of commitments – conceptual, theoretical, instrumental, and methodological' (Kuhn 1970: 42). In later writings he identified two aspects of scientific activity that the term 'paradigm' was intended to capture (Kuhn 1977). First of all the notion of a paradigm refers to a past scientific success that serves to exemplify the nature of the scientific enterprise and thus conceptualises 'normal science'. Second, he used the term paradigm in a broader sense to denote the common assumptions and commitments that unite a particular group of scientists and regulate their experiments. In this sense, a paradigm is a 'disciplinary matrix' that defines what counts as scientific knowledge, guides and directs scientific research, and generates expectations concerning the results of new experiments or research.

Kuhn's notion of a paradigm or model has been widely influential beyond his original use of it to describe the nature of science and of scientific enquiry. The term has come to be used more widely for any broad ranging and integrated set of beliefs, assumptions and values that structures theorising and practice within a particular discipline or field of enquiry. In this wider sense, the language and the associated understanding of models, paradigm shifts and even crisis-states are illuminative of the intellectual and social history of religious education in Britain, which, since the end of the Second World War has been dominated by contrasting and competing disciplinary models that have determined its nature and practice.

What are these broadly successive sets of beliefs and values? One can identify a confessional model that enjoyed dominance in state schools up until the late 1960s and early 1970s. This model still endures, particularly in Catholic schools, and has recently received new impetus with the creation of state funded Muslim schools, but confessionalism is no longer regarded as appropriate to state schools that are intended to cater for all pupils (for convenience, these may be referred to as 'common' schools). Confessional religious education gave way to non-confessional religious education. It would have made for easier comprehension and a simpler narrative if the subsequent history of non-confessional religious education in Britain was explicable in terms of commitment to a single, educationally dominant non-confessional model. Indeed from the 1970s until the 1990s one particular model of religious education did enjoy dominance in common schools, and still enjoys influence up to the present. This model was indebted to and determined by liberal theological commitments and values, and for this reason it may be characterised as a *liberal* model of religious education (naturally what this means will be the subject of later analysis and discussion). Since the 1990s, however, this liberal model has been competing with a further distinguishable model of non-confessional religious education, this time a model that is strongly influenced by postmodern accents and commitments – a *postmodern* model of religious education. In some respects the current situation in religious education is what Kuhn would describe as 'a period of crisis', as a liberal model of religious education vies with a postmodern model for educational dominance. On a more critical note, the position pursued here is that neither a liberal model nor a postmodern model, as currently configured (or any combination of the two), is capable of meeting the challenges posed by diversity in society to education and schools. A different model of religious education is required that instantiates different foundational beliefs and values.

The task ahead

Our discussion will be structured in the following way. In Chapter 1 close attention is given to the increasingly vocal expressions of successfulness that accompany the practice of religious education in schools in England and Wales. Such claims are critically examined, alongside an account of the reasons why official representatives of the institutions and associations of religious education are so vociferous in their praise for contemporary religious education and so reluctant to criticise it publicly. The chapter concludes with an overview of empirical evidence that suggests that religious education is failing to motivate pupils and in all probability is contributing little to their moral and social development. Chapters 2 and 3 explore and analyse the notion of diversity in society, chiefly using the tools of sociological analysis. Attention is given to the demographics of diversity in Britain; to the changing character of diversity in society alongside changing *perceptions* of the character of this diversity, and to the specific nature of the challenges posed by diversity to society and schools. Chapter 4 turns explicitly to the subject of religious education and lays the foundation for what follows by providing a short overview of confessional religious education in Britain. It is not necessary for our purposes to delve deeply into the institutional history of the confessional model, but it is important to grasp something of its history and character in order to appreciate more fully the nature of the contrast between it and that which succeeded it, namely non-confessional religious education. A fundamental opposition between confessional and non-confessional religious education is foundational to modern British religious education and to much educational theorising.

Chapters 5 to 10, in one way or another, are concerned with the liberal model of religious education and the various forms and methodologies in which it is expressed. Chapter 5 reviews the contribution of Ninian Smart to religious education and his advocacy of a phenomenological approach in *Working Paper 36: Religious Education in the Secondary School* (1971). The focus of Chapter 6 falls on exploring and explaining the commitments and axioms of the phenomenology of religion as these are expressed and developed by prominent and influential representatives. Chapter 7 traces the translation of the methodology and commitments of the phenomenology of religion into the idiom of religious education, chiefly in the form of the phenomenological approach, but also in the form of experiential religious education and recent educational accounts of spirituality and spiritual development. Chapter 8 moves beyond analysis and begins to engage in criticism of the central epistemological tenets of the phenomenological approach to religion and its distinctive interpretation of religion. This criticism naturally invites questions about the nature of religion and how religion is to be interpreted and represented within religious education; consequently, the chapter concludes with a positive constructive response to these questions. Chapter 9 seeks to identify and analyse the central beliefs and commitments of the liberal model of religious education, that is, the beliefs and commitments that are foundational not just to phenomenological religious education and the experiential approach but to all forms of the liberal paradigm. This is done chiefly through a close analysis and review of the work and writings of the influential religious educator John Hull. The position of Hull is then compared with Enlightenment interpretations of religions in order to identify similarities and dependence. Chapter 10 concludes discussion of the liberal model of religious education by providing a detailed critique of its central commitments and explaining why it is conceptually incapable of challenging intolerance and contributing to the social and moral aims of liberal education.

The focus shifts from the modern model of religious education to a postmodern model in Chapters 11 to 13. Chapter 11 provides an overview of the nature and commitments of postmodern thinking, and equips us to recognise its influence in religious education. In Chapter 12 Robert Jackson's interpretive approach is identified with a postmodern model and a detailed account of it is given. Chapter 13 assesses the strengths and weaknesses of an interpretive approach, particularly with regard to its representation of the nature of religion and to its effectiveness in challenging cultural and religious prejudice.

The important relationship of religious education to moral education is considered in Chapter 14. A case is made for reconnecting religious education with moral education and for education to take advantage of the potential that religious conceptions of morality bring to the moral development of pupils and to the social development of communities.

Chapter 15 draws the threads of the argument together and outlines the beliefs and commitments of a new post-liberal model of religious education. This new integrated set of beliefs, commitments and values is intended to enable religious education to make a positive contribution to the creation of a tolerant, cohesive society where people are respectful of each other and responsible socially.

It may be acknowledged that there is a negative quality to much of what is said and this will be unwelcome to some, particularly to those who extol the virtues of current provision in British religious education and those who enjoy power and prestige as a result of professional and academic influence. The issue is not about personalities and reputations: it is about developing strategies and policies that will enable religious education to fulfil its potential to advance the causes of social inclusion and respectful relationships between individuals from different communities and religions. This potential will be realised, however, only when educators fully acknowledge the 'intractable' nature of religious difference and implement strategies and policies that predicate respect for others on personhood rather than on either theological assumptions about the essential agreement between religions or on deconstructive strategies that effectively evacuate religions of their normative force and appeal.

A note on terminology

The term 'British' religious education is used to draw attention to ideas and influences that are common across religious education in the three nations of England, Scotland and Wales, though it may be conceded that some of the ideas considered and criticised in what follows are more characteristic of English religious education and educators than of the Scottish or Welsh. At no stage is credence given to the idea that religious education is uniform across Britain: it is acknowledged that there are differences as well as similarities between religious education in England, Scotland and Wales.

1

THE RHETORIC OF SUCCESS AND THE REALITY OF UNDERACHIEVEMENT IN BRITISH RELIGIOUS EDUCATION

Defences of the existing *status quo* in British religious education are increasingly strained and unconvincing, yet, ironically, they are increasingly vocal, no doubt a reaction, in part, to increasing criticism.

The rhetoric of success

In the January 2005 issue of the *British Journal of Religious Education*, Professor John Hull recommended the British model of 'neutral and secular' religious education as appropriate to the German situation and characterised an alternative 'dialogical' model, which allows for an element of Christian nurture in education, as an 'interim' solution on the way to open, multi-faith religious education of the form practised in Britain (Hull 2005). The logic of Hull's position is clear: as countries become more conscious of internal moral and religious diversity, so they will come to appreciate the strengths of the British version of multi-faith religious education as the model best equipped to secure in pupils the values of toleration, moral integrity and civic virtue (Hull 2005: 8–10). Indeed the view that other countries can learn positively from the example of Britain has been a common refrain in recent years. Brian Gates, speaking at the annual conference of the Association of RE Advisers, Inspectors and Consultants in July 2006, stated that 'RE in this country has never had it so good; no wonder that we are viewed by our continental European colleagues as in an enviable position' (Gates 2007: 5). John Keast (2006: 15) expresses a similar opinion:

> RE in much of the UK is in a good position to help other parts of Europe
> . . . RE of the kind needed across Europe is being articulated and provided
> in the UK.

The theme that Britain leads Europe in terms of achievement in religious education is also voiced by Bill Gent (2009: 3), though he purports to be reporting the view of Continental educators:

> In its experience of integrating religious education into the public education system, many European educators, it is said, see Britain as a trail-blazer.

In the same edition of the journal from which the quotation by Gent is taken, Joyce Miller (2009: 6) speaks of Britain as a 'world leader in religious education in public schools', a view echoed by the Religious Education Council of England and Wales (RE Council; www.religiouseducationcouncil.org) in a publicity leaflet that states that 'RE in British schools is admired across the world'; and affirmed again by Denise Cush on behalf of the Association of University Lecturers in Religion and Education (AULRE) in an open letter to Michael Gove, the Secretary of State for Education:

> . . . there is one subject [i.e. religious education] in which England is recognised to be a world-leader . . . The role of AULRE in linking research with classroom practice enables us to be aware of the high prestige in which English religious education is held around the world.
>
> *Cush, 6 December, 2010; published on the*
> *aulre.org website on 8 December 2010*

It would be unwise to take these statements at face value and to fail to recognise the apologetic and ideological purposes that they are intended to serve (or the constituencies they are intended to impress). A closer examination of them should caution against an over-optimistic view of the achievements of British religious education or of the esteem in which it is held by religious educators elsewhere. The conclusion that British religious education is the envy of Europe would be better justified by reference to European educators expressing their admiration and emulating our policies than for proponents of British religious education to inform us of how widely *their* achievements are recognised. Apart from the *British Journal of Religious Education* (in which Hull extolled 'neutral and secular' religious education to Germans), which attracts an international readership, the above quotations are taken from national sources intended to serve a national readership. British religious educators are being informed by British religious educators that their philosophy of religious education and their practice are the envy of Europe! Moreover, some of the writers who are commending British religious education have been instrumental in shaping and directing recent policy in relation to religious education in Britain. Brian Gates, for example, was until recently Chair of the RE Council, which represents the collective interests of a wide variety of professional associations and faith communities in religious education; John Keast is a former Principal Officer with responsibility for religious education at the Qualifications and Curriculum

Authority (QCA) and current Chair of the RE Council. It was under his direction that the *Non-Statutory National Framework for Religious Education* (QCA 2004) was produced – and it is the policies advocated in this document that he believes equip British religious education to help other parts of Europe (Keast 2006: 15). Both men have been highly influential and both men have seen their ideas officially endorsed. The other three individuals quoted, Bill Gent, Joyce Miller and Denise Cush, are respectively the current and the past editor of *Resource* (the journal of the National Association of Teachers of Religious Education) and the Chair of the Association of University Lecturers in Religion and Education: none of the three could be described as an entirely disinterested observer of religious education in Britain.

Interestingly, the article in which Hull commended the British version of multi-faith religious education to an international audience drew a sharp retort from Friedrich Schweitzer of the University of Tübingen. According to him, 'the British model [of religious education] does not make sense for Germany' (Schweitzer 2006: 149). Schweitzer raises a number of objections to the assumptions and commitments of modern British religious education (as do other Continental religious educators; see Ziebertz 2003: 111–112 and 118–120, for example). In Schweitzer's opinion (2006: 149) the nature of religious education, conditioned as it is by a particular cultural, national and religious setting, requires 'a pluralism of different models even in a limited area like the European Union'.

There are undoubtedly Continental educators who do appreciate aspects of the theory and practice of religious education in Britain, and there are aspects of British religious education that should be appreciated, but it is simply false to suggest that British religious education is either the envy of Europe or the best in the world. This is apologetic rhetoric and not a genuine reflection of the variety of estimates of the worth and quality of British religious education that are held by educators from Britain and from elsewhere.

Once one moves beyond self-serving expressions of the success of religious education in England and Wales by those organisations and individuals that have been influential in directing educational policy in this area, the picture becomes complex and contested. Indeed, to couch the debate on British religious education in terms of its successfulness or otherwise, most likely fails to capture the nuances of the situation. The question of 'success' invites a simple positive or negative response: religious education is or is not successful. 'Reality', however, does not always conform to our binary linguistic oppositions. There are a number of considerations that bear on the notion of educational successfulness. For example, success can be defined in different ways, and consequently there are different measures of what constitutes success – successful for what and for whom! Is success the only relevant criterion, and can all other considerations be subsumed under it? What about the contribution of religious education to social cohesion or the relevance of the subject to the interests and lives of pupils? These two issues are raised, precisely because there are prominent critics who allege that contemporary religious education in England and Wales has failed in these particular respects. Of course it is possible to fail in one respect but be successful in others: it is possible to hold that religious education has failed to equip pupils to evaluate and assess religious beliefs and practices while being successful in interesting them in religion and in fostering good community relationships. There is no simple measure of successfulness and no algorithm to determine how successful or not religious education is: it is a matter of personal judgement on the basis of the available evidence.

It is probably best to think of the overall worth and value of religious education as determined by the degree of success recorded across a range of criteria, such as the contribution of religious education to fostering social cohesion, developing respect for persons, imparting an understanding of religion, and so on, rather than by reference to a single uniform measure that fails to acknowledge the different ways in which worth and value can be defined and measured. The use of a range of criteria to measure success might make a contribution to defusing the polarised nature of the debate on religious education, where all too often unbridled criticism is met with assertions of unqualified success and dismissal of the evidence that is offered. In one sense, rejection of criticism of the ruling model of British religious education is not unexpected, in that many religious educators are aware of the controversial status of religious education in the curriculum and are reluctant to engage in 'public' debate on the matter. There are good historical reasons why British religious educators are defensive in relation to their commitments and practices, and it is important to be aware of these so that their opposition to criticism can be seen in the best light.

The 'ambiguous' status of religious education in Britain

The acknowledgement of some weaknesses, even alongside acknowledgement of positive achievements, is difficult for some British religious educators, even though it is understandable. Religious education has an ambiguous status in British education. This is reflected in the subject being placed outside the National Curriculum in the 1988 Education Reform Act; in the retention of a parental withdrawal clause for religious education; and in the oft repeated description of it as being the 'Cinderella' subject of the curriculum – under-financed and lacking in high quality resources (Baumfield 2004: 115). In addition, religious education is often perceived by parents and pupils alike as irrelevant to the career prospects of pupils.

Over the years the subject has also been harried from without by those who call for the end of religious education in state maintained schools. For example, in 1994, David Hargreaves, at that time Professor of Education at the University of Cambridge and subsequently Chief Executive of the Qualifications and Curriculum Authority (one of the then chief official policy advising and implementation agencies in the United Kingdom), while advocating an expansion of religious schools within the state system, argued that religious education in non-religious schools should be abolished and replaced by citizenship education, on the grounds that such education can only underwrite moral education in schools that are religiously uniform (as in faith schools) and not in religiously diverse 'secular schools'. Interestingly, he went on to characterise multi-faith religious education as a 'pick 'n' mix tour of religions' that 'trivialises each faith's claims to truth' (Hargreaves 1994: 34), a viewpoint not uncommon among educators generally but fiercely resisted by religious educators. More recently, Professor John White (2004) has similarly questioned the contribution of religious education to moral education, and by implication its contribution to the social aims of education; he concluded that it should become an optional rather than a compulsory subject for pupils.

Such proposals (and of course criticisms of the form raised by Hargreaves) create a sense of vulnerability among religious educators: knowing that there are those within the wider educational community who are critical of the contribution of religious education to the school curriculum means that they are naturally defensive and therefore reluctant to admit weaknesses that may contribute to the further undermining of the status of religious education and to its eventual demise as a compulsory subject within the curriculum. This feeling of vulnerability is (perhaps unknowingly) captured by Julian Stern (2006: 5) when he asks how religious education can 'bridge the gap between its own self-image as a vital and vibrant subject, and the image of it portrayed by some inspectors and even some pupils, parents and teachers as something of a backwater'. Here we have a dichotomy expressed between the self-perception of religious educators as contributing something vital to the curriculum alongside the recognition that those outside religious education regard it is a backwater. Lack of appreciation of the contribution of religious education to education by those outside the profession has unfortunately had the effect of arresting debate and self-criticism from within. Religious educators believe that their subject is secure in its role in schools only if it is seen to be successful: criticism from without is typically met by accusations from within of misunderstanding and the recitation of the rhetoric of success.

A further contributory factor to the inherent defensiveness of many British religious educators is the fear that any admission of failure, however slight, will be (and is) seized upon either by those in society, such as the Christian right, that seek to reinstate confessional Christian education (see Chapter 4) in state schools or those that wish to dispense with religious education in schools altogether. The ghost of confessionalism still haunts many modern British religious educators. Accordingly, criticism must be resisted for fear that support is given to a return to Christian confessionalism in education. The result is that criticism of current theory and practice in multi-faith religious education is too hastily dismissed and legitimate educational concerns become secondary to ideological disputes. As in most examples of references to the Christian Right in academic discourse, it is clear where the sympathies of the author lie: criticism from this quarter should not be taken seriously. By contrast some secularists and atheists campaign against the inclusion of religious education in the curriculum, believing that even to study it, however dispassionately, gives credibility to a subject that in all probability frustrates proper and legitimate educational objectives and goals.

To illustrate the point that religious education in Britain is much too defensive in reaction to criticism and that this defensiveness manifests itself in a tendency not to engage fully with criticism, it is worth looking in some detail at the long-standing complaint that certain forms of multi-faith religious education confuse pupils. Consideration of this also serves as an introduction to some of the criticisms that are frequently brought against modern multi-faith religious education in Britain.

Mishmash in British religious education

One of the most enduring criticisms of multi-faith religious education has been the accusation that it confuses pupils, largely because the content of the different religions is often presented thematically – organised under a range of generic headings, such as sacred places, festivals, rites of passage and pilgrimage. Thematic teaching, as opposed to systematic teaching, where the different religions are presented serially and separately, became the staple diet of RE syllabuses in the late 1970s, and still continues to this day. Part of the appeal of thematic teaching is that it is believed by some of its proponents to emphasise the similarities between religions (and as we shall note in later chapters, this accords well with the ecumenical theological assumptions that are constitutive of post-confessional British religious education).

Criticism of thematic teaching in religious education became particularly vocal in parliamentary debates surrounding the 1988 Education Reform Act. Thematic teaching was accused not just of confusing pupils but of failing to respect the integrity of the different religions, particularly Christianity. A vocal lobby in the House of Lords (see Alves 1991) expressed the view that the historical, social and religious contribution of Christianity in Britain was depreciated by thematic approaches that treated each religion equally: no recognition was given to Christianity's unique role in shaping the history and social institutions of Britain. Multi-faith thematic religious education was disparagingly characterised as 'a cocktail of faith', 'a value-free hotch-potch', and 'a mishmash of beliefs and practices' (see Hull 1991: 9–13).

In response, a number of prominent religious educators wrote in defence of thematic teaching, none more elegantly than Professor John Hull, then of the University of Birmingham. Hull took up the metaphor of mishmash as used by opponents and subjected it to close analysis and scrutiny (Hull 1991). He traced the term's origins to the fifteenth century and explored its developing usage and application across the centuries. More critically, he explored its metaphorical use to condemn what the speaker or writer believes to be the corruption of culture and of (pure) religion by external influences on indigenous beliefs and practices: the unholy mixing of faiths, cultures and nations is analogous to the improper mixing of different types of foods. Behind (continuing) accusations of mishmash in religious education, Hull detects inappropriate associations of Christianity with Britishness (an association developed in Hart 1993, for example, and analysed sociologically in the context of religious education by Tamney 1994) and the vestiges of Christian triumphalism in education. Hull concluded that criticism of thematic teaching is a thinly veiled attempt to reinstate Christian confessionalism in the classroom (as in Burn and Hart 1988).

Hull's defence of thematic multi-faith religious education is widely regarded as successful. Lat Blaylock (2004: 19), for example, refers to it as 'the funniest analysis of the defensive tendency of the religious right'; and there is substance to his claim that the individuals with whom Hull engages harbour desires to reintroduce Christian nurture in state maintained schools and to revive what he considers to be misguided and inappropriate links between Christianity and citizenship. Nevertheless, the debate on the appropriateness of thematic teaching should not be concluded by religious educators on this basis. Hull's careful study shows that some of those who criticise thematic teaching are inspired by unworthy motives. He does not address the educational complaint that thematic teaching confuses pupils and consequently lowers their levels of attainment in terms of religious knowledge and understanding, and he fails to acknowledge, let alone answer, other criticisms of thematic religious education that are widely discussed by religious educators and with which he should/would have been familiar at the time of writing. Here is the late Terence Copley's (2005: 119–120) summary of the criticisms brought against thematic religious education in the 1980s (he also acknowledges that thematic teaching is still a feature of religious education in some schools):

> First, it is conceptual nonsense to imagine that one might understand a religion by seeing one slice of it alongside slices of other religions . . . Second, it [thematic teaching] encouraged unintentionally a dangerous concept of equivalence. That is, that the Christian Bible is the equivalent of the Quran to Muslims, the Guru Granth Sahib for Sikhs, or the Upanishads for Hindus. Or in a similar way, that a rabbi is a 'Jewish vicar', a gurdwara is a 'Sikh church', etc. Third, the themes selected were always phenomenological and nearly always secular. Units [of work] rarely appeared on God, revelation, sin, mysticism or prayer.

Copley adds the issue of pupil confusion as a further criticism, which is the only criticism that Hull considers.

The debate around thematic teaching illustrates the point that assessments of the strengths and weaknesses of different aspects of multi-faith approaches in British religious education have become polarised and ideological in nature (as in Brown 1995, for example). In what has become an increasingly acrimonious and sterile discussion, 'conservative' criticism of multi-faith religious education seems largely intended to advance Christian claims to supremacy and to marginalise adherents of other religions, politically and socially. By contrast, 'liberal' defences simply presuppose the validity and appropriateness of multi-faith religious education and are content to expose conservative prejudices. A multi-faith approach is assumed to accord with the values of individual autonomy, openness and social justice, and such values are regarded as above question and constitutive of the liberal tradition. Some commentators have gone as far as suggesting that the professionalism of religious education teachers and the integrity of religious education as a school discipline are threatened by criticism of a multi-faith approach (as in Hull 1993 and 1995). Such comments, however, must not be allowed to muddy the waters or stultify the debate by leading educators to exaggerate the strengths of multi-faith religious education and ignore its weaknesses (for the reasons discussed earlier, see pp. 13–15).

Philosophers speak wisely of the genetic fallacy, which is that fallacious line of reasoning by which a perceived defect in the origin of a claim or thing is taken to be evidence that discredits the claim or thing itself. That some are inspired by unworthy and inappropriate motives to challenge developments in modern religious education is ultimately irrelevant to the evaluation of their arguments. The question of motives and motivation is superfluous to the issue of assessment and evaluation; it is because of this that philosophers tend to distinguish between causes and reasons (Gaskin 1984), and subsume the issue of motives under the former. What really matters is the reasons offered and the evidence adduced. The important point to stress to religious educators is that criticism of modern British religious education can be legitimately inspired by educational concerns that are appropriate to and reflective of the need to develop a form of education that is critical, inclusive and relevant.

Thankfully, some years on from the original debate about the educational appropriateness of thematic teaching, there is now empirical evidence that is relevant to its assessment. In an important survey of 2,879 Year 8 pupils in schools in England and Wales, William Kay and Linnet Smith found that there was little to choose between systematic and thematic studies of religion as far as religious understanding and comprehension are concerned (provided no more than four religions are studied), but that a combination of systematic and thematic teaching tended to confuse pupils. More importantly, their research revealed that pupils who studied the different religions systematically rather than thematically tended to have a more positive view of religion (see Kay and Smith 2000; Smith and Kay 2000). These findings (particularly the latter), which tilt the balance in favour of systematic teaching over thematic teaching in the secondary school (for the research was conducted with secondary school pupils), have not entirely defused the debate.

Internal criticism of British religious education

The original criticism that multi-faith religious education confuses pupils, as has been noted, did not originate among professional religious educators but among conservative Christians who wanted to reinstate Christian confessionalism in state maintained schools. It is this identification that provides the substance of Hull's *ad hominem* argument considered above. In the 1980s the battle lines over multi-faith religious education were clearly drawn as that between professional educators and conservative, reactionary Christians. What has happened since is that support for current versions of multi-faith religious education has weakened considerably among both professional religious educators and members of religious communities (see Ansari 2004: 312–339, for example). However, this weakening support among professional religious educators does not mean that there are increasing calls within the profession for a return to confessionalism. Increasing criticism from within the ranks of professional religious educators is not of multi-faith religious education *per se*, but of the particular forms multi-faith religious education has taken in Britain.

The concern by faith community members about how their beliefs and practices are portrayed and treated in schools (see RE Council, Sept. 2005) has been given further substance by the contention of Copley (2005) that Christian confessionalism in schools has largely been replaced by secular confessionalism, whereby pupils are effectively indoctrinated into secular beliefs and values. Copley gives examples from religious education lessons that illustrate how familiar religious material such as the story of Joseph, the story of David and Goliath and the Parable of the Prodigal Son are divested of their original religious meaning and significance and reinterpreted to serve moral and social education: 'Be faithful to yourself'; 'Stand up to bullies'; and 'Always forgive'. Religious beliefs and the religious context of the stories are overlooked, yet the lessons purport to provide *religious* education. The charge that 'RE has sometimes secularized its own subject matter' (Copley 2005: 121) is telling, not only because Copley refers to actual lessons and quotations from the responses of pupils but also because he is the author of the standard critical history of religious education in modern Britain and is an undoubted authority on the subject (Copley 2008). Others allege that neutral and non-judgemental presentations of religious phenomena in the classroom invite religious indifference (Watson 1993: 43–46). Such criticisms are being voiced, not by those nostalgic for a recently lost Christian society in Britain, which largely disappeared in the 1950s, but by those who are committed to broadly liberal educational aims and who believe that religious education has a positive contribution to make to the creation of a just, sustainable and peaceful society.

A recent Ofsted report (2007: 7) on religious education, entitled *Making Sense of Religion*, concludes that 'the subject's potential to contribute to community cohesion, education for diversity and citizenship is not being fully realised'. Given the controversial nature of religion and of religious education (it remains after all a subject from which parents can withdraw their children), and the circumspection that usually attends official comments on controversial issues, the expression of such reservation is significant, as are the final words of the report (2007: 41):

> RE cannot ignore its role in fostering community cohesion and in educating for diversity. This goal has never been far from good RE teaching

but the current changes in society give this renewed urgency. Pupils have opinions, attitudes, feelings, prejudices and stereotypes. Developing respect for the commitments of others while retaining the right to question, criticise and evaluate different viewpoints is not just an academic exercise: it involves creating opportunities for children and young people to meet those with different viewpoints. They need to grasp how powerful religion is in people's lives. RE should engage pupils' feelings and emotions, as well as their intellect.

One may presume that the comments in this Ofsted report are based upon observation by inspectors of actual lessons, and it is this empirical element that gives substance to its conclusions.

The contribution of religious education to social inclusion

Overall there is a paucity of evidence and research on the subject of religious education's contribution to social cohesion and to the development of positive attitudes to religious diversity among pupils. Certainly there is evidence that members of religious minority communities, particularly the Muslim community, are forsaking community schools for faith schools, where there is the opportunity to do so without serious financial penalty, and this is in part because of the perceived secularism of community schools, including the perceived secularism of religious education. David Freeman (2012: 5) has recently commented that 'one factor uniting . . . [Muslim] groups is their common opposition to the secular nature of modern Britain and, in particular, to the secularism underlying British educational practices'. There is irony in this situation in that although secularism is often promoted as inclusive and neutral, it can actually effect greater division in society by alienating religious parents and pupils from common schools, who then seek to establish (or to avail themselves of currently existing) religious schools that they perceive to be more inclusive of their particular religious identity, commitments and values.

For the most part we simply do not know if multi-faith religious education contributes to social cohesion and develops respect in pupils for those who belong to different communities and espouse different values. The limited empirical evidence that is available does not directly address this issue. This is surprising, and clearly it is an omission to which researchers need to give attention, particularly given that the contribution of religious education to challenging religious intolerance is one of the reasons originally advanced in favour of multi-faith religious education. Forty years after its introduction in Britain we do not know if there is a positive correlation between multi-faith religious education and respect for others.

There is empirical evidence and research, however, on matters that are of tangential interest to our concerns, which is worth briefly discussing. At a presentation entitled 'Learning to live together? The impact of religious diversity or homogeneity in Dutch schools for secondary education' at the International Seminar on Religious Education and Values in Ankara, July 2008, Gerdien Bertram-Troost provided a report on an empirical investigation that addressed the question of the extent to which different types of schools equipped pupils to deal with religious diversity in society. A series of questions were administered to 14- to 16-year-old pupils in four different types of school in the Netherlands that reflected different religious and secular commitments and exhibited different degrees of internal diversity: Van Prinsteren College, a segregated Christian school, where pupils receive confessional Christian education; El Habib, a segregated Islamic school, where pupils receive confessional Islamic education; Het Kompas, a state school with pupils from a range of religious and non-religious backgrounds who receive no formal religious education; and Da Vinci Lyceum, a Catholic school, where pupils receive a broad based religious education that focuses on different worldviews.

A series of questions was put to pupils to ascertain the extent to which they related both in school and socially to pupils who belonged to different religious backgrounds. A further series of questions explored the attitudes of pupils towards those who held different religious viewpoints from themselves. The conclusions were not what one might have expected:

> [g]etting knowledge about different religions as such, does not necessarily contribute to learning to have respect for everyone, irrespective of their religion ... the correlation between 'At school I get knowledge about different religions' and 'At school, I learn to have respect for everyone, whatever their religion' is not very high ($r = .371$).
>
> *Bertram-Troost 2008*

Bertram-Troost concluded that there was no clear-cut relationship between religious diversity in schools and 'learning to live together and learning how to be good citizens' in a society that was religiously diverse. She commented:

> This result corresponds with the results of a recent Dutch study by Bakker and others [unreferenced] on the effects of ethnic class composition and inter-ethnic contact between students on students' ethnic attitudes. The researchers found that the ethnic composition of the school class (primary school) did not seem to affect students' attitudes; neither did the number of inter-ethnic contacts, nor the amount of intercultural education.
>
> An important conclusion from this small study ... is that religious diversity at school as such is not a clear predictor of getting knowledge about different religions and/or learning to have respect for others.
>
> ... we learn that religious diversity or homogeneity in schools does not necessarily hinder the personal religious identity development at the one hand, but that it does also not necessarily stimulate or hinder the openness

of pupils to religious diversity in society and/or the possibilities to live together.

Bertram-Troost 2008: 5

Bertram-Troost wisely refers to the need for further research into the relationship between the attitudes of pupils in different types of schools to the issue of social diversity.

Bertram-Troost's conclusions are broadly complementary to research findings elsewhere. A major study of religious attitudes and prejudice among school pupils in Northern Ireland by John Greer (1985: 275) concluded that there was a positive relationship between attitude to religion and openness: 'young people [in Northern Ireland] most favourably disposed to [the Christian] religion being most open to the other religious tradition . . .'. Greer's research seems to give substance to the view that pupils who were confident of their own religious beliefs and commitments (and such confidence in this case was no doubt enhanced by confessional religious education) were more positive towards those with whom they differed religiously than those who had limited or negative attitudes towards religion. More recently, Professor Leslie Francis concluded, on the basis of a sample of 802 young people aged 15–16 years in the United Kingdom, who completed a range of standard psychological tests, that positive attitudes towards Christianity are unrelated to dogmatism. Given that empirical research has already established that there is a positive correlation between dogmatism and prejudice, this means that commitment to religion, or more particularly commitment to the Christian religion, is in all probability not necessarily associated with or conducive to prejudice and intolerance. (The same research was later replicated among undergraduate students and yielded similar results; see Francis and Robbins 2003). Francis (2001a: 221) notes that the data he analyses 'lend no support to the criticism that Christianity is bad for young people in that it fosters closed-mindedness and promotes prejudice'.

It may be granted that such empirical research is of limited relevance to assessments of multi-faith religious education. What is clear is that commitment to the truth of one's own religion is quite compatible with liberal and positive attitudes towards those of different religious convictions and persuasions. This finding certainly challenges those who condemn confessional schools on the grounds that they promote religious prejudice and intolerance. The research in Northern Ireland is also interesting in that it shows that Christian nurture and exclusively Christian content in religious education are compatible with positive attitudes to people of a different religious persuasion from oneself. There is no necessary connection between confessionalism and intolerance of others. This finding certainly calls into question one of the chief reasons that was originally advanced for the introduction of multi-faith religious education in Britain, namely that Christian confessionalism in education encourages negative attitudes towards non-Christians. It may do, but there again it may not.

There are, of course, good educational reasons for preferring that a range of religions be taught to pupils in British schools (to which I subscribe, see Chapter 4), but they should not include tendentious associations between confessional education (or exclusively Christian content in religious education) and intolerance. The pertinent question to ask of today's multi-faith religious education is whether, according to its current interpretation and instantiation in classrooms, it is successful in developing pupil respect for those who belong to different religions and communities. The answer to this must remain tentative and conjectural, as the necessary empirical research has not been conducted. There is no empirical evidence to substantiate a positive connection between multi-faith religious education and respectful attitudes towards members of minority religions and cultures.

The contribution of religious education to moral and spiritual development

If there is little evidence of the historical contribution of multi-faith religious education in Britain to the development of positive attitudes and mutual respect between individuals and communities, is there evidence that the subject is regarded as relevant and important by pupils? What value do pupils place on multi-faith religious education as currently practised in Britain? What positive contribution does religious education make to their moral, social and spiritual development? In this case, there is empirical evidence that is recent, pertinent and troubling.

In 2004 Penny Jennings conducted a large-scale questionnaire survey in Cornwall's state maintained secondary schools of pupils' attitudes toward religious education across a range of spiritual and moral issues (Jennings 2004). The questionnaires were completed by 3,823 pupils (1,962 from Year 9 and 1,861 from Year 10) from 24 schools (i.e. over three-quarters of the total number) that were representative of the different variables obtaining in Cornwall's secondary schools; thus making this one of the largest surveys conducted into pupil attitudes and values in Britain. Here are some of her findings with regard to pupils' attitudes to different aspects of religious education (see Table 1.1 on p. 23).

The statistics speak for themselves: they make depressing reading and certainly give substance to the charge that for the most part religious education currently fails to engage the imagination and interest of pupils. Negative attitudes outweigh positive attitudes: only 29% find religious education interesting; only 16% believe that it helps them to think about their identity; only 9% believe RE helps them to live a better life; and 53% find the lessons boring. On the basis of her research (which includes data on pupils' attitudes to a range of moral and religious issues as well as attitudes to religious education), Jennings (2004: 3) concludes that 'the majority of the students do not feel that religious education is relevant to their own spiritual or moral development'.

TABLE 1.1 Attitudes towards RE

Item	Yes (%)	Unsure (%)	No (%)
RE is usually interesting	29	24	48
RE is a waste of time	37	22	41
RE helps me to understand what God is really like	21	27	51
I enjoy learning about different religions	27	22	51
RE helps me to make sense of my life	15	22	63
RE is boring	53	18	29
RE wastes time I could spend on exam subjects	50	23	27
RE helps me to find rules to live by	14	26	60
It is interesting to learn about life after death	41	21	38
RE helps me to choose a faith to live by	9	22	69
RE helps me to sort out my problems	8	19	73
RE provides relaxation in a busy timetable	21	19	60
I enjoy discussing moral problems in RE	28	21	52
RE helps me to think about who I really am	16	21	62
RE is fun	17	23	60
RE helps me to lead a better life	9	23	68
It is important to know what people of other faiths believe	47	22	31
I enjoy debates in RE	44	19	37
Studying the Bible in RE is boring	63	21	16
RE helps me to think about why I am here	23	27	50
RE helps me to believe in God	11	21	68

Source: Jennings (2004)

There is one important positive point revealed in Jennings' survey of pupils' attitudes: although only 27% enjoy learning about different religions, 47% think it is important to know what people of other faiths believe, compared to 31% who do not. This suggests that there is support among pupils for multi-faith religious education or some component of multi-faith education within religious education. The contradiction between the two statistics is most naturally explained by a degree of pupil disillusionment with contemporary forms of multi-faith religious education. This in turn alerts us to an important qualification. That pupils are dissatisfied with current interpretations of multi-faith religious education in Britain does not mean that it cannot be taught in relevant and educationally appropriate forms. The models of theory and practice in religious education that were dominant in British state schools from the 1970s up to the present are not the only ones available. The term multi-faith religious education can denote different combinations of educational strategy, beliefs and practices, and an appreciation of this latitude of usage is important.

Although it will be argued that much multi-faith religious education in Britain has revealed itself as not particularly well suited to preparing pupils to live as respectful neighbours and to participate as responsible citizens in a multicultural society, there is no insurmountable reason why it cannot combine good pedagogical practice with accurate representations of religion in such a way as to make a real contribution to the development in pupils of religious toleration and respect for cultural and religious difference. The focus of the criticisms that are developed in later chapters is not against multi-faith religious education *per se*, but against the culturally and educationally dominant models used in British schools.

It is not necessary at this stage to explore the full range of criticisms brought against contemporary religious education in England and Wales; later chapters will engage more fully with them and attempt to explain both their historical and genealogical provenance and the ways in which they reflect deeper and more enduring weaknesses in how the subject is theorised and interpreted. What has been said in this chapter is sufficient to illustrate the point that, despite the rhetoric of success, there are serious criticisms of religious education in Britain that suggest that current theory and practice is failing to realise some of the aims that are frequently advanced by educators as central to the case for its compulsory inclusion in the school curriculum; namely, its contribution both to social cohesion (an aim that subsumes under it the notion of challenging religious intolerance and discrimination) and to the moral, social and spiritual development of pupils.

2

TRADITIONAL AND MODERN DIVERSITY

The aim of this chapter and the next is to provide an overview of both the changing contours of diversity in British society and the changing perceptions regarding the significance of diversity for society and for public institutions, particularly the education system and schools. It is important to have a clear grasp of the nature of social and religious diversity, and of the challenges posed to society by diversity, before a review and assessment of the response of religious education can begin. Although different aspects of diversity are considered, consistent with our focus on religious education, the nature of religious diversity will naturally command most attention. Religious diversity (which in many cases also subsumes other forms of diversity – ethnic, racial and cultural) is relevant in two chief ways to religious education. First, there is the issue of how religious diversity is interpreted and represented in the classroom; and second, there is the issue of how and to what extent religious education contributes to the social aims of education by challenging religious intolerance and improving relations between different religious communities.

The content relevant to our concerns is structured in the following way. An introductory account is provided of the nature and character of human diversity and how diversity relates to social and group identity, and how this in turn creates the potential for community and social division and strife. This is followed by an overview of religious diversity in Britain. These two sections are preparatory to a critical analysis of the changing nature of social diversity in Britain – this analysis extends into a second chapter. Three different historically successive forms of diversity in society are identified and discussed: traditional, modern, and late modern diversity.

The nature and challenge of diversity

Why should diversity in society be a matter of concern? What challenges does diversity pose to society and its institutions? In a straightforward sense diversity is a feature of 'the rich tapestry of life' and always has been: people differ physically, emotionally, culturally, religiously, and so on. Yet people – individuals, who by their independent existence differ from each other – are also connected to each other in a complex web of shifting relationships of various forms of choice and necessity. Some of these connections and identifications are regarded as more important than others and some can come to be central to an individual's sense of self-identity (or even worth). Society, by extension, is made up of people relating to each other in a multiplicity of ways, sharing with others certain features of their lives, differing from others in certain respects, belonging to certain groups and not belonging to certain groups. There is a dialectical and shifting relationship between human unity and human diversity, and this tension is experienced at the level of the individual.

Group membership is a complex notion, chiefly because membership of certain groups becomes part of our shared and individual identity. We share interests and characteristics with others and we identify with these and with them; as the importance of these interests and our connections with other people increase, so we begin to identify ourselves (or indeed be identified by others) with certain constituencies and groups, sometimes formally and sometimes informally. Moreover, our membership of different groups can be arranged hierarchically, with certain aspects of our identity assuming more importance and becoming more constitutive of our self-identity. A cautionary note is needed, however, because we must not think of self-identity as something necessarily freely chosen (or as fixed, for that matter), for identity is fashioned in social settings under the influence of others in ways that are not always obvious or apparent, even to ourselves. Certain attachments and identifications become more important and inclusive of other less important attachments – Christian, husband, parent, teacher and so on. There is no straightforward hierarchical ordering of different identifications and commitments, and only on rare occasions do individuals have to choose between groups and attachments – say, for example, when one's membership of a union is challenged by a call to strike action that is adjudged to be self-serving and unwarranted or when one's identification as a citizen of a particular country is challenged by important political decisions that one believes to be undemocratic and unsupportable morally. Even our ultimate commitments can be revisable.

The existence of different human groups witnesses to human diversity, for groups are formed on the basis of identifications and classifications that are selective and partial. Not all people enjoy the same interests or attachments and commitments; not all share the same identity. It is at this point that the potential for division and conflict between individuals and between groups in society can occur. There seems to be a natural human propensity to regard one's own interests, choices and commitments, even biological characteristics, as superior to others, and this in turn may lead to negative attitudes and behaviour towards those with different interests and commitments.

Differences between individuals may arise at every level of human experience, and although most are managed successfully, within the context of on-going relationships, they can, when a difference is interpreted as significant, become the occasion for division. Understandably, differences between groups, at points which are perceived as important and which are central to a group's sense of identity, have much greater potential to result in attitudes and actions that threaten the well-being and efficient functioning of society than differences between individuals. Equally, groups are protective of interests and privileges that result from group membership; and in turn privileges and benefits that some groups enjoy (or are perceived as enjoying) can arouse hostility from other groups. There is a competitive element to life and this competitive element takes different forms in different contexts. To this can be traced the roots of much division in society, though division in society can also result when there is no competitive dimension.

What constitutes difference, in the sense of which differences are regarded as significant, is culturally and socially conditioned. There are reasons why particular differences assume importance and why some particular difference is perceived as salient, all other similarities apart. People can become defined by a single characteristic and hence stereotypes are created. Individual identity is overlooked and a common (often negative) identity with others is regarded as determinative of character and personhood. Individual identity is replaced by a single ascribed, collective or group identity. The concept of the scapegoat, that is of the individual or group that is blamed for the ills of 'the community' is common to different cultures and societies. The 'community' in question is invariably exclusionary and 'the other', who for the purpose of community expiation becomes the scapegoat, necessarily differs in some respect, even if that difference lies not in reality but in some 'constructed' or 'imagined' difference (see Girard 1986). Difference may be in the eye of the beholder; it is manufactured to give vent to one's own frustrations and inner conflicts.

It has already been noted how differences between groups have the potential to result in attitudes and actions that threaten the well-being of society. Typically, the more inclusive of identity membership of a particular group is or becomes, the greater the depth of division that results when that particular marker of identity is perceived by its members to be challenged by some other group. This means effectively that those with different racial, ethnic, cultural and religious origins in society can be perceived as a threat by the majority, simply because these differences are believed to express or signify fundamental differences that challenge the privileges, benefits, status and commitments of the majority, indigenous community; and to some what is perceived as a threat gives support to prejudice, intolerance and active discrimination. Historically, since the Protestant Reformation, Europe has had to respond to the challenge of accommodating religious diversity within nation states, but in more recent times the countries of Europe have had to accommodate increasing numbers of immigrants who differ racially, ethnically, culturally or religiously from the majority. Often these categories are overlapping and indivisible. The important point is that each category individually or in combination describes a difference that has the potential to create deep divisions in society.

It is easy to appreciate why religion becomes constitutive of identity and a marker of group membership, and therefore also how it becomes a symbol and a cause of division in society. Followers of the same religion (or denomination) typically hold beliefs in common, follow common practices and perform common rituals. Recognition of the ability of religion to foster group identity and a sense of community was central to Émile Durkheim's interpretation of the nature of religion ([1912] 2008), which he believed focused on the distinction between the sacred and the profane. For him, certain things are sacred because they provide a focus for community loyalty. The sacred binds individuals together to form 'a moral community'; and this sense of community often brings people together for the common good. Durkheim wrote at a time, in the early twentieth century, when a single religion commanded the allegiance of most of the citizens of an individual national state. By the last decades of the twentieth century, however, this situation had changed and most of the nations of Western Europe were exhibiting increasing levels of religious diversity. Whereas religion was once a unifying force, in many places it now acquires the potential to divide societies in ways that threaten public order and community cohesion.

Religious diversity in Britain

This section provides a snapshot of contemporary religious diversity in Britain. Subsequent sections and the next chapter address the precise ways in which British society, and Western Europe more generally, have become more plural and diverse. Attention is also given to the specific challenges posed to education in Britain by diversity.

Interpreting recent census statistics is not without its challenges, both internal and external. Internal challenges relate to the fact that the question on religious identity was answered by respondents on a voluntary basis and that the data from the three different nations do not represent responses to the same identically worded question: the 2011 England and Wales census asked about 'affiliation', whereas the 2011 Scotland census asked about 'belonging' (Office for National Statistics 2013). External challenges relate to the consistency of results with those of empirical measures of religiosity.

Other datasets present a different picture, indicating much lower levels of commitment to religion than might be inferred from census results. For example, in the 2013 British Social Attitudes Survey 48% of respondents claimed that they do not belong to a religion (www.bsa-30.natcen.ac.uk). Clearly affiliation to religion does not necessarily correlate to a strong appreciation of the importance of religion in one's life. Equally, there is evidence that formal religious affiliation does not always translate into either religious practice or commitment to religious beliefs consistent with affiliation: only 15 per cent of adults in the United Kingdom attend church at least once a month (Ashworth and Farthing 2007: 6), and while approximately two in three people in Britain believe in God (similar, earlier evidence prompted Grace Davie in 1994 to speak of 'believing without belonging'), only one in four believe in a *personal* God (Barley 2007: 1). This is not the context to attempt to resolve such issues (if they can be resolved): empirical studies of religion typically show that people are not always consistent in their religious beliefs, in the sense that contrary and even contradictory beliefs are held by the same person; and belief and practice may also be inconsistent.

Table 2.1 provides the most recent and reliable data on the religious composition of Britain and reveals the broad contours of diversity in Britain; comment will be confined to the statistics that are most relevant to religious education. Clearly Christianity commands the greatest number of adherents throughout Britain, and by a sizeable margin, though it has decreased significantly from the 2001 Census, from just over 70 per cent to just below 60 per cent. The statistical significance of Christianity is of course complemented by its cultural, historical, legal, political and social significance as well. Table 2.1 also shows that Islam is the largest minority religion in Britain, though its strength in Britain varies from over 2.7 million Muslims in England to just over 42,500 in Scotland. Alongside Muslims there are adherents of all the major 'world' religions and the diverse and numerous religious traditions and movements that one would expect to find in a modern European, liberal democratic state with a colonial history. Altogether, however, as the table shows, less than 8 per cent of the population in Britain belong to a religion other than Christianity.

TABLE 2.1 2011 Census: Collating data from the Censuses in England and Wales and in Scotland

Religion	England	Scotland	Wales	Total	Britain (%)
Buddhist	238,626	6830	9117	254,573	0.4
Christian	31,479,876	3,294,545	1,763,299	36,537,720	59.8
Hindu	806,199	5564	10434	822,197	1.3
Jewish	261,282	6448	2064	269,794	0.4
Muslim	2,660,116	42557	45950	2,748,623	4.5
Sikh	420,196	6572	2962	429,730	0.7
Other Religion	227,825	26974	12705	267,504	0.4
Total	36,094,120	3,389,490	1,846,531	41,330,141	67.7
No Religion	13,114,232	1,394,460	982,997	15,491,689	25.3
Not stated	3,804,104	278,061	233,928	4,316,093	7.1

Source: Census data collated by the author.

Table 2.1 also shows that the distribution of this 8 per cent is not uniform across the three different nations: other data from the censuses show the equally variable distribution levels of religious adherents in different areas and regions within the different countries. One of the effects of differentiated patterns of religious distribution is that outside the main, industrial cities and the main areas of 'new' religious settlement, which followed immigration to Britain in the 1950s and 1960s, many schools are much less diverse religiously than one might have imagined from acquaintance with overall statistics. Yet a note of qualification needs to be sounded immediately, for the term religious diversity need not apply only to diversity between religions, diversity is also a feature within religions. One naturally thinks of the denominational variety within Christianity, the Sufi/Sunni division within Islam, the schools and sects of Hinduism, and so on. These conventional distinctions within religions, however, often fail to capture the diversity of practice and belief at the level of lived experience in diverse social and community settings; and some religions are more diverse than others, although if recent research is to be believed, British Muslims are one of the most homogenous religious groups in all of Europe with regard to beliefs and to moral valuations (Gallup 2009: 30–33; see Chapter 13). Recognition of this, however, does not detract from the central point about the existence of diversity within religions.

The acknowledgement of diversity within religions and religious traditions raises an issue for educational provision that takes us back to the disparity we noted between the number of adherents to Christianity in Britain and empirical measures of their commitment to traditional Christian beliefs, practices and values. Research reveals a wide diversity of beliefs and values among Christian 'adherents', with some expressing scepticism not only towards distinctively Christian beliefs but also towards basic theistic beliefs, such as belief in a personal God or in the afterlife, for example. Moreover, this scepticism is most marked among those of secondary school age. When this evidence is complemented by empirical measures of religious agnosticism and atheism (in the Census for England and Wales 25 per cent of the population describe themselves as having 'no religion') it becomes clear that the concept of religious diversity, if it is to be both meaningful as a descriptive term and relevant to curriculum planning and pedagogy, needs to include some reference to the different varieties and degrees of religious scepticism that exist within Britain.

Conceptualising diversity and its implications for education

Religious diversity in the United Kingdom has increased in the last 50–60 years in at least three distinguishable ways: an increase in the variety of religions that are practised; an increase in the diversity within religions and religious traditions; and finally growth in the number of people who are either entirely sceptical about religion or sceptical about some of the central claims of religion. Ironically, in the first half of the twentieth century the prevailing intellectual orthodoxy confidently anticipated the demise of religion in response to the forces of scientific materialism and rationalism. As early as 1905, A. E. Crawley reported that 'the opinion is everywhere gaining ground that religion is a mere survival from a primitive . . . age, and its extinction only a matter of time' (1905: 8). The progress of modernity would sweep away the last vestiges of religious enthusiasm and practice. It was even anticipated that the second and third generations of 'new' immigrants that came to Britain after World War II would renounce the 'outdated beliefs' of their parents and embrace secular norms and values or, if this was too demanding a prospect, at least espouse a genteel form of religion of the kind favoured by their host community. Continuing immigration, increasing knowledge and interest in 'other' religions, reactions to Enlightenment rationalism, the influence of capitalism, the demise of state religious monopolies and other factors have contributed to create a very different and more plural Britain from that anticipated in the 1950s.

It is not just that religious diversity *per se* has increased, it is also that perceptions of the importance and social relevance of diversity have undergone profound changes. The nature of these changes justifies distinguishing three different (historically successive) forms of religious diversity in Britain and in most other European nations: traditional, modern and late modern diversity. These different forms are correlated to wider shifts in intellectual history, which in turn are related to patterns of practice and pedagogy in religious education. There is effectively a triangulation between diversity, intellectual movements and religious education. Yet while religious education is subject to the influence of the other two and chiefly reactive to their influence, even as reactive it does not simply mirror these (external) influences but reinterprets and reshapes them in accordance with its own interests and aims. The purpose of this chapter and the next is to explore the diversity pole of this triangular relationship.

Traditional diversity

From the sixteenth and seventeenth centuries religious diversity has been an internally recognised feature of most European nation states, though some version of Christian orthodoxy typically held sway politically and with varying degrees of enthusiasm and success attempted to expunge all other versions. As the centuries advanced, formal discriminatory practices gradually declined, as did efforts to press a uniform religious identity on all citizens. Open hostility and illegality gave way to toleration, and in time the toleration enjoyed by 'sectarian' Christian groups was extended to incorporate adherents of other religions, a feature which in turn facilitated further immigration and hence further diversity. Other religions were accorded minority status, in keeping with their numbers. Viewed from the perspective of mainstream culture, the beliefs and values of non-Christian religions were, for the most part, socially and culturally invisible; more critically Barry Troyna (1993: 24) spoke of 'the suppression and depreciation of ethnic, linguistic and cultural differences' and to this may be added the suppression of religious differences. Non-Christian communities were typically politically powerless (though from the nineteenth century certain accommodations gave Jews a political significance lacked by other non-Christian religious groups).

Up until the late 1960s adherents of other religions in Britain existed in a Christian society where a particular form of 'established' Christianity enjoyed cultural hegemony, and pertinent to our concerns, educational hegemony. Members of the majority culture (which was a curious amalgam of religious and secular elements) believed it to embody civilised, universal values, the virtues of which, through cultural influence and education, would increasingly be appreciated and assimilated by members of 'minority' cultures. The task of education was to transmit and inculcate these civilised and civilising universal values in the young. The situation so described corresponds to what can be referred to as traditional diversity.

Modern diversity

In the 1970s traditional diversity gave way gradually to modern diversity. At one level modern diversity differs from its predecessor in straightforward quantitative terms: society becomes more diverse morally and religiously. An important catalyst of modern diversity in Britain was the collapse of the cultural power and prestige of mainstream Christianity. Such an interpretation naturally raises the issue of secularisation, for this includes within its (contested and not always consistent) range of meanings the process by which Christianity loses both personal and social significance in particular societies (as for example in McLeod 2000). Secularisation carries other connotations as well and its use as an explanatory concept need not be confined to Christian societies (as here) and their transformation under the influence of modernity (a convenient label that subsumes a range of factors and influences), but this meaning is sufficient for introductory purposes.

Although it is correct to trace the process of secularisation in British society to the nineteenth century (though its intellectual and social roots can be identified much further back, see Taylor 2007), there is compelling evidence that in the 1960s secularisation took a much deeper turn and undermined the credibility of any future description of Britain as 'a Christian society' (Brown 2009). Formal measures of Christian commitment, such as church attendance, church weddings, baptism and confirmation, all declined dramatically across the different denominations throughout the 1960s and early 1970s, a decline, which, although less precipitous in succeeding decades, continues. Loss of confidence in Christianity and the diminution of its social and cultural influence resulted in a similar decline in the prevalence of specifically Christian belief. For some, loss of confidence in Christianity was compensated by a new positive appreciation of alternative 'Eastern' spiritualities; others embraced agnosticism or atheism; the 'silent' majority remained religious in an indeterminate way that combined beliefs from different sources without obvious enthusiasm or commitment. A secular mentality came to prevail, according to which religion is a private or individual affair unrelated and inappropriate to social and political issues.

Alongside an increase in the level of religious diversity within society, and more characteristically constitutive of modern diversity, came social and political recognition of ethnic minority communities and the need to address the inequalities of power and influence that attended this recognition. Inequalities were evident in employment, housing and education. There was also increasing evidence of discrimination across both private and public institutions and service providers in society. A different but perhaps more genealogically accurate account of the origins of modern diversity in Britain is to state that recognition of racial and ethnic discrimination, and of the inequalities of power and privilege this exposed, gave a new social and political salience to religious diversity. Race riots in Brixton in south London in 1981, followed by further riots in cities in the West Midlands and in Liverpool's Toxteth area, underlined the serious nature of the problem.

Perceptions of diversity and its challenge to society throughout the late 1970s and the following decade focused on two related issues, that of racial prejudice and that of the cultural marginalisation of minority communities. Race and colour can be highly visible markers of identity and individuals distinctive in these ways were often subject to abuse and discrimination; the inspiration for which is found in a combination of economic, historical, sociological and psychological causes (that discrimination is morally wrong shall simply be assumed). Racial and religious intolerance represents one pole of the negative reaction to diversity by some members of the majority culture, whereas lack of recognition and appreciation of the cultures of minority communities is at the other pole. Situating these two negative responses to diversity at opposite ends of the same continuum makes the point that they are intimately connected and that the alienation felt by members of a minority community can be plotted on a sliding scale of intensity as one moves from cultural and social anonymity (powerlessness) to experiences of racial and religious discrimination.

Attention to the two poles of our continuum on negative responses to diversity is also helpful in understanding the nature and character of educational responses: antiracist educational programmes were devised, as the name implies, to counteract racial discrimination; whereas multicultural programmes were devised to give recognition to the cultures of minority communities in the school curriculum. Although distinguishable, the two types of programme share common concerns and overlap in significant ways. Anti-discrimination legislation was introduced in 1965, but significantly strengthened by the Race Relations Act of 1976, which made both direct and indirect discrimination an offence and gave those affected by discrimination redress through employment tribunals and the courts. This Act provided fresh stimulus to educational programmes in schools that focused on racism and its relation to imperialism/colonialism (see Mullard 1984; Brandt 1986; Cohen 1988). Some argued that racism, which formerly characterised the attitude of (British) colonialists abroad to indigenous cultures and peoples, was now 'internal' to the modern British state. By contrast, multicultural programmes of education focused on the equality of different cultures and sought ways to give recognition in the school curriculum to the cultural, ethnic and linguistic identities of minority communities. According to Marta Araújo and Hélia Santos (2006: 4) multicultural education was based on two fundamental assumptions: first, that non-recognition of minority cultures results in pupils from ethnic minority communities having lower self-esteem, which in turn contributes to educational underachievement; second, the claim that prejudice is a result of ignorance. The appropriate educational response to both assumptions is to widen the curriculum to include minority cultures and values: 'multicultural education proposed to achieve mutual understanding and "tolerance" by teaching about minority cultures' (Araújo and Santos 2006: 4).

> For the curriculum to have meaning and relevance for all pupils now in our schools, its content, emphasis and the values and assumptions contained must reflect the wide range of cultures, histories and lifestyles in our multiracial society.
>
> *Home Office 1978: 6*

> Education for diversity and for social and racial harmony suggests that the richness of cultural variety in Britain, let alone over the world, should be appreciated and utilised in education curricula.
>
> *CNAA Multicultural Working Group, quoted in Swann 1985: 318*

> Cultures should be empathetically described in their own terms and not judged against some notion of 'ethnocentric' or 'Euro-centric' culture.
>
> *Schools Council, quoted in Swann 1985: 329*

Underlying this commitment to cultural equality was a philosophy of pluralism, which affirmed that all cultures are worthwhile and valuable and that judgements between cultures (and aspects of culture) are (morally and epistemically) impossible or politically and socially inappropriate. According to Barry Troyna (1987: 313), one of the propositions central to multicultural education of this period was that of cultural relativism, which is the view that cultures can be evaluated internally only by those who share the beliefs and values of the particular culture in question. This commitment is clearly expressed in the final quotation above from the Schools Council; in fact the request for different cultures to be 'empathetically described' not only entails that non-European cultures should not be criticised but that the beliefs, values and practices of other cultures should be regarded in a positive light and appreciated. The fallacy that underlies much of the multicultural agenda is that cultures are 'distinct wholes' that are static and unchanging, without internal diversity; it is recognition of diversity within cultures that creates the possibility of criticising specific aspects of a particular culture while affirming the positive nature of the culture generally.

Both anti-racist and multicultural programmes of education have been widely challenged (particularly at the political level), and despite the commonalities between them advocates of both have often engaged in mutual criticism. For example, Barry Troyna, an influential advocate of anti-racist education (and from whom we have already quoted), accused multicultural education of overlooking the institutional nature of racism and of superficiality in its treatment of cultures: he equated multicultural education with a 'saris, samosas and steel band' approach that focused on the 'exotic and the primitive' (1993: 5). Such a form of education he believed only accentuated the differences between cultures and in a perverse way reinforced 'British' cultural superiority. In response, multicultural critics accused anti-racist educators of narrowing the category of discrimination to that of race and overlooking all other kinds of difference that can become a source of discrimination. The respective merits of these two educational programmes and their prescriptions for classroom practice are not our major concern. What they illustrate with regard to their conception of diversity, however, is significant; and it takes us back to our earlier discussion of secularisation.

Both antiracist and multicultural education gave limited attention to religion. Under the influence of perceived secularisation in society, and enamoured by secularisation theory that predicted the hasty demise of religion, many social commentators and educators concluded that religion was peripheral to culture. In a sense this conclusion mirrored the experience of many within the ranks of the intellectual elite, who had long departed from formal religious practice in deference to Enlightenment rationality and inflated views of the competence of science and scientific methodology. It should also be noted that the 1950s and early 1960s were the high-water mark of Logical Positivism in philosophy and the view that theological language, not being capable of empirical verification, was literally meaningless. This was the period when the future social commentators and educators of the following two decades received their higher education. They imbided the notion that religion was meaningless in cognitive terms, and continued believing such long after analytic philosophers had concluded that linguistic meaning and experience are not connected in the way Logical Positivists imagined. Social commentators and educationalists who persisted with the philosophically naive view that religion was meaningless in cognitive terms concluded that whatever other non-cognitive functions religion fulfilled, these eventually would cease, as scientific rationality extended its scope to all areas of social existence. Such a view is not inconsistent with standard liberal, Marxist social theory, which consigns religion to the superstructure of society and not to its foundation. Religious beliefs and practices are not a motivating force for communities but rather are viewed as giving expression to more deep-seated economic and political alienation.

On reflection it can now be appreciated that perceptions of the ongoing march of secularisation were not entirely true of British society and certainly not true of places elsewhere, say in South America and in many parts of Africa. The problem in particular for sociologists of education and educationalists is that their commitment to the theory of secularisation blinded them to the social significance of religion, particularly for minority communities. Gerald Grace (2004: 47) captures the limited and distorted vision of much social theorising by sociologists and educationalists when he writes:

> The problem for the sociology of education has been that it has operated within a 'secularisation of consciousness' paradigm which has limited both the depth and scope of its intellectual enquiries. Sociological analysis which elides a religious dimension not only presents an oversimplified view of social relations in 'the modern West', but also fails to make an authentic engagement with many socio-cultural and educational situations internationally where God is far from dead.

His criticism is directed more widely, but it certainly applies to social theorists in Britain and elsewhere who wrote in the 1970s and 1980s.

If religious decline was a necessary accompaniment of modernity, which *seemed to be* the case in Britain, then it was only a matter of time before 'disenchantment' (Weber) would be extended to incorporate minority communities as well as the majority community. The inevitable result was that the significance of religion in relation to the identity of minority communities could simply be overlooked: religion was 'erased' from the cultural and social experience of minority groups. For example, the Race Relations Act 1976 protects against discrimination 'on the basis of race, ethnic or national origins, colour or nationality', but not religion. The description of minority groups by academics and by government as 'ethnic communities' or as 'ethnic minority communities' (as in, for example, Lord Swann's Report, *Education for all*, 1985) also reveals the perceived centrality of ethnicity to group formation and identity and the relative unimportance of religion. The social and political irrelevance of religion meant that the nuances of religious description and difference could be overlooked. Race matters; ethnicity matters; hence the preoccupation with them in the educational literature of the period. Moreover, the description of those who are perceived as ethnically different is chiefly in terms of group membership: people belong to minority 'communities'.

Diversity is conceptualised chiefly in terms of the group to which one belongs. There are two explanations for this: one external, by way of ascription, the other internal, by way of self-identification. The external reason why people who are perceived as different are typically categorised in collective terms is because to members of the majority community the identity of others from minority groups is defined by a single common difference; all other points of similarity are overlooked and all other differences are subsumed under one category of description so that stereotyping becomes possible. The internal reason why people who are regarded as different by members of the majority community see themselves in collective terms is because in reaction to discrimination they accentuate the aspects of their identity that they share with others within their own group and in reaction to accusations of cultural inferiority they elevate the importance of their collective cultural traditions to themselves and to others: what they share becomes a source of pride; the hostility of the dominant culture is met with cultural unity and pride in their cultural traditions. Even those within minority communities who do not participate in religious activities can have strong emotional attachments to the religion of the group.

Both external ascription and internal self-identification reinforce each other and lead to a heightened sense of community identity among minority groups. These same factors also work to create the perception that minority cultures are fixed, clearly bounded, separate and homogenous entities. There is even a sense in which members of a community, not least members of a minority community, actively work to reinforce cultural boundaries and to differentiate themselves from other communities. The greater the number of barriers that are erected and the 'higher' they are perceived to be by 'insiders', the less likelihood there is of defections from the community. Both political and personal influence are conditioned by numbers, that is, the number of people over whom power is exercised and the number of people who can enjoy exercising power over others. The issue of power is integral to both personal and community identity, and not simply the power of one community in relation to another but also the power of individuals in relation to other communities and in relation to their own communities.

3

LATE MODERN DIVERSITY

In the last chapter the distinctive nature of both traditional and modern diversity was reviewed and consideration given to the challenges posed to education by them. In this chapter a more recent form of diversity is distinguished and attention given to its implications for education.

The case for late modern diversity

By the 1990s modern diversity in Britain was giving way to what can be termed *late modern* diversity: alternative designations that carry broadly similar connotations are 'deep diversity' (Capek and Mead 2006; Kymlicka 2009) and 'super-diversity' (Vertovec 2006). Some social commentators refer to 'postmodern' diversity, but this is contested by others who point out (see Atkinson 2010; Heaphy 2007) that the term postmodern is used to refer to developments in too many different areas – philosophy, art, architecture and culture, for example, and hence is potentially confusing. In any case, the use of the designation 'late modern' is more typically restricted to social reality, and therefore more appropriate to descriptions of diversity in society. The point has substance, hence the preference here for that designation. It is worth noting, however, that perceptions of the social and educational significance of late modern diversity have connections to postmodern currents in philosophy and the history of ideas, connections that will be identified and considered in later chapters.

In the last ten to fifteen years in Britain there has been a significant rise in net immigration and a diversification of countries of origin (Vertovec 2006: 4). According to figures released by the Office for National Statistics (ONS) in December 2010 the number of people living in Britain who were born abroad has more than doubled in the past 30 years, rising from 3.4 million in 1981 to 6.9 million in 2009, which is 11% of the total population (see Matheson 2010: 5–6).

The statistic often cited is that over 300 different languages are spoken within the boundaries of London; of the (wider) city's eight million inhabitants, three million do not have English as their mother tongue. In some years of the first decade of this century up to three-quarters of a million people came to live in the United Kingdom. In part this reflects the expansion of the European Union in 2004, which resulted in a surge in new arrivals from Eastern Europe. Even so, according to figures released by the ONS, the largest single group of immigrants in 2004, for example, came from 'New Commonwealth' nations, principally Pakistan, Bangladesh, India and Sri Lanka (Matheson 2010). Unlike earlier patterns of immigration between the 1950s and 1970s, when the majority of new arrivals spoke English and had some experience of British culture, albeit in a colonial setting or one conditioned by colonialism, many new immigrants have limited knowledge of British culture or language. (Steps have been taken to rectify the situation: on 1 November 2005 a 45-minute test on British society, history and culture was introduced for all those who wished to become British citizens, and from 29 November 2010 all new immigrants originating from outside the European Union have had to take a compulsory English language proficiency examination.)

Late modern diversity is not distinguished from modern diversity in quantitative terms alone (just as quantitative terms alone do not fully distinguish between traditional and modern forms of diversity); the two forms differ in ways that are both complex and contested. Much depends on which social forces are regarded as determinative and on the nature of their interaction in different social contexts. Social forces not only do not act singly or uniformly in different contexts but are identified and constructed on the basis of our human reading of complex human interactions. Recognition that 'we' as purposive agents are involved in social processes, which in the sociological literature is often referred to as the principle of 'reflexivity' (see Giddens 1984: 1–5), can carry a number of meanings, two of which are relevant in this context. First, it denotes the fact that our (particular) values, beliefs, political commitments and social identities enter into our reading and interpretation of social reality; and second, it denotes that our reactions to social forces and influences become part of the social phenomenon in question:

> The point is that reflection on social processes (theories, and observations about them) continually enter into, become disentangled with and re-enter the universe of events they describe. No such phenomenon exists in the world of inanimate nature, which is indifferent to whatever human beings might claim to know about it . . .
>
> *Giddens 1984: xxxiii*

It is on the basis of this second meaning that different forms of diversity should be distinguished, in that perceptions (in a particular socio-political context) of the significance of diversity for individuals and for society enter into the meaning of diversity. Diversity becomes a challenge to human society when human actors in society perceive it as a challenge; and different perceptions of diversity give rise to different construals of its significance for us. This does not mean that 'diversity' is exclusively in the eye of the beholder: diversity is present in society and has been present in society. The intellectual challenge is both to explain the nature of this diversity and to account for its changing historical character; and part of its historical character is its significance in different socio-political contexts.

Implicit in what is said above is that social forces and influences are not discrete entities that can be clearly differentiated from each other. Different social influences overlap, conjoin, mutually modify each other and even produce different effects in different contexts. This means that the question of the causal chains of social influence in (a particular) society and how the causes are related to each other is not easily answered. There is also the challenge of finding a suitable vocabulary to capture and express the character of social processes. The same explanatory concept can subsume different social influences and this in turn may lead to mistaken conclusions and inaccurate depictions of social change.

José Casanova's celebrated discussion of secularisation provides an illustration of a number of these points (see also Hanson 1997). In *Public Religions in the Modern World* (1994), he noted how the term 'secularisation' is used by social theorists to describe a range of different social processes, and this he argues leads to mistaken interpretations of the interaction between the forces of modernity and religion, and of course inaccurate predictions of the course of social change in societies that are in the process of modernising. In his view most formulations of the secularisation thesis inappropriately conflate three related but distinct processes: (1) the differentiation of modern society into semi-autonomous secular (non-religious) spheres; (2) the decline of religious beliefs and practices; and (3) the marginalisation of religion into a private sphere. According to him, the first of these processes expresses the most important aspect of the influence of modernity on religion, the other two only follow in a social context where an alliance between the church and the state exists and the European Enlightenment critique of religion is culturally influential. In other words, there is no *necessary* connection between these three different processes in different national contexts.

What are the social forces and influences that have combined to give a new salience to diversity in British society and to the case for distinguishing late modern from modern diversity? Given that increasing diversity is a feature of most (late-) modern, Western liberal, democratic societies, it is natural to look to social influences that are common to them as determinative. For this reason attention will centre on globalisation, individualisation and the resurgence of religion. Confining ourselves to these three particular social influences is less restrictive than it initially sounds. This is because the discussion will range more widely and subsume under it reference to other influences that some writers treat separately.

Globalisation

Globalisation may not seem an obvious topic for inclusion in an analysis of contemporary diversity. Does globalisation not denote the development and evolution of a truly global society, where the same rights and privileges, products and services, ideas and values are shared across different regions and countries? Is the process of globalisation not necessarily homogenising? In part, yes; yet it is also true that the same social processes that are identified with globalisation have also contributed to a new appreciation of diversity, where what was once distant and esoteric is now accessible and exoteric. For example, central to the emergence of globalisation is the importance of new technologies and digital forms of communication, creating new possibilities of interaction and communication. Regional and national identities can now be maintained across geographical and political barriers and consequently a sense of community can transcend spatio-temporal limitations. Events in a distant country become immediately and graphically accessible to others and on occasions can stimulate political tensions and protests in countries geographically removed from the events in question. This is particularly the case among 'immigrant communities', who continue to identify with their country or region of origin and who react with enthusiasm or opprobrium to events there. Clashes involving Sikhs and Hindus in the Punjab can have implications for community relations in British cities (see Shani 2007: 100–127), as can British military 'interventions' in foreign states.

The challenge of alienation and the need for democratic governments to command broad-based support have encouraged the development of policies and practices that are intended to secure the allegiance of minority communities (Young 1990). Such policies may bestow privileges on particular communities (however defined) or offer exemptions not available to others, and are often supported by financial incentives that release funds for 'social' projects. The largesse of national governments towards minority cultural and 'interest' groups, in the name of and in pursuit of inclusion, has in turn stimulated greater diversity as other groups seek financial support for their particular interests. The 'politics of identity' has increasingly become differentiated into ever smaller groups claiming community recognition and state (financial) support; where recognition can mean both recognition from the (mainstream) community and recognition as a distinct community, with special rights and privileges (for criticism, see Barry 2002). In a paradoxical way the democratic nation state extends its influence over the lives of its citizens through a variety of legal and bureaucratic measures, which collectively aim to create a level of social uniformity (social justice), while simultaneously, as benefactor, supporting a range of measures that foster and legitimise diversity in ways that are often exclusionary and partisan (positive discrimination for particular groups is a case in point).

Central to the concept of globalisation is the exchange of goods, services and finance on an international basis. Improvements in travel and communication have created innovative entrepreneurial possibilities, and as a result national economies have become connected and dependent on each other in new and novel ways. For the first time in history there is truly a global market, in which multi-national corporations are ideally placed to take financial advantage. The overall effect of these developments is to weaken the power of the nation state and its ability to regulate the internal market within its borders (cf. Osmer and Schweitzer 2003: 31–32). The shift to an information and digital economy, from a manufacturing economy, also opens the way for reduced labour costs as jobs can be 'out-sourced' in countries where wages are considerably lower than that of the 'developed' world. This raises the spectre of rising unemployment in the developed nations, alongside the increasingly limited possibilities of the nation state to initiate economic policies independently of the broader international economy. Apart from the economic cost of unemployment, there is also its social cost in alienation from society and the danger that members of minority communities, who in some cases are more likely to be less well qualified educationally, will not only suffer higher levels of unemployment but will also be perceived as a threat to the employment prospects of those who belong to the majority culture. In this way the process of globalisation, with its attendant threat to jobs, can aggravate already felt community tensions and heighten the sense of felt diversity in society.

A further effect of economic globalisation is that of multiplying choice for the consumer, as goods, products and personal services once remote become accessible. The rich diversity of interests and proclivities that is represented on the internet, for example, has the effect of cultivating and stimulated further diversity. Alternative lifestyles are fostered by the realisation that there are other people, however remote geographically, who share similar interests. Diversity fosters diversity. Increasing awareness of diversity has a legitimising effect and therefore encourages it further.

This insight can be complemented by reference to Peter Berger's notion of 'pluralisation,' which he first used in the early 1970s to explain the process of modernisation in society, but which he also believes is a continuing feature of contemporary society. In *The Homeless Mind* (1974), along with Brigitte Berger and Hansfried Kellner, he identified pluralisation as one of a range of social processes constitutive of modernisation in society; others processes identified include secularisation, increasing bureaucracy and the emergence of a dichotomy between the public and the private aspects of life (Berger later famously recanted the view that secularisation and modernity go together; see below). The combined effect of these influences is to create a sense of anonymity and alienation, what is referred to as 'homelessness', and hence the title of the book.

Pluralisation is the process whereby 'the authority of different lifestyles, values and beliefs' (Berger and Luckmann 1966: 203) is diminished as a consequence of the increasingly plural nature of modern society. First, under the conditions of modernity religious convictions are not held with the same confidence or strength of conviction as formerly, under pre-modern conditions. In more traditional times when one particular form of religion received state sanction and society was socially and religiously uniform, greater certainty attached to one's religious commitment and convictions. Second, under modernity individuals are required to make a conscious choice both about whether to be religious or not and about which particular beliefs and practices to endorse: 'Modernity, in many ways, can be described as a movement in human existence, *from fate to choice*' (Berger 1981: 34, my emphasis). In pre-modern societies religious commitment is inherited; in modern societies a conscious choice is required. Moreover, commitment is chosen from among a range of religious and non-religious options. Basically there is a loss of religious authority in the modern world and beliefs once taken for granted have lost much of their certitude in a world dominated by relativity. 'Modernity pluralizes the lifeworlds of individuals and consequently undermines all taken-for-granted certainties' (Berger 2001: 449); clearly the further increase in diversity in society associated with late modernity exacerbates this process.

Individualisation

We have charted the course from modernity, through pluralisation to the developing capacity of individuals to determine their own lifestyles and commitments. This capacity for personal choice is often referred to as individualisation, and although in some respects its origins can be traced to the social forces associated with modernity, it is widely regarded as becoming more prominent over the last few decades, and therefore it is an important catalyst and aspect of (what is here termed) late modern diversity.

In negative terms, individualisation denotes the gradual disappearance of the traditional authority of social institutions and relationships such as the church, social class, or the family. This does not mean that these institutions and relationships entirely lose their significance, only that it is no longer possible to 'type-cast' the individual on the basis of them. To take an obvious example, someone who identifies himself or herself as Roman Catholic does not necessarily believe in the infallibility of the Pope, be opposed to the use of contraceptives, attend confession on a yearly basis (at least), or perhaps even believe in life after death. More positively, individualisation denotes 'the tendency towards increasingly flexible self-awareness as the individual must make decisions and choose identities from among an increasingly complex range of options' (Wallace 1995, cited by James E. Côté and Seth J. Schwartz 2002: 573). The two-fold nature of individualisation is also stressed by Ulrick Beck. For him, individuals are disembedded from 'historically prescribed social forms and commitments' (Beck 1992: 128) and re-embedded in new ways of life in which they 'produce, stage, and cobble together their biographies themselves' (Beck 1997: 95). 'Cobbling together biographies' is an interesting expression: it suggests a relatively unsystematic, *ad hoc* process. Different identities are stitched together without obvious pattern or design, either to the observer or to the subject. The idea of self-identity is interpreted as fluid, even fragile and contested from within.

Increasing freedom to choose one's identity and to live life as one pleases challenges older interpretations that regard personal identity as relatively stable and fixed over time. The criticism is often made that modernity (as both a philosophical and social movement) subscribed to an essentialist understanding of the self. This is the view that within each person there is an innate identity (defined by such characteristics as race, class, gender and aptitude) waiting to develop and express itself along pre-determined lines. However, social mobility, urban and digital anonymity, the rejection of external authorities and (particularly) the sharp differentiation of roles and rules of behaviour in different contexts in post-industrial societies combine to create new possibilities for the construction of 'the authentic self' (see Taylor 1992). The authentic self is a creation of the self. Individuals have responsibility for creating themselves (cf. Berger 1985: 327); though this idea of 'self-creation' needs to be complemented by recognition of the socially constructed nature of the self.

Identity is the product of self-perception and the perception of others. Accordingly, identity is ours to change and amend, but equally possibilities for change are conditioned by cultural and social environments, and of course self-perception is significantly conditioned by cultural and social environments. That said, the freedom that individuals now enjoy to construct their own identities, to be what they want to be and to seek 'self-fulfilment' (cf. Robert Bellah's notion of 'expressive individualism,' see Bellah *et al* 1996) contrasts markedly with earlier periods in human history. A number of social theorists have identified such emphases as distinctively modern, in particular as reflecting post-Enlightenment, Romantic attachments (Taylor 2007: 473–504). This may be conceded. What justifies their consideration under the heading of late modern diversity is that such freedoms are no longer the preserve of the cultural and academic elites, as they were under modernity, but are now *self-consciously* shared across society. Furthermore, a case can be made that the modern self, while suspicious of external authorities, was relatively unproblematic to itself, unlike the late modern self, which is inherently reflexive and epistemologically unstable (see Zweig 1995). In fact in this context it becomes appropriate to speak of the postmodern self, in that late modern diversity is interpreted through a distinctively postmodern philosophical lens (see Chapter 11). In any case, identity is no longer conceived of as unified or as consistent across different contexts. Indeed some writers now speak of the human capacity to create multiple identities, not just serially but concurrently. As Walter Truett Anderson has claimed: 'In the postmodern world, you just don't get to be a single and consistent somebody' (1999: 11).

This freedom to create and conjoin (what may be) inconsistent beliefs, roles and identities is also, some suggest, reflected in the fate of religion in contemporary society. In an American context, Robert Wuthnow (2002) has spoken of 'patchwork religion' to describe the way in which individuals pick and choose from a range of religious options and identities. Others have made much the same point, only using different terminology. For example, Wade Clark Roof and

William McKinney (1987) refer to the 'new voluntarism'; Nancy Ammerman (2006) refers to 'everyday religion' and David Voas (2009), writing in a British context, speaks of 'fuzzy fidelity'; other equivalent terms in the literature are 'hybrid religion' and even 'playful religion'. The same form of patchwork or extempore religion has been identified more broadly across Europe by Danièle Hervieu-Léger. In her view European church members now practise 'religion à la carte', paying less and less attention to religious authorities or church pronouncements. She makes use of Claude Lévi-Strauss's term 'bricolage' to refer to a religion that is improvised and made up of originally disconnected beliefs and practices (Hervieu-Léger 1999). Ideas from different religious sources are brought together in an unlikely and unsystematic way, leading to highly personal and personalised forms of religion. Indeed some that construct beliefs in this way would demur from this reference to religion. Religion is taken to connote order, structure and sets of pre-packaged historical religions, discrete from each other. Spirituality may be a more appropriate and illuminating descriptive term, with its connotations of inwardness, personal quest and tentativeness regarding dogma, institutions and communal rituals (see Heelas and Woodhead 2004).

There is a danger, however, both in exaggerating the freedom that one enjoys in constructing identity and in unqualified notions of multiple identities or of a plural self. It can be acknowledged that the self is historical and open to revision, and certainly in a fast changing social world the ability to revise and reassess one's identity is important. Yet there are constraints, biologically, psychologically and socially. In all probability we are less free than we imagine ourselves to be and less free than some social commentators assume us to be. There is good evidence that shows that market capitalism intrudes in all kinds of ways to revise our identities in the direction of stimulating the ongoing consumption of market goods (see Edwards 2000). There still remain social, economic and personal restraints on freedom of choice. An obvious source of restraint is that of conservative religion, which in the case of minority communities still exerts a powerful influence on behaviour and lifestyle. This suggests that a differentiated concept of individualisation is needed to take account of different personal and social commitments and circumstances. The rich typically have more choices than the poor; the young more than the old; men more than women; and those who belong to 'mainstream' culture more than those who belong to religious minority groups.

The extension of personal choice, however, is not necessarily a good thing, when judged in terms of outcomes, either for individuals or for society (cf. Berger's point about 'the *homeless* mind'). Freedom of choice brings with it the freedom to make bad choices and to choose self-centred lifestyles that undermine community cohesion and the common good. In Britain increasing freedom of choice among young people to manage and conduct their own affairs is accompanied by increasing disengagement from political participation. There is reliable evidence that the numbers of 18- to 24-year-olds voting in national and local elections is falling rapidly (see Graham 2004). There is also evidence that a diminishing number of people participate in civil society and in public life, a point provocatively made in relation to North America by Robert Putnam in *Bowling Alone* (2000). He argues that people are now less inclined to commit themselves to local forms of community – voluntary associations and church groups, for example. The result of this is a decline in 'social capital', which he defines as the 'connections among individuals – social networks and the norms of reciprocity and trustworthiness that arise from them' (Putnam 2000: 19). In his view, interaction enables people to build communities, create a sense of mutual belonging and encourage civic virtue and the creation of formal and informal bonds of social support and assistance. Putman's conclusions, while controversial, are widely regarded as capturing something significant about the changing nature of contemporary liberal societies (an independent and less controversial statement that shares the same broad sociological analysis is made by Robert Wuthnow 2002, particularly pp. 58–82).

Our discussion of individualisation has been largely sociological in nature and little attention has been given to the intellectual sources that complement social causes to create a distinctively late modern form of diversity. Individualisation may be the term preferred by social theorists and sociologists to draw attention to the social forces that create greater freedom of choice for the individual, but obviously the growth of individualisation as a social phenomenon is not divorced from deeper and historically extended intellectual and philosophical ideas about freedom and personal autonomy. There is a fundamental connection between social and epistemic formation (see Foucault 2001).

The idea of freedom has a long history in Western thought, from the ancient Greeks to Isaiah Berlin and John Rawls. Modern freedom can be traced to the Protestant Reformation and the increasing recognition of the virtue of religious toleration. Kant and others moved towards a more positive idea of freedom in the nineteenth century, to that of personal autonomy, understood as self-governance or self-determination. Such an understanding naturally related to earlier notions of political freedom and natural rights, nascent in Locke, which in more recent times have been extended to incorporate ideas about popular sovereignty, democracy and human rights. Freedom to live as one pleases, then, while taking account of legal constraints, is not a novel notion. Yet legal constraints on personal freedom have historically not been the only constraints on freedom and lifestyle choice. There is also the weight of accepted tradition and public opinion. What is distinctive of late modern societies (and diversity) is not only that the sphere of personal freedom and choice has been legally extended and enlarged but that conditions have been created for individuals to express themselves through behaviour and lifestyles that once were subject to public opprobrium. Such a form of freedom was proposed by J. S. Mill ([1859] 1972) in the nineteenth century; his ideas have now come to (social) fruition. The historical trajectory of freedom is the story of increasing personal freedom and decreasing social censure of individual lifestyle choices, correlated to increasing moral diversity in society.

Moral diversity is, in turn, refracted and conditioned by other forms of overlapping diversity – social, economic, religious, racial, cultural and ethnic.

The resurgence of religion

In 1968, Peter Berger (1968: 3) told the *New York Times* that by 'the 21st century, religious believers are likely to be found only in small sects, huddled together to resist a worldwide secular culture'. Just less than thirty years later, he (Berger 1997: 974) admitted that what he 'and most other sociologists of religion wrote in the 1960s about secularization was a mistake'.

> Our underlying argument was that secularization and modernity go hand in hand. With more modernization comes more secularization. It wasn't a crazy theory. There was some evidence for it. But I think it's basically wrong. Most of the world today is certainly not secular. It's very religious.

Berger's startling new conclusion is that the world is 'very religious'. Just how religious, and just how dangerous, this post-secular world is was dramatically illustrated by the events of 9/11, when a group of Islamists from the Middle East launched a series of attacks on prominent government and economic targets in the United States of America, killing somewhere in the region of three thousand people. Four years later on 7 July 2005 (often referred to as 7/7) a group of British Islamists, all of whom were born in England and educated in (state) community schools there, launched a further series of coordinated suicide attacks upon London's public transport system during the morning rush hour. Fifty-two civilians were killed in the attacks and around 700 were injured. All four bombers also died in the explosions, which were caused by homemade, organic peroxide-based devices, packed into rucksacks. The bombers were motivated by the teachings of Osama bin Laden, opposition to British support of Saudi Arabia, and anger against Britain's involvement in the Iraq War. All believed themselves to be acting in the name of Allah and in defence of the worldwide Muslim community, the *ummah*.

The challenge of militant Islam to civil society and to the democratic institutions of society in Britain led to a flurry of government initiatives (as elsewhere): financial support for moderate Islamic groups and for the training of British born imams; the appointment of Muslim advisors by the then Labour government to review social policy that would impact on Muslim communities; and a new community cohesion agenda for public institutions, particularly schools. In addition there were obvious, and in some cases controversial, security measures; for example, the number of days a person can be detained before charges are brought was increased. Worth noting in this connection is that the only official reference to religious education made by Gordon Brown in his time as Prime Minister of the United Kingdom (2007–2010) was to commend the *Religious Education: The Non-Statutory Framework* (QCA 2004) to schools in the context of a formal statement to the House of Commons on 'national security' (Brown 2007). Clearly for him religious education should chiefly serve the political interests of the nation state, in this case in the form of indirectly contributing to national security.

Many date the modern resurgence of religion in the world to the Iranian revolution of 1979, which saw the overthrow of Iran's monarchy (Pahlavi dynasty) under Shah Mohammad Reza Pahlavi and its replacement with an Islamic republic under Ayatollah Ruhollah Khomeini, the leader of the revolution. This event contributed to Muslim self-confidence and initiated new efforts to develop social forms of Islam, which, rather than reflect or defer to secular beliefs in the public realm, sought to develop an authentically Muslim foundation for the organisation of society. Such attempts looked to the original sources of Islam in the Qur'an and in the life and traditions of the Prophet Muhammad and his immediate successors for inspiration (and to perceptions of a 'golden age of Islam', under the Abbasids, which lasted from the mid-seventh century to the mid-thirteenth century). The 'aim was no longer to modernize Islam but to "Islamize modernity" ' (Kepel 1993: 2).

Modernity, for many Muslims, is synonymous with colonialism and the imposition of secular laws and values on Muslim populations – the same laws and values that have produced what Muslims believe are decadent and corrupt societies in the West, exhibiting high levels of crime, political corruption and drug and alcohol abuse. Secularism, and to a lesser extent Christianity, were the ideologies of the oppressing colonial powers. The increasing wealth of the Islamic oil-producing states from the 1970s onwards, which allowed them to export traditional forms of Islam to Muslims elsewhere, and the alignment of Islam with post-colonial nationalism in countries such as Turkey and Indonesia, stimulated the worldwide Muslim *ummah* to more fervent religious devotion and commitment. Ernst Gellner (1992: 5) has commented that '[w]hereas other religions . . . declined in the twentieth century, Islam is as strong – or stronger – than a century ago'. In the last few decades European Muslims, buoyed by high levels of religious commitment and practice within the Muslim community, have begun to speak of the 'second evangelisation of Europe' (the first was when Muslims ruled in Spain from the eight to the fifteenth century) and to plan accordingly.

In 1980, the year after the Iranian Revolution, Ronald Regan was elected to the presidency of the United States, a victory brought about in part by support from conservative Christians. At a time when most British Christians concluded that religion was either irrelevant to politics or indistinguishable in its application from non-religious commitments, American Christians were coming to quite different conclusions. It was time to restore America to its former glory and to roll back legislation and influences that excluded religion from the 'public square'. 'The wall of separation between church and state', to use Thomas Jefferson's summary of the 'religion clauses' of the First Amendment, which were originally intended to protect the free exercise of religion, had, according to conservatives, been used by the liberal elite and the judiciary to banish Judaeo-Christian beliefs and values from public institutions (the same complaint is increasingly being voiced in the United Kingdom with regard to the application and interpretation of recent human rights legislation such as the Equality Act of 2010). American liberal democracy's much vaunted neutrality was in fact a covert attempt to divest religion of its social influence and to substitute secular and effectively anti-religious commitments and values, or so the story goes. The election of President Regan was a mandate to challenge the marginalisation of Christianity, culturally and socially. His election revealed the importance of religion in America and the political ambitions of conservative Christians.

It is not necessary to trace the rise of the 'Christian right' in America (Martin 2005), or to chart its various political successes and failures over the last few decades (see Bruce 1988, 1998: 143–189; Lienesch 2006; Northcott 2004). Political Christianity remains to this day a potent force in American politics, and it is a potent force precisely because traditional forms of Christianity hold sway over a large percentage of the American population. To describe the political activity of conservative Christians in America as an expression of political Christianity is not entirely uncontroversial, for many conservatives see their activity as opposing political interpretations of Christianity by liberal Christians who endorse secular over religious values and reinterpret the gospel of Christ as a progressive social agenda rather than as a transformative personal experience. Whatever nomenclature is used, however, the same basic conclusion stands: the most technologically advanced modern society in the world is confidently religious, and arguably has become more religious in certain respects in the last twenty to thirty years.

Attention to the situation in other countries confirms that throughout the 1980s and 1990s many countries across Africa, Asia and Latin America were also becoming more rather than less religious. To get a flavour of this, we can quote from the sociologist David Martin, commenting on the growth of Protestantism (chiefly Pentecostalism) in Latin America: 'Not since the mass baptisms of Indians by the conquering Spanish in the 16th century has Latin America witnessed a religious conversion of such magnitude' (quoted in Westmeier 2000: 14; see also Martin 1993); other commentators refer to 'a Protestant Reformation' in Latin America (Stoll 1990: 44–48). There is no shortage of studies and statistics to substantiate the point that religion at the end of the twentieth century and in the first decade of the twenty-first enjoyed a revival in many places (Berger 1999; Micklethwait and Wooldridge 2010).

The religious situation in most countries of Western Europe, including Britain, is different. Scholars have begun to recognise this and to speak of 'European exceptionalism' with regard to religion (Davie 2002). The nature of the differences between Europe and elsewhere had already been noted, though not conceptualised in this way: the decline of traditional Christian denominations, closely related to a similar decline in church attendance and religious practice; the rise of less dogmatic, eclectic or 'hybrid' forms of spirituality; increasing numbers of people who regard themselves as atheists or agnostics, and so on. Yet there are numerous ironies and contradictions. High levels of religious belief and practice are maintained by Muslim communities across Europe, particularly in Britain (see the 'Islam in Britain Report', Institute for the Study of Islam and Christianity 2005: 10). More generally, minority 'immigrant' communities retain much higher levels of religious participation and practice than the 'indigenous' population, and new forms of Christianity, typically conservative or charismatic, are flourishing in many cities, particularly in the United Kingdom and in Ireland. The difference between Europe and elsewhere is not absolute. In many countries outside Europe hybrid forms of spirituality are evolving and religious scepticism is increasing, but these features exist alongside the practice of traditional versions of religion, which continue to command the commitment of the majority.

A number of explanations have been put forward to explain why Europe is more highly secularised than elsewhere. One of the most interesting is that associated with Rodney Stark (see Stark and Finke 2000: 218–258). According to him, levels of religious participation in a society reflect the degree of competition there is between religions: all things being equal, the greater the number of religious choices available to people, the greater the degree of religious commitment and practice. High levels of religious diversity provide greater choice and in turn this elicits greater public participation. On this interpretation religious pluralism stimulates rather than corrodes active commitment to religion. How does this insight explain European exceptionalism? Stark contends that, historically, European countries operated state religious monopolies, by which is meant that one particular church or denomination enjoyed official support and was regarded as the 'state church' to which everyone belonged. Citizenship and churchmanship were conjoined and religion effectively reduced to a single species. Official state churches enjoy special privileges, often benefitting from religious taxes or other state revenues. Historically, legal and social penalties were endured by those whose religious allegiance was directed elsewhere; even though some state churches have been disestablished and others have lost privileges, they still benefit from historical associations with the nation state. In real terms there was no true religious competition in much of Europe for centuries. In Stark's view the effect of religions competing for adherents on an equal footing in a particular locality or state is to stimulate the religious market. This explains the vibrancy and the extent of religious commitment in America. The historical effect of state monopolies in religion is to suppress religious innovation and competition and thus religious commitment. This accounts for the more secular character of Europe compared with the rest of the world.

Our discussion of the resurgence of religion in this section has focused chiefly on political religion. This does not mean that political religion is a sufficient condition of late modern societies, or indeed that it is a necessary condition. If it were the former then societies in Iran and in numerous other Islamic states should be regarded as late modern societies; they should not be so regarded. Our discussion is more circumspect and contextually orientated. Late modern diversity describes a feature of societies where there is a wide diversity of beliefs and practices and no overarching comprehensive framework, constitutionally, morally, religiously or culturally. Deep diversity with regard to religion includes varieties of political or public religion, orthodox religions, extemporary, *ad hoc* religious expressions and various degrees of religious scepticism and indifference. Diversity of this kind is a necessary condition of a late modern society. Political or public religion is one aspect of such societies in the West, and is one subset of the diversity of belief and practices that characterises them.

Diversity, religion and education: a preliminary summary

The emergence of late modern diversity accentuates many of the same challenges to society as those associated with modern diversity, challenges which, given our discussion in Chapter 2, ultimately centre upon the issue of difference and how difference can be sustained and accommodated in human relationships without resulting in divisions in society that are expressed as disrespectfulness, resentment, discrimination, intolerance, and even unrest and civil disturbance. Late modern diversity deepens the challenges to society because people are exposed to difference in ways and on occasions in which they were not exposed before; other factors, such as the economic situation and the prevailing political ethos, play an influential role as well. Obviously, in democratic societies such as the United Kingdom and the countries of the European Union, where human rights are embedded in legislation, there is a requirement on governments to ensure that all citizens are treated fairly. Ironically, on occasions, the efforts of governments to challenge intolerance and to create more inclusive societies are perceived by some as exacerbating divisions by imposing restrictions on traditional freedoms and entitlements (see Trigg 2007).

Clearly the increasing degree of religious diversity in society and its changing form have important implications both for education generally and for religious education in particular. For example, in Britain there is the issue of whether religious schools should receive state funding or not. Traditionally Christian and Jewish schools have benefited from state financial support, and naturally other religious communities have aspired to and increasingly are receiving state funds to provide faith schools. There are opponents of religious schools who maintain that they are socially divisive and indoctrinatory. There is the issue of the extent to which the scruples of religious parents should be accommodated in the school curriculum. Should parents have the right to withdraw their children from sex education classes that condone practices such as homosexuality that are contrary to their religion? There is also the topical issue of whether certain forms of traditional religious clothing are appropriately worn in schools (see Gereluk 2008). Examples such as these could easily be multiplied, for religious diversity touches on almost every aspect of school life and the school curriculum.

Of course, although the effects of religious diversity are apparent in schools, it is in religious education that its reality and influence are often most keenly felt. It is for this reason, as well as to keep our discussion within manageable limits, that the focus here is on religious education and not on the wider aspects of the challenge of diversity to education. Increasing religious diversity in society raises questions about the aims of religious education, curriculum content, how religion should be represented in the classroom, methodology, and so on. It also raises the question of how successful religious education in Britain has been in contributing to the social aims of education. If we believe the rhetoric, religious education has been in the forefront of challenging religious intolerance and in effecting positive relationships between the different religious communities. Is this the case? Our review of empirical research in Chapter 1 suggests that more modest conclusions are required. The argument that follows reinforces the need for a greater degree of honesty and of self-criticism than has up to now characterised the conclusions of British religious educators, while laying the theoretical foundations for a more culturally and educationally relevant model of religious education that offers the prospect of it making a real contribution to interreligious and intercultural understanding.

4

THE DEMISE OF CONFESSIONAL RELIGIOUS EDUCATION

Modern religious education in Britain can be defined as the form of religious education that succeeded Christian confessionalism in state maintained schools in the late 1960s and early 1970s. It explicitly eschews confessionalism and conforms itself to post-Enlightenment beliefs and values. In other words, modern religious education, so understood, denotes the post-confessional history of religious education as dominated by the beliefs, commitments and values of the philosophical legacy of the Enlightenment, or in shorter form, the philosophical commitments of modernity. Modern religious education is self-consciously critical in a way confessional religious education is not. It is not necessary for our purposes to delve deeply into the institutional history of the confessional model, but it is important to grasp something of its history and character in order to appreciate more fully the nature of the contrast between it and that which succeeded it, namely non-confessional religious education. A fundamental opposition between these two models is foundational to modern British religious education.

Confessional religious education

Religious education has always enjoyed a fairly prominent, if controversial, role in British education, and for the greater part of its history it was confessional. This no doubt reflects the fact that the modern British education system can be traced back to the initiative and financial support of the Christian churches and that historically almost everyone was formally regarded as Christian. From the early nineteenth century the churches founded schools, trained teachers and organised the daily curriculum for millions of pupils. The British and Foreign School Society (Free Church) was formed in 1808 with the purpose of providing schools for the children of parents who were 'nonconformists', that is, parents whose beliefs and practices did not conform to the teachings of the Church of England. In 1811 a rival Anglican society was founded, the National Society for Promoting the Education of the Poor in the Principles of the Established Church. Beginning in 1833, grants were given by Parliament to both societies; and when in 1847 the Roman Catholic Church established the Catholic Poor School Committee, it too became entitled to state grants.

It was only in 1870, through the Elementary Education Act, that the state, recognising that the churches were failing to keep pace with population growth, reluctantly stepped into the educational arena and began providing Board schools (named after the local school boards set up to run them) to fill the gaps in the provision provided by the voluntary Christian societies. But what kind of religious instruction, if any, should be provided in board schools? There were three different constituencies whose views had to be taken into account: the majority, who were members of the established church; a significant minority of nonconformist and Roman Catholic Christians; and finally a small but growing body of atheists and agnostics (see Budd 1977). The Act contained a series of measures, which could equally be described as a series of compromises, in order to win popular support. The first measure was a deliberate act of omission: the legislation did not require schools to provide religious instruction, though most followed the example of the voluntary societies and met the expectations of the majority of parents by providing it; however, a small number of schools did not. The second measure provided to parents a right of withdrawal from religious instruction and from religious observance; this right was described as a 'Conscience Clause' by W. E. Forster, who introduced the act to Parliament. Section 7 of the 1870 Elementary Education Act states:

> It shall not be required, as a condition of any child being admitted into or continuing in the school, that he shall attend or abstain from attending any Sunday school, or any place of religious worship, or that he shall attend any religious observance or any instruction in religious subjects in the school or elsewhere, from which observance or instruction he may be withdrawn by his parent, or that he shall, if withdrawn by his parent, attend the school on any day exclusively set apart for religious observance by the religious body to which his parent belongs.

In order to facilitate withdrawals, the period of religious instruction was restricted to a fixed time at the beginning or at the end of an educational session, thus giving withdrawn pupils the opportunity to remove themselves from the classroom. The wording also makes it clear that admission to or continuance in a school may not be affected either positively or negatively by attendance or non–attendance at religious worship. The third measure was introduced by Francis Cowper-Temple, the Liberal MP for South Hampshire, on the second reading of the Bill, and has become known as the Cowper-Temple clause: 'No religious catechism or religious formulary which is distinctive of any religious denomination shall be taught in the [Board] school'. Positively, the clause provided for instruction in a broad, non-denominational form of Christianity; negatively, the clause excluded denominational specific teaching. The aim was to provide a form of religious instruction that was as religiously inclusive as possible.

This is an early example of religious education confronting the challenge of religious diversity in society. There is an attempt to achieve the broadest possible agreement on the issue of religion in public education, in this case achieved by providing a non-denominational form of Christian nurture. Those who objected to this, whether secularists or religious adherents of unorthodox disposition or adherents of a religion other than Christianity, had the right to absent their children from all religious instruction and observance. Even at this stage there was growing recognition of the principle that religion is a matter of private conscience and that the state does not have the right to impose religion on its subjects. The following year, for example, the Universities Test Act in 1871 abrogated the requirement for men attending or teaching at Oxford, Durham and Cambridge Universities 'to subscribe to any article or formulary of faith' or to be practising members of the Church of England.[1] The clauses of the 1870 Education Act can be seen as both inclusive and anti-discriminatory in embryonic form.

The decades that followed witnessed the gradual knitting together of church schools and Board schools into one integrated system administered through Local Education Authorities. The final convergence of these two types of school into one state 'maintained' system was achieved by the 1944 Education Act, in what has been described by Ken Jones (2003: 18) as trading 'influence for cash' as the state gained influence in church schools in return for state funding. Nevertheless, the Act distinguished between and legislated for 'county schools' and 'voluntary schools', the latter being those schools originally established and funded, for the most part, by the churches through their various societies. Voluntary schools were further distinguished into 'aided', 'controlled' and 'special agreement' schools (with regard to religious education, nothing turns on the distinction between aided and special agreement schools; see O'Keeffe 1988: 187). Controlled voluntary schools, like county schools, received full state funding; and in acknowledgement of their founding role the churches were granted a limited number of representatives on the boards of governors, thus contrasting with county schools, where the churches did not enjoy rights of representation. In voluntary-aided schools, in return for continuing contributions towards the cost of buildings and their maintenance (all other costs were met by the state), the founding religious body retained more influence and enjoyed majority rights on the Board of Governors. Most voluntary-aided schools were typically either Church of England or Roman Catholic, though there were a few Christian schools associated with other denominations and, significantly, a few Jewish schools. As we shall see, these distinctions within the Act between different types of maintained school carried implications for the nature and content of religious education.

Under the terms of the Act, 'religious instruction' and religious observance in the form of 'collective worship' (which according to the Act together comprise religious *education*) were established as compulsory elements of the school curriculum of all county and voluntary schools; in keeping with earlier legislative compromises, provisions for withdrawal by pupils and exemption by teachers on grounds of conscience from both were included. In his memoirs, the chief architect of the 1944 Act, R. A. Butler, was later to comment that when religious instruction was made a statutory requirement the only serious objections raised were by those who questioned if it was necessary to make compulsory what was in most schools already accepted practice (Butler 1971: 99). Interestingly, the Act did not specify which religion was to be taught and what type of worship was to be conducted in schools, though we can safely assume on the basis of the speeches in both Houses of Parliament in support of the then Bill, that the religion intended was Christianity (see Leeson 1947: 194). The Act did, however, specify that religious instruction in both county and voluntary controlled schools was to be according to an 'agreed syllabus'. Such syllabuses had to be either drawn up by the local authority or adopted from some other authority that had produced its own syllabus.

The notion of locally produced religious education syllabuses, endorsed by different Christian denominations, had already proved successful on a voluntary basis in some authorities (e.g. the 1923 West Riding of Yorkshire Syllabus) and this encouraged the government to legislate for such an approach throughout England and Wales. In order to construct an agreed syllabus a local education authority had to convene a Syllabus Conference consisting of four panels: one representing the Church of England; one representing other denominations; one representing the local authority; and one representing teachers' organisations. Nothing could be included in syllabus content to which any of the panels took exception, hence the title *Agreed* Syllabus (the current legal situation with regard to agreed syllabuses is described in Barnes 2008). The 1870 Cowper-Temple clause, which stated that syllabus content had to be non-denominational in character, was re-enacted in Section 26 of the legislation to ensure that religious education was uncontroversial and as inclusive as possible. By contrast, voluntary-aided schools could provide religious instruction in a form appropriate to the beliefs and interests of the founding church or body; in other words, they could provide denominational religious education.

The religious provisions of the 1944 Education Act remained in effect until 1988, some forty-four years, when they were superseded by the religious clauses of the Education Reform Act. If the success of legislation is indicated by the duration of its applicability then the 1944 Act must be regarded as highly successful; it certainly contrasts with the relatively short 'shelf-life' of much recent legislation on social and educational matters. A number of commentators have suggested that this success was in part due to the Act's imprecision with regard to the content of religious education. Content was to be locally determined according to agreed syllabuses, thus effectively distancing central government from a potentially controversial issue. Furthermore, as has already been noted, Christianity is not referred to by name in the legislation, and this ambiguity may have been deliberately created to accommodate state supported Jewish schools: it was also an ambiguity that was able to be exploited in the 1970s by proponents of multi-faith religious education to introduce the study of religions other than Christianity into the curriculum.

There is no need to settle the matter of the proper interpretation of the religious clauses of the 1944 Act. Like other parts of the legislation, the clauses on religion were intended to achieve a compromise between different parties to the educational enterprise. The crucial point with regard to religious education is that the Act effectively established a confessional form of religious education in 'maintained' schools, that is, schools funded in part or whole by the state. Without exception the agreed syllabuses produced between 1944 and the late 1960s assumed the truth of Christianity and presumed that the aim of religious education was to nurture Christian faith (see Loosemore 1993: 83). The Surrey Syllabus of 1947 stated in its preamble that its general aim was to give children 'knowledge of the common Christian faith held by their fathers for 2000 years' and to help them to 'seek for themselves in Christianity, principles which would give purpose to life and a guide to all its problems' (quoted in Cox 1983: 6). The Cambridge Syllabus of 1949 stated explicitly that its aim was 'to lead children to an experience of God, His Church, and His Word, an experience based on worship, fellowship and service' (quoted in Cox 1983: 30). Many more statements in a similar vein could be added. A review of the provision of religious education by the Institute of Christian Education (1957: 27) summarised the confessional nature of the type of religious education advocated by agreed syllabuses in this way:

> The agreed syllabuses from 1940 onwards reveal a great change of emphasis. Increasing attention is paid in them to worship and the aim of the teaching is declared to be that children should understand and accept the Christian faith and follow the Christian way of life . . . the hope is expressed that school worship and religious instruction will in the words of the Introduction to the Lindsey syllabus, 'increasingly lead pupils to become and remain full members of a worshipping community outside the school'.

The content of the agreed syllabuses was chiefly Bible based, comprising passages from the Old and New Testaments (for this reason Edwin Cox referred in 1956: 97 to religious education as 'the Scripture lesson'), though attention was also given to biblical history and the history of Christianity in Britain, often with a particular focus on the coming of Christianity and on local saints in the geographical region of the local education authority that produced the syllabus.

There was widespread cultural, political and educational support for such syllabuses. It is not as if a confessional form of religious education was foisted on authorities by central government. Local panels independently produced or adopted confessional syllabuses, which were then ratified at council level. Furthermore, up until the 1960s there were few dissenting voices with regard to the confessional character of religious education in schools (see Mitchell 1984). A few humanists and radical socialists raised objections but such voices originated from the ideologically liberal or secular intellectual margins of society. The syllabuses reflected the thinking of the time, which was that Britain was a Christian country and that the school had an important role to play in the promotion and continuation of Christian culture and Christian democracy (see Day 1985: 56). By teaching a broad non-denominational version of Christianity in a nurturing environment it was hoped to inculcate Christian beliefs and values in the young and thus lay down a firm moral foundation for post-war recovery. The apparatus of church and state worked together to further Christian discipleship and civic virtue: religion and morality were inextricably linked in the eyes of the politicians and educators of the day. Confessional commitments characterised religious education throughout the 1950s.

The social and political consensus on the educational appropriateness of confessional religious education began to be challenged in the 1960s (see Copley 2008: 61–88). Economic, social and intellectual influences all contributed to create a new cultural situation where traditional authorities and familiar institutions were subject to widespread criticism. Progressive and liberal ideas became the currency of public debates and discussions. Naturally education was not immune from these influences. There was a radical reassessment of the aims of education and of the aims of religious education in particular (as in Edwin Cox 1966). In the case of religious education this reassessment proceeded against the background of diminishing numerical support for institutional religion (Bruce 1995; Brown 2001: 170–192), widespread questioning of traditional Christian beliefs and values (questioning initiated in part by Christian theologians themselves, e.g. Robinson 1963; Vidler 1966), and, chiefly as a result of post-war immigration from former colonies, a growing awareness of the multi-faith nature of modern Britain. Within the field of religious education critical voices were also raised against the prevailing orthodoxy. Research seemed to indicate that the staple diet of bible study and church history, so central to the post-war agreed syllabuses, was meeting with limited success in terms of capturing pupils' interest in Christianity and in terms of advancing their understanding and comprehension of basic Christian beliefs (Sheffield Institute of Education 1961; Loukes 1961). This last point was reinforced by empirical research into the development of children's religious thinking by Ronald Goldman (1964). He contended that much of the material presented to pupils in religious education was unsuitable because it was unintelligible in terms of their experience, and presupposed capacities for thought and understanding not possessed by most until a much later stage of their intellectual development. Controversially he concluded that '[t]he Bible . . . is demonstrably not a children's book' (Goldman 1964: 203).

How should religious educators respond to this new situation? Some argued that what was needed was a more experientially focused (Loukes 1961) or life-centred approach to religious education (Hubrey 1960). Others, such as Brigid Brophy (1967) and A. J. Ayer (DES 1967: 489–92) advocated a more radical solution and called for the subject to be replaced with secular moral education. Whatever the difference between proposals, however, one thing was clear: it was becoming controversial to maintain that publicly funded schools should commend and nurture Christian faith. The received wisdom of former generations of educationalists and politicians, in part a wisdom informed by knowledge of the religious roots of the modern British education system, did not seem to resonate with the same conviction and certainty in an increasingly secular and pluralist society (as, for example, in Smith 1969). In 1966, H. F. Matthews, after reviewing developments in psychology and theology and considering their implications for education, concluded that a 'revolution' in religious education was occurring. His book, while noteworthy and useful as a review of the work of others, failed to identify a new direction for the teaching of religion in schools. That new direction, however, was to come five years later with the publication in 1971 of *Working Paper 36: Religious Education in the Secondary School*, produced by the Schools Council but written under the guidance and direction of Professor Ninian Smart of Lancaster University.

Criticisms of confessional religious education

Although *Working Paper 36* (Schools Council 1971) is best known for its advocacy of a phenomenological approach to religious education, which will be considered in the next chapter, it was also influential at the time in dismissing confessional education on the grounds that it is indoctrinatory. Two different arguments or considerations can be identified in the text, though neither is developed: the accusation that confessional religious education entails indoctrination; and the complaint that confessionalism is inappropriate in a secular and pluralist society.

The publication tersely states that the confessional or (what it terms) 'dogmatic' approach to religious education 'begins with the assumption that the aim of religious education is intellectual and cultic indoctrination' (Schools Council 1971: 21). This suggests that the indoctrinatory nature of confessional religious education is openly acknowledged by its supporters to be such. There may well be supporters of confessionalism in education who admit to indoctrination (though it is unlikely that those who do, use the term in the pejorative way *Working Paper 36* does) but there are others who do not equate inducting pupils into (Christian) faith as indoctrinatory. In any case, the paper assumes a necessary connection between confessional religious education and indoctrination, although no argument is developed or evidence adduced to substantiate the claim. This of course is not to say that the equation is without support; it may be that the framers of the document believed the evidence for an identification of confessional religious education with indoctrination to be so well known and so widely acknowledged that they could simply dispense with the need to develop an argument.[2] The subject of indoctrination in religious education had been a prominent topic in educational debates throughout the 1960s and there was a perception among some educationalists that the religious education of the sort practised in state maintained schools was either straightforwardly indoctrinatory, or at least indoctrinatory in some subtle or disguised sense. R. F. Dearden (1968: 59) is typical of many philosophers of education of the period when he concluded that 'the introduction of religious beliefs and initiation of children into religious practices . . . [should have] no proper part of the primary school curriculum'.[3]

The conviction that confessional religious education is indoctrinatory often rests upon two assumptions. First, that indoctrination can be distinguished from education (for present purposes we shall simply assume that this can be done);[4] and secondly, on the basis of this distinction, that it can be further established that there is a *necessary* connection between confessionalism in education and indoctrination. The connection must be necessary, for if it is not necessary (that is, if there is only a contingent relationship between confessionalism and indoctrination) then some forms of confessional religious education are compatible with the process of education. This would mean that *indoctrinatory* confessional religious education, if and where it exists, could and should be replaced by genuinely educational, confessional religious education. Are all forms of confessional religious education indoctrinatory? To answer this we need a clearer understanding of what constitutes (illegitimate) indoctrination in an educational context.

Intuitively, we tend to think of indoctrination describing a situation where pupils are not encouraged to think for themselves or to question the beliefs and values of the worldview into which they are being inducted, or when they are given a partial and distorted view of things. Institutions indoctrinate when they are selective in the information and knowledge they transmit, forbid and censure criticism, and when individuals are treated differentially on the basis of their commitment to the beliefs and values of the institution, and so on. More philosophically, indoctrination is often interpreted as any attempt to frustrate the growth of pupils towards normal and realistic rational autonomy (Laura and Leahy 1989).[5]

Does confessional religious education (or religious schooling for that matter) frustrate the growth of pupils towards (normal and realistic) rational autonomy? It may do. Confessional religious education may use unworthy and educationally illegitimate means of eliciting and maintaining religious faith, and in the process frustrate and arrest the development of normal rational autonomy. Perhaps the beliefs and values of other religions and non-religious communities are simply ignored, misrepresented, or falsified in a way that is unfair and sectarian; perhaps pupils are not encouraged to think for themselves; and perhaps pupils are encouraged to believe uncritically what they are taught about religion. Yet there is no reason why confessional religious education or religious schools must of necessity indoctrinate. In fact there are positive reasons why confessional educators should ensure that indoctrination does not happen.

The first is that religions in general and Christianity in particular acknowledge that religious belief and conviction must be freely chosen to be religiously valuable: a point made by John Locke in *A Letter Concerning Toleration* (1689):

'Faith only and inward acceptance are the things that procure acceptance with God' (Locke 1955: 34). One may compel belief by social pressure or psychological technique but genuine conviction and belief cannot be compelled in this way; and presumably God has the requisite perfections to know whether an individual's faith is genuine and authentic or not. Second, in liberal Western societies, where individuals are invariably exposed to different belief and value systems, there is some evidence to suggest that attempts to establish and inculcate religious beliefs in schools by exclusively non-rational means are ultimately self-defeating, in that the convictions are renounced upon leaving the indoctrinatory educational context. In other words, indoctrination does not work in a liberal democratic context where contrary beliefs and worldviews abound and are widely publicised, and where individuals enjoy freedom of belief.[6]

Finally, religious adherents typically claim that religious belief and practice can enhance personal autonomy by freeing individuals from the desires, motivations, and actions that impede responsible, self-directed decisions and behaviour. In light of these considerations it is not at all obvious that confessional religious education must be indoctrinatory or that reflective and committed religious believers would wish it to be indoctrinatory. It is surely possible to nurture religious commitment within a context where pupils' autonomy and personal integrity are not compromised; that is, in a context where pupils are encouraged to think, reflect upon and even question religious values and where appeals are made to reason and to evidence where appropriate.[7]

The second objection to confessionalism in schools adduced by *Working Paper 36* is a different kind of consideration entirely. It is a social argument that appeals to the particular constituency of modern Britain, more precisely to the multi-faith and value pluralist nature of modern Britain. Like the equation of confessionalism with indoctrination, however, the argument is not developed or defended. Be that as it may, it will be concluded that such a consideration is convincing, albeit up to a point. This qualification is important.

There are two parts to the argument that confessional religious education is inappropriate to a pluralist society. First, presumably, is the assertion that Britain in the 1960s–1970s was properly characterised as a secular, multi-racial, pluralist society; and secondly, because of this (in a yet to be specified sense), confessional religious education was and (presumably) is inappropriate.

The question whether Britain in that period was truly a multicultural, pluralist society initially suggests itself to be capable of a fairly straightforward answer – a simple yes or no. But initial impressions are deceptive. This is because what appears to be an empirical question about diversity in society actually raises complex conceptual issues. What degree of pluralism is required for a society to be properly characterised as pluralist? How many different cultures need to be represented in a society (and to what extent) for it to be considered multicultural? There is then the issue of determining whether British society in the late 1960s and early 1970s was pluralist and multicultural in our conceptually agreed sense. Some degree of historical reconstruction of the period is needed to gain an answer. Rather than pursue these issues in relation to the social situation that obtained in Britain at that time, however, it is more important to ask the same question of recent British society. Is British society over the last few decades appropriately described as multicultural and pluralist? This is the crucial question, for it tests whether the social argument adduced by *Working Paper 36* against confessional religious education *still carries force*, irrespective of its historical significance in contributing to the decline of confessional religious education in maintained schools. The matter of the nature of British society in the 1960s and 1970s may simply be overlooked.

Whatever evidence can be claimed in support of the judgement that by the end of the 1960s Britain was a pluralist society, a much stronger case can be made for the pluralist nature of contemporary Britain. There is no need to repeat the evidence and discussions of Chapters 2 and 3 in order to substantiate the point. Perhaps a case can be mounted for questioning the multicultural and plural nature of some of the smaller communities and regions within Britain, but such exceptions do not seriously challenge the appropriateness of describing modern Britain as pluralist. What implications for education follow from this? *Working Paper 36* simply assumes that confessional religious education is inappropriate to the educational needs of a pluralist society. Why is it inappropriate? We have already concluded that it is not inappropriate because it is necessarily indoctrinatory in some way. Are there other considerations? There is no reason to draw this discussion out. The most convincing reason why confessional religious education is inappropriate in state maintained (community) schools is because it is not what parents want. It is not because society is pluralist *per se*, it is because it is pluralist in the precise sense that there is no consensus or broad agreement on the subject of religion in society, and consequently no public consensus or broad agreement on the nature and role of religious education in schools. In such a context it is inappropriate to use publicly funded schools, which are by intention and design open to all, to pursue particular religious ends. In a society where most individuals/parents do not subscribe to Christian orthodoxy, practise Christianity or worship according to a Christian rubric, and where there is no widespread support for Christian nurture in state schools, then it is inappropriate. In other words, the existence and nature of religious diversity in society effectively undermines the case for exclusively confessional schools.

At one time there may well have been support for Christian nurture in state schools, but this is not now the case. In a situation where a large number of parents want to avail themselves of a state education but for whatever reason (perhaps they adhere to a different religion than Christianity or are simply indifferent to religion) do not want their children nurtured in Christian faith, then they should not be required to have them so nurtured, and for this reason confessional religious education should be abandoned.[8] This is a fairly circumscribed conclusion and certainly challenges the popular view that *Working Paper 36* provides some kind of universal or normative justification for non-confessional religious education. What it does do is provide a reasonable case, within the context of a multicultural and pluralist society, where different religious viewpoints obtain, for the conclusion that state schools, *which are by design and intention open to all*, should not proselytise on behalf of one 'comprehensive doctrine' (Rawls 1988). It does not establish the negative conclusion that it is illegitimate for *any* school within a multicultural and pluralist, liberal democratic society to pursue one comprehensive doctrine.

The suggestion that confessional religious education may be appropriate in some contexts and in some schools is at odds with the position of *Working Paper 36*, which asserts that such education is inappropriate in all schools, whether run by the state or church. It is this conclusion with which *Working Paper 36* is now associated. The impression has been created in generations of religious educators that confessional religious education is in some sense always educationally unworthy and illegitimate. The argument for challenging the propriety of confessional religious education in both state *and* church (or faith) schools is made in the document on the principle that 'the same educational principles need to be observed by all schools' (Schools Council 1971: 96). Confessionalism is incompatible with educational principles: there is a confessional approach to religious education and there is an educational approach (cf. Horder 1971: 11–12). Schools, both church and state, should be guided by educational principles, therefore confessional religious education is inappropriate in any school. This conclusion is unwarranted and overstated.

We have already discounted the accusations that confessional religious education entails indoctrination and that confessionalism involves a form of commitment that is subversive of true education. The social argument that confessional religious education is inappropriate in some contexts, and that *certain* state funded schools in Britain constitute such a context, is more successful. However, it does not establish the conclusion that confessional religious education is inappropriate in *all* schools of whatever religious, cultural, and social constituency (or whether church schools and faith schools generally should receive state funding). Properly interpreted and assessed, *Working Paper 36* fails to make a convincing case for the exclusion of confessional religious education from all schools, even though such is its intention, and historically part of its legacy has been to discredit confessional education in the eyes of many educators, religious educators included. Weaknesses in the argument of *Working Paper 36* leave room for a form of confessional religious education in faith schools that can claim to be as truly educational as it is truly religious. Of course such a form of confessional education must accommodate the rights of the child, the educational aim of autonomy (interpreted in terms of critical openness), parental wishes, and so on, but there are no insuperable educational or philosophical reasons why this cannot be done.

Notes

1   For the full text of the legislation, see http://bit.ly/1fIY896 (accessed 2 October 2013).

2   Much of the anti-confessional *animus* that pervaded British educational thought in the 1960s and early 1970s was due to the influence of Paul Hirst, who in a series of influential articles argued that Christian confessionalism is incompatible with the aims of education. A particular provocative statement of this opinion is given in Hirst (1972).

3   See also Snook (1972), which draws together and reflects upon philosophical discussions of indoctrination throughout the 1960s.

4   It is not at all obvious that a clear distinction between indoctrination and education can always be drawn. Although some educators equate indoctrination with non-rational methods of teaching, it can be argued that in the early formative years of schooling much of education is non-rational, whereby pupils accept ideas and beliefs on the strength of the teacher's authority; without such acceptance pupils would never reach the point where training and instruction gave way to education proper.

5   I acknowledge that some interpretations of rational autonomy may conflict with religious commitment; however, I do not judge the conflict to be necessary, see Shortt (1986).

6   Fred Hughes' unpublished paper, delivered at the International Seminar on RE and Values, Carmarthen, Wales, August 1998, 'Serving Many Masters: the place and nature of Christian nurture', provides some evidence for this conclusion.

7   A critic might contend that a definition of indoctrination in terms of frustrating the growth of pupils towards normal and realistic rational autonomy does not effectively capture the term's true nature and meaning, and it is because of this tendentious interpretation that confessional religious education is found to be compatible with legitimate and proper educational processes and procedures. Two points can be made in reply to this. The first is to insist that the interpretation employed is entirely defensible and that given greater space its adequacy and appropriateness could be shown. The second is to note that a number of rival interpretations of indoctrination, from which the conclusion that confessional religious education is indoctrinatory is thought necessarily to follow, upon examination either condemn other subjects and processes that are commonly regarded as genuinely educational or else fail to establish a necessary connection between confessionalism and indoctrination. Thiessen (1993) provides a philosophically sophisticated defence of the view that Christian nurture is compatible with the ideals and principles of a reflective liberal education; he rejects the idea that confessionalism implies indoctrination.

8   The crucial point to note is that a negative conclusion with regard to the appropriateness of Christian nurture in state maintained schools depends upon the fact that a reasonably large number of parents do not want their children so nurtured. The objections of a small number of parents could be overcome by encouraging them to exercise their legal right of withdrawal on behalf of their children. This strategy becomes unrealistic when the numbers become considerable.

5

NINIAN SMART, *WORKING PAPER 36* AND THE ORIGINS OF PHENOMENOLOGICAL RELIGIOUS EDUCATION

In the last chapter it was noted that the Schools Council publication *Working Paper 36: Religious Education in the Secondary School* (1971), written under the guidance and direction of Professor Ninian Smart of Lancaster University, heralded a new direction for religious education in Britain. The paper introduced a non-confessional, phenomenological approach to the teaching of religion, and to this day Smart's name is synonymous with such an approach, and with all that is best and 'professional' in British religious education (see O'Grady 2005). Unfortunately, the result of these associations is that Smart's contribution in Britain and elsewhere is often valorised and not subjected to the same level of critical scrutiny as that of others.

Although Smart introduced the phenomenological approach to religious education, his was not the only voice that enjoyed influence in schools – others took up the challenge of explaining the phenomenology of religion to teachers and of adapting it to classroom use. Michael Grimmitt, Robin Minney and Eric Sharpe are prominent examples, and these writers more self-consciously reflected and espoused the central axioms and commitments of the phenomenology of religion proper than did Smart. The point to be noted is that it is historically inaccurate to treat Smart's interpretation of phenomenology as the only one that enjoyed educational influence in schools. After *Working Paper 36* Smart wrote very little on religious education. Furthermore, the paper (1971: 5) was intended 'to raise questions for public discussion and to invite comments from those concerned with education'; it was not chiefly concerned with methodology but covered the full spectrum of issues relevant to religious education – legislation, aims, moral education, and so on. While advocating a phenomenological approach to religious education, *Working Paper 36* did not provide a fully worked out model of the form such an approach should take in schools. In fact it provided only a sketch, with just over seven pages out of 108 being explicitly devoted to explaining the nature of phenomenological religious education. The result of this is that it was largely left to others, albeit stimulated by the advocacy of Smart, to develop and to apply phenomenology to the classroom.

Ironically, the reason for the historical focus on Smart's interpretation of phenomenological religious education to the exclusion of other interpreters and interpretations is not just to attribute a uniformity of purpose and practice to religious education that never existed in reality but also to deflect criticism. There is an appreciation, in retrospect, by some religious educators that Smart's account of the phenomenology of religion is less vulnerable to criticism than that of other accounts. Consequently, and in order to maintain the fiction that religious education has an ongoing rational history, constantly developing and improving to meet new challenges, it is necessary to deny the historical influence of other interpretations in case some substance is given to the conclusion that, historically, British religious education has been largely uncritical and unreflective. The truth (which is argued for and acknowledged here) is that Smart's version of phenomenology is indeed much less vulnerable to criticism than that of others, but it is historically inaccurate to identify this form of religious education, as it was theorised and practised in Britain throughout the 1970s and 1980s, as consistently faithful to his vision and interpretation. As will be noted, at certain points British phenomenological religious education departed from Smart's position, and often in ways detrimental to the relevance and success of religious education.[1] More critically, in relation to Smart, there are also reasons for concluding that even his interpretation of phenomenological religious education is subject to weaknesses, and that these endured long after the demise of this educational approach.

From what has been said already it is obvious that the legacy of Smart in religious education is both significant and contested. An accurate estimate of his influence, however, presupposes a proper account of his position; and in order to attain this, it is necessary to trace the development of his thinking about religious education from his earliest to his later writings. This is both because Smart's developing position anticipated the direction in which most professional religious educators were moving (often on the strength of his arguments) and because his interpretation of religion and of religious education was deeply marked by Enlightenment values and commitments, that is, the values and commitments of modernity.

Ninian Smart's early writings on religious education

Professor Smart made his first contribution to the emerging debate on the nature and purpose of religious education in 1966, with the publication of *The Teacher and Christian Belief*. Although some of the themes and arguments that came to characterise his later work are anticipated, there is little to suggest the influence he would come to exert on British religious education in subsequent decades (see O'Grady 2009). His chief aim in this work was 'to discuss certain key issues about Christian belief which are relevant to those engaged in the teaching of religion' (Smart 1966: 7). Most of the book is given over to a fairly sophisticated philosophical discussion of the relationship of Christian belief to contemporary knowledge and experience, in order to acquaint teachers with a form of Christianity that he believes to be intellectually credible in the light of modern knowledge and to urge that such a form of Christianity should be the subject of study in schools. Pupils, in his opinion, should be aware both of the challenges to Christian belief, posed by science and biblical criticism, and of Christian responses, so that 'a synthesis between contemporary knowledge and the essence of Christian belief is possible' (Smart 1966: 170). There is clearly an apologetic note sounded here, though it is softened somewhat by his insistence that Christianity should not be forced upon pupils. This tension between Christian confessionalism and educational neutrality runs throughout the book. For example, at p. 140 he advocates a study of other religions alongside Christianity, in order for pupils to be freed from 'a narrow cultural and religious outlook'. But he also supports this position by a theological argument to the effect that the Christian God is revealed, through mystical and prophetic experiences, in all religions, albeit to a lesser extent than in Christianity. In other words, there is a theological justification for the study of world religions in education: other religions should be studied because (the Christian) God is also revealed and active to save in them.

Perhaps part of the tension between confessionalism and educational neutrality in *The Teacher and Christian Belief* is relieved by recognition that Ninian Smart is more concerned with developing a Christian perspective on religious education, and with encouraging Christian teachers to engage their pupils in a critical dialogue between modern knowledge and Christian belief, than with directly addressing the role of religious education in schools and in society. In addition, although there is an element of Christian confessionalism within his thinking, it is a chastened or attenuated confessionalism. Schools should endeavour, he believes, to show the coherence of Christianity and its consistency with modern knowledge for the purpose of furthering an understanding of religion and not for the purpose of eliciting faith; but then in his opinion fanatical confessionalism is self-defeating and raises the suspicion among pupils that Christianity may not be true (Smart 1966: 12). One is left wondering whether Christian confessionalism in schools (not just the fanatical version to which he refers) is inappropriate because of some educationally valid reason or because it is ineffective as a means of eliciting Christian commitment; in other words, it is not successful in awakening and nurturing Christian faith.

If there is a lingering tension within Smart's understanding of the relationship of Christian confessionalism to educational neutrality in *The Teacher and Christian Belief*, it is a tension that he settles in favour of the latter in *Secular Education and the Logic of Religion*, published two years later in 1968. Here the tension is identified as lying at the heart of contemporary theory and practice in religious education: Smart (1968: 90 and 91) refers to it as 'the schizophrenia' of modern religious education:

> The schizophrenia consists in the twin facts that Christian education is entrenched in our school system (through the 1944 Education Act) and that the typical modern institution of higher education is secular – that is, it is neutralist in regard to religious or ideological commitment . . . Neutralism is in part a reflection of the plural society in which we live . . . Ours is a society where only a minority is firmly wedded to orthodox Christian belief and practice.
>
> It is odd that an open and religiously uncommitted society should yet attempt, in its schools, to purvey some form of faith.

The suggestion that purveying faith in schools is 'odd' indicates that, for Smart, the schizophrenia of modern British religious education is to be resolved by the rejection of confessionalism and the adoption of an open and religiously neutral approach that aims to provide an understanding of religion.[2] In his view (1968: 7),[3] attention to the logic of the subject of religious studies and to 'the consequences of that logic in a secular or religiously neutralist society such as ours in Britain' establishes the case for 'non-dogmatic' religious education.

According to Professor Smart (1968: 9), the content and methodology appropriate to the study of religion, at any level, for '[t]here is an organic connection between the teaching and study of religion in all forms and stages of education', should be determined by the nature of religion. But what is religion's distinctive nature? Religion, he believes, consists of six interrelated strands or dimensions: the doctrinal, mythological, ethical, ritual, experiential and the social (cf. Smart 1971).[4] The dimensions are mutually dependent and interrelated, though combined with different degrees of emphasis in the different religions: some religions emphasise doctrines, some emphasise experience, and so on. The interrelationships and juxtapositions between the different dimensions give to the various religions their distinctive characters and spiritual sensibilities. There is no need to expand upon this aspect of Smart's work. His account of the multi-dimensional character of religion will be familiar to most students of religion. It has been highly influential, and, as Eric J. Sharpe (1983: 94) remarked, 'at the time when it was put forward it represented a new and creative way of looking at the totality of religion'.

The next step in Smart's argument is to point out that religion can be viewed from two different perspectives (1968: 12).

> We can consider religious phenomena and beliefs from a purely historical and descriptive point of view . . . and we can approach them as relevant to, or enshrining, claims about the nature of reality.

Thus there can be a descriptive study of religion, which deals with the facts of religion (i.e. with religious beliefs and the way in which religion is practised), and there can be what he calls a 'parahistorical' study of religion, which goes beyond description and considers the reasons and arguments advanced for the truth or value of religion. The question of whether Jesus lived in Galilee or whether Jesus thought he died for sin is on his usage an historical question; but the question of whether Jesus *did* die for sin is a parahistorical question, and one that is subject to different answers depending on whether one believes in the truth of Christianity or not. These two contrasting approaches derive from the character of religion itself. Typically religions claim to be true, to describe reality as it is; this in turn invites some kind of judgement and some acquaintance with the ways in which religion may be evaluated. Equally, religion is a social phenomenon, to be described and interpreted (Smart 1968: 12–15).

The central chapters of *Secular Education and the Logic of Religion* are given over to illustrating the way in which Smart believes attention to the nature of religion and to the claims typically made by religious adherents on the basis of their beliefs requires students of religion to pursue both descriptive and parahistorical studies (or alternatively, to include both elements within a study of religion). Again, it is not necessary for our purposes to follow the details of his argument. What is interesting, from our perspective, is his additional claim, made within the context of a discussion of religious experience, that 'a comparative study of religion' is a necessary and essential element of an educationally valid study of the subject (Smart 1968: 29 and 70–89). Given the relevance and importance of this conclusion for his later reflections and recommendations for religious education, it is appropriate to consider his position at this point in more detail.

According to Smart (1968: 90), an analysis of religious experience drives theology outwards to 'the wider world of . . . the comparative study of religion'. He notes how there are structural and experiential similarities both within and across the different religions and that these similarities combine and coalesce to produce distinctive patterns of religious belief and practice. In effect he develops a typology of religious phenomena (though he eschews the term *typology*). Different broad forms of religious belief, experience and practice are identified across the different religions and cultures. For example, he distinguishes between prophetic experiences, where God's transcendence is emphasised, and mystical experiences, which highlight God's nearness and immanent nature. He distinguishes between belief in a personal God, belief in an impersonal Absolute, and so on. He also draws attention to the way in which religious experiences can be overlaid and expanded by doctrinal interpretations. Strikingly similar religious experiences may, in Smart's view, be interpreted differently – the interpretation typically following the subject of the experiencer's prior religious commitment. The interplay between the different dimensions, experiences and doctrines results in similar and contrasting cross-cultural patterns of religion.[5]

Smart's position is more complex than this brief discussion suggests, but enough has been said to indicate the way in which his analysis of the nature of religion necessitates a comparative study of religion. In his view a descriptive study of religion needs to take account of the fact that broadly similar experiences are recorded within different religions and a parahistorical study of religion needs to appreciate that these similar experiences are used by adherents to justify the existence of different spiritual beings and different metaphysical beliefs.

In the final chapter of *Secular Education and the Logic of Religion*, Smart draws out the implication of his analysis of religion for religious education. His position is quite straightforward and predictable. On the basis of 'the essential unity of education' (Smart 1968: 99), the same logic that requires third-level students of theology and religious studies (for it is to this level that he has addressed his argument so far) to undertake a neutral and non-confessional study of different religions, which includes descriptive and parahistorical elements, should likewise inform the study of religion in schools (a position anticipated in Smart 1966). In other words, religious education should take precisely the same form in schools as the newly emerging discipline (under the influence of Professor Smart himself) of religious studies in universities. Both should attend to the different dimensions of religion and both should aim to create 'certain capacities to understand and think about religion' (Smart 1968: 90) and not aim to evangelise. In his view, confessional theology misinterprets and distorts the nature of religion; religious studies reflects and preserves it. If religious education wants to establish its educational credentials, it should allow its content and methodology to be determined by the nature of religion and follow the university discipline of religious studies in adopting a non-confessional, multi-faith approach. Although Smart (1968: 96) believes that confessional religious education is 'incompatible with the demands of a secular, neutralist society', he does, however, grant that it should be available to pupils 'if a majority of people [in a democratic society], for whatever reason, wish . . . though with due safeguards for those with conscientious objections to the kind of religious instruction given'.

Smart (1968: 106) concludes his study with a set of theses that conveniently summarise his position.

> First, religious education should transcend the informative.
>
> Second, it should do so not in the direction of evangelising, but in the direction of initiation into understanding the meaning of, and into questions about the truth and worth of, religion.
>
> Third, religious studies do not exclude a committed approach, provided that it is open and so does not artificially restrict understanding and choice.
>
> Fourth, religious studies should provide a service in helping people to understand history and other cultures than our own. It can thus play a vital role in breaking the limits of European cultural tribalism.
>
> Fifth, religious studies should emphasise the descriptive, historical side of religion, but need thereby to enter into dialogue with the parahistorical claims of religious and anti-religious outlooks.

Working Paper 36: Religious education in secondary schools

In 1969, one year after the publication of *Secular Education and the Logic of Religion*, Professor Smart was appointed Director of the Schools Council Project on Religious Education in the Secondary School and in 1971 an indication of the project's direction and thinking was presented to the public in *Working Paper 36*. Unsurprisingly it repeats many of the same arguments and endorses many of the same conclusions as *Secular Education and the Logic of Religion*. For example, it recommends that a number of religions should be studied across their (six) different dimensions and that religious learning should be structured according to the nature of the subject. Yet there is also novelty and some subtle shifts of interpretation and emphasis that create a degree of tension with his earlier position. Attention will be given to this in the context of a review of the central *positive* contentions of *Working Paper 36* and their supporting arguments – we have already considered the negative arguments adduced by the paper against Christian nurture, and more broadly against all forms of religious confessionalism, in the preceding chapter. Critical discussion of the position of Smart and *Working Paper 36* is reserved for the next chapter.

Phenomenological religious education

Working Paper 36's equation of a phenomenological approach to religious education with 'an undogmatic approach' (alongside the equation of confessional religious education with 'a dogmatic approach') did much to ensure that it became the dominant methodology in British schools, even though this has also brought other, less welcome, consequences. In the late 1970s and early 1980s, for example, when criticisms were beginning to be raised against phenomenology, some professional educators reacted defensively on the assumption that its rejection heralded a return to some form of Christian confessionalism in education (see Bates 1994). The alternatives were clear: either confessional religious education or (non-confessional) multi-faith, phenomenological religious education. Such a set of oppositions, while faithful to the distinctions drawn in *Working Paper 36*, is unwarranted and has served only to frustrate genuine concerns about the educational appropriateness of post-confessional approaches and methodologies in British education.

Working Paper 36's endorsement of a phenomenological approach related religious education to intellectual developments in the emerging 'discipline' of religious studies, though the theological and religious commitments of the phenomenology of religion are not discussed but simply assumed. Attention is given, however, to the application of phenomenology to religious education and to the educational benefits that accrue. The approach is commended on the basis of its 'openness' and 'objectivity', and for its promotion of 'empathic' understanding (Schools Council 1971: 21) – by virtue of imagination and empathy human beings are able to transcend their own situations and enter creatively into the subjectivity of others. Religious understanding is achieved through self-transcendence, which enables individuals to escape the 'prison of their own subjectivity' and 'by the power of imagination . . . participate in the subjectivity of others' (22). More simply expressed, the phenomenological approach enables one to 'share the life and though of another person' and 'to experience the world through someone else's eyes' (22). At the heart of phenomenology lies the notion of bracketing the issue of religious truth and freeing pupils to enter into the situation and experience of others. True religious understanding is achieved by penetrating and entering the 'inner life' of the religious believer.

We will have much more to say about phenomenology in the next chapter, but it is important to note at this stage that Smart's position with regard to attaining an understanding of religion has changed in *Working Paper 36* from the position he earlier espoused in *Secular Education and the Logic of Religion*. In the latter there is no reliance upon the phenomenological techniques of bracketing out one's own commitments and attempting to enter imaginatively into the experience of others. Religious understanding is simply equated with, first, an appreciation of the different dimensions of religion and the ways in which they relate to each other and, second, the ways in which different religions stress the importance of some dimensions over others. There is also a change of emphasis and a subtle shift of interpretation in the notion of religious truth in the two books. In *Secular Education and the Logic of Religion*, Smart argues that descriptive, historical studies of religion need to be supplemented by parahistorical studies that focus upon the truth-asserting nature of religion and provide students with opportunities to develop the necessary skills to evaluate religious beliefs and practices. By contrast, in *Working Paper 36* no mention is made of parahistorical studies, and the critical element of assessing and evaluating religious truth almost disappears: the emphasis instead falls on understanding religion and providing pupils with a non-reductive interpretation of religion. Arguably, as will be shown, these shifts in Smart's interpretation of religion brought about a much closer alignment of his position with that of the phenomenology of religion proper.

Religious tolerance and mutual understanding

Clearly schools have a role to play in combating racism and religious intolerance in society, and *Working Paper 36* is attentive to this issue (Schools Council 1971: 64 and 65).

> Pupils belonging to minority faiths need to feel that their way of life is understood and its true worth appreciated.
>
> We believe that in a multi-racial and pluralistic society there must be dialogue between those holding different beliefs and growth in mutual understanding, not the widening of inherited divisions.

As a response, *Working Paper 36* suggests that the phenomenological study of a number of different religions will further the aim of advancing religious tolerance and mutual understanding. The paper presents the view that there is a positive relationship between religious understanding and an affirmative view of others who hold different religious viewpoints, in fact they can be construed as two sides of the same coin. As religious understanding increases so does an appreciation of difference (cf. Jackson 1997; see Chapters 12 and 13 for discussion and critique). By suspending judgement and bracketing out one's own commitments, one is enabled to enter into the experience of others, and in this way one gains a 'sympathetic understanding of the[ir] inner life' (Schools Council 1971: 23). The result is a new found appreciation of the value of 'the other's' experience and beliefs. What distinguishes this publication from earlier confessional accounts of religious education is the realisation that social harmony will not be achieved by attempting to induct pupils into a common religio-cultural inheritance. Unfortunately, however, its own attempt to challenge religious prejudice and promote social harmony was also severely limited in terms of application and success, as will be noted and considered in later chapters.

Religious education and moral education

One of the most important conclusions of *Working Paper 36*, which remains influential to this day in British education, is that moral education should be distinguished from religious education and that the latter should and can be pursued as an autonomous discipline in its own right. Given the importance and influence of this position, the issue of the (changing) relationship of religious education to moral education is a subject in its own right and for this reason it is discussed separately in Chapter 14, alongside an attempt to reconnect moral education and religious education, within a different 'post-liberal model' of religious education. What is said here is confined to setting out the position of *Working Paper 36* on the relationship between religious and moral education.

Section VIII of *Working Paper 36*, entitled 'Religious education and moral education' begins with the assertion that 'moral philosophers argue that the study of ethics and the study of religion are separate and distinct academic disciplines or areas of study' (67). The subsequent four pages can be described as footnotes to this assertion. It may be granted that the assertion reflected the views of most moral philosophers at the time of writing; and it is in a sense entirely predictable. Moral philosophy is a subdivision within philosophy, and philosophy since the Enlightenment has asserted its independence of theology. Philosophy traces its origins to the sixteenth century and the beginning of the process of the secularisation of knowledge and of education (the writings of Hugo Grotius (1583–1645) may be cited as a convenient starting point for *moral* philosophy). In an important sense the *modus operandi* of moral philosophy is to describe and explain moral principles, beliefs and practices in non-religious terms, without recourse to religious beliefs and concepts. In the 1970s particularly, many moral philosophers and philosophers of education also worked under the assumption that ethical principles and rules can be stated (and derived) independently of metaphysical and ontological commitments. This was the heyday of conceptual and linguistic analysis, which, following in the wake of Logical Positivism, still looked askance upon such commitments. For example, in his 1974 restatement and revision of his 'forms of knowledge thesis', the influential philosopher of education, Paul Hirst, while purporting to eschew metaphysical and ontological beliefs, identified morality as a discrete domain of rational (propositional) knowledge, with distinctive concepts that can be tested, defended and refined on the basis of appropriate methods of enquiry and ways of assessing their epistemological status. Hirst (in this context) regarded morality and religion as autonomous domains of human knowledge. Morality is not derived from religion and religion does not provide a foundation for morality. Accordingly, moral education is an entirely secular undertaking, appealing (necessarily) to secular, non-religious norms of reason that govern behaviour.

Working Paper 36 simply reiterated (secular) philosophical orthodoxy about the relationship of religion to morality, though attention was given to explaining why religion and moral education have traditionally been linked: religions prescribe a code of behaviour; religion and morality have features in common, for each is concerned with attitudes and beliefs; Christian moral teaching is enshrined in the law in Britain (this of course is now much less the case); and finally, 'the Christian Church has played a central role in the history and development of education in this country' (68). In other words, there are historical reasons why moral education and religious education have been linked in the imagination of the public and of politicians and educators. Nevertheless, there is no logical connection between religion and morality: 'Moral knowledge is autonomous' (70) and 'morality is an autonomous area of study' (69). One of the conclusions to this section states that '[i]f morals are not founded upon a religious view of life, they must have some adequate foundation' (70). This suggests that there is an adequate secular foundation for morals, though interestingly, no indication of what this adequate foundation might be is given.[6]

Whether there is an adequate secular foundation for morals, as *Working Paper 36* presumes, or not, is not an issue that is likely to be resolved in this context. What is important and of direct relevance to our concerns is its suggestion that religious education should be concerned with religion, not morality: 'There is no reason why moral education in schools should be regarded as the responsibility of the RE department' (Schools Council 1971: 70). *Working Paper 36* simply asserts that morality and religion are (logically) independent of each other; no supporting argument is given. We have already noted that this stance reflected much educational opinion at the time, but it also reflected the stance and commitments of the phenomenology of religion, which was espoused and recommended to schools by this paper. Almost without exception the original founders and practitioners of the phenomenology of religion were liberal Protestants who looked to (inner) religious experience and not morality as the determining and justifying heart of religion; much of this was in conscious opposition to Kant's reinterpretation of religion in exclusively moral terms, with God as a postulate of 'pure practical reason'. Rudolf Otto is typical of such opposition. He identified holiness as the essence of religion and rejected equating holiness with goodness, and consequently identified 'the holy' with 'the good'; and this not because God is not morally good and perfect, as the theistic religions teach, but because holiness and the holy 'includes in addition . . . a clear overplus (*sic*) of meaning' (Otto 1950: 5) – something above and beyond moral goodness. It is this 'overplus', which is manifest in experience, that Otto wishes to isolate and explicate, and which he believes gives to religion its distinctive nature.

The combined effect of the phenomenology of religion's identification of religious experience with the essence of religion and analytical philosophy's divorce of morality from religion was to re-orientate religious education around exclusively religious content and to diminish the role of religious education in providing moral education. In other words, the combined effect of the two influences was to support and consolidate a theoretical framework for religious education that minimises the importance of the (material) contribution of religious education to moral education. Religion and morality are autonomous realms, each with its distinctive content and each with an independent claim to be part of a liberal curriculum.

Ninian Smart and the legacy of *Working Paper 36*

Tensions have already been identified between Smart's early writings on religious education (as in *The Teacher and Christian Belief* and *Secular Education and the Logic of Religion*) and his mature view as set out in *Working Paper 36*. Equally, there are tensions between the ideas espoused in that paper and subsequent developments in British religious education, which are also frequently overlooked by his interpreters. These later tensions are important for two reasons. In the first place, departures from the kind of religious education envisaged by *Working Paper 36* arguably render the phenomenological approach more vulnerable to criticism; and secondly, the departures are concerned with pedagogy, an issue that directly influences classroom teaching and practice.

The aim of the Schools Council Project on Religious Education was to initiate curriculum development in schools, and alongside the publication of *Working Paper 36* the Project also produced classroom materials and resources. What is interesting is that the position espoused by the working paper, and exemplified in the associated curriculum resources, conflicts in places with later practice in British religious education. For example, it is affirmed that 'the teaching of the Christian religion will continue to be the dominant motif in religious education' (Schools Council 1971: 83). Such a position, where prominence is assigned to Christianity over other religions, is in agreement with the later 1988 Education Reform Act, when it affirms that all new locally agreed syllabuses must 'reflect the fact that religious traditions in Britain are in the main Christian' (Harte 1989;

Poulter 1990). Those who are familiar with the debate surrounding the religious provisions of the 1988 Act, however, will recognise the irony in this. Many advocates of a phenomenological approach to religious education criticised the Act and opposed the legislation on the grounds that the prominence given to Christianity, *inter alia*, was inconsistent with an open and neutral form of religious education and with the cause of furthering religious tolerance in education (for example, see Bates 1994; Robson 1996).

The original proponents of a phenomenological approach (i.e. Ninian Smart and the contributors to the Schools Council Project on Religious Education) clearly saw no such inconsistency. They assumed, with some degree of plausibility, that religious education should reflect the cultural and religious context within which it is set. British history, literature, religious practice, and so on, have been more influenced by Christianity than any other religion, therefore recognition of this influence should be reflected in the proportion of curriculum time allocated to the treatment of Christianity within religious education. The point is not that Christianity should always dominate the religious education curriculum but that the religious education curriculum should reflect its historical and cultural context. The aim of neutrality and the quest for social justice do not require that each religion receives an equal allocation of class time, as some later supporters of the phenomenological approach in the 1980s contended.

The second point at which *Working Paper 36* reaches a conclusion that contrasts with later practice in phenomenological religious education is the issue of whether different religions should be taught systematically (serially and separately) or taught thematically. This issue was discussed in Chapter 1 and our treatment here can be confined to the point at issue in this context. In *Working Paper 36* a thematic presentation of the different religions is recommended for pupils in the primary school and during the first few years of secondary school. A systematic presentation is recommended for pupils in the later years of secondary education (Schools Council 1971: 87). This original statement, however, requires qualification in the light of the curricular materials that were produced by the project team for use in secondary schools. There we find a systematic presentation alongside a thematic presentation adopted in curriculum materials throughout. More pertinently, at *all levels* of education separate units of work are used to introduce the different religions. There are separate booklets on Christianity, Islam, Judaism and Hinduism. This shows that the early proponents of a phenomenological approach did not identify it exclusively or even chiefly with a thematic presentation of religion. Despite this, however, it should be acknowledged that Smart's dimensional theory of religion was certainly influential in providing intellectual credibility to thematic teaching: it is not unnatural to move from recognition that there are dimensions common to all religions (e.g. founders, worship and myths) to the conclusion that religious phenomena are best presented thematically under these common dimensions.

The third point of contrast between the position of *Working Paper 36* and later practice in phenomenological religious education is the balance struck between providing pupils with knowledge and understanding of religion and addressing their existential concerns as they search for meaning in experience. Over the years the phenomenological approach for the most part came to be associated with pursuing only the former: the phenomenological approach concerns itself only with the explicit phenomena of religion. Examples of school texts that fail sufficiently to engage with the concerns and interests of pupils are David Simmonds, *Believers All* (1984), J. R. S. Whiting, *Religions of Man* (1983) and a selection of texts produced by Geoffrey Parrinder in 1973 to satisfy the need for reliable classroom material on world religions. It is precisely this lack of concern with pupil interests that has produced the most strident criticisms. The accusation is made that in phenomenological religious education pupils learn about religion but they do not learn from religion, because their own experience and their quest to make sense of their experience are ignored in the classroom. Such criticisms are widely canvassed and their force widely acknowledged, even by those sympathetic to phenomenology. For example, Robert Jackson cites and discusses it in his overview of phenomenology in *Religious Education: An Interpretive Approach* (1997: 10–14; cf. Wright 2004: 185), and it is also a criticism expressly made by Edwin Cox (1983: 132) and pursued by Nicola Slee (1989: 130–131).

This particular criticism serves to illustrate clearly the difference between the original phenomenological approach as advocated by *Working Paper 36* and the phenomenological approach as it came to be interpreted by later commentators and practised by many teachers in schools. *Working Paper 36* (1971: 43) counsels that 'religious education must include *both* the personal search for meaning and the objective study of the phenomena of religion' [my emphasis]. If this call had been followed, phenomenological religious education would have been much more effective in capturing pupils' imagination and creating a context within which learning from religion would have proceeded alongside learning about religion; and thus escaped much of the criticism that has been directed against it. Part of the failure of subsequent religious educators to address pupils' concerns and questions, however, may be attributed to the paper itself. Although religious education is interpreted in the document as including both the personal search for meaning and the objective study of the phenomena of religion, the emphasis falls on the latter. In addition, for those unacquainted with the detail of *Working Paper 36*, the name 'phenomenological religious education' gives the impression that religious phenomena alone provide the subject matter.

One of the undoubted strengths of Smart's account of religious education is that it raises the important issue of how religion is to be represented in an educational context. He was able to show convincingly that the exclusively historical and biblical orientation of confessional religious education misrepresents the character of religion. Other dimensions of religion, such as the experiential and the mythological, were simply overlooked. Yet he failed to appreciate fully that his own identification of non-confessional religious education with the phenomenology of religion committed him to an alternative account of religion that is equally problematic. One cannot quibble with his insight that the study of religion should be determined by the distinctive nature of the subject; this is a welcome reminder in an age when subject knowledge is widely disparaged and thinking *skills* are believed by some to be independent of content and context. The problem is that his espousal of phenomenology commits him to an understanding of religion that is now criticised by contemporary scholars as misrepresenting and falsifying its true character. Commitments that are central to the phenomenology of religion are now widely challenged within the scholarly community, whereas among many religious educators these same commitments remain unacknowledged, or when acknowledged deemed uncontroversial. The reputation of Ninian Smart in religious education endures, whereas in religious studies his legacy is widely contested and subject to quite different estimates.

Notes

1   Cf. my earlier judgement: as the 'phenomenological approach developed . . . it became vulnerable to criticisms that did not apply to its earliest [Smartian] interpretation' (Barnes 2000: 324).

2   At the same time as Smart was advocating neutrality within religious education, Lawrence Stenhouse, Director of the Schools Council Nuffield Humanities Project, 1967–72, was advocating the same value neutral approach for humanities teachers in schools.

3   Although the title of Smart 1968 refers to 'the logic of religion', in the book he more characteristically refers to 'the logic of religious studies', which he argues should be determined by the *nature* of religion.

4   This is Smart's first use of his multi-dimensional model of religion. A few flourishes are added to it in his 1973 publication. In later writings (1989 and 1996) he distinguishes a further 'material' dimension of religion, buildings, works of art and other creations; something hinted at in Smart 1973: 43.

5   This 'structural' interpretation of patterns of religion was first introduced in Smart 1958, and then explored and developed in later writings, e.g. Smart 1964. In Smart 1981 he uses it to develop a pluralist theology that regards Christianity and Buddhism as complementary revelations of the Sacred; see Barnes 1987.

6   Writing over 40 years later, it is worth noting that contemporary philosophers are much less positive and much more divided about the intellectual plausibility of secular justifications of morality. For example, after discussing and considering a range of six different secular ethical theories, the moral philosopher Gordon Graham (2004:178) concludes starkly that 'every one of them [is] . . . deficient'; a similar judgement is expressed by the (religiously agnostic) political philosopher John Gray. In *Enlightenment's Wake* (1995) he reviews the progressive ambitions of secular post-Enlightenment liberalism and its quest for a rational, humanistic ethic and concludes that the notion of a rational morality of universal scope and application is not intellectually credible or politically achievable; see Barnes (2010).

6

THE PHENOMENOLOGY OF RELIGION

Working Paper 36: Religious Education in the Secondary School (Schools Council 1971) concluded that the phenomenological approach to religious education is the one best suited to the promotion of both religious understanding and a positive attitude towards those who belong to minority ethnic and religious communities. The descriptive nature of the phenomenological approach and its (purported) neutral stance towards the truth of religion were believed to distance teachers from the charge of indoctrination while simultaneously securing for the subject a fully educational foundation. Interestingly, despite its recommendation and use of the terminology of phenomenology, *Working Paper 36* does not provide a systematic or critical introduction to the phenomenology of religion and its distinctive methodological approach to the study of religion. Consequently, the focus of this chapter will fall on exploring and explaining the commitments and procedures of the phenomenology of religion and Chapter 7 will consider their translation into the idiom of education by prominent religious educators. This is done in some detail, to give credence and substance to the claim that the adoption of the phenomenological approach determined the subsequent character and direction of religious education in Britain. It is when there is clarity about the theoretical commitments and underlying assumptions of phenomenology that its influence in later developments and practices can be recognised.

The theological and philosophical roots of the phenomenology of religion

The roots of the phenomenology of religion go back to nineteenth-century liberal Protestant attempts to respond both to Enlightenment critiques of revealed religion and to confessional theology's attitude of superiority to religious beliefs and practices that existed beyond the narrow boundaries of each particular denomination's confessional interpretation of Christian orthodoxy. The background to this reassessment (and ultimately reinterpretation) of the nature of religion, and of Christianity in particular, was the perceived collapse of natural theology in response to the criticism of Hume (see Gaskin 1987) and Kant (see Reardon 1988). Their critique (and historically Kant undoubtedly had the greater influence) convinced many that the path from public and demonstrable knowledge to the existence of God was at best inconclusive and at worst intellectually bankrupt. In response, following Schleiermacher ([1799] 1958 and [1821–22] 1928), theology turned inwards, to the experience of the divine within the self.

Against Kant's strictures of revealed religion, Schleiermacher affirmed that religion has 'a province of its own' (Schleiermacher 1958: 21), distinct from the domains of both pure and practical reason; in other words, separate from both metaphysics and morality. Accordingly, religion is free from the requirement of justifying itself at the bar of reason or commending itself as a justification for morality. Rational apologetics, Schleiermacher believed, cannot support religion, and rational and moral criticism cannot effectively criticise it either. Instead, the essence of religion is 'a feeling for the Infinite': this is how he expresses himself in his early work, *On Religion: Lectures to its Cultural Despisers* (1958). In his later, more systematic exposition of Christian faith, he speaks plainly of religion possessing its own peculiar form of consciousness; and this peculiarity derives and finds its origin in 'the [human] feeling of absolute dependence' (*das schlechthinige Abhangigkeitsgefuhl*, Schleiermacher 1928: 12). His claim is that the reality and truth of religion are encountered in religious feeling.

By 'feeling' (*Gefuhl*) Schleiermacher obviously did not mean (mere) emotion. Having a feeling of absolute dependence is not the same as having a feeling of anger or of pleasure. It is, for him, a form of self-consciousness, an experiential form of knowledge, which may be attended by emotion, but is not to be identified with emotion. Dependence, unlike freedom, he believed, can be experienced to an absolute degree: we are conscious of ourselves as standing in relation to something that we do not determine at all. At the level of absolute dependence, human experience takes the form of religious experience, and we become aware of 'the Infinite in the midst of the finite'. The feeling of absolute or 'unmixed' (as the German *schlechthinige* can also be translated) dependence is the ground and essential source of religion; from it religious assertions gain their meaning: 'Christian doctrines are accounts of the Christian religious affections set forth in speech' (Schleiermacher 1928: 76–78). In other words, Christian theology is nothing more nor less than the articulation of the content of Christian experience.

The task of theology begins, Schleiermacher observed, when the experience of absolute dependence is felt and attempts are made to express it in religious terms. The experience has priority over its conceptualisation. This suggests a dichotomy between religious experience and theological descriptions of religious experience. For Schleiermacher, religious experience, which is for him equivalent to revelation, is essentially pre-conceptual. The conceptualisation of religious experience is secondary, and hence for him religious doctrines, at best, only approximate to the 'experienced', felt truth of religion: it is because of this that religious doctrines are capable of revision and restatement. There is no definitive form of Christian dogma. The heart of religion is located in the 'pre-reflective experiential depths of the self', and the public or outer features of religion are to be regarded as 'expressive and evocative objectifications (i.e. non-discursive symbols) of internal experience' (Lindbeck 1984: 21). Those familiar with the history of modern philosophy will recognise that this reinterpretation of religion in terms of experience apes the Cartesian, foundationalist quest for inner epistemic certainty – the chief difference being that Schleiermacher, unlike Descartes (who in other respects as a religious rationalist was supportive of religion), extended the range of justifying experiences to include religious experience.

The Romantic appeal to religious experience, initiated by Schleiermacher, set the pattern for *modern* theology (Gerrish 1984). The reinterpretation of religion in terms of inner subjectivity and commitment brought obvious advantages to the liberal Christian apologist, for if the ground of religion is situated within the self in private experience, free rein can be given to criticism of the public aspects of religion. A lively faith is compatible with a thorough-going scepticism towards the historical, moral and philosophical aspects of religious belief. Such compatibility in the late nineteenth century offered a welcome accommodation with the increasingly critical results of the emerging discipline of biblical criticism and its efforts to reconstruct biblical history on rationalist lines. A faith confined to inner experience could also avoid conflict with the pretensions of science and its claim of universality for naturalistic explanations of nature and human origins. Even traditional doctrines were not above criticism, for doctrines, as Schleiermacher insisted, are second-hand and necessarily inexact and inaccurate attempts to set forth the religious affections in speech. The essence of religion lies beyond discursive reason and rationality and is penetrated only by intuition and encounter, within the deepest recesses of the self. Effectively, religion is removed from the realm of public knowledge and the realm of the sacred privatised. The result is that public knowledge becomes equivalent to secular knowledge. By contrast, religious knowledge is deeply personal, divorced from history and non-political; and also essentially good, in that this inner experience provides a sense of personal worth and significance, which in turn issues in socially positive actions. Such a reading of religion supports an easy accommodation with culture, for religion focuses on subjectivity (cf. Schools Council 1971: 22–23) and the inner world of the spirit (for criticism, see Bartley 1984). Religion tactically withdraws from the public world of economics, ethics, social policy and politics.

Schleiermacher's account of religion also opened the way for more positive interpretations of 'other' religions, though on this subject there are important differences between his earlier, more speculative and philosophical, exposition of the nature of religion in *On Religion: Speeches to Its Cultured Despisers* and his later constructive account of Christian belief in *The Christian Faith*. In both,

Schleiermacher affirmed the universality of religious experience, and hence the universality of genuine faith, but the latter, with its emphasis upon the centrality of Christ for Christian self-consciousness, justified him in endorsing the superiority of Christianity over all other religions. The different religions, although expressing 'pious self-consciousness' in varying degrees, and thus allowing them to be plotted on an evolutionary scale of human religious development, nevertheless fall short of the full depth of religious piety that is expressed in Christianity. His earlier account, which lacks the Christological orientation of *The Christian Faith*, more deliberately underlines the theme that religion is 'great and *common*' (my emphasis, Schleiermacher 1958: 217):

> The whole of religion is nothing but the sum of all relations of man to God, apprehended in all the possible ways in which any man can be immediately conscious in his life. In this sense there is but one religion.

Even though Schleiermacher held to the superiority of Christianity, the logic of his position lends itself to a positive interpretation of other faiths that regards them as complementary to the Christian revelation. If religious experience has priority over its conceptualisation in beliefs and doctrines, and if the historical specificities of Christian faith are relegated to the level of secondary importance, then it is relatively unproblematic to move to the conclusion that there is essential agreement among the religions at the level of experience. The religions can posit agreement at the foundational level of experience, while acknowledging that the same (or complementary) experience can be expressed in different doctrinal ways in the different religions. God is manifest through all the great religions of humankind. The appeal to inner experience by Schleiermacher creates the possibility of reconciling the religions to each other; both theologians and phenomenologists of religion exploited this possibility in the twentieth century.

The intellectual and apologetic commitments of modern liberal Protestant theology were integrated into the phenomenological approach to religion. In fact as most contemporary historians of religion point out, the phenomenology of religion is one important stream of development within modern liberal Christian thought (a point recently stressed by James Cox (2006) in his historical, critical overview of the phenomenology of religion). Throughout the nineteenth century there had been a growing awareness that non-Christian religions were frequently misrepresented and misinterpreted in the West by attempts both to conform them to Christian apologetic concerns and to compare them unfavourably to Christianity (Sharpe 1975c: 28–29). There was a need for more descriptive, broad ranging and objective studies of the different religions and the development of methodological approaches that were less driven by Christian polemics and more conscious of the divisive legacy of religion in the modern world. The First World War illustrated the degree to which liberal religion could be exploited to serve national self-interest;[1] and the growing secularism of the cosmopolitan intelligentsia across Europe, which followed the war, convinced many religious thinkers that the differences between religions should be set aside in attempts to forge a new interreligious foundation for civil society and civilisation. Religion should become a unifying force among the nations rather than a stimulus to suspicion, distrust and division. This was the view, for example, embraced by William Hocking in *Re-Thinking Missions* (1932), a report commissioned by six (American) Protestant Christian denominations on foreign mission.

The influence of the apologetic orientation of liberal Protestantism over the phenomenology of religion is also seen in the latter's defence of religion against the pretensions of science. A naturalistic view of science came to prominence in the nineteenth century, of which the theory of evolution played no small part, and it threatened both to reduce all knowledge to scientific knowledge and to explain all of reality in (deterministic) scientific terms. Natural science presumed to account for all of reality and to do so in a way that not only rendered appeals to the divine (or any cause external to the universe) otiose but defined human beliefs and values in terms of impersonal processes susceptible to causal, deductive-nomological (or 'covering law') explanations (see Hempel 1965: 331–496). On this understanding human freedom is a chimera, for human choices are fully explicable in terms of casual, impersonal laws. The shadow of determinism and the loss of human freedom thus characterise the modern self. The problem is anticipated in Kant, and his distinction between the *noumenal* world, where human freedom is required to vindicate the moral law, and the *phenomenal* world, where human behaviour is fully explicable in scientific terms, is one attempt to overcome it, though one beset with philosophical difficulties (see Acton 1970: 53–59).[2]

Both twentieth-century philosophical phenomenology and the phenomenology of religion (however the relationship between them is construed) affirm human meaning and purpose in contrast to scientific determinism and the reduction of reality to impersonal laws in which 'man' simply becomes a 'cog in the machine'. Both can be interpreted as seeking to maintain the value of the individual and of lived experience, over against 'scientism' and its efforts to go beyond appearances ('phenomena') to identify some deeper reality accessible only to a scientific methodology and explicable in exclusively naturalistic terms. By contrast, philosophical phenomenology and the phenomenology of religion seek to prioritise phenomena, that is, to prioritise the lived word of experience (what Edmund Husserl, Alfred Schütz and others refer to as *die Lebenswelt*, 'the Lifeworld'). The world of experience as it 'appears' to us is much more than an object of scientific curiosity and in seeking to understand this world we are often more interested in the meaning and relation of other human subjects and objects to ourselves than in their constitution and causality. As persons we are more interested in looking for the meaning of events than in identifying their cause. Science is concerned with explanation, whereas phenomenology is concerned with meaning and purpose; and central to meaning, according to phenomenologists, is the concept of intentionality. Human experience is intentional experience, experience directed towards an object, for experience is always of something – of another human subject or an object – and experience has significance and meaning for the (experiencing) subject; as Husserl says (1931: 119), intentional experience is 'a consciousness of something' and its attendant meaning.

This orientation to persons, intersubjectivity and lived experience (*Erlebnis*)[3] is characteristic of all schools of phenomenology, both secular and religious, and consequently it is maintained that 'the study of man and society' requires a different methodology from the study of nature and external processes (this distinction in content and methodology began to be denoted in Germany in the nineteenth century by the use of two different words, *Geistenwissenschaften* and *Naturwissenschaften*). The essential function of the human sciences is interpretive, as efforts are made to gain an understanding (*Verstehen*) of the subjective meaning (for individuals) of objects and actions. Such an understanding is gained through 're-living' (*nacherleben*) the experience of others by stepping into their shoes on the basis of 'empathy', or what Husserl calls 'transcendental empathy', which he interprets as entering into the other's cognitions and establishing an intersubjective transcendental consciousness.

The phenomenology of religion

The actual term 'the phenomenology of religion' was coined by Professor P. D. Chantepie de la Saussaye of the University of Amsterdam in his *Lehrbuch der Religionsgeschichte*, first published in 1887. His aim was to bring together and describe common themes across a number of religions, what he called 'groups of religious phenomena' (*Gruppen von religiösen Erscheinungen*), such as sacrifice, prayer, and the object of worship. The main stimulus for Chantepie's attempt to organise religious phenomena along typological lines was Hegel's distinction between the essence (*Wesen*) of a thing and its manifestations (*Erscheinungen*) to consciousness. While accepting, following Schleiermacher, that there was such a thing as the essence of religion, Chantepie wanted to underline the different and diverse manifestations of religion across common themes (see Wiebe 2000: 31–50 for discussion).

This distinction between the essence of religion and its different manifestations was taken up by a number of Continental writers in the twentieth century whose studies are now commonly associated with the phenomenological study of religion: Rudolf Otto's *The Idea of the Holy* (1950 [1917]); Gerardus van der Leeuw's *Religion in Essence and Manifestation: A Study in Phenomenology* (1964 [1933]); Friedrich Heiler's *Erscheinungsformen und Wesen der Religion* (1961); W. B. Kristensen's *The Meaning of Religion* (1960); and Mircea Eliade's *Patterns in Comparative Religion* (1958). Of these studies, that of Otto and that of van der Leeuw were the most influential. Otto focused on the foundational nature of religious experience for religion whereas van der Leeuw developed a distinctive methodology that provided justification for regarding the phenomenology of religion as a separate 'scientific discipline,' different in character and form from confessional and dogmatic Christian theology. A short review of the work of both men will clarify the nature of the phenomenology of religion as an academic discipline and introduce some of the assumptions and commitments that are central to phenomenological interpretations of religion.

Rudolf Otto and experience of the holy

Rudolf Otto was in agreement with Schleiermacher's general account of religion and religious knowledge, and spoke appreciatively of him as having 'rediscovered' religion (Otto 1931: 68–77). Like Schleiermacher, he regarded religious experience as the heart of religion, and, like him, he regarded the rational approach to religious knowledge as effectively undermined by the criticisms of Kant and Hume. He was much better informed, however, through travel and education, of the content and complexity of non-Christian religions; for it was only in the late nineteenth and early twentieth centuries that accurate knowledge of these 'other' religions was becoming available to scholars. Similarly, writing later, he was able to take account of the findings of literary and historical criticism in his reconstruction of the origins and development of the religions in a way Schleiermacher was not. These findings caused Otto to question Schleiermacher's characterisation of the essence of religion in terms of 'a feeling of absolute dependence,' on the grounds that it blurred the distinction between the holy and the profane, a distinction that Otto believes is foundational to religion, wherever practised. According to Schleiermacher, religious experience and ordinary experience are two poles at opposite ends of the same continuum: the religious feeling of absolute dependence differing only by degree from natural feelings of relative dependence. This, Otto believes, misrepresents the religious consciousness: experience of the holy is, he contends, *sui generis* (see Otto 1950: 7 and 44), different in quality or kind from natural feelings. There can be no derivation of religious experience from natural experience, and no direct passage from one to the other in discourse.

Immediately this fundamental difference between Otto and Schleiermacher is noted, those familiar with the history of religious education in Britain will recognise the influence these contrasting views of the nature of religion have had. Schleiermacher's view of religion, particularly as mediated and interpreted by Paul Tillich, lends supports to the view that religious experience is latent in ordinary human experience.[4] Tillich could affirm that '[h]e who knows about depth knows about God' (Tillich: 1948: 57). This viewpoint was the inspiration of 'implicit religious education', a movement associated with Harold Loukes (1965), Violet Madge (1965) and Sir Richard Acland (1966), which enjoyed a brief period of popularity in the 1960s. The basic theological premise was that God was present and revealed in all of life, indeed more revealed in the joys and pains of everyday living than in institutional religion and abstract religious doctrines – such a position found support in the 'honest to God' theology popularised by Bishop John Robinson (1963). The educational form of this theology contended that close attention to the interests and concerns of pupils would ultimately yield religious insights as their experiences were plumbed for religious meaning and significance. The problem is readily apparent in that all too often the experience of pupils is rooted firmly in secular interests and activities, and accordingly religious education, if consistently pursued on this basis, operates without reference to religious content or religious language.

By contrast, Otto's view of religion, which is a view he shares with phenomenologists of religion generally, accentuates the contrast between everyday experience and religious experience. The reality of the divine is vouchsafed to individuals through dramatic encounters that transcend the ordinary. Such encounters are felt as immediate and direct; and provide the existential ground of religious certainty. This interpretation of the nature of religious experience, though not entirely dissimilar from that of Schleiermacher's, in that both are equally indebted to post-Enlightenment assumptions and commitments, lends itself more naturally to the development of a distinctive methodology that reveals the essence of religion (in the sense that a *distinctive* experience that can be clearly distinguished from 'ordinary' experiences is more likely to revel itself to a *distinctive* methodology). The unique nature of religion and religious knowledge is central to Otto's interpretation of religion, as is the distinctive nature of the methodology to capture the nature of religion that is central to van der Leeuw's interpretation.[5]

According to Otto in *The Idea of the Holy* (1950: 5), experience of the holy, or as he more characteristically calls it, *numinous* experience, is 'the innermost essence of religion', and that which gives religion its distinctiveness: 'Holiness – "the holy" – is a category of interpretation and valuation peculiar to the sphere of religion'. Otto derived the word *numinous* from *numen*, the Latin term for 'a divine spirit or power manifest or latent in a sacred place or object'. In his view, numinous states of mind point towards a numinous object, 'objective and ultimate,' 'precious beyond all conceiving,' and in an 'absolute sense worthy to be praised' (Otto 1950: 51–52). In numinous experience one encounters a holy presence that is majestic, frightening and transcendent. The holy has both a rational and a non-rational aspect or nature. Its rational nature allows it to be described and classified, whereas its non-rational aspect, which Otto believes is the more basic and original, is beyond description and communication. At its deepest level the holy is 'ineffable' and 'inexpressible'. Human experience of the holy is similarly beyond description and qualitatively unlike any other experience, yet it constitutes the essential source of knowledge of the divine. Numinous experience 'is a religious feeling providing a unique form of religious knowledge inaccessible to our ordinary rational understanding' (Schlamm 1992: 533).

Much of Otto's account of the holy focuses on the relationship of the rational to the non-rational in religion (with the aim of giving priority to the latter), in contradistinction to what he viewed as the prevailing religious rationalism of his day. His account of this relationship is also integrally bound up with an equally nuanced and controversial interpretation of the nature and function of religious language. For Otto, the truth of religion extends beyond the boundaries of language. There are religious truths too deep for words, in the sense that there are certain religious experiences which cannot be described but which nevertheless convey knowledge of the holy. Religious experience is primarily a feeling that defies conceptual understanding and lies beyond the domain of discursive reason. Consequently, what is distinctive of religion cannot be adequately communicated through language. Even when all that can be said about religion is said, that which is most vital to it, experience of the holy, evades description. In other words, religious language is chiefly evocative rather than descriptive; it seeks to evoke the experience of the holy rather than describe it. Although strictly speaking numinous experience cannot be described, it nevertheless initiates a genuine encounter with the holy, and as such partakes of the character of personal, existential knowledge. For Otto, there are two species of religious knowledge: immediate awareness, which is non-conceptual or pre-conceptual in form, and rational (because conceptual) knowledge; the former has priority over the latter. He writes accordingly (Otto 1950: 135):

> Something may be profoundly and intimately known in feeling for the bliss it brings or the agitation it produces, and yet the understanding may find no concept for it. To know and to understand conceptually are two different things, and are often even mutually exclusive and contrasted. The mysterious obscurity of the *numen* is by no means tantamount to unknowableness. The rational dimension of religious faith is dependent upon a non-rational and non-verbal core.

In Chapter 8 criticisms are brought to bear on Otto's account of religious knowledge and his related interpretations of religious experience and of religious language, but before moving on it is important to note the apologetic use to which Otto puts his distinctive ideas. Carefully integrated into his account of the nature of religion is a defensive strategy to protect religious truth claims. That this is the motive behind much of Otto's analysis and many of the distinctions he employs is made explicit in a number of places, none more clearly than in the quoted passage that follows. The passage needs to be placed in context. It comes at the end of the chapter 'Divination in Christianity Today', divination here being a technical term for that human faculty by which one 'genuinely' (Otto's word) apprehends the holy (1950: 144). Ironically, Otto is referring to the lack of epistemic force numinous experience has for those without such experience. Yet the point is made that numinous experience does have epistemic force for those who do have the experience. From this he goes on to conclude that the rational criticism of those who do not have the experience is of no relevance for those who have, and even more controversially still, and again implicitly, that the truth and proper content of religion entirely depends upon numinous experience (it is after all the essence of religion). Given that what is important in religion is non-rational, it follows for Otto that rational apologetics cannot commend religion, and more importantly, rational criticism cannot effectively criticise religion. This is the implication, as Otto himself notes (1950: 174, author's emphasis):

> There can naturally be no defence of the worth and validity of . . . religious intuitions of pure feeling that will convince a person who is not prepared to take the religious consciousness itself for granted. Mere general argument, even moral demonstrations, are in this case useless, are indeed for obvious reasons impossible from the outset. On the one hand the criticisms and confutations attempted by such a person are unsound from the start. His weapons are far too short to touch his adversary, for the assailant is always standing right outside the arena! But if these intuitions, these separate responses to the impress of the Gospel story and the central person to it − if these intuitions are immune from rational criticism, they are equally unaffected by the fluctuating results of biblical exegesis and the laboured justifications of historical apologetics. For they are possible without these, springing, as they do, from firsthand *personal divination*.

From this it is quite clear that Otto is attempting to do much more than accurately describe religion. His intention is quite explicitly to defend religion against criticism, and he does this by locating what is essential to religion beyond the domain of rational knowledge, by opposing religious intuitions of pure feeling to our normal categories of knowing. It is at this point that one of the central uses of his distinction between non-conceptual and conceptual knowledge is most obviously seen for what it is: an apologetic device to safeguard the autonomy of religion and protect religious truth claims from rational criticism.

Methodology, the phenomenology of religion and van der Leeuw

Gerardus van der Leeuw's *Religion in Essence and Manifestation* ([1933] 1964) has been described by Mirce Eliade (1964)[6] as 'the most adequate analysis of the phenomenology of religion available in any language'. The book is encyclopaedic in scope and conception, providing a comprehensive morphological description of the subject of religion (the emphasis on morphology reflects the influence of Lévy-Brühl). For those who give attention only to succeeding chapters and their headings the work appears sprawling and poorly organised, but for those who are more attentive to the broader scope of the book, taking account of its various subdivisions, there is a discernible structure, which revolves around the complexities and possibilities that result from challenging the traditional philosophical opposition between subject and object; challenging this distinction is characteristic of phenomenology generally (cf. Moran 2000: 13).

First, van der Leeuw (1964: 23) considers the object of religion, which following Otto he equates with 'a *highly exceptional* and *extremely impressive* "[holy] *Other*"' [my emphasis]. This is followed by an extended discussion of the human subjects of religion; that is, by a discussion of the human roles and positions that are culturally and historically connected with representing, manifesting and communicating with the sacred: the King, the medicine man (*sic*), the priest, and so on. Next, van der Leeuw considers the 'object and subject in their reciprocal operation'. As with Schleiermacher and Otto there is a post-Enlightenment Romantic emphasis upon 'feeling' and the subjective aspect of religious experience, and as with Otto there is a corresponding stress upon the objective aspect of experience. Apologetically, religious feeling is not to be equated with 'utmost subjectivity' (van der Leeuw 1964: 461). Religious content (which he can gloss as 'revelation') and religious experience are one, as are religious facts and religious meanings; by these identifications van der Leeuw (462) means that the objective reality and truth of religion is 'revealed' in religious experience:

> [The meaning of religious experience] is an ultimate meaning . . . But it could not attain this significance were it not primary and initial; thus its meaning becomes experienced as 'wholly other', and its essence as relation . . . Like all experience . . . religious experience is related to the object, and this indeed in a pre-eminent sense . . . In religious experience . . . this orientation is a presence, subsequently an encounter, and finally a union. And in this presence not he who experiences is primary, but He who is present; for He is the holy, the transcendently Powerful.

The final two sections of *Religion in Essence and Manifestation* provide a detailed treatment both of the different religious conceptions of 'the world' and of different forms of religion, particularly as these forms of religion relate to different types of 'founder figures'. In an 'epilegomena', he offers some short reflections on methodology in the phenomenology of religion and its relationship to the reality of religion.

Up to his concluding discussion of methodology, van der Leeuw has added little by way of originality or depth to Otto's interpretation of religion. Certainly he has provided more detail and discussion of religious phenomena in their cultural variations, but theologically and philosophically the accents and lines of interpretation are similar to Otto's. For example, the same account of the 'ineffability' of religious experience and, by extension, of the religious object, is found: speaking of the 'strange element' of religious awareness, which 'has no name whatever', he goes on (van der Leeuw 1964: 681):

> Otto has suggested 'the numinous' [as a title], probably because this expression says nothing at all! This foreign element again, can be approached only *per viam negationis*; and here again it is Otto who has found the correct term in his designation 'the Wholly Other'.

It is only in the last 30 of over 700 pages, when he adds some final comments on methodology, that van der Leeuw distinguishes his work from others'. His ideas and terminological distinctions are not themselves original, but he makes explicit and develops what is implicit in the work of earlier interpreters of religion such as Otto. Moreover, the methodology that he proposes is not unique to him. What claim he has to originality lies not in the discovery of new ideas but in his appropriation and application of philosophical phenomenology to the study of religion. By drawing on the work of philosophical phenomenologists and adapting their methodology and terminology to the study of religion, he constituted the phenomenology of religion as a distinctive discipline, clearly demarcated from that of confessional theology and from confessional approaches to religion. According to van der Leeuw, understanding the unique, *sui generis* nature of religion is facilitated by a unique methodology.

Van der Leeuw believed that his detailed analysis and descriptions of religious phenomena in *Religion in Essence and Manifestation* demonstrate and instantiate both the nature and the virtue of his methodology. Consequently his formal reflections on the subject in his 'epilogue' are not intended to be comprehensive and systematic. The appropriateness of his methodology to the task of understanding religion, he believed, is best revealed in use, in the detailed descriptions and analyses that it produces, rather than in abstract accounts explaining how it is to be used. This, coupled with lengthy debates among his interpreters about his indebtedness to philosophical phenomenology in his understanding of methodology, and the influence of particular figures within this philosophical tradition (with most interpreters conceding that he drew heavily on the thought of Edmund Husserl[7]), have meant that his comments on methodology are less clear and more difficult to interpret than one would wish. The briefest outline of his position only will be presented, for the most part ignoring the detailed secondary literature that seeks to clarify and synthesise his thoughts on this matter (for example, see Cox 2006: 115–128; Strenski 2006: 186–191; Wiebe 2000: 173–190). In any case, the chief principles of his methodology are easily appreciated and relatively straightforward when placed in the context of a wider discussion of the phenomenology of religion, as they are here. Furthermore, it was what is only easily accessible and straightforward in van der Leeuw that was of interest to those religious educators in the 1970s who were charged with the task of translating the methodology, originally devised for the academic study of religion, into a form suitable for use by pupils in primary and secondary schools.

An important point to note is that van der Leeuw does not construe either his interpretation of religion or the form of methodology that he believes is appropriate to the study of religion as *theoretical*. He does not regard his work as concerned with developing a theory about religion. His account of religion is believed by him to be descriptive and objective; and his methodology is intended to reveal the nature of religion as it is, unobscured by theoretical presuppositions. In his preface to the German edition he voices his opposition to theories (van der

Leeuw 1964: vi): 'I have tried to avoid, above all else,' he tells us, 'any imperiously dominating theory, and in this Volume there will be found neither evolutionary, nor so-called anti-evolutionary, nor indeed any other theories' (vi). Clearly, there are polemical concerns at work here, and these concerns resurface in his later summary of the phenomenological method:

> This entire . . . procedure [i.e. the phenomenological methodology] . . . has ultimately no other goal than pure objectivity. Phenomenology aims not at things, still less at their mutual relations, and least of all the 'thing in itself'. It desires to gain access to the facts themselves, and for this it requires a meaning, because it cannot experience the facts just as it pleases. This meaning, however, is purely objective . . . It [phenomenology] holds itself quite apart from modern thought, which would teach us 'to contemplate the world as unformed material, which we must first of all form, and conduct ourselves as lords of the world'. It has in fact one sole desire: to testify to what has been manifest to it. This can be done only by indirect methods, by a second experience of the event, by a thorough reconstruction . . . To see face to face is denied us. But much can be observed in a mirror; and it is possible to speak about things seen.
>
> *van der Leeuw 1964: 677–678*

In this passage van der Leeuw is clearly criticising a Kantian (Idealist) approach to knowledge and understanding, according to which human experience is (necessarily, *a priori*) conformed to the limiting structures imposed by the mind on the material of the senses in such a way that there is no perception of the true nature of reality. But equally, he is concerned to deny what Kant also denies: that we can enjoy experience of the 'thing in itself' (*Ding an sich*), if by this is meant a 'direct' and unmediated experience of reality. Van der Leeuw wants to maintain that human *experience* is open to the transcendent (unlike Kant), and that phenomenological analysis requires us to take seriously what is reported in experience by religious people. For van der Leeuw the focus of religion is the objects and events that are experienced as religious. Accordingly, the focus of the study of religion should not be on religion *per se* – its beliefs, practices, history, and so on – but on religious phenomena experienced by religious subjects as sacred and 'other'. Objectivity in the study of religion is, he tells us, 'to testify to what has been manifest to' the experiencing self. But how is the phenomenologist of religion to testify to what is manifest in religious experience? Van der Leeuw's answer to this in the passage quoted above is terse and gnomic: 'This can be done only by indirect methods, by a second experience of the event, by a thorough reconstruction . . .' What does he mean? How is the event of religious revelation to be experienced a second time?

Van der Leeuw believes that it is possible to enter into the experience of others, not in the sense of experiencing the event through them, but in experiencing the same event within oneself. He refers (1964: 674) to this as the 'interpolation of the phenomenon into our own lives'; we relive the experience 'intentionally and methodically'. In order to achieve this, the phenomenologist must first 'assign names' to religious phenomena: for van der Leeuw this is a quasi-technical term describing the cross-cultural grouping and classification of religious phenomena. This is followed by the practice of 'restraint', which he immediately glosses as 'epoché' and the employment of 'brackets' (1964: 675). This restraint or bracketing is the suspension of value judgements and the adoption of a neutral stance towards the object of one's attention. It is not just the methodological device of setting one's presuppositions aside in order to appreciate the religious phenomena on its own terms, it also connotes a positive attitude towards religious phenomena and a conscious effort to enter into and contemplate the religious object. Restraint brackets out what is accidental in appearances to obtain insight into the essence of things (Van der Leeuw 1964: 676). Such an understanding calls to mind and betrays the influence of Edmund Husserl, who identified epoché with 'phenomenological reduction' and stressed the need for empathy (*Einfühlung*) with phenomena in order to discern their ultimate essence. In any case by bracketing and attending to the structure of religious phenomena, the essence of religion is made manifest to the trained observer.[8]

The reference to 'the *trained* observer' (van der Leeuw 1964: 675) is important because, for van der Leeuw, religious understanding (*Verstehen*) is an intuitive process, which although facilitated by the use of a phenomenological methodology, does not automatically result from following the method. Religious understanding is 'more an art than a science' (679). This is because religious empathy is the ability to enter into the emotions and feelings elicited by religious phenomena in the religious participant, and such ability admits of lesser or greater degrees; equally not everyone is able to suspend value judgements when attending to religious phenomena.[9] Yet if the task is difficult and requires concentration and commitment, it is not impossible. The phenomenology of religion is able to give the trained observer access 'to the reality of primal experience [which is] itself wholly inaccessible' (673); to gain such access is what van der Leeuw (677–678) means when he speaks of the aim of phenomenology being 'to testify to what is manifest' in religious phenomena. In this way, the phenomenologist of religion gains 'a second experience of the [sacred] event' (678). The reality and power of religion is felt within the inner self 'in our own consciousness' (675).

Notes

1 Upon reading, in April 1914, a published statement by 93 German intellectuals, including a number of prominent theologians, supporting the German war effort, Karl Barth (1959: 57) concluded that he could no longer 'accept their ethics and dogmatics, their biblical exegesis, their interpretation of history'. As is well known, this event did not lead him to renounce theology but to develop a new kind of confessional theology – 'neo-orthodoxy.'

2 Kant famously argued in the *Critique of Pure Reason* ([1781] 1991a) that objects of human experience are all subject to complete causal determinism, yet at the same

time he affirmed belief in (libertarian) free will, which is necessary for moral accountability: the phenomena/noumena distinction is his attempt to solve this apparent contradiction.

3   This is a somewhat technical term in modern German philosophical language (see Gadamer 1975: 55–63).

4   The relationship between Schleiermacher and Otto is discussed in McKelway 1964: 20–23.

5   An often unacknowledged source that was influential in introducing Otto's ideas about religious experience into British religious education is Ronald Goldman; see Goldman 1964: 116–127. It should be noted, however, that there are other aspects of the work and writings of Goldman that seem more indebted to Schleiermacher's interpretation of religious experience; see Goldman 1965, and the 'Readiness for Religion Series of Workbooks' for pupils, edited by Goldman. See Cliff 1968, for discussion of the curricular materials by one who was involved in the project.

6   The original title in German was *Phänomenologie der Religion*; the quotation from Eliade is taken from the flyleaf of the 1964 English edition of Leeuw's book.

7   Van der Leeuw claimed that his religious phenomenology was an adaptation of the philosophical phenomenology of the German philosopher Edmund Husserl, though his claim was only made with the publication of the second edition of *Religion in Essence and Manifestation*.

8   Van der Leeuw does refer to the essence of religion, but he more characteristically refers to a range of 'ideal types' that are encountered in and through religious phenomena, and specifically refers to the soul as an ideal type. In some places he equates ideal types with religious 'meaning'. It may be helpful to think of ideal types as forms of transcendental meaning, which are timeless (see van der Leeuw 1964: 673–674); such a reading suggests parallels with Plato's notion of the Eternal Forms. Yet the comparison with Plato should not be pressed, as immediately after insisting that a type is timeless, van der Leeuw describes it as 'not real', with the qualification that 'it is alive and appears to us' (674). We will leave the resolution of this particular interpretative conundrum to authorities on the work of van der Leeuw. More broadly, van der Leeuw can be interpreted as believing that the ideal types grasped by phenomenological analysis and the use of a phenomenological methodology manifest and participate in the sacred.

9   An appeal to the need for empathy is not as prominent in *Religion in Essence and Manifestation* (1964) as it is in some of the earlier writings of van der Leeuw; cf. the qualified approval of empathy on p. 674 with the enthusiastic endorsement of it in his early works, extracts from which are included in Waardenburg 1973: 401–404, and 406. However, although the term *Einfühlung* is little used in *Religion in Essence and Manifestation* what it connotes is assumed.

7

THE PHENOMENOLOGICAL APPROACH TO RELIGIOUS EDUCATION

If modern British religious education traces its origins to the rejection of confessionalism in education, it was the adoption of the phenomenological approach that determined its subsequent character and direction. Most religious educators received the endorsement by *Working Paper 36* (Schools Council 1971) of phenomenological religious education uncritically and took advantage of the increasing number of publications that sought to enshrine its principles and methodology in classroom materials. The fact that the phenomenology of religion had already established its academic credentials at university level no doubt contributed to its favourable reception by teachers, as did the perception that the phenomenological approach was the only viable alternative to confessionalism. The vocabulary and procedures of the phenomenology of religion became the currency of religious education and its principles came to be enshrined in numerous textbooks, agreed syllabuses and Local Education Authority handbooks; its theological and philosophical assumptions were disseminated through numerous conferences for teachers, through the work of the Shap Working Party for World Religions in Education (www.shapworkingparty.org. uk/index.html) and through the journal, *Learning for Living*. Religion is regarded as the distinctive realm of the sacred (or the divine), which is revealed in diverse ways through religious phenomena; by bracketing out one's presuppositions and through the practice of empathy one can gain a 'second experience of the [original, religious] event' (van der Leeuw 1964: 677–678).

Education and the phenomenological study of religion

It has already been noted that *Working Paper 36*, while advocating a phenomenological approach, did little more than introduce the subject. The task of explaining the distinctive nature of a phenomenological interpretation of religion to teachers and of adapting its methodology for educational use was taken up by religious educators and those eager to support non-confessional initiatives in the classroom. It is important to trace the influence of the phenomenology of religion in education, and to identify the extent to which this approach to teaching the subject mirrors the basic commitments, beliefs and values of phenomenology proper, in order to illustrate the extent to which British religious education (for the most part) uncritically appropriated the axioms and commitments of the phenomenology of religion.

This is an important step in the argument, for there are contemporary religious educators who simply equate a phenomenological approach with non-confessionalism and the inclusion of religions other than Christianity in the curriculum. While both equations have merit (though reservations are expressed about the first in subsequent chapters), and there are good educational reasons for adopting non-confessional, multi-faith religious education (if not phenomenological religious education specifically) in schools that aim to accommodate those of different religious persuasions or none, this is often as deep as the analysis goes. There is often no engagement with phenomenological religious education as it was theorised and practised in the 1970s and 1980s; no consideration of the axioms, epistemic commitments and methodological procedures of a phenomenological approach; and more importantly, no serious assessment of the worth of a phenomenological approach in realising liberal educational aims compared with other approaches. Basically, phenomenological religious education is viewed from a distance – not just in the sense that the further removed in time from the period of its most explicit influence in British education the more its achievements are cited and its weaknesses minimised, but also in the sense that it is portrayed in broad, general terms. Any intellectually credible evaluation of phenomenological religious education in Britain, however, must attend to what it meant for teachers and pupils in the period when it enjoyed almost unrivalled influence in education; this is revealed in the work of teacher educators who translated the phenomenology of religion into a form suitable for classroom use.

When it was first published in 1973, *What Can I do in RE?*, by Michael Grimmitt, was in the vanguard of attempts to promote and develop a new experiential/phenomenological approach for religious education, following the collapse of confessional and neo-confessional models. In 1982, Dr John Hull could claim that *What Can I do in RE?* was one of a few books that 'to a large extent' created religious education as a 'new subject' in the 1970s (Hull 1982: xiv). It soon became a standard text for teachers and student teachers of religious education: it went through a number of editions and remained in use in higher education institutions until the end of the 1980s. Moreover, the orientation of the book was practical, in that it was written to facilitate the successful translation of educational theory into classroom practice. It aimed '[t]o provide students and teachers – especially non-specialists in RE – with an opportunity to . . . practise and acquire the skills involved in designing and implementing schemes of work and lessons in RE in accordance with educational criteria' (Grimmitt 1973: ix). For many teachers the distinctive phenomenological interpretation of religion and the form phenomenological religious education should take in schools were mediated through this book of Grimmitt's.

What understanding of religion does Grimmitt associate with phenomenological religious education? Here is a representative quotation (1973: 95):

> ... the experiential dimension is central to religion and provides the justification for the other dimensions. It is this dimension which points us more precisely to the essence or nature of religion and religious belief. Indeed, it is the presence of an experiential dimension which distinguishes a 'religion' from other types of belief system.

Here we have the familiar identification of religious experience as the essence of religion and the assertion that it is by reference to this essence that religion is both (epistemically) justified and distinguished from other 'belief systems'. This understanding of religion translates into a model lesson where the aim is to 'initiate children into Religion as a *unique* mode of thought and awareness ...' (Grimmitt 1973: 215); this of course exactly mirrors the phenomenological idea of religion as a *sui generis* category of experience.

The relationship between religious experience and religious doctrine is revealed in the following cantena of quotations (Grimmitt 1973: 96 and 97):

> ... he [the teacher] can help them [the pupils] to become aware of the all important 'feeling' side of religion and, at the same time, gain more accurate and meaningful insight into traditional religious concepts. In subsequent work he [the teacher] will need to show how the religious interpretation given to these experiences results in a person committing himself to a particular perspective from which to view life, and how it counts for his willingness to subscribe to religious doctrines ...
>
> If our only concern when introducing such accounts [i.e. Moses and the Burning Bush, ... Paul's experience of the Risen Christ on the Damascus Road, Muhammad's revelationary experiences and so on] was to foster understanding at an *intellectual* level, there would be little point in using them in the primary school ... We have chosen ... to give priority in our work with children of primary school age to the task of *sensitising them to the feelings which underlie religious beliefs and practices.* [my emphasis]
>
> ... mythological and ritual dimensions of religion ... fulfil their task as expressions of the experiential dimension.

Grimmitt (1973: 97) maintains that the 'conceptual bridges' between religious experience and understanding 'may be supplied in three ways ...: through acts of worship in schools, through films and tapes and through stories ...'. But why are conceptual bridges needed? It is because religious experience is primarily a feeling that defies conceptual understanding. One hears the echo of the voices of Schleiermacher and Otto in such a comment. Like them he believes that religious language is an inadequate vehicle for expressing religious cognition and truth. Strictly speaking, religious truth does not translate into language. The experiential essence of religion lies beyond the domain of discursive reason. Accordingly, religious language is chiefly evocative rather than descriptive; it seeks to evoke experience of the sacred rather than describe. Central to this reading of religion are two philosophical assumptions that Grimmitt shares with phenomenologists of religion proper, namely, first, that the parameters of religious experience and truth extend beyond the parameters of religious language, and secondly, that religious knowledge transcends conceptual knowledge.

The same assumptions about the nature of religion are widely evidenced in the writings of religious educators throughout the 1970s and 1980s. Here is an extract from another influential book written by a prominent religious educator. The extract is taken from his discussion of the form of religious education suitable for Year 10 pupils in a secondary school.

> . . . religion for all its many forms and manifestations is something basic and essential to what is human. The attempt to express this verbally also will, or at least ought to, emphasise that most of these forms are non-verbal. They are wordless because they are too deep, arising from the depths of the human and divine encounter. Even within the allegiance to one faith there are countless forms and expressions, and yet what gleams through the differences is precisely the unity of mankind in our primal destiny and in our relation to God. In practice students have quite spontaneously declared that an understanding and respect for the religions of other men (*sic*) has deepened and clarified their personal faith within their own religious tradition.
>
> *Minney 1975: 223*

As with Grimmitt, so with Minney, the same phenomenological commitments are present: religion is an essential element of human nature; the different religions reveal 'our primal destiny and our relation to God'; the essence of religion is 'non-verbal' religious encounter; and so on. Interestingly, Minney makes explicit the idea that recognition of the complementary nature of the different religions provides an educational foundation for respect 'for the religions of other men', a commitment that is implicit in the work of other religious educators of the period who were influenced by the phenomenology of religion and the broader stream of post-Enlightenment liberal theology.

These examples are sufficient to illustrate the point that phenomenological religious education in many instances was faithful to the basic axioms and commitments of a phenomenological interpretation of religion. Two different examples will illustrate the further point that this basic faithfulness extends to include the distinctive methodology of the phenomenology of religion. Both are taken from the foremost professional journal for teachers of religious education in Britain, *Learning for Living* (which in 1978 changed its title to the *British Journal of Religious Education*): they are 'The Phenomenology of Religion' (1975a), by Eric J. Sharpe; and 'Phenomenology and the Future of Religious Education' (1976), by John Marvell. These articles were highly influential in translating the methodology of the phenomenology of religion into the idiom of education.

John Hull wrote a summary of Marvell's article to serve as an introduction to its inclusion in an edited collection of previously published articles under the title *New Directions in Religious Education* (1982: 52), and this is a good place to begin.

> John Marvell contrasts the 'theological', the 'empirical' and [what Marvell advocates] the 'phenomenological' approaches. Pupils can be given experiences of the numinous, and religious education will thus be affective as well as cognitive. But these experiences will be related to the religions of the world . . .

The emphasis in this summary by Hull is on the cognitive nature of religious experience and that such cognitive experiences are not confined to any one religious tradition (for discussion of Hull at this point see Chapter 9). This summary tells us as much about Hull's own convictions and stance as a religious educator as it does about the convictions and stance of Marvell.

Marvell notes that the phenomenological approach to religion 'finds its basis in the work of the philosopher Husserl', though he also mentions that one of the key scholars who applies the methodology to religion and illustrates its fruitfulness is van der Leeuw. He then cites the position of Otto that 'religious experience is unique and *sui generis*. Religion in all its forms is a response to the experience of a revelation of the "numinous"'. Phenomenology 'seeks by way of "bracketing out" one's own understanding and experience to enter sympathetically into the "knowing situation" of the other person'. 'Phenomenology of religion, then, is concerned with a "presuppositionless" approach to that which is essential and unique to the essence and manifestation of religion' (all the above quotations are taken from Marvell 1982: 71). Marvell (74) goes on to recommend the production of new teaching materials that are 'evocative of the numinous', so that pupils can appreciate that 'man's [*sic*] religious experience is distinctive from any other form of experience'.

Eric J. Sharpe provides a more nuanced and detailed description of the methodology of the phenomenological approach to religion and its historical development for teachers. He refers to the influence of Husserl and to the importance of van der Leeuw in fully integrating the insights of philosophical phenomenology into the study of religion (Sharpe 1975a: 6). Two methodological principles, epoché and eidetic vision, are presented as central to the discipline. Epoché connotes the 'suspension of judgement, the exclusion from one's mind of every presupposition' (6). The term is derived from the Greek verb *epecho*, 'I hold', in this case to hold one's beliefs and values in abeyance. Ideally, according to phenomenologists of religion, all prior beliefs, commitments and value judgements should be bracketed out when the subject matter of religion is concerned. One simply observes, describes and reports. Eidetic vision is similarly derived from a Greek word, *eidos* – 'that which is seen' (i.e. form, shape or essence). According to Sharpe (6), '[e]idetic vision is the capacity for seeing the essentials of a situation, or in the case of a phenomenon, its essence'. This two-fold hermeneutical process of epoché and eidetic vision, or two-fold 'reduction' (Husserl), defines the nature of the phenomenological approach to religion. Attention is given to the religious phenomenon under discussion with all prior beliefs and assumptions suspended, then, in this focused state, the observer enters into the basic structures and thought world of religion and intuits the meaning of the experience for the believer and thus lays bare the essence of religion. Sharpe (8) notes that for most phenomenologists of religion, 'the purpose of their enquiry [is] to understand the nature of man's response to a transcendent reality, summed up as a rule under the words "the sacred" or "the holy"'.

Sharpe concludes his article on phenomenology of religion and its implications for education in a somewhat sombre mood. He cautions against use of the specialist vocabulary of phenomenology and speculates that part of the attractiveness of this approach to religion may be because 'it provides a useful alternative to rejected orthodoxies.' The implicit message in this comment is that phenomenology is attractive to teachers and educators because of its non-confessional nature rather than because of its obvious educational and pedagogical strengths. Interestingly, in a collection of essays entitled *New Movements in Religious Education*, published in the same year, Sharpe (1975b: 195) reflected further on the reasons for the increasing popularity among educators of what he calls 'comparative religion' (it is clear in this context that comparative religion is equated with the phenomenology of religion):

> Now if it should prove to be the case that the comparative religionist, by reason of the many systems of religious belief and practice which pass under his gaze, is expected to demonstrate the relative unimportance of creeds and authorities, priests and sacraments, hassocks and hymnbooks, and to demonstrate what the Hindu, and increasingly some Christians too, would call the transcendental unity of all religions (or rather all religion), then we have another reason for his [i.e. the 'comparative religionist's'] current popularity.

This was a deeply perceptive, even prescient remark, as will become clear in subsequent chapters. What was to endure in British religious education after the demise of a phenomenological approach and the use of its specialist terminology was the conviction that all the different religions mediate truth and salvation: the thesis of the 'transcendental unity of all religions' was to come to provide a generation of religious educators with a *religious* foundation both to challenge religious intolerance and to develop respect for others.

Influence and criticism

The attractiveness of a phenomenological approach to teachers should be obvious. Phenomenological religious education claims to be multi-faith, inclusive, neutral and 'objective' – no religion is privileged over another. Formally, the critical evaluation of religious beliefs and practices can be set aside, bracketed out as the phenomenology of religion's methodology demands, yet informally the truth of religion is assumed: the irreducible truth of religious experience of the sacred that reveals itself through intuition and encounter (i.e. eidetic vision). In this way religious believers can be persuaded that their ultimate commitments will be unchallenged in the educational domain and religious educators can believe themselves to be contributing to religious understanding. Through empathy insight is gained into the religious world of 'the other'; and true to the liberal Protestant foundations of the phenomenology of religion, the religious world of 'the other' is found to be centred on and expressive of the transcendent mystery that lies at the heart of all religion. As Marvell (1982: 74) maintains, every religion evokes 'the numinous'. On this basis one of the most controversial issues in relation to religion is overlooked: that of evaluating religious claims to truth and adjudicating between rival doctrinal beliefs.

Religion is not chiefly about doctrines and beliefs but about experience of the sacred, which the different religions facilitate, and in turn, express in different culturally conditioned ways. Furthermore, following the demise of Christian confessionalism in education, there was a certain embarrassment with the doctrinal element of religion, and the phenomenological approach provided a welcome justification for diminishing the role of doctrine in religion, and consequently the role of doctrine and beliefs in religious education. Religious education is thus freed from challenge and possible controversy. What could be fairer than that the different religions are treated equally, for all are believed to facilitate an encounter with divine mystery! Thus the principle of equality is affirmed, in this the religious case. The phenomenological approach provides the means of endorsing religion while favouring none.

This endorsement of religion was important, against a background in education and in society where the relevance and significance of religion was often overlooked. In the discussion of modern diversity in Chapter 2 it was noted how education and schools attached salience to ethnic and racial differences, but for the most part disregarded religion and religious differences. The intellectual elite viewed religion as an epiphenomenon that reflected more fundamental economic or psychological realities; in any case commitment to the secularisation thesis predicted that religion was in terminal decline. Against this intellectual background many religious educators in the 1970s and 1980s regarded themselves as witnessing to the importance of religion and to its positive contribution to society. In a situation where religion was culturally despised, it was natural to underline the similarities between religions and thus present them as collectively opposed to secularism and the cultural disparagement of religion.

The phenomenological approach commended itself to religious educators on the grounds that not only did it uphold the principle of religious equality but it also had both a commitment to the elimination of religious prejudice and a strategy to achieve this. *Working Paper 36* (Schools Council 1971: 64) affirmed the need for members of 'minority faiths' to feel that their ways of life were understood and valued; and in keeping with the phenomenology of religion, it linked religious understanding to an appreciation of religious difference. By bracketing out prior commitments and beliefs, pupils are enabled to enter into the meaning of religious phenomena. As religious understanding develops and deepens, so an appreciation of the power and force of religious beliefs and values is gained; in this way pupils come to respect religious difference. By developing this form of religious understanding, religious educators believed themselves to be promoting religious tolerance and contributing positively to preparing pupils for life in a multicultural, multiracial society.

As multi-faith, phenomenological religious education rose to prominence in the 1970s, however, certain weaknesses about its capacity to further the social aims of multicultural education soon became apparent to teachers. The notion that acquaintance with the beliefs and values of minority groups *by itself* will considerably reduce religious prejudice enjoyed little support from experience. More specifically, questions began to be raised about the capability of pupils to enter into the experience of others and to develop a positive attitude to them on the basis of the phenomenological technique of 'bracketing out' their own convictions and commitments. A psychological perspective on children's cognitive development suggests that most pupils in primary schools are incapable (conceptually) of adopting a viewpoint contrary to their own (the evidence is summarised and discussed in Kay 1997). At this stage in their cognitive development pupils are not able to adopt a third person perspective on situations and experiences. The method of bracketing one's own beliefs and entering into the mind-state and experience of others in order to gain an appreciation of their beliefs is compromised by the psychological and imaginative limitations of many pupils; in some cases limitations that endure until well into secondary level education. There is also the complaint that by setting aside one's own values and commitments and attempting to place oneself in the situation of the experiencing subject, tacit support is given to moral and religious relativism − from the perspective of the 'insider' everything that is experienced in religion is valid and true.

Such considerations should have caused proponents of phenomenological religious education to question its fundamental assumptions and commitments. They did not, and this for two reasons. First, being true to the position of *Working Paper 36*, most religious educators equated a broadly phenomenological approach to religious education with a non-confessional, anti-dogmatic stance, which alone was regarded as educationally responsible. Second, prior theological commitment to the transcendental unity of the religions by the major proponents of a phenomenological approach acted as an obstacle to a proper assessment of its educational suitability and effectiveness to challenge and overcome religious intolerance. This criticism will be pressed home in later chapters.

Alongside a growing awareness of its limitations, the influence of phenomenological religious education in Britain increased steadily throughout the 1970s and 1980s. The endorsement of religion by religious educators through the phenomenological approach was viewed by them as challenging prejudice and as affirming the social significance of religion. In 1985 an official government inquiry into the 'Education of Children from Ethnic Minority Groups', chaired by Lord Swann, concluded that the phenomenological approach provided the 'best and only means of enabling all pupils, from whatever religious background, to understand the nature of religious belief, the religious dimension of human experience and the plurality of faiths in contemporary Britain' (Swann/DES 1985: 518). The inquiry concluded that the phenomenological approach was an ideal vehicle for advancing tolerance and harmony between different religious groups and communities in society.

In retrospect, it is clear that official support for phenomenological religious education by the Swann Report represented the nadir of its influence in British religious education. By the late 1980s, in acknowledgement both of weaknesses and of new developments, the term 'phenomenological religious education' gradually fell into disuse, to be replaced by 'multi-faith religious education'. The 'official' history of British religious education cites this shift of nomenclature, along with the associated revision of the phenomenological approach, as evidence of the ongoing development of the subject as it adapts to new challenges and corrects itself in response to criticism and rational reflection. By contrast, the view that is pursued here is that the underlying assumptions, beliefs and values of phenomenology continued to determine the nature and character of religious education as the ruling intellectual paradigm until the 1990s, and remain influential to this day.

Professional responses to criticism of phenomenological religious education

Although many of the criticisms that are brought against phenomenological religious education have already been mentioned, and in some cases considered in detail (e.g. the accusation that treating religions thematically at secondary level leads to pupil confusion), it is useful to set these out more systematically, using Robert Jackson's helpful overview and summary of them. He notes that critics 'have focused on five main characteristics of the approach' (Jackson 1997: 10), which (paraphrased) are listed below:

1. The phenomenological approach focuses on the observable phenomena of religion and the external actions of religious believers to the neglect of the spiritual and experiential dimension that provides the motivation and stimulus for religious belief and practice.

2. Too many religions are covered, resulting in superficiality.
3. The juxtaposition of material from different religions on common themes confuses pupils, and contributes to superficial learning.
4. The subject matter is remote from the experiences and concerns of pupils.
5. There is a failure to address the issue of religious truth, which results in giving implicit support to religious relativism.

Jackson has provided a fairly accurate account of representative criticisms of phenomenological religious education and, if necessary, reference could be made to specific writers who actually express these criticisms. I say *fairly accurate* account of criticisms because he omits entirely any discussion of the complaint that the phenomenological approach is not particularly successful in challenging religious intolerance or developing respectful attitudes in pupils towards those who hold different convictions. There is also the concern that Jackson has not appreciated the full force of the criticisms. What stands out, in the light of our earlier review of empirical evidence that records the negative pupil attitudes to religious education in Chapter 1, is the complaint that the subject matter of religious education is remote from the experiences and concerns of pupils. This was a criticism whose force was particularly felt by Michael Grimmitt, who although an influential early advocate of phenomenological religious education, and we quoted him to this effect at the beginning of this chapter, was increasingly troubled by its apparent failure to engage the interests and concerns of pupils (Grimmitt 1987: 45).

> For pupils to gain personally from the study [of religion], education must enable them to relate what they learn to their own experience and to become aware of the ways in which their own perceptions of what they are studying influence their understanding. This is precisely what the phenomenological method ... cannot permit because it infringes its requirement that procedures for studying religion are neutral.

In a later passage in the same book, he elaborates on this criticism (Grimmitt 1987: 209):

> ... although religious phenomena can be an object of much fascination for some children and good teaching can stimulate the interest of others, expecting children and young people to exhibit a sustained willingness to explore religion 'from the point of view of those who are religious' is unrealistic if, at the same time, such exploration does not also meet their own needs and relate to their own experiences and interests.

In the same passage, Grimmitt (1987: 209) also expresses the view that 'the phenomenological principle of "bracketing" one's own questions and experiences (and any beliefs or values derived from them or informing them) is in direct conflict with the central principle of all child-related conceptions of education'. By contrast, he believes, a good religious education curriculum 'should seek to encourage pupils to make personal evaluations of the truth, significance and value of what they are studying' (Grimmitt 1987: 211). There is a natural progression in Grimmitt's criticism of phenomenology: beginning with recognition of the fact that an exclusive focus on religion and religious phenomena often fails to relate to the life experience and existential concerns of pupils, he moves to the conclusion that educational attempts to relate religion to their lifeworld (*Lebenswelt*) necessarily require attention to be given to the issue of religious truth. In other words, to stimulate pupils' interest in a subject requires them to see its relevance to their experience, and relevance in turn naturally invites them to consider its value and significance, and of course its truth. Grimmitt effectively shows how the fourth criticism in our list above gives rise to the fifth, that is, a failure to relate religion to the lives of pupils naturally leads to the issue of religious truth and the relevance of religion to them being overlooked. Ironically, the book in which Grimmitt expressed his initial (chiefly uncritical) support for phenomenology, namely *What Can I Do in RE?* (1973), remained influential long after he had concluded that 'the principles of phenomenology ... do not, and cannot, purport to provide adequate educational grounds for religious education in schools, nor a sufficient methodology for teaching the subject' (Grimmitt 1987: 209).

The attitude of most professional religious educators, however, unlike Grimmitt, is that criticisms of a phenomenological approach are surmountable and can be (and have been) accommodated. One form of defence is to argue that the original or 'canonical' form of phenomenological religious education is not vulnerable to criticism in the same way as later versions or translations. This strategy acknowledges that there are weaknesses in phenomenological religious education but that these can be corrected by reference to the original statement of phenomenology in *Working Paper 36* (Schools Council 1971). A not dissimilar strategy is adopted by Robert Jackson. After reviewing and discussing the standard objections to a phenomenological approach (his summary of which we made use of above), he concludes that they are not valid as 'objections to phenomenology *per se*', 'being applicable only to poorly designed materials which misapply principles from phenomenology' (Jackson 1997: 27). There is some plausibility in Jackson's defence of phenomenological religious education, even though it is not fully convincing, not just because he fails to consider some of the most important criticisms of phenomenology but because his defence at specific points often appeals to materials and sources that are not representative of materials in use in schools. In other words, Jackson fails to relate his discussion to phenomenological religious education as practised in schools and in classrooms. For example, he point outs that 'phenomenology as a methodology does not require attention to a wide range of faiths concurrently,' and then proceeds to cite the examples of Kim Knott's (1986) study of Hindus in Leeds and Peter McKenzie's (1998) encyclopaedic (and somewhat idiosyncratic) study of

Christianity as important phenomenological studies focused on one religion. The problem is that neither of these books is a school text. The majority of school texts that employ a phenomenological approach typically cover five or six religions thematically (see Simmonds 1984; Whiting 1983).

This section will conclude by considering in further detail the criticism that the phenomenological approach fails to address the issue of religious truth. Some writers have contended that the enjoined bracketing of religious truth is solely a procedural act designed to give religion a fair hearing within an educational context. This interpretation would be convincing if it can be shown that once religious beliefs and practices have been accurately portrayed by phenomenology, some attention is then given to the truth and validity of religion, not as settled matters but as matters of public disagreement and dispute. This is not the case, as acquaintance with text books and curricular material shows.

The positive epistemic status accorded to religion is a presupposition of phenomenological enquiry, and this presupposition is never allowed to be interrogated and challenged by pupils. To raise the issue of the truth of religion as an *explicit* question, on which pupils are invited to reflect and respond, is, we are told by phenomenologists, to undermine the *sui generis* quality of religion and to threaten to reduce religion to something else. Part of the motivation for this neglect of ontological and epistemological questions is undoubtedly to avoid the charge of indoctrination and to observe methodological neutrality. The problem with this position is that it fails to address the cultural situation of pupils where the truth of religion is publicly disputed and acknowledged to be deeply ambiguous. One of the fundamental questions upon which pupils have to make up their own minds is whether religion is true or not. Does God exist? How do I know? The educational point is that pupils must make up their *own* minds, which entails that schools should not determine their answers; in other words pupil autonomy must be respected.

Given that decisions about the worth and truth of religion will be made by pupils, either explicitly or implicitly, consciously or unconsciously, whatever happens in schools, it is surely incumbent upon schools to enable pupils to be critical and reflective in reaching their decisions. The privileged epistemic status effectively accorded to religion by the phenomenological approach to religious education, an axiom that will be further criticised in Chapter 10, is incompatible with a critical and democratic education in a pluralist society. Pupils in school should have opportunities to reflect upon and discuss the truth of religion.

The experiential approach to religious education

One of the most common and enduring criticisms of the phenomenological approach is that it is concerned with the observable phenomena of religion and the external actions of religious believers to the neglect of the spiritual and experiential dimension that provides the motivation for religious belief and practice (see Burn and Hart 1988: 15; Edwin Cox 1983: 27 and 132). How true is this? Clearly this criticism is not true of the writings of Ninian Smart, Michael Grimmitt, Robin Minney and others who translated the phenomenology of religion into the idiom of education. In a sense, for them, the description of religious phenomena was preparatory to an existential encounter with the reality of religion as it revealed itself to the attentive observer who entered into the religious world of the believer. Nevertheless, many of the textbooks that purported to express a phenomenological approach to religious education amounted to little more than a catalogue of religious phenomena arranged thematically (see Cole 1984, for example). This neglect of the experiential dimension in religion was challenged by David Hay and others, who collectively developed an approach that focused on the cultivation of the 'inner, spiritual experiences of pupils', which they regarded as foundational for later religious commitment.

A focus on religious experience was central to the phenomenology of religion, while acknowledging that its significance was often overlooked in classroom materials. In fact British educational interest in religious experience can be traced back to the 1960s when Harold Loukes (1961) and Douglas Hubrey (1968) stressed the importance of utilising pupils' experience as a bridge to understanding religion. Their work was complemented by the pioneering research of Sir Alister Hardy, a distinguished Oxford zoologist, into the nature and forms of spiritual and religious experience. Hardy believed that religious experience evolved through the process of natural selection because of its survival value for the individual. In his 1965 Gifford Lectures at the University of Aberdeen, published as *The Divine Flame: An Essay Towards a Natural History of Religion* (1966), he argued that there is a form of awareness, different from and transcending everyday awareness, which is potentially present in all human beings and which plays a positive function in helping individuals to survive in their natural environment. This transcendent awareness, Hardy contended, is the common experiential source of religion. The difference between religions is to be explained by the diversity and range of human cultures through which the same spiritual awareness comes to expression. Accordingly, spirituality is not the exclusive property of any one religion or for that matter of religion in general. In Hardy's view, those who are alienated from religion and traditional religious language may well express their spiritual awareness in unconventional or even secular terms.

Hardy believed that recognition of the widespread occurrence and the distinctive nature of spiritual experience supported his interpretation of the utility of religion, and he devoted the energies and commitment of his later years, following official retirement, to setting up the Religious Experience Research Unit in Oxford and to the collection and recording of first-hand evidence of religious experience. This work was carried on after his death, first by Edwin Robinson (at the renamed Alister Hardy Research Centre) and then by David Hay. Under Robinson's direction the Centre's research and publications began to focus more explicitly on the occurrence and significance of childhood religious experiences and their implications for education. This orientation was further developed by David Hay, who headed a research project into religious experience and education at the University of Nottingham. The culmination of this project was the publication in 1990 of *New Methods in RE Teaching: An Experiential Approach.*

Although some commentators stress the difference between the experiential and the phenomenological approaches (with the potential to commend the former and to criticise the latter), this was not the view of Hay and his collaborators. They argued that the experiential approach actually expresses and recovers the original form of phenomenological religious education as envisaged by Ninian Smart in *Working Paper 36:*

> The approach to religious education advocated in this book . . . is based on the phenomenological approach to RE and provides teachers with ways of communicating the spiritual insights of the religious traditions of the world. Experiential learning uses the tools of phenomenology, in particular the device of 'bracketing out' or putting aside, our personal assumptions when attempting to understand the life world of another person. This helps to develop the skill of 'seeing' or perceiving the world through the eyes of that person.
>
> *Hay,* et al. *1990: 198; cf. 6*

As originally conceived (and as already noted) the phenomenological approach involved two distinguishable hermeneutical steps: suspending critical judgement in attending to religious phenomena, followed by an act of intuitive awareness – laying bare the essence of the believer's experience. Hay and colleagues allege that this approach, as it came to be practised and taught in schools, involved only the first step – a neutral or objective presentation of religious phenomena – with no attempt, as a necessary second step, to go beyond descriptions of these phenomena to discover the essence of religion in immediate experience. The experiential approach aims to correct this omission by providing resources and ideas that enable pupils to enter their 'own and other's personal worlds' and in this way to uncover the experiential roots of religion and spirituality within the self (1990: 6). Through self-awareness exercises, guided meditations and visualisations pupils are taught to explore their own subjective states, and then to use these as a creative resource to gain an appreciation of the nature of spiritual experience and of the way different cultural and religious metaphors can be used to express deep emotions, feelings and experiences.

There are strengths in the experiential approach to religious education and in its extension to include the subject of spirituality across the curriculum: the pupil's own experiences are taken seriously; the importance of personal experience in religion and personal learning are stressed; there is an unmasking of secular influences in education and the way in which religion and spirituality have been marginalised; and a word of caution is sounded against content-dominated and unduly academic curriculum programmes or syllabuses. But there are also weaknesses.

A number of critics have pointed out that the experiential approach is only loosely related to religion. Its focus is more on personal experience and self-awareness than religion. The social and corporate dimensions of religion are largely ignored and the false impression is given that the religious believer constructs religion out of his or her immediate experience. This diminishes the role of sacred writings and religious authorities and the way in which they structure and condition experience. The deliberate cultivation of spiritual or religious experience in the classroom is also problematic. Is every pupil capable of religious experience? Are the kinds of experience gained as a result of guided meditations or self-awareness exercises genuinely religious experiences? Are they even analogous to religious experiences? More seriously, is it legitimate to pursue (presumed) religious or spiritual experiences self-consciously in the classroom? Is this a covert form of religious indoctrination? These are widely regarded as questions to which advocates of experiential religious education do not provide fully convincing answers.

Some writers, for example, maintain that the phenomenological and the experiential approaches complement each other. The weaknesses of one are overcome by the strengths of the other and vice versa; thus both together provide a balanced picture of religion. Certainly the phenomenological approach and the experiential approach belong together, though it is more accurate to conclude that the experiential approach attempts to achieve and to fulfil the original vision of a phenomenological approach: in a strict sense it is not a different approach. The development of the experiential approach would have been unnecessary had the commitments of phenomenology been successfully and fully integrated into classroom materials and lessons. At the very point, however, where the experiential approach is most frequently regarded as complementing phenomenological religious education (that is, where it exalts the importance of religious experience), it is arguably most vulnerable to criticism. This is because experiential religious education shares the same disquieting assumptions and commitments as the phenomenological approach: that religious experience is the source and foundation of religion; that religious/spiritual experience has priority over its conceptual interpretation; and that the same spiritual experience can be expressed in a variety of theological and cultural languages. Before engaging in criticism, it is important to establish the point that the assumptions identified in phenomenology are equally central to the experiential approach, as developed by Hay and others.

According to *New Methods in RE Teaching* (Hay *et al.* 1990: 6), the aim of the experiential approach is to 'appreciate what the world looks and feels like to other people' and to enter into their experience; 'religion . . . needs to be entered into in order to be appreciated properly'. It is important to become 'more sensitively aware of our own subjective experience if we are to be free to appreciate that [i.e. the religious lifeworld] of others'. The view is expressed that the capacity for religion is universal, for religious awareness is universal. Reference is made to Plato, who viewed education as the challenge of helping 'pupils to recognise what they already potentially know. This process of "freeing the mind" is not easy and includes removing taboos or rigidities that may prevent children from having conscious access to what they know' (1990: 7). There is an echo here of Schleiermacher's notion of the divine as universally present, but often unrecognised, in experience; the appeal to 'free the mind' resonates with the phenomenological technique of epoché, of excluding presuppositions from the mind in order to appreciate the religious reality that is given in and through experience. The phenomenological emphasis on 'inner experience' (1990: 7) as the essence of religion is affirmed, as is the phenomenological dichotomy between immediate awareness and religious beliefs: 'churches, temples, synagogues, festivals, gatherings for worship, doctrinal and creedal statements' are all deemed to be public phenomena (1990: 10):

> But for the religiously committed, there is another dimension which is more important than these public phenomena. Believing members of religious communities are aware of a sacred realm of personal *experience* for which the public aspects of their faith provide context and the interpretation. The historical religions, endlessly colourful, creative, tangled up with politics and every other dimension of life, are in all cases the public expression of an inner experience of the sacred.
>
> Hay et al. *1990: 10 [author's emphasis]*

> The exercises in this book attempt to explore the often hidden dimensions of religion – their spiritual cores . . .
>
> Hay et al. *1990: 198*

New Methods in RE Teaching was first published in 1990, almost twenty years after the introduction of the phenomenological approach in British religious education, yet its commitments and values directly mirror the commitments and values of the chief exponents of both the phenomenology of religion and phenomenological religious education, as originally conceived and practised. (To substantiate the point further compare the quotations above from *New Methods in RE Teaching* with the quotations from Michael Grimmitt, quoted earlier on p. 96.)

The enduring influence of phenomenological assumptions and commitments

Much of the writing and theorising on spiritual development up to the present expresses the same interpretation of religion as that associated with the phenomenology of religion, even though this common framework is typically unacknowledged. An appreciation of this is important, for some contemporary religious educators contend that the weaknesses of the phenomenological approach to religious education have been overcome in more recent approaches and initiatives. Accordingly, attention to this approach is regarded as of historical interest only and of no relevance to current theorising or practice. This is not the case, as may be briefly illustrated.

Writing in the 1980s, Jack Priestley distinguished between the primary apprehension of religious meaning through imagination and the secondary analytic concerns of the theologian. The spiritual dimension of existence, he believes, can be grasped only in the 'attempt always to go beyond what is "sayable", to try to communicate that which lies beyond, which is to be apprehended through the imagination because it cannot be fully comprehended by the mind' (Priestley 1981: 23). Again we meet the notion that there are religious truths too deep for words, truths beyond conceptual and linguistic communication.

A further illustration of the continuing significance of phenomenological axioms and commitments (and behind them the liberal Protestant tradition in theology) is provided by a recent article entitled, 'Religious experience and experiential learning', by Peter Jarvis, published in the international peer reviewed journal *Religious Education* in 2008. In this case the use of quotations is intended both to confirm that phenomenological commitments continue to enjoy influential educational supporters in Britain and to remind ourselves of the precise nature of these commitments in preparation for the critique that follows.

The focus in Jarvis's article is on experiential learning and on facilitating experiential learning in religious education. The 'abstract' presents a faithful summary of his position (2008: 553):

> Learning is both experiential and existential and a theory of learning is examined here in considerable detail to show how we interpret religious experiences. This learning provides the basis of theological systems although it is argued here that we cannot learn religious experience, only interpretations that provide us with mediated religious experience. These interpretations usually come from within a culture or a faith community. The interpretations, when they are shared, are secondary experiences: they constitute the basis of theological explanations, which are then taught. But teaching religion academically creates a tension between approaches to study, faith, and experience that has to be resolved in a satisfactory manner.

What understanding of religion is expressed here? There is a distinction between (immediate) religious experience, which is the essence of religion, and secondary mediated interpretations; theology and theological doctrines are derived from these secondary mediated interpretations; finally, religious experiences are subject to different interpretations, the interpretation 'usually coming from within a culture or a faith community'. Although no explicit mention is made of the phenomenology of religion or phenomenological religious education (which is interesting in itself) there are references to the work and writings of William James and Rudolf Otto, who are interpreted by Jarvis (2008: 556) as 'pointing to the idea that religious experiences are primary experiences; that they leave us with a sense of the unknown, even unknowable'. On p. 557 he testifies to his own experiences of 'a Wholly Other, the Numinous' and he endorses the claim that immediate religious experiences are strictly ineffable and beyond description. 'Fundamentally religious experiences are primary experiences and they are disjunctural [sic] because we cannot explain or give meaning to them'. Some form of language must nevertheless be used to convey and communicate the experience to others and typically the language used 'reflects . . . [the] religious history and culture of those who enjoy the experiences'.

> The meaning, or the interpretation, is dependent on both the time and the culture within which the experience occurs but in each case a meaning given to it is learned. It would, however, have been possible for me to try to interpret my experiences not from within the framework of academic discussion but from a Christian theological perspective, or had I been a Jew or a Muslim or a Hindu, or a member of any other faith, I could have given it a meaning that reflected my faith community. This is indisputable. Once we start from the idea that religious experience is fundamental to our understanding of religion, it is natural from within learning theory to see how we learn the meanings associated with our lifeworld and that these meanings are associated with either our faith communities or our cultures, or both. Once we recognize that it is the meanings that are disputed rather than the experiences, we can see the significance of inter-faith dialogue as part of our own religious education, as well as a significant movement in community development and religious understanding of the world.
>
> *Jarvis 2008: 557*

According to Jarvis the same spiritual experience could equally be described and interpreted in Jewish, Muslim or Hindu terms, for as he says, the interpretation is contingent; and in an uncharacteristic display of academic confidence he affirms that this account of religion and religious experience 'is indisputable'. In the last sentence of the above quotation he begins to draw out the implications of the reality of common cultural and religious experiences. Clearly religious dialogue takes on a new meaning when it is 'discovered' that the different world religions are based upon such experiences. The implications for religious education are drawn out by him is his final paragraph.

> We cannot teach the primary experience but only learn from it but we can teach religious belief systems. Perhaps the significant fact is that we all have these experiences but that we differ in the way that we interpret them but these differences have led to major cultural conflicts – conflicts that can only be resolved if we try to reach back and recognize that these experiences are fundamental to our humanity whereas the explanations reflect only the cultures within which they were had – the explanations are not the

experiences! We learn our cultural heritage and our interpretations are secondary but our experiences are at the heart of our humanity and in this contemporary world we might wish to shift the debate from secondary interpretations to the human experience and what we learn about the Wholly Other – something that words cannot contain.

Jarvis 2008: 566

Religious education can contribute to positive community relations by teaching pupils to identify and appreciate the common spiritual source of the different religions, for they all provide access to the same indescribable 'wholly other'. Recognition of the common experiential roots of religion, for Jarvis, will make a significant contribution to resolving religious and cultural conflicts. What greater contribution to education and to society can religious education make than this!

This chapter has illustrated the extent to which religious education in Britain has been influenced by axioms and commitments associated with the phenomenology of religion, not only during the period of phenomenology's greatest influence in the 1970s and 1980s but also more recently in writings and proposals concerned with spiritual development and experiential learning in religious education. The next chapter will move beyond analysis and begin to engage in criticism of phenomenology and its distinctive interpretation of religion.

8

RELIGION, PHENOMENOLOGY AND RELIGIOUS UNDERSTANDING

One of the chief aims of this chapter is to begin to question and criticise phenomenological approaches to religion and their employment in education. The focus of criticism will be on phenomenology's distinctive interpretation of religion and not on the elements it shares with the wider liberal theological framework, of which it is an expression; further analysis and criticism of the wider framework will follow in subsequent chapters. Criticism of the distinctive aspects of phenomenology, which effectively means the central epistemological tenets of the phenomenological interpretation of the nature of religion, naturally invites questions about the true nature of religion and how it is to be interpreted and understood within religious education. These questions will be addressed once the criticisms of phenomenology are set out and developed.

A phenomenological understanding of religion: a Wittgensteinian critique

Is a phenomenological understanding of religion intellectually credible? Does phenomenology faithfully reflect the nature of religion? Grave doubts have been expressed by those influenced by the philosophical writings of the 'later' Wittgenstein over the enterprise of the phenomenology of religion as it was originally conceived and as it has developed; such doubts naturally extend to include the use of phenomenology in religious education. The central assumptions of the phenomenological approach to religion are widely rejected by those who hold to a post-Wittgensteinian understanding of the nature of language and its relation to human experience: that there is such a thing as the essence of religion; that this essence is to be found in religious experience and that religious experience is *sui generis* – different in quality and kind from all other experiences. These assumptions are as prominent in phenomenological and experiential approaches to religious education, and in more recent writings on spiritual education and on experiential learning, as they are in the writings of 'classical' phenomenologists such as Otto, van der Leeuw and Mircea Eliade. Moreover, as in the phenomenology of religion, in religious education these assumptions are typically predicated on a basic distinction or dichotomy between religious experience and religious language.[1] The common understanding is that religious experience, as a form of awareness, is meaningful and cognitive, yet exists prior to and independently of conceptual understanding. The former is in some sense direct and immediate (even self-certifying), the latter secondary and indirect. Unlike thought, feelings, awareness or emotions cannot be accurately conveyed to another in words, but can be known only by acquaintance. For feelings to be known they must be experienced at first hand. The experiencing self enjoys a privileged epistemic position: the self that experiences alone knows and the experiencing self alone knows that it is entitled to know.

Familiarity with the later philosophy of Wittgenstein challenges any assumed directness of feelings and emotions and their priority over beliefs and language; as it also challenges the solitary experiencing self as the final arbiter of knowledge. In the *Philosophical Investigations* (1958), Wittgenstein questions the epistemic priority of the first person, a view which until the time of his writing had dominated modern philosophy in both its empiricist and rationalist forms. In contradistinction, Wittgenstein gave priority to the 'third-person perspective'. From the perspective of the third person he analysed and described a number of complex mental phenomena – perception, intention, desire and expectation. The upshot of his family of arguments is that nothing about the essence of the mental (or about the essence of anything, including religion) can be learnt from the study of the isolated (Cartesian) self. 'The "immediacy" of the first person case,' as Roger Scruton has noted, 'is an index only of its shallowness' (1981: 283). The Cartesian notion of the inner thinking self abstracted from the categories of public thought and understanding which communicates privately with itself is incoherent.

Experiences in general, and religious experiences in particular, do not constitute an autonomous realm of meaning that only subsequently comes to be symbolised in linguistic form. Rather, religious concepts and religious language together structure and condition religious experience. Public concepts and language have priority over 'inner' experience. There is no private world of meaning and experience which either transcends or relates contingently to public discourse. According to Wittgenstein human feelings and emotions are dependent upon our acquisition of language and conceptual understanding, for it is in linguistic and conceptual terms that emotions and feelings are to be distinguished. Our use of affective terms presupposes an interpretative framework of meaning, conceptual and linguistic rules and a shared public world. Without the appropriate public language and the necessary linguistic distinctions there would be no inner or subjective experience. Feelings (or the feeling of the sacred for that matter) do not enjoy some kind of privileged epistemic status over discursive reason and conceptual thought. Feelings – religious feelings – are structured and conditioned according to conceptual beliefs. In the case of religion, without the appropriate religious concepts and language, there would be no religious experience.

How can there be experience of an external object (a being that transcends the self), as the sacred is believed to be, which does not involve conceptual understanding? Can religious feelings be isolated from religious concepts without loss of meaning? A post-Wittgenstein view of the nature of language and of human experience suggests that if the feeling of the divine is intentional then it cannot be specified apart from reference to its object, and thus it cannot be independent of thought. The real difficulty for phenomenologists and their notion of (non-conceptual) religious experience as the essence of religion is that *religious* experience cannot be specified without reference to a holy object and this in turn requires, or presupposes, that the feeling, the religious feeling, is the result of divine operation; without this judgement the experience remains without religious import. But to invoke the holy as the cause of experience or feeling is to employ concepts, and quite complex concepts at that, of divine agency – the notion of an invisible, powerful, personal spirit, etc. The criteria for identifying religious experience include reference not only to concepts but also to specific beliefs about how the experience is to be explained and interpreted. Explanation, and thus conceptual understanding, enter into experience from the outset. There is no direct speaking of the divine into the human heart, there is only a presence of the divine (if at all) conditioned by conceptual, linguistic and cultural modes of mediation. Once we acknowledge this, the issue of the meaning of religious discourse is raised, and also, importantly, its appropriateness, reliability and truth. If personal experience of the divine is structured and conditioned by the *public* symbols of faith then the immunity of religion to (public) rational criticism and assessment, which proceeds from the mistaken (phenomenological) assumption of the essential directness and privacy of religious experience, is undermined. There is no privileged domain of introspective knowledge. Private experience is a function of public discourse, intrinsically dependent on the latter. Understanding religion is not achieved by attempts to intuit its essence but by coming to know its public discourse and the public world of beliefs and practices of which that discourse is an expression and a part. An appreciation of religious beliefs and doctrines provides the necessary preliminary context for an understanding of the individual's religious experience, rather than vice versa. Furthermore, where beliefs differ, so experiences differ; there is no common religious or spiritual experience underlying the different religions.

Recognition of the public character of beliefs and practices also provides the means of overcoming a further (alleged) dichotomy that is believed to pose a challenge to the (educational) study of religion: that of insider and outsider accounts of religion. This challenge is sometimes interpreted to mean that insiders alone understand a religion and that those who are not insiders and participate in the religious life do not and cannot understand it. One must be committed to a religion to gain an understanding of it. Our earlier discussion of Wittgenstein's account of the public nature of human language, thought and behaviour effectively undermines any kind of sharp distinction between a first person and a third person perspective with regard to religion. Insiders and outsiders will differ in their estimates of the truth of religion or truth of some particular religion, and this may well be reflected in their overall theory regarding it; but if beliefs shape practice, and beliefs by their nature are public (in the sense that they are expressed in language that is public) then there is no necessary reason why insider and outsider accounts of the nature of religion should differ. This is in contrast to theories regarding religion, which may well reflect opposing epistemological stances to the truth of religion. In addition, there are other problems that attend posing too sharp a distinction between insider and outsider accounts. The first is that the contrast is often cast in absolute terms that are false to human experience. The issue of religious identity is reduced to an overly simplistic contrast between belonging or not belonging. This fails to appreciate that there are 'degrees of belonging (e.g. complete insiders, partial insiders, occasional insiders, marginal insiders, complete outsiders, etc.), and it fails to take account of multiple and overlapping dimensions of identity' (Gardner and Engler 2012: 242). Second, the phenomenon of conversion seems to require that the person who converts has an appreciation and understanding of that to which he or she has converted. In other words, outsiders are able to acquire a sufficient understanding of a religion to be able to make an informed choice about whether to commit to its beliefs and practices or not.

Nothing that has been said above should be interpreted to deny that religious experience *is* important in religion, and clearly there is a difference between knowing about a religion and experiencing religion: there is a difference between knowing the Christian theology of grace and knowing God through being justified by grace through faith in Christ. The issue with phenomenologists is that they fail to appreciate the role and constitutive power of language, for it is the language of religion that makes religious experience possible. Yet, equally, one needs to appreciate the role and constitutive power of language if religion is to be understood and properly interpreted. In one sense, to introduce the language and concepts of religion to pupils is necessarily to create the possibility of personal commitment, though personal commitment is not necessary to understanding the concepts of religion and becoming familiar with the distinctive logic and uses of religious language. One can have an understanding of religion without commitment, and in many schools the aim of religious education is properly confined to simply enabling an understanding of the nature of religion. There is a difference between understanding a religion and believing in God. Both involve understanding but both do not involve personal commitment and trust. The aim of non-confessional religious education is to impart an understanding of religion, not a commitment to it. The aim of confessional religious education is to both impart an understanding of religion and elicit or nurture a commitment to it.

The ineffability thesis

Phenomenologists of religion also typically affirm that God is 'wholly other', beyond description, and literally ineffable. In Chapter 6 we quoted from van der Leeuw to the effect that, in his view, Otto used the title of 'the numinous' for the Holy precisely because it 'says nothing at all' (van der Leeuw 1964: 681) and this, van der Leeuw affirmed, captures the essence of authentic religious experience. Some religious educators similarly support this interpretation of the nature of the divine: in the last chapter we quoted Robin Minney as stating that most of the forms that express what is basic and essential to religion are 'non-verbal' and 'wordless' (Minney 1975: 223); Jack Priestley (1981: 23) equated the spiritual dimension of religion with what cannot be said; and Peter Jarvis (2008) endorsed Otto's idea of God as the 'Wholly Other'. This commitment to the ineffability of God is philosophically problematic.

The term ineffability is derived from two Latin words – *in* and *effabilis* – literally, 'not speak-able', and hence our English translation as inexpressible, unutterable and indescribable. The word can be used in different contexts, not all of them religious or theological, though it is religious usage which exclusively concerns us. In religious contexts it is invariably the object or certain (usually mystical) experiences that are regarded as ineffable. These two applications are naturally related: because some religious experiences appear to their subjects as beyond description, it is frequently thought to follow (and with a certain plausibility) that the object encountered in such experiences is similarly beyond description. There are other reasons which have prompted theologians to claim ineffability for God. Some regard ineffability as a consequence of God's infinity; others as a consequence of God's transcendence: God so transcends human beings as to be 'wholly other'.

A thing is ineffable only if it cannot be expressed in language. Ineffability has no degrees, strictly speaking – it is logically impossible for one thing to be more ineffable than another. Ineffability entails silence about the object of religion; nothing can or should be said about the divine. In fact we can think of the predicate 'the divine' as a place holder for 'something' about which nothing can be said. What would a religion be based on silence? No creed, no beliefs, no religious instruction, not even religious practices, for such practices would have nothing to express. What is the difference between a spiritual object about which nothing can be said and no spiritual object at all? If the divine is ineffable, no words can express the difference. But an empty 'concept' of God is of no serious interest to religion, or morality, or for that matter to anything.

If the ineffability thesis is true then all distinctions and descriptions of God are equally invalid; this would include traditional religious and moral predicates, for example that God exists, or that God is all good (one could with equal justification say that God does not exist, or God is all evil). Very few adherents of the main religions would be happy with such a conclusion. Most would want to say that the ascription of existence and moral goodness to God is preferable to the ascription of non-existence and turpitude. The point is not just that adherents of religion do make assertions about God, suggesting that for some, at least, God is not ineffable, it is deeper still: basically if any (one) proposition of the form, 'The spiritual object is *x*', or 'is better described in terms of *x* than *y*' (where *x* and *y* are predicates), is true, then the ineffability thesis is refuted. For example, if the proposition 'God is love' is true, then God is not ineffable.

> . . . divine ineffability is incompatible with there being any theology, any account of the properties and actions of God. The simple consequence of divine ineffability is that Christian (or any monotheistic) theology and ethics (which in turn provide the point and content of institutions and practices) become 'cognitively meaningless' – neither true nor false. Similarly, we can conclude that if Christian (or any monotheistic) theology or ethics can be shown to be either true or false, then the claim that God is ineffable must be false.
>
> *Yandell 1984: 125*

Rejection of the ineffability thesis, however, should not be taken to imply that no mystery attaches to the divine object. To say that the divine is not *totally* mysterious is not to say that the divine is not mysterious at all. The different religions typically teach that the religious object is beyond human comprehension, but this does not entail that God cannot be comprehended *tout court*. Rather it means that God cannot be fully comprehended. For the religious believer (in the theistic religions at least) there is conceptual and propositional knowledge of God, but it is not exhaustive knowledge. For religion and theology to be meaningful, divine mystery must be interpreted to leave room for the ascription of content to God.

Most followers of theistic religions do not endorse the ineffability thesis. This is because Christians, Jews and Muslims believe that God has revealed himself in history and through chosen spokespersons. God is not silent: he has taken the initiative and revealed his character to humankind and he has published his laws and commands. For example, Muslims affirm that God is one, gracious and merciful; that peace with God is gained through following the teaching of Islam; that God revealed his message to a line of prophets, beginning with Adam and culminating in Muhammad, who received God's final word, which was then faithfully recorded in the Qur'an. Muslims speak of the nature and character of God because God has spoken and revealed his character and nature to humankind. Although there are some mystics in Islam who (occasionally) speak of the ineffability of God, attention to context often shows that ineffability is predicated of the experience rather than of the object of experience. Equally, attention to context reveals that references to ineffability in religious devotional literature often function as literary tropes that are intended to underline the significance of experiences of God for the individual. Language is felt to be inadequate to the challenge of describing an experience that is essentially 'other-worldly'. In a sense words fail, because words cannot convey the profundity of the experience. Often the point of appeals to ineffability (or implied appeals) is to underline the difference between having intellectual knowledge of God and having experience of God; this is the case with Al Ghazzali, for example (see Watt 1963).

Understanding religion

One of the interesting points to emerge in scholarly reflections upon Ninian Smart's analysis of the multidimensional nature of religion is that the same dimensions apply equally to secular ideologies and to worldviews more generally: Smart himself applied his dimensional understanding of the nature of religion to Maoism to illustrate its fruitfulness, and in later writings he advocated that there should be a study of worldviews in education. This does not mean that Smart dismissed all definitions of religion as unsuccessful or that he concluded that religions cannot be distinguished from secular ideologies or worldviews; like most phenomenologists he did on occasions identify religion with the sacred (see Smart 1996; for discussion, see Fitzgerald 2000: 54–71). His dimensional model of religion, however, did have the effect of blurring the distinction between religion and non-religious worldviews and has encouraged some more recent religious educators to conclude that secular worldviews or ideologies should, on this basis alone or in conjunction with other considerations, come under the purview of religious education In Britain this kind of thinking often underlies appeals for the inclusion of secular humanism within religious education. These observations suggest that an attempt to understand the nature of religion must begin with the contested matter of its connotations and denotations.

The challenge of defining religion is one of the stock subjects of introductions to both the academic and the philosophy study of religion: a long list of definitions is often set out and then each definition analysed for its strengths and weaknesses, with the conclusion sometimes reached that religion is impossible to define. Often such analyses distinguish between different types of definition, such as, say, functional, substantive, normative, theological or legal. In addition, since Wittgenstein introduced the notion in the *Investigations*, many interpreters refer to, and some prefer, a 'family resemblance' account – that there is no one defining characteristic of religion (e.g. belief in God) but rather a range of overlapping characteristics, none of which is common to all. For example, a number of religions believe in heaven and hell, but not all of them do; a number believe in the existence of angels and demons, but, again not all of them (the most sustained example of this type of analysis is Edwards 1972).

The challenge of definition is resolved in different ways. Some writers simply decide to follow conventional usage and record that Buddhism, Christianity, Hinduism, Islam and Judaism (and others, for the list is not meant to be exhaustive) are commonly referred to as religions, and leave the matter there; some refer to religions and quasi-religions, or religions and border-line cases, and so on. A number of writers, following the example of Wilfred Cantwell Smith, have drawn attention to the ideological and theological interests that lurk behind both definitions of religion and the origins and historical uses of the denominating term religion and its cognates (this position will be considered in relation to Robert Jackson and interpretive religious education in Chapters 12 and 13). Some recent writers even urge that the term religion should be excised from the scholar's lectionary and the work of the scholar of religion subsumed under cultural studies, where 'religion' is just one more symbolic system among others that is open to exclusively naturalistic analysis and interpretation.

Can religion be successfully defined? It is not strictly necessary for religious educators to have a clear answer to this, and there is room for honest disagreement. Nevertheless, attention to the challenge of defining religion and the consideration of different proposed solutions are useful activities not just for students and scholars of religion but for pupils in school as well, albeit for the latter at a level appropriate to their age and aptitude. Such engagement raises interesting and provocative issues in relation to understanding the nature of religion, particularly as a generic category of interpretation, even if there is no generally accepted definition that emerges from the discussion. There may be forms of belief and practice where there is uncertainty about the aptness of regarding them as religions or as religious in some significant sense. That English usage is on occasions inexact and ambiguous is not a new or unusual phenomenon: ambiguity of application and meaning can equally attend such terms as chair, mountain, institutions, citizenship and rights (in fact we could add to this list almost any abstract noun), just as it attends the term religion and its cognates. Nevertheless, aside from popular or common usage, it might be maintained that terms should have a fairly clearly defined content if they are to be used as interpretive tools of cultural and social analysis or used cross-culturally to identify and classify similar phenomena. More pointedly, can a sufficiently determinate meaning be given to religion (and its cognates) for it to be used descriptively and objectively to distinguish religious from non-religious worldviews and hence religions from secular worldviews? Such a definition could lend some support to the view that religious education can be concerned with religions and religious content alone and not with secular worldviews and content. (It may be granted that the issue of definition should not exclusively determine the content of religious education and that other considerations are relevant.)

Religion may be construed as a human concern with a supernatural reality that transcends the ordinary world revealed by sense perception and by the use of a scientific methodology; as Thomas Nagel (2012: 26) would say, it is a reality that is 'not part of the natural order' (incidentally, a reality whose existence he rejects). Moreover, this supernatural reality, from the perspective of those who believe in it, is not ultimately explicable in terms of (natural) causes internal to the universe. Minimally, one may define (and appropriately describe) as religious any belief or practice that expresses or implies the existence of supernatural beings or states: angels, ghosts, Nirvana, God and Brahman, for example.

Religious beliefs and practices, however, singly or collectively, may not constitute *a* religion. The term religion is appropriate:

1. in the context of belief in a transcendent or supernatural reality that is regarded as unconditionally and non-dependently real, and as such, should be regarded (in a stipulative sense) as divine; in other words, that what is regarded as unconditional and non-dependent is appropriately designated 'divine';
2. where there is a distinctive account of the nature of the divine that is integrated into a wider form of life that incorporates both other beliefs, say about human origins, personhood and human salvation, and practices that typically involve (religious) functionaries, institutions and rituals.

It is the integrated and extended nature of religions as distinctive forms of belief and life that is implicit in Clifford Geertz's influential definition of religion

> as *a system* of symbols which acts to establish powerful, pervasive, and long-lasting moods and motivations in men *by formulating conceptions of a general order of existence* and clothing these conceptions with such an aura of factuality that the moods and motivations seem uniquely realistic.
>
> Geertz 1985: 4 [my emphasis]

Religions typically centre on what people believe to be divine, and people may, and in fact do, disagree widely on what can be identified as such. Different interpretations of the divine and humans in relation to the divine give rise to different religions.

It is not necessary in this context to set out and defend a fully worked out nomenclature for the field of analysis and interpretation that focuses on beliefs about supernatural reality and the divine, say to distinguish further between religious traditions (within a religion), religious movements and so on. The meaning of the divine when confined to supernatural or transcendent reality, as exemplified by belief in a supernatural being (or beings), or in supernatural states or principles, is sufficient to distinguish religions from other patterns of human belief and behaviour. Religion falls on one side of the distinction between supernatural or transcendent reality and the natural universe of space and time and secular ideologies fall on the other: beliefs, values and practices that express and relate individuals to the divine are appropriately thought of as *religious*. It does not follow from this that the divine exists in reality, in the sense there is a supernatural reality, only that certain people and groups believe that the divine exists and regulate their existence in ways influenced by their (religious) beliefs about the divine. This interpretation of religion does not purport to include all of the features that religions typically possess but to distinguish between religion (and religions) and non-religion by identifying what is distinctive about religion, namely the claim that there is a supernatural level of reality that transcends the natural world.

This minimal definition and conceptualisation of religion, as focused on supernatural reality and the divine, provides a natural starting point for exploring and understanding the nature of religion. It reinforces our earlier Wittgensteinian point that beliefs are constitutive of experience, emotions, attitudes, and more broadly of different ways of life and (predictably enough) *belief* systems or world-views. It follows, if this analysis is correct, that belief in some form of supernatural reality is both constitutive and distinctive of religion; and belief in the divine is constitutive and distinctive of *a* religion – Buddhism, Christianity and Taoism, for example. For Christians the divine takes the form of a Trinitarian God; for (Advaita) Hindus the divine often takes the form of *Brahman*, the Absolute Undifferentiated One; for Theravada Buddhists the divine is Nirvana, and so on.

Different conceptions of the divine in turn determine the different ways in which the divine can be known and experienced by humans. The means and form of revelation and salvation are different for a personal God from that of an impersonal principle. It may even be that certain conceptions of the divine exclude the concept of revelation altogether, for an impersonal principle or (claimed) ineffable divine state (of being) cannot (in the strict sense) reveal 'itself' through spokespersons, history or sacred books. In addition, if there is divine knowledge, this knowledge must be existential in some sense; in other words, it must relate to human nature, and to human interests and aspirations in some way. Therefore, implicit in all claims to knowledge of the divine is some account of human nature, of salvation and how salvation is achieved: basically some account of how and on what basis human beings find their fulfilment (or release) in the divine. In order to understand a religion it is necessary to understand the beliefs that characterise the religion. It is the distinctive set of beliefs about the divine, salvation/liberation, human nature and so on that distinguishes one religion from another and gives meaning to religious practices, experiences, activities and, in its broadest sense, the religious way of life.

An appreciation of the nature of religion is gained by acquaintance with religious vocabulary and the uses to which it is put within the religious life. To understand the religious believer's world one needs to understand the beliefs and values that give purpose and meaning to his or her actions and behaviour. One becomes aware of the role of doctrines and beliefs in facilitating experience and the way in which religious rituals and practices give expression to beliefs and values. The implications of this for teaching and learning are clear. A focus on religious language and religious concepts facilitates an understanding of religion. Pupils need to be acquainted with religious beliefs and doctrines, not as something peripheral to religion, as phenomenologists maintain, but as something central. Accounts of religious activities and practices that fail to refer to the beliefs and values that shape and give meaning to them provide only a limited understanding of the practices, and of the religion more generally, for these activities and practices make sense only in the context of the shared beliefs of the religious community and the wider forms of life of which the activities or practices are a part.

Let us consider the example of fasting in Islam. A proper appreciation of the Pillar of Fasting requires not only an acquaintance with 'the facts' of the matter, how and when it is observed, the provisions for exemptions, and so on, but also the reasons for fasting and how these reasons relate to the wider framework of Muslim belief and practice – the requirement of fasting by God and the notion of a God who reveals his will to humans; the purposes of fasting to promote righteousness of life and to overcome temptation; and of course the rewards that fasting brings to the individual and to the community, and so on. A proper understanding of fasting in Islam needs to go beyond the structural similarities of religion to engage with the particular beliefs, values, hopes and aspirations of Muslims who engage in fasting. Certainly the practice of fasting is common to different religions but its meaning varies depending on the context in which it occurs.

Recognition of the centrality of beliefs to the nature and practice of religion does not entail that religious education in schools should be transformed into a form of theology, whereby pupils attend chiefly to the meaning and logic of religious doctrines. Religious beliefs may be constitutive of religion, but their meaning and importance are mediated to believers through participation in the religious life, through rituals, observances, moral imperatives, and spiritual disciplines; in addition religious beliefs are derived from sacred scriptures and are conveyed through stories, historical narratives, and personal encounters. It is at this point that Smart's account of religion again becomes relevant, for it alerts us to its different dimensions and aspects. Pupils need to become acquainted with the rich phenomena of religion; including the music that it inspires, religious works of art, religious drama, and so on, for religion engages not just the intellect but directs the will and stimulates the senses.

There may be an educational case for concluding that one or other dimension of religion makes an overall understanding of its nature more accessible to pupils at different stages in their cognitive development. Perhaps the narrative and experiential dimensions of religion relate more effectively to the mental capacities of pupils in primary school, whereas some of the other dimensions are better suited to conveying an understanding of religion to older pupils. This is an issue in which religious educators should defer to psychologists and those who are experts in child development and how children best learn. What is important is that efforts are made throughout the years of schooling to engage the interests and concerns of pupils in the content of religion at a level appropriate to their cognitive capacities and also reflective of the nature of religion.

Although Smart's dimensional analysis of religion has certain educational benefits, it does not provide a fully rounded account of the nature of religion, chiefly because it gives insufficient attention to the active role of the individual in appropriating and interpreting it. Certainly Smart takes account of the role and importance of religious founders and of subsequent interpreters of the traditions, and he stresses the importance of personal religious experience; what is understated, however, is the way individuals appropriate, revise and even reject elements of the religion to which they belong. In Smart's account, the individual believer seems to be cast either in a passive role of receiving and affirming the tradition or in an active role of contesting the tradition. Creativity attaches to religious reformers and passivity attaches to religious believers; the impression is given (and it is probably unintentional) that the distinction between these two is absolute, whereas in reality they are better viewed as two poles of a continuum. Such an understanding easily lends itself to a rarefied view of religion as unchanging and of religious communities as homogeneous, united in thought and practice. Attention is given by Smart to diversity within religions, but his account of this is typically along predictable and conventional lines, by which is meant that he attends to the schismatic divisions within religions: Sunni and Shi'a Islam; Protestant and Roman Catholic Christianity, for example. While this is important historically, and remains important, it needs to be complemented by recognition of the diversity of 'ordinary' religious life, where individuals adopt a 'pick and mix' approach and combine different religious and spiritual sources in an eclectic, unsystematic way. Attention to these features was drawn in our earlier discussion of modern and late modern diversity (see Chapter 2 and Chapter 3) and their significance will be further underlined in the consideration of interpretive religious education in Chapters 12 and 13.

The positive interpretation of religion that has been developed in this chapter is largely indebted to analytic philosophy and to Wittgenstein-inspired developments in the philosophy of language. What is important for the future of religious education, however, is that the principle that the study of religion should reflect its nature ought to be accepted as providing the rule against which models of religious education and methodologies for the study of religion in education are assessed. Smart was right at this point. Where his followers in British religious education, past and present, have gone wrong is by valorising his interpretation of religion and remaining wedded to phenomenological axioms and commitments long after scholars in the field of religious studies have moved on to identify their inadequacy and develop more convincing accounts of religion. One of the strengths of a postmodern model of religious education (which will be considered in later chapters) is that it does represent an attempt to engage in dialogue with contemporary developments in philosophy and in the academic study of religion; the problem is that it often takes up ideas that are new and fashionable without subjecting them to proper analysis and scrutiny. Clearly judgements on these matters will not be unanimous and there will be disagreement. This is all part of academic debate and is to be expected. There is no *final* interpretation of religion. The intellectual challenge is to show why some interpretations of religion are more objective than others, broader in scope, greater in explanatory power, and so on. Not to attend to the nature of religion in education only increases the potential for the subject to be conformed to the ideological agenda of the nation state or of some particular religious or secular constituency that wants to impose its beliefs and values on the wider public without debate or democratic accountability.

Note

1   Michael Grimmitt (1973) distinguishes between religious awareness and conceptual thought, Alison Leech (1989) between 'naive experience' and interpretation, and John Marvell (1976) between experience of the 'holy' and its explanation or 'schematization' (in this case explicitly borrowing the technical terminology of Otto).

9

JOHN HULL, THE ENLIGHTENMENT PROJECT AND THE LIBERAL MODEL OF RELIGIOUS EDUCATION

Much of the last chapter was devoted to criticism of phenomenology's distinctive interpretation of religion and not to the elements it shares with the wider liberal theological model of religious education. This chapter will seek to identify and analyse the central axioms, commitments and values of the liberal model, that is, the axioms, commitments and values that are foundational not just to phenomenological religious education and the experiential approach but to all versions of 'liberal' religious education; the following chapter engages in criticism. Our analysis, in the first instance, will focus on the work of Professor John Hull, who exemplifies the beliefs and commitments of the liberal paradigm of religious education. A consideration of Hull is also appropriate because his historical influence chiefly followed that of phenomenology, which fell into decline in the 1980s (albeit with appropriate qualifications, as has been argued and illustrated in earlier chapters). Hull represents the liberal model in its purest form: what is implicit in phenomenology and the experiential approach is explicit in Hull.

John Hull and modern religious education

No one person has had more influence on the development and promotion of religious education in virtually all of its aspects in the UK and internationally over the past thirty years of significant social, religious and educational change than John Hull.

Bates 2006: 19

Anyone familiar with the modern history of religious education in the English-speaking world and beyond will know that such a description is entirely appropriate to express the contribution and achievements of John Hull, the noted

British-Australian religious educator. Dr Hull is currently Emeritus Professor of Religious Education in the University of Birmingham and Honorary Professor of Practical Theology in the Queen's Foundation for Ecumenical Theological Education, Birmingham. In 1989 he was awarded a personal chair in religious education and became the first Professor of Religious Education in a university in the United Kingdom. From 1971 to 1996 he was editor of the *British Journal of Religious Education* (called *Learning for Living* until 1978); and from 1977 to 2010 he was General Secretary of the International Seminar for Religious Education and Values, an international academic association of religious educators, which he founded in 1977 with the late American religious educator, Dr John Peatling.

Of all the religious educators discussed in this book, the work of Professor Hull is by far the most wide-ranging and extensive. Something of the breadth of his interests and publications is captured by his own identification of the 'main themes' on which he has written: blindness and disability; religious education and collective worship; money and globalisation; reconstructing Christian faith; spiritual development and spiritual education; Christian education; and finally (what he designates as) 'training for prophetic ministry'. On each of these themes he has published widely, but by far the theme on which he has published most is that of religious education in schools; and within this theme much of his work has focused on the issue of diversity (or as he prefers, 'pluralism') in society and the challenges posed to education by local, national and international religious diversity. That much of his work has been directed to meeting the challenges of diversity to education is widely recognised and is illustrated by the description by the editors of a recent collection of essays that honour Professor Hull's contribution to religious education. The editors state:

> This volume is a tribute to our esteemed colleague Professor John Martin Hull for his exceptional academic achievements in the field of religious education. Especially worth mentioning are his worldwide continuous efforts in trying to realize interreligious education and interreligious learning in public schools. In his approach there is a strong emphasis on openness, dialogue, and encounter.
>
> *Editors' description on publisher's website, Miedema, 2009*[1]

The focus of our discussion will be Hull's account of the form 'interreligious education and interreligious learning in public schools' should take. Detailed consideration of his position is appropriate for two reasons. First, because of his influence nationally and internationally, and second, because he exemplifies the commitments and values of a liberal model of religious education and the values and commitments of modernity (i.e. what John Gray has characterised as claims to universality and a prejudice against 'particularisms, ethnic and religious'; 1995: 145).

According to Hull, commitment to modernity, in the case of religion, requires the privatising of religious beliefs and religious forms of life, and the conforming of religion to public reason and the requirements of public ethics. Hull is *the* modern religious educator *par excellence*. Indeed he has spoken positively of secular religious education in Britain of the type he advocates as 'a legitimate heir of the European Enlightenment' (in a section entitled 'The Prophetic Role of the Secular', Hull 2003: 57–58). To identify himself with the commitments of the Enlightenment and modernity in this way, however, alerts us to the need for a qualification to be added to Dennis Bates' claim (quoted at the beginning of this chapter) regarding the extent of Professor Hull's influence as a religious educator. Few would demur from this judgement, though it needs to be supplemented by the further (updated) observation that Professor Hull's influence is less than it was and that the reasons for this are significant. Although the liberal model of religious education, of which Hull's contribution is the clearest example, was dominant in the British classroom from the demise of Christian confessionalism in the 1970s until the 1990s, this period of almost unchallenged dominance has now ended. The last twenty years have seen the emergence of a range of new approaches to religious education, some of which can broadly be characterised as postmodern. This currently vies with the liberal model for educational and political influence and for this reason will be the subject of detailed discussion in Chapters 11 to 13.

Religionism

Professor Hull has been at the forefront of new developments in religious education throughout his professional career, and the challenge of diversity to religious education has been central to his writings. Throughout the 1970s, for example, he advocated a 'secular' form of religious education, on the grounds that increasing pluralism and secularism in society undermined forms that were specifically Christian. Although with hindsight there is nothing particularly controversial about this, curiously he also believed that a secular form of religious education was not only consistent with Christian commitment but actually required by it. Secular religious education, for him, expresses a 'theology which no longer serves the needs of the religious community but is at the service of the secular world, of the secular school' (Hull 2003; quoting from what is in part a retrospective article that refers to the development of his ideas as a religious educator). Clearly such a reading of the nature and function of theology by Hull reflects the theological currents of the late 1960s and the 1970s when radical theologians embraced secular ideas (see Cox, H. 1966). For Hull, commitment to the secular values of the Enlightenment and to modern religious liberalism remains intellectually credible. This observation does not mean that Hull is not a confessional theologian, for as we shall see, his 'secular vision for religious education' clearly reflects his theological commitments, rather he is a *liberal* confessional theologian.

Throughout the 1980s Hull continued to reflect on the challenges of diversity to religious education and it was during this period that he wrote his defence of thematic religious education against the charge that it confuses pupils (see Chapter 1 for discussion and criticism). In the 1990s his focus shifted from defending multi-faith religious education in Britain against its critics to engaging more deeply with the reality of social exclusion and the continuing nature of religious intolerance and religious discrimination in society. This marked a more constructive turn in his thought as he sought to uncover resources within the educationally dominant liberal model of religious education to meet the ongoing challenges of diversity to society and to public institutions. This constructive turn was signalled by a provocative, programmatic editorial article in the *British Journal of Religious Education* entitled 'The transmission of religious prejudice' (Hull 1992). The basic position set out in this article remains foundational to his ongoing interpretation of the nature and role of religious education (see Hull 1993, 1996, 1998, 2000); in many respects his later writings reiterate, refine and develop his original ideas but add little new of substance. For this reason the argument of 'The transmission of religious prejudice' will be considered in detail, though reference will be made to later writings where they offer fuller argumentation and elaboration of his original position.

At the beginning of 'The transmission of religious prejudice', Hull engages in an analysis of the nature of religious bigotry and intolerance in dialogue with *The Song of Roland*, a prose poem, which evolved over the period of the Crusades when Christian and Muslim hostility was at its height, and which describes a supposed encounter in the eighth century between devout Christian knights, led by Roland, and 'infidel' Saracens. A battle ensued in which the much smaller Christian force defeated the large Muslim army: most of the 'heathen' were killed and those that remained, disillusioned with their God and their religion, converted to Christianity. Roland is presented as a symbol of Christian heroism and valour struggling against tyrannical Islam. The story is included in the *Legacy Library* (1962) along with other stories, such as 'Jason and the Golden Fleece', 'The Adventures of Ulysses', and 'The Arthurian Legends'. Hull (1992: 70) perceptively remarks:

> 'In view of the Gulf war [of 1991; presumably if he were writing now, he would refer to the events of 11 September 2001 and the ensuing wars in Iraq and Afghanistan] and the ancient resentments which it has aroused, it is most unfortunate that a work of this kind is still to be found on the shelves of school libraries. Not only does *The Song of Roland* show Europe and the Middle East locked in a religious conflict, but its descriptions of Muslims and Islam are both inaccurate and offensive.

Hull's use of this example is not confined to the identification of offensive and insensitive religious material in school textbooks and libraries, and to urge their removal from public institutions (see 1992: 71–72). If he stopped at this point there would be little debate or controversy. Teachers should be alerted to triumphalist Christian propaganda that glorifies violence and to teaching materials on other religions that are inaccurate, prejudicial and partisan. But Hull, not unreasonably perhaps, wants to go further and identify the beliefs and attitudes that give rise to the production of religiously unsuitable and insensitive educational materials, and in light of this, arrive at an adequate educational response (see Hull 1996).

To identify and clarify the attitudes that inspire such material as *The Song of Roland* and which in turn give rise to religious intolerance, Hull uses the word 'religionism' (1992: 70; cf. Hull 2000: 76).

> Religionism describes an adherence to a particular religion which involves the identity of the adherent so as to support tribalistic or nationalistic solidarity. The identity which is fostered by religionism depends upon rejection and exclusion. We are better than they. We are orthodox; they are infidel. We are believers; they are unbelievers. We are right; they are wrong. The other is identified as the pagan, the heathen, the alien, the stranger, the invader, the one who threatens us and our way of life. Religion is in principle universal in its outlook but religionism is committed to the partial.

Moreover, '[r]eligionism always involves prejudice against other religions' (Hull 1992: 70), though the notion of prejudice does not exhaust its meaning.

> The expression 'religious prejudice' is not sufficient to describe the phenomenon in question, because prejudice is a psychological matter. There is a distinction between racism and racial prejudice . . . Although prejudice may be a significant part of racism, to reduce racism to nothing but prejudice is to seriously misunderstand the power and meaning of racism.
>
> The same is true of religion, religious prejudice and religionism. Religionism is present in institutions, in ideologies, in the relationship between entire cultures. It has social and historical roots. Religious prejudice is but a small part of it. Religionism falls as a shadow upon the heart and mind of the individual in the form of religious prejudice, but its structures go beyond the individual.
>
> *Hull 1992: 70; cf. Hull 2000: 77*

For Professor Hull, religionism subsumes both the notion that one's religion is true to a degree denied to other religions and the attitude of superiority that expresses itself as intolerance towards adherents of other religions. In this sense religionism, he believes, is rather like racism – there is the racist belief that one's own race is better than others and there are racist attitudes that show themselves in acts of discrimination against individuals from other races. Belief and attitudes are linked, though strictly speaking, in his view, it is the belief that has priority. With regard to religion, it is the denial of the truth of religious traditions other than one's own that is the cause of religious bigotry and intolerance.

Armed with this understanding of what he means by religionism, Hull identified the role it has played in the growth and evolution of the different historical religions. He acknowledges that 'it seems difficult for religions to evolve without taking on religionist tendencies' (Hull 1992: 70). As examples of the 'religionist tendency' of nascent religious movements he cites Christianity's differentiation of itself from Judaism in the early Christian centuries and Protestantism's divorce from Scholastic Catholicism in the sixteenth century.

In drawing out the implications of a proper educational response to religionism, Hull calls for the implementation of special educational programmes in both schools and churches to combat this problem. In the case of the former, 'anti-religionist education' should become a feature of all agreed syllabuses, and in the case of the latter, anti-religionist teaching should become part of the churches' ministry to both the young and adults alike. He is tantalisingly brief in putting flesh on these bare bones. Positively, he speaks of overcoming religionism 'by the genuinely religious features of the spiritual tradition' (Hull 1992: 71). This seems to mean that religionism is to be combated by explicit teaching on the universalist thrust of religion – the notion that followers of a tradition are working to extend God's kingdom in the world, and that followers of different religious traditions recognise each other as working towards the same end (Hull 1993, 1999: 6–7). Less positively, he speaks of the need to distinguish between 'genuinely religious mission and activities which are merely religionist' (Hull 1992: 71). Genuine missionary endeavour has to do with working for peace and justice, and with mediating God's presence to others. Religionist missionary activity has to do with criticising and condemning the religious beliefs and values of others and with seeking converts (Hull 1998: 340–341).

Hull is quite insistent that '[i]t is not enough for religious education to encourage a *tolerant* attitude towards other religions' (Hull 1992: 71, my emphasis). If we interpret tolerance as essentially the idea of putting up with or enduring something with which one disagrees (which is the natural interpretation) then he patently does not believe that an attitude of tolerance goes far enough. He wants to see a positive attitude fostered by schools towards the different religions. By this he does not mean only that the different faiths and traditions should receive a parity of esteem and treatment within schools and education generally, though this is undoubtedly part of his meaning, in addition he means that within schools pupils should be explicitly taught that all religions are equal (i.e. epistemically equal as to their truth), in the sense that no one religion should be presented as *regarding itself* as superior to others.

According to Hull, religious education should teach that the different religions are not in competition with each other, and this interpretation should also become part of the self-identity and self-understanding of the different religious communities themselves (cf. Toynbee 1957: 83–112; Bernhardt 1994; Knitter 1995). In his view the division between Judaism and Christianity is both unnecessary and mistaken. Christianity in the first few centuries of its existence should not have attempted to foster a sense of separate identity from Judaism, and consequently should not regard itself as superior to Judaism in the sense that it is right and Judaism wrong, or presumably that one provides salvation and the other does not (Hull 1992: 70; cf. Hull 2000: 77–78). The historical process by which religions have differentiated themselves into separate, competitive units is in Hull's opinion mistaken. Different traditions may quite properly witness to different aspects of religious truth, but when this witness extends itself to criticise and challenge the truth of other religions (implicitly or explicitly) then the spirit of religionism is released, with deleterious effects for the individual and for society. In order to challenge such a misunderstanding, Professor Hull (1992: 71) urges the setting up of adult anti-religionist educational programmes in 'mosques, temples and synagogues'. In the cause of good community relations and in the attempt to overcome religious discrimination and prejudice, religious believers must revise their traditional claims to absolute truth and come to recognise the relative or non-absolute character of religious truth. Religions, he believes, need to divest themselves of those religionist features that support 'a tribalistic or nationalistic solidarity' (1992: 70) and encourage intolerance. Realistically, he acknowledges that the process of revising and reinterpreting traditional religious beliefs may well be resisted by some religious believers in the name of preserving the integrity of some particular religious tradition or other.

John Hull and the Enlightenment tradition

The origins of modernity and modern (as opposed to postmodern) ways of thinking about religion are properly traced to the eighteenth century and the period of intense intellectual effort and speculation that we associate with the Enlightenment. Naturally, like any other period of intellectual history, the Enlightenment encompassed diversity, difference and even contradiction. The same age that defined itself in terms of commitment to reason and rational argument also saw the emergence in Germany of mesmeric healing and in America of religious revivalism, in the form of the Great Awakening. The influence and scope of 'enlightened' thinking was not uniform across national boundaries; it is for this reason that some writers caution against historical generalisations and therefore now distinguish between the American, French, German and Scottish Enlightenments. Generalisations are appropriate, however, when suitably qualified and contextualised; and religion is a subject on which Enlightenment thinkers from different countries often expressed broadly similar views, French atheism excepted.

What precise form did reasonable religion take for progressive Enlightenment thinkers? This question has recently been addressed by Robert B. Louden (2007), and it is instructive to compare his account of Enlightenment interpretations of religion with the contemporary interpretation espoused and expressed by John Hull and others. While Louden acknowledges the existence of a diversity of interpretations of religion among Enlightenment thinkers, he also adduces evidence to show that there are 'fundamental points of agreement between different Enlightenment intellectuals' and these collectively give substance to the notion of a distinctive Enlightenment view of religion. He identifies three core ideas about religion 'shared by a wide number of Enlightenment intellectuals from different countries' (Louden 2007: 16). These are the unity thesis, the morality thesis and toleration.

The unity thesis

Louden (2007: 16) notes that most European Enlightenment intellectuals were convinced that religion, if properly interpreted, could serve as a progressive force for the social and moral reform of society and contribute to the formation of a more cosmopolitan moral community. A key strategy in Enlightenment attempts to reform religion is what he calls the *unity thesis*, that is, the belief 'that all historical faiths are manifestations of one universal religion' (2007: 16); among its supporters Louden cites Gotthold Lessing, Pierre Bayle, Lord Edward Herbert of Cherbury, Thomas Paine and Immanuel Kant.

What is interesting about Louden's list of prominent and influential supporters of the unity thesis is that most of them are appropriately classified as deists, though Louden does not make this identification. Deism can be characterised as: (1) belief in a single god, who set the universe in motion or caused it to exist, and whose existence can be arrived at through reasoning alone; and (2) the denial that this god reveals himself in any special way in the world. The deist emphasises the ability of human reason to arrive at religious knowledge, and to attain religious truth, without invoking revelation. The deist view is that the body of truth about God attainable by reason is sufficiently extensive of itself to generate a religion on its own. No need for revelation, or to attempt to adjudicate between competing interpretations and sources of revelation. Everyone can unite in a religion of reason, a religion that best serves the public interest, and which includes within itself 'man's' natural knowledge of God and morality. Revelation can be dispensed with, and any associated belief which thinks of God acting specifically or particularly in the world. Gotthold Lessing (1957: 82; for commentary see Yasukata 2002: 89–116) expressed his questioning of the religious relevance of historical revelation with the celebrated remark that '[r]evelation gives nothing to the human race which human reason could not arrive at on its own'. Positively, Lessing believed that reason *on its own* can justify a form of religion that all can affirm, precisely because it is founded on reason, a universal human faculty.

The reasons for the attraction of deism to Enlightenment thinkers are also interesting. In cultural, social and intellectual terms the Enlightenment succeed the Reformation period. The Reformation signalled the end of the religious hegemony enjoyed by the Roman Catholic Church in Europe and heralded the creation of new national Protestant churches; it also gave rise to sectarianism, persecution, civil strife and religious wars that continued on and off for over a hundred years. Against this background it is hardly surprising that many within the intellectual community came to view both rival claims to religious revelation and rival interpretations of the same revelation as inimical to social harmony, human welfare and political progress. What was needed was a religion purged of superstition and intolerance, a religion founded on reason, to which all men and women could assent.

Although this particular historical narrative of the origins and commitments of the Enlightenment was widely influential among commentators at the time and still rightly commands a degree of support among professional historians, it does not provide a fully convincing historical explanation of the religious wars of the seventeenth and eighteenth centuries. This is because it is now widely appreciated that the 'wars of religion' were closely related to the birth of the modern nation state and can just as convincingly be described as 'the wars of the birth of the modern nation state'. Moreover, the modern nation state is secular, and consequently the notion of 'the secular' and the process of secularisation are connected to this same historical narrative. The essential point is that what has been called 'the myth of the wars of religion' (Cavanaugh 2009: 124) was used by Enlightenment thinkers and continues to be used by social commentators and social reformers to justify the existence of a centralised, secular nation state that alone dispenses 'justice' through its monopoly of the means of inflicting violence on 'its' citizens. While this is not the place to pursue such arguments (see Cavanaugh 2009: 123–180), it does alert us to the fact that appeals to rational religion in the service of humanity may not be as ideologically pure and disinterested as they are often presented or presumed to be. This is turn provides a critical perspective from which to view Hull's commitment to *secular* religious education and his equation of a secular approach with an approach that accords priority to rational criticism of religion.

The morality thesis

A second characteristic feature of Enlightenment interpretations of religion is the conviction that 'the content and orientation of religion should be directed primarily toward *moral* concerns' (Louden 2007: 20). Anyone familiar with the history of modern thought will immediately associate Kant with this position and recognise him as its most influential spokesperson.

In *Religion within the Limits of Reason Alone* ([1793] 1998), Kant distinguishes 'a pure moral religion' from 'a statutory religion'. The former consists of commitment to moral autonomy and respect for persons as the service that is pleasing to God (to treat persons as 'ends' rather than as 'means to ends'), whereas the latter consists of the doctrines, rites and practices of the different historical religions. The former is essential to religion; the latter is not essential. Pure religion is moral religion, religion as it serves moral ends. Anything that goes beyond this is for Kant of secondary importance, and strictly superfluous. Even to ascribe properties to God beyond those strictly required by the moral law is unacceptable, both because it is unwarranted and because it undermines the true nature of religion by deflecting it from its essentially moral purpose. He acknowledges that the doctrinal, liturgical, and miraculous aspects of religion may help 'simple minds' to appropriate moral truth, but for the 'more able' these aspects of religion can be dispensed with, leaving religion in sole service to morality. What is true in religion is what conforms to the moral law and what inspires moral action. 'Apart from a good-life conduct, anything which the human being supposes he can do to become well-pleasing to God is mere delusion and counterfeit service of God' (Kant 1998: 166).

Naturally, the thesis that the purpose of religion is essentially moral was often linked to the unity thesis. The key elements of this alignment between religion and morality are:

> All human beings are children of the same father [the doctrine of divine fatherhood]; all human beings are moral equals; all human beings are morally obliged to treat each other justly and beneficently.
>
> *Louden 2007: 22*

Underlying the different religions was a common morality that encouraged and rewarded virtue and condemned and punished vice. This common morality was based on reason, which was regarded as potentially universal in scope and application, given that reason was the defining feature of 'enlightened' human nature. Typically, God is believed to superintend the operation of the moral law by apportioning final rewards and punishments; God does not provide a justification for morality in the strict sense. Most Enlightenment thinkers concurred with the judgement of Kant (1998: 33) that 'morality in no way needs religion (whether objectively, as regards willing, or subjectively, as regards capability) but is rather self-sufficient by virtue of pure practical reason'. Duty, which for Kant is the defining feature of morality, can be known and fulfilled without reference to God.

Toleration

As Kant is associated with assigning priority to the moral function of religion, so the English philosopher John Locke is associated with the Enlightenment idea of toleration. In part this latter association is polemical, for as typically presented it advances the thesis that religious toleration was a distinctively Enlightenment 'invention', which in turn distinguishes the ongoing Western Age of Enlightenment from the preceding religious age when conflict and sectarianism reigned. There may be evidence in support of this thesis but it is clearly overstated. Historical scholarship reveals that the emergence of the idea of religious toleration in the West was a much more gradual affair than the received liberal narrative that suggests a dramatic change from religious intolerance to Enlightenment secular toleration. Moreover, the emergence of the idea of religious toleration often drew on and was inspired by religious ideas and values. The idea that

Enlightenment scepticism about religion was the sole and determining cause of religious toleration is unsustainable historically and intellectually. Our focus, however, is not on defending religion from its detractors but on reviewing the commitment of the Enlightenment to religious toleration. Clearly, the desire to lessen the disruptive social effects of some forms and some aspects of religion is a pervasive aim of much Enlightenment thinking on this subject, even if these disruptive effects were exaggerated for ideological reasons.

In *A Letter Concerning Toleration* ([1689] 1955), Locke argued for the view that the state has no business interfering in the matter of religious belief: in part, because no individual who consents to government would think it appropriate to entrust matters of salvation to the decision of 'the magistrate'; in part, because other people are not harmed by the religious beliefs and practices of others; and, in part, because religious belief cannot be coerced. In later writings this last point was further amplified: persecution and coercion may change a person's practice and behaviour but they cannot change a person's beliefs. True belief can only be produced by 'light and evidence', and from a religious perspective, without true belief there can be no salvation. As is well known, Locke cited exceptions to his case for religious toleration. First, he believed that toleration should not be extended to atheists because they could not be relied upon to keep their promises or to Roman Catholics because they were a threat to national security (their primary political allegiance being to the Pope in Rome, who made inappropriate claims to religious and *temporal* sovereignty). Second, in some cases Locke accepted that aspects of religious *practice* may constitute legitimate subjects for state interference and legislation (the nature of his argument and its application need not detain us). Nevertheless, despite these restrictions, he begins his *Letter* by affirming 'toleration to be the chief characteristic mark of the true church' (Louden 2007: 23). Interestingly, recent engagements with the political philosophy of Locke, as for example that of John Dunn (1982) and Jeremy Waldron (2002), have revealed the extent to which his support for liberal political ideas such as liberty, natural rights and equality are derived from distinctively religious and theological premises and commitments.

'A more radical theory of religious toleration', according to Louden, is advocated by Pierre Bayle. According to Bayle, religious believers (and state magistrates) should tolerate each others' conflicting beliefs because 'it is impossible in our present condition to know with certainty . . . absolute truth' (Louden 2007: 23). There is no doubt that Bayle's position strikes a decidedly modern note. The essential idea is that there is a degree of agnosticism that attaches to religious claims to truth and consequently to religious beliefs; therefore no one can ever know with certainty whether his or her (chosen or inherited) religious beliefs are true. No individual enjoys a privileged epistemic situation with regard to religious truth and no one really knows which religion, if any, is true; and in such a situation one should extend tolerance to those who hold different religious beliefs and conclusions.

A similar position is also taken by the writer and theologian Gotthold Ephraim Lessing (1729–1781) in his dramatic poem, *Nathan the Wise*, which is set in the

Middle Ages at the time of the Crusades. In response to a question by Saladin, the leader of the Muslims, regarding which religion was 'the truest and best', Nathan, a Jewish merchant, told the story of a man who possessed a precious ring and whoever wore the ring was endowed with the magic power to win both the love of other people and of God. When the owner of the ring died, he left it to his favourite son; and when the son died, he in turn left it to his favourite son. Finally the ring descended to the father of three sons, who could not decide which son should have the ring, because all were equally loved and dear to him. Consequently he had two more rings made, so exactly like the first that even he was unable to distinguish between them; a ring was given to each son. The sons, however, fought among themselves, each claiming to have the original. This situation, Nathan pointed out, is analogous to conflicts between the Jews, the Muslims (termed Mohammedans in the drama) and the Christians. Asked for his own advice, Nathan refers Saladin to the counsel of the judge to whom the sons presented their respective cases:

> So let each believe his ring the true one.
> Tis possible your father would no longer tolerate
> The tyranny of this one ring in his family,
> And surely loved you all – and all alike,
> And that he would not oppress
> By favouring the third.

Lessing's point is that his readers should be tolerant in religious matters because God loves 'all alike' and would not favour one religion over another. The argument is broadly consistent with the account of 'genuine religion' given by Schleiermacher in *On Religion: Speeches to Its Cultured Despisers*. In Speech 4 Schleiermacher (1958: 146–209) commends religious toleration on the grounds that religious feeling is universal and therefore faith is universal. Some might argue that there is only a semantic difference between these positions and the proposals of 'pluralist' theologians such as John Hick (1973), Paul Knitter (1985) and Alan Race (1983). In fact the late John Hick, who was one of the most renowned twentieth-century advocates of the 'pluralist thesis' that all religions mediate salvation, has argued that the logic of interpretations of religious experience such as Schleiermacher's is that all the different religions should properly be regarded as religiously valid.

One further feature of Enlightenment thinking about religion is worth discussing here. It is not considered by Louden but is relevant to religious education.

The private/public distinction

The Enlightenment's gradual elevation of reason over revelation had far reaching implications in the social and political realms. Only those parts of religion which conformed to autonomous reason should be regarded as attaining the character of knowledge. Those parts or doctrines of religion that did not conform to reason, such as original sin, the deity of Christ and the notion of atonement, were regarded as matters of belief or opinion, at best simply unwarranted, at worst superstitious. So a distinction between the public and private domains of religion began to emerge. Religious beliefs which both conformed to reason and endorsed the social and political order enjoyed the status of public knowledge, whereas those religious beliefs which did not conform to reason and upon which there was dispute were consigned to the realm of private opinion.

The above paragraph summarises and necessarily simplifies the emergence of a distinction between the public and the private as it relates to religion in Enlightenment thought. We have already encountered the notion of conforming religion to the dictates of morality in Kant, and in a sense his reinterpretation of religion represents an attempt to do this not just in moral terms but in moral terms that serve the public good. Morality for Kant is necessarily universal and public, as is its truth; consequently in pursuing a moral interpretation of religion Kant gave it a public role – it became a servant of public morality. Kant was also a fierce critic of sectarian and superstitious religion and his account of religion is intended to show the form *public* religion must take. Religion as the servant of pure practical reason has a public role to play in the cosmopolitan society; this is one of the conclusions reached in his essay 'What is Enlightenment?' ([1784] 1991). Any form of religion, however, that does not conform to pure practical reason must be excluded from public life. In some respects there is a family resemblance between the view of Kant and that of Hobbes in *Leviathan* ([1651] 1998); we should also note that some historians date the period of the Enlightenment from 1650 to the end of the eighteenth century; on this dating, *Leviathan* qualifies as a text of the Enlightenment. Hobbes, like Kant, believed in a public role for religion, but rather than tailoring religion to the dictates of morality, Hobbes counselled that religion should be tailored to the dictates of the sovereign. For Hobbes, the sovereign has the right both to determine what religion should be and to enforce commitment to this form of civil religion. Both Hobbes and Kant recognised the threat from religion to civil and political order and both endeavoured in different ways to harness religion to positive social ends.

As in so many areas, the Enlightenment did not speak with one voice and different streams of Enlightenment thought have resulted in two distinguishable accounts of the public role of religion. This is another way of saying that the trajectory of Enlightenment ideas about the role of religion in society has produced two contrasting positions. The first position (which is identified with Hobbes above) is that of the idea of civil religion and the belief that religion should serve the interests of society, which may now be glossed as the common good or the good of society – for Hobbes it was peace and security. The second position is that religion should be a private affair, with religious beliefs and values excluded from influence in the public sphere.

It may be conceded that what can be conceptually distinguished for the purpose of clarification, in this case that religion may either act as a force to confirm the interests of the nation state or withdraw to its own private domain, is often blurred in reality. There are various modifications of both positions that combine elements of each. For example, some aspects of religion may be regarded as private and others as public, and these in turn will relate in different ways and form different partnerships with the social and political agendas of the political classes and the nation state. The legacy of the Enlightenment in this regard is complex and even contested. It is also interesting to reflect on the possible influence that diversity has had on revising and reinterpreting Enlightenment ideas about the public role of religion. Both Hobbes and Kant wrote at a time when religion, namely the Christian religion, was still seen as potentially a source of unity and a force for amity in society and it is this potential that encouraged them to think in terms of the positive value of civil religion. Whether they would have endorsed the idea of civil religion in our modern pluralist societies or instead have endorsed a principled distinction between private religion and public virtue, can only be speculated. The historical situation, at least in Britain, is that religion has increasingly become a matter of private opinion, which seems to have resulted in it becoming a matter of public indifference.

The liberal model of religious education

Hull's account of the nature and purpose of religious education clearly exemplifies the central commitments and values of the European Enlightenment and justifies speaking of a liberal model of religious education, that is, a model that self-consciously seeks to embody and perpetuate Enlightenment (or modern) values in and through religious education. At every point Hull endorses the central commitments of Enlightenment interpretations of religion and he believes that religious education should express these commitments. First, he supports what Louden calls the unity thesis, that each religion is valid in its own terms and that this religious validity excludes the appropriateness of attempts to convert religious adherents from one religion to another. Second, he affirms the priority of morality over religion and the conviction that religious beliefs and values should be revised on the basis of moral commitments. This may sound innocuous enough, but in the hands of Hull, as in the hands of Kant and other Enlightenment thinkers, it yields quite radical conclusions that challenge traditional religious orthodoxies. Third, his interpretation of the nature of toleration accords with those later Enlightenment figures who believed that religious intolerance finds its origin in the notion of religious superiority and that explicit recognition of equality among the religions would undermine religious intolerance and strife. Finally, Hull believes that representations of religion in education should be tailored to serve the case of religious unity, which in turn, he believes, will contribute to social harmony. For him, religion is chiefly a private affair and where it does impinge on public matters it should endorse liberal political and social values.

How does this liberal model of religious education, which at this stage has been identified with the position of John Hull, relate to our earlier discussion of phenomenological religious education? Certainly there are differences. For example, there is a conspicuous absence of any appeal by Hull to the use of a phenomenological methodology, with its emphasis upon empathy and intuition; he also has no interest in identifying the essence of religion or in attempting to identify and explain what is distinctive about it. Nevertheless, while acknowledging that there are differences between Hull and proponents of a phenomenological approach to religious education, these are insignificant compared with the similarities. Both Hull and phenomenological religious educators trace their intellectual commitments and values to the Enlightenment critique of religion and to the emergence of Liberal Protestantism in the nineteenth century. Both perceive a common spiritual dynamic in the different religions and both believe that the divine is present and is active to save in all religions; and on the basis of these commitments both believe that religious intolerance and discrimination can be effectively challenged in schools. Phenomenological religious education and Hull's 'anti-religionist' form of religious education are in fundamental agreement and for this reason they are both properly interpreted as two different expressions of the same liberal model of religious education (as is the experiential approach also).

A model of religious education provides the framework within which learning and teaching occurs, yet within a particular framework there is room for innovation and 'progress': different content, pedagogical methodologies, classroom practices and attitudes to specific educational policies may all be equally consistent with the beliefs, values and commitments of a particular framework. A model, while prescriptive and exclusive in certain respects, is also non-prescriptive and accommodating in others. It is part of the nature of different models to hold certain beliefs constant while accommodating some degree of diversity of belief and practice. The ability of 'disciplinary models' to accommodate a degree of diversity is what allows the liberal model of religious education to take a variety of forms, which while distinctive are properly viewed as different expressions of the same fundamental beliefs and values.

This aspect of models, in relation to scientific models, has been explored by Imre Lakatos (1970) and what he has to say on the issue is helpful and illuminates our consideration of the role of models in religious education. Lakatos thinks of scientific models as research programmes (for commentary and discussion, see Larvor 1998). A research programme, like a model, comprises a set of assumptions, beliefs and commitments. Typically, one basic assumption or commitment is central to a particular research programme; he refers to this as its 'hard core'. According to him the *negative heuristic* of a programme involves the stipulation that the basic hard core commitment (or commitments) must not be rejected or modified: the hard core of a research programme is rendered unfalsifiable by 'the methodological decision of its protagonists' (Chalmers 1982: 81). Any scientist who modifies the hard core has opted out of that particular research programme. Conjoined to the core is a set of auxiliary commitments and hypotheses that flesh out the central commitment and enable it to be explicated and applied in different contexts. The 'auxiliary hypotheses' also form a 'protective belt' around the 'hard core'; they have the ability to be modified and revised when potentially falsifying data are found. Lakatos also speaks of the *positive heuristic* of a research programme, which is that aspect of the model that indicates to its supporters the kind of things they should do in the light of acceptance of the hard core (or core commitment), though he acknowledges that the positive things to be done that follow from the research programme are often vague and difficult to characterise in advance of assuming its truth and applying the programme.

The relevance of this to our discussion of a liberal model of religious education should be obvious. What is the 'hard core' of the liberal model of religious education? What is the central commitment that justifies regarding phe-nomenological religious education, John Hull's anti-religionist programme and the experiential approach to religious education as different versions of the same model of religious education? It is the conviction that the religions are different but complementary expressions of the divine. This is the foundational belief of the liberal model of religious education, and around it is a cluster of auxiliary beliefs and hypotheses: that religious intolerance in pupils is effectively challenged by an appreciation of the spiritual unity of the different religions; that religious experience is central to religion; that religious doctrines are secondary to experience and revisable; that morality and religion are for the most part distinct; that religion is chiefly a private affair, and so on. There is a contingent relationship between these secondary beliefs and the core belief in the universality of God's revelation through the different religions. It is also the contingent nature of these secondary beliefs that provides the latitude of belief and commitment for there to be different expressions of the liberal model of religious education. The core belief can be applied in different ways in conjunction with a range of secondary hypotheses and commitments: what remains constant is the core belief.

One other point worth stressing at this stage is that adherence to a particular model of religious education does not require that one knowingly and consciously subscribes to it. Certainly the chief proponents of a particular model argue for, identify and appreciate the role of its core commitment(s) and typically adhere to most of the secondary convictions and beliefs that cluster around the core, yet this type of principled support is not necessary for practitioners. This is because classroom practice (all human practices in fact) are not only historically grounded and inherently theory laden but are often simply taken for granted as appropriate and self-evident.

> All our practices . . . have theories behind and within them. We may not notice the theories in our practices. We are so embedded in our practices, take them so much for granted, and view them as so natural and self-evident that we never take time to abstract the theory from the practice and look at it as something in itself.
>
> *Browning 1983: 6*

The enduring significance of the liberal model of religious education in British education

The conviction that the different religions are each spiritually valid is the core belief of the liberal model of religious education and is constitutive of much post-confessional religious education in Britain. It is often implicit, as in phenomenological religious education in the 1970s and early 1980s (see Marvell 1976; Hay 1977), but is increasingly explicit in later forms of multi-faith religious education (as in Johnston 1996; Radford 1999). The liberal model may not now enjoy the dominance it once did, yet it remains influential. To reinforce this point, the chapter will conclude by citing some examples of the continuing influence of the liberal model of religious education in British education, in order to show that the critique that follows in the next chapter is not of historical interest only.

In the immediate aftermath of the '9/11' Islamist attacks on America in 2001, a group of prominent religious educators from the University of Birmingham (which included Professor John Hull) and elsewhere signed and published a declaration that affirmed their commitment to liberal theological principles, which implied the essential spiritual unity of Christianity and Islam (the declaration was widely circulated at the time and was posted on the www. studyoverseas.com website on 23 October 2001):

> . . . we call upon our fellow Christians and Muslims *to abandon the competition* which has defiled our mutual relations for centuries. We confess that *this spirit of competition* has contributed to the climate in which extremism and fanaticism appears in both Christianity and Islam. We invite our fellow Christians and Muslims to enter into a new partnership in which we will work together for the good of humanity . . . [my emphasis]
>
> . . . [religious education, conceived in this way, will] provide an education for understanding in both these two religions [i.e. Christianity and Islam], so that ignorance, prejudice and intolerance may be eliminated.

The connection is made between claims to religious uniqueness (in this case with regard to Christianity and Islam) and 'extremism and fanaticism', to which the solution is for Christians and Muslims to abandon their exclusive claims to truth and result in the elimination of 'ignorance, prejudice and intolerance.' There would be no competition between religious adherents if they acknowledged the common spiritual validity and vitality of the different religions.

The next example is more recent still. In an article published in 2005, Geoff Teece contended that the influential British philosopher and theologian John Hick's theological advocacy of religious pluralism (according to which there are many equally valid and authentic ways of salvation) provides a 'foundation' for religious education in multi-cultural Britain. The obvious question to ask is: why does religious education in community ('state maintained') schools in a pluralist democracy need a theological foundation? The assumption that the different religions represent different but complementary revelations of the divine, he believes, supports learning and teaching in religious education, and its inculcation in the young will contribute to a 'fruitful' and 'appropriate critical education for the twentieth-first century' (Teece 2005: 9; for a reply, see Barnes and Wright 2006).

As one would expect, a liberal model of religious education is also influential and evident in classrooms. A recent ethnographic research project into religious education in Anglican voluntary-aided secondary schools (that is, schools that retain their distinctive Christian identity and aim to provide a Christian form of religious education) has produced some interesting evidence that reveals the extent to which respect for adherents of other religions is predicated on commitment to a 'universalist' or pluralist theology. Here is a representative quotation from the head of a religious education department in an Anglican school:

> I would want them all [i.e. pupils] to realise that we all have different understandings [of religion] but *we're not wrong*, we're different, we come from different perspectives and therefore it is good for us . . . *to respect everybody's believing system.*
>
> *quoted in Street 2007: 125, [my emphasis]*

The unstated assumption is that respect for others excludes the possibility of honest disagreement between people on substantial matters such as religion.

In his report the researcher commented that this interview and others like it reflect 'a theology which sees all religions as either equally valid cultural expressions of personal experience or expressions of one common transcendent reality' (Street 2007: 125). In thinking and expressing themselves in this way teachers are reflecting the commitments and assumptions of the liberal model of multi-faith religious education.

Interestingly, in a relatively recent review of different approaches to religious education in Europe, the Dutch educator Bert Roebben identifies British multi-faith religious education with the theological assumption that 'God represents himself in different historically contingent forms of religious experience' (Roebben 2007: 42). According to him, British multi-faith religious education 'legitimises' itself on this basis (noteworthy in the light of our earlier discussion in Chapter 1 of the official rhetoric that educators from other parts of Europe envy the British form of religious education). Roebben goes on to criticise the British, multi-faith model.

In this chapter the writings of John Hull on the issue of religious diversity have served as a focus to identify the core commitments of a liberal model of religious education and their influence and prevalence in Britain. The auxiliary commitments, which are frequently employed to support and protect the core ones (most typically those associated with a phenomenological interpretation of religion), have already been criticised in Chapter 8; consequently, what remains to be examined are the central distinctive commitments of the liberal model of religious education.

Note

1   'Religious Education as Encounter: A tribute to John Hull'. Online. Available http:// bit.ly/1c0AlMT (accessed 9 October 2013).

10

THE LIBERAL MODEL OF RELIGIOUS EDUCATION: A FINAL CRITIQUE

Criticism up to now has focused on the commitments and beliefs that constitute the outer core of the liberal model of religious education – the divorce of religious beliefs and doctrines from essential religious experience, the private nature of religious experience, and so on. It follows that in showing the weaknesses in these secondary commitments, the central 'hard-core' ones are also weakened, or more precisely, they are weakened to the extent that they depend upon the secondary commitments for support and justification, and some such justification is ultimately necessary. For example, if the distinction between non-conceptual (ineffable) religious experience and conceptual religious beliefs cannot be maintained in the way assumed by phenomenologists of religion then there are no grounds for concluding that the different religions should be viewed as complementary, within the terms of that particular account of religion: religious educators who rely on phenomenology are relying on a defective interpretation of the nature of religion and advancing religious understanding on an intellectually flawed philosophical basis.

Hull, unlike the phenomenologists of religion, simply overlooks the challenge of showing how the different religions and their different doctrines can be reconciled. He simply assumes that the different religions are complementary and that religious education pursued on this basis would effectively (in his opinion) undermine religious intolerance and discrimination. His is a straightforward ideological reading of religion: he believes that positive social outcomes will be achieved by teaching pupils in schools that every religion mediates the presence of God and salvation. If our review and analysis in preceding chapters is correct, the liberal theological thesis that the divine is revealed in different religions is the core determining principle of much post-confessional religious education in Britain. It provides the rationale for the subject to contribute to the moral and social aims of education and to challenge intolerance – and religious intolerance, it is contended, finds justification in the notion of religious supremacy. Is this not a reasonable and educationally responsible position? Hull makes explicit what is implicit in much phenomenological religious education and in many of the versions of multi-faith religious education influenced by phenomenology. There are clear advantages then in considering Hull's position in detail. His account of the nature and purpose of religious education exemplifies the central commitments and values of the liberal model. Moreover, a focus on his position concentrates attention on these alone without the potentially distracting arguments and debates that surround secondary commitments. In other words, Hull provides an opportunity to consider the liberal model of religious education in its purest form, namely its commitment to the thesis of religious unity and its associated strategy for undermining religious intolerance, without the various subsidiary arguments that are commonly used to support the position. If the position of Hull is flawed, so too is the entire liberal model, for he encapsulates its essential features, divested of any reliance on contingent secondary considerations and commitments.

The deconstruction of John Hull's *religionism*

There are two central strands in Hull's position (as outlined in the last chapter): first, the thesis that the different religions are complementary and, second, the educational strategy that follows from this – namely that the complementary nature of the different religions should be explicitly taught in schools and pupils should be disabused of the idea that one religion is superior to others. This position and its associated educational strategy, as advanced by Hull, are difficult to assess. This is because it is not always easy to separate the different strands of his argument, and indeed he does not attempt to develop an *argument* in any rigorous sense of the term. Points are often conflated and crucial premises unacknowledged. For the purposes of analysis and assessment, however, his position can be stated more formally.

1. There is religious intolerance and discrimination.
2. This precipitates community, national and international conflict and disharmony.
3. The cause of religious intolerance and discrimination is religious claims to uniqueness and superiority.

Therefore:

4. Religions and the different religious adherents should relinquish claims to uniqueness.

This entails:

5. The religions should be regarded as complementary.
6. The full weight of the educational process should be thrown behind attempts to deconstruct religious uniqueness.

7.   Religious intolerance, and of course the threat to social, national and international order represented by religion, will be overcome.

The advantage of setting out the argument in this way is that it shows that support for the liberal model of religious education may be advanced on educational grounds without an appeal to explicitly religious or theological considerations, though the argument does make theological assumptions and does carry theological implications, as will be shown in what follows.

Propositions 1 to 3 are premises, from which conclusions 4 to 7 are believed to follow. Premises 1 and 2 are well supported by evidence, and we can simply accept them as true. This leaves 3 as the crucial premise.

Premise 3 states that the cause of religious intolerance and discrimination is religious claims to uniqueness and supremacy. Let us first consider what is meant by this. Part of my contention is that Hull's position appears more plausible than it is, precisely because religious intolerance is considered in the abstract, without any further analysis of its meaning or human context. This lack of analysis tends to isolate *religious* intolerance from other forms of intolerance, and thus Hull's suggested solution appears much less controversial and more convincing than it actually is.

Tolerance has traditionally been interpreted to mean 'enduring or putting up with something of which one disapproves'. Positively, it requires our acceptance of someone who holds different beliefs, values or practices. Consequently, intolerance carries the connotation of not enduring something of which one disapproves and not accepting someone who holds different beliefs, values or practices (see King 1976: 12–13 and 21–72; Newman 1978). Additionally, in normal usage intolerance carries a pejorative meaning: tolerance is a virtue whereas intolerance is a vice.[1] Moreover, intolerance is not just disagreeing with someone over some belief or practice, it is on occasions, as *The Alberta Report of the Committee on Tolerance and Understanding* (1984; quoted by Laplante 1989: 148) puts it: 'the damning of one person or group by another and the intent to subject that person or group to suffering'. Recognition needs to be given both to the essentially personal nature of intolerance, for tolerance and intolerance are concepts of personal relationship, and to the evil intent which frequently underlies intolerance: the intention is to inflict pain and harm on others, be it physical or mental. Ultimately, intolerance of other beliefs, values and behaviour is intolerance of other persons. (There are also structural forms of intolerance and discrimination but given that their influence is on persons, they can also be regarded as ultimately personal in nature.)

Intolerance subsumes under it at least two components: a certain attitude towards others and some kind of discriminatory behaviour towards them. At root it is an attitude or disposition that is not prepared to countenance difference (see Chapter 2); it is an attitude of superiority which often looks down on or disdains those who hold different beliefs and values. As Evelina Orteza y Miranda (1994: 24) has commented, '[f]or questions and problems of tolerance to arise, it must be the case that plurality and diversity of practices, expressed opinions and so on must exist'. Intolerance is essentially an active word; it is something one does. The term *intolerance* and its cognates refer to actual and specific behaviour. People may have prejudiced attitudes which they never act on, but intolerance encompasses the notion of behaviour and activity.

What causes intolerance? In Chapter 2 we considered this issue and it is not necessary to repeat what was said there. What we concluded was that psychological and sociological factors are both involved. A sociological perspective alerts us to the importance of groups and the need for people to belong to and to identify with groups. Group membership distinguishes between individuals, thus 'we' and 'they', our group and your group, and in certain contexts and over certain issues there will be competition between groups: over resources, status, power, even truth itself. A psychological perspective draws attention to the inner dynamics involved: the way in which experiences and individuals are categorised, and the development of stereotypes which, sometimes, are ill-formed and rigid. It was also concluded that intolerance presupposes the perception of difference, whether real or imagined. The perception of difference, however construed, is the crucial matter.

Intolerance, moreover, is a general phenomenon. It is not something confined to religious contexts and religious individuals. Alongside religious intolerance there are many other varieties – racial and ethnic, for example. Intolerance and discrimination are not confined to one particular situation, context or group of people. Intolerance can be directed against those of a different social class, different culture, different political persuasion, and so on; the list is endless. At all the points at which people recognise difference, there is the potential to develop and foster attitudes which diminish and demean other human beings. While intolerance is often revealed at the social level and directed against certain groups within society, it is also revealed in closer relationships of kinship and friendship. The person who is intolerant of blacks or Catholics or women or Christians or secularists is typically intolerant of other family members or community members when they diverge in judgement and behaviour from what is expected or approved. Certainly intolerance towards minority groups within society increases the threat to the well-being and harmony of society as a whole, and for this reason requires a more reflective and sustained educational response, though this does not diminish the seriousness of intolerance at the family level. Intolerance discloses itself both in intimate personal relationships and less personal group relations. Any adequate educational response to intolerance must address both forms and recognise the connection between the two.

A consideration of the general concept of intolerance provides the necessary context to appreciate and interpret the specific notion of religious intolerance. This is but one species of a wider genus, similar in form and in its consequences for individuals and for groups – lower status, lower self-esteem, social discrimination and so on. The distinction between religious intolerance and other forms is that individuals are discriminated against on the basis of their *religious* commitment. This brings us back to Professor Hull's position: premise (3) of his argument states that the cause of religious intolerance and discrimination is religious claims to uniqueness and supremacy.

In order to assess the contribution of religion to religious intolerance there are a number of preliminary issues which first need to be addressed. For one thing, a clear understanding of what counts as intolerance is needed. What activities and actions should be regarded as exhibiting religious intolerance? This is a question of definition. It is not an issue which can be settled by reference to empirical data. For example, if all efforts to convert individuals from one religion to another are regarded as exhibiting intolerance then, clearly, religion is a major source of it. It follows from this that religious intolerance would be greatly reduced if adherents of one religion never attempted to win converts from any other. But of course on such an interpretation, the point at issue is simply assumed. By definition, all those who attempt to convert others from one religion to a different one, by whatever means, are guilty of intolerance.

This does not seem a sensible or compelling position. Its unreasonableness can be seen if we apply the same logic to other situations. In the political context attempts are made by politicians and others to challenge and change peoples' convictions across a wide range of social, economic and political issues, yet such actions are not normally regarded as illegitimate and thought to spring from some basic intolerance of other peoples' opinions and a desire to impugn their dignity. In fact, providing opportunities for debate and discussion seems to be an essential feature of an open and democratic society. Freedom of speech is one of the cardinal principles of modern political liberalism. It may be concluded that certain forms of political persuasion are morally unacceptable, though this does not detract from the conclusion that they may take proper and legitimate forms, such as those that appeal to reason and argument and that respect the integrity and autonomy of individuals. The same is true in a religious context. Certain forms of appeal and persuasion may well be unworthy of religion but not all forms of persuasion should be regarded as illegitimate and thought to originate in a basic intolerance of other people and their opinions.

A proper, sensible and convincing analysis of exactly what constitutes religious intolerance is needed: if a community's values and commitments are conveniently ignored or held up to ridicule, or if individuals from a particular group are socially and legally discriminated against; such provide clear examples. The point of departure for analysing the nature of intolerance should be the examination of unambiguous cases, examples which are obvious and uncontroversial and where there are clear infringements of justice. Following this, attention can be given to more controversial cases, where there is some dispute between parties about whether intolerance is actually present and whether the term intolerance and its cognates have a legitimate application.

Keeping these observations in mind, the precise nature of the relationship between religion and intolerance may be considered. Hull rests his case on the assumption that there is a direct causal relationship between belief in the exclusive truth of one's own religion and acts of intolerance. Premise 3 states that religious claims to uniqueness are the cause of religious intolerance and discrimination. But what kind of causal agency is involved here? Is Professor Hull simply asserting that there is an empirical connection between religious superiority and religious intolerance, in the sense that those who assert the exclusive truth and supremacy of their own religion are more likely to *exhibit* religious intolerance in their relations with adherents of other religions, or is he claiming something more? A close reading of what he says suggests that he does mean something more. He seems to be of the opinion that there is some kind of *deductive* and *justificatory* link between religious superiority and religious intolerance. For him, religious supremacy entails religious intolerance, not chiefly in the sense that individuals who assert the supremacy of their own religion *often happen to be* intolerant of adherents of other religions, but in the stronger sense that belief in religious superiority *sanctions* or *justifies* religious intolerance, and this justification is deductive in form: the attitude of intolerance logically follows from belief in the uniqueness and superiority of one's religion.

That this is the correct and natural reading of Professor Hull's position is worth pursuing. For one thing, it makes best sense of the language he employs to express his position. His entire discussion of religious intolerance and religious prejudice focuses on definitions and the way in which one concept is derived from or subsumed under another. For example, he equates religionism both with the view that one's religion is right and others' wrong and with the adverse social consequences which he believes accompany this equation. 'Religionism' he tells us '*always involves* prejudice against other religions' (Hull 1992: 70; my emphasis), and, as he immediately goes on to say, religionism is more than simply prejudice, it also involves 'rejection and exclusion'. The derivation of the one from the other is based on his analysis of terms and the way in which one term or category is extended by definition and deduction to incorporate new and broader meanings. This suggests that his argument is logical and deductive rather than empirical – an interpretation further strengthened by the fact that he makes no appeal to empirical evidence or research. We have also to take into consideration his absolute and implacable opposition to the notion that a religion might be true and other religions false. His position, as he expresses it, does not appear to stand or fall by reference to a contingent link between assertions of religious uniqueness and intolerant behaviour, and the extent to which religion can be identified as the determining factor: the connection to his mind is deductive and necessary.

Such a connection is not easily established. At one level it runs foul of the philosophical dictum that you cannot derive an 'ought' from an 'is'. Factual beliefs do not yield imperatives for action, or at least not all that easily or uncontroversially (unless one believes that factual beliefs are set within a wider context where values are already affirmed and endorsed). Thus the belief that Christianity is the only true religion may not imply that Christians are required ('ought') to be intolerant of adherents of other religions, even if they do hold them to be in error. Furthermore, recent criticism of the (supposed) logical independence of value judgements from factual beliefs would seem to do little to advance Hull's position that religious uniqueness necessarily entails religious intolerance. Alasdair MacIntyre (1985 and 1988), for example, has argued that it is possible to derive moral values from factual considerations, but only within the context of a larger metaphysical framework, such as Aristotelianism or Thomistic Christianity, with their essential commitment to teleology. This line of reasoning, however, is unlikely to appeal to Hull, for it presupposes the intellectual and moral superiority of some metaphysical views or worldviews over others. His argument against the notion of exclusive religious truth is predicated on the assumption that no one religion has an epistemic advantage over any other; consequently he may be reluctant to countenance the idea that some religions constitute more plausible candidates for justifying moral values and moral discourse than others.

Dr Hull is caught on the horns of a dilemma. Moral (or immoral) valuations either can or cannot be derived from factual claims, and if the latter is true then his premise that religious uniqueness (logically) entails intolerance is simply false. The most credible argument for the positive conclusion that moral claims can be derived from factual considerations, however, may entail a high view of the truth of some particular religion (perhaps even some group of religions), a view of truth which may not necessarily be shared with other religions, say non-theistic ones.

It may be contended that Hull's position has been misrepresented, or correctly interpreted but perhaps not in accordance with what he really meant to say. Perhaps rather than proposing a logical and deductive relationship between religious supremacy and intolerance he was really insisting, despite all appearances and evidence to the contrary, that the relationship was empirical and contingent, yet nonetheless causal: people who believe in the uniqueness of their own religion are caused by this to be intolerant of other religious adherents. (For illustrative purposes discussion will focus on Christianity.)

The fact that intolerance is not confined to religion, however, cautions against a straightforward causal relationship between negative judgements on the truth of other religions and religious intolerance. It has already been noted that the potential for misunderstanding the nature of religious intolerance and consequently ineffective and inappropriate educational responses is greatly increased by Hull's exclusive focus on religious intolerance and discrimination without looking at the phenomenon more widely. Intolerance is not confined to religion and to religious people. This alone suggests that the cause of intolerance is to be found in some general feature of the human self or personality rather than in some particular and peculiar feature of the religious consciousness, and this in turn fits in with our earlier discussion of the nature of difference and the ways in which difference (and perceptions of 'alterity') becomes an excuse for intolerance. For some people it may be the case that believing themselves to be right provides the stimulus for intolerant attitudes, but being right and regarding others as wrong does not sanction intolerance.

Intolerance of whatever form is an expression of a person's personality and of choices made, though no doubt choices are reflective of social and community attitudes. In the case of religion it may be that intolerant attitudes are encouraged and endorsed by some religious authorities, be they sacred books or sacred individuals, and it is entirely proper that such uses of religion should be challenged and criticised in educational contexts (the same comment could be made in relation to political intolerance). Hull makes this point and it should be endorsed, but criticism should also be directed against the extension of this point into an educational strategy for inculcating pupils into the belief that the different religions are complementary avenues to religious truth. Such a move is open to serious objections, and also fails either to address the real problem of religious intolerance or to provide a strategy that can effectively challenge it.

This wider perspective on intolerance, however, may not fully absolve religion from (moral) blame. There is empirical research that suggests that church members are more prejudiced than non-church members (Gorsuch 1988) and perhaps familiarity with this oft repeated conclusion has encouraged some, like Hull, to believe that there is a simple causal relationship between religious superiority and intolerance. Certainly there are researchers who have concluded that religion is a cause of prejudice and intolerance. Yet this conclusion may be too simplistic, for empirical research has also identified a curvilinear relationship between prejudice and church attendance. Those who go to church frequently are the least prejudiced; those who go to church infrequently are the most prejudiced. This finding led Gordon Allport (1966) to postulate a distinction between what he called 'intrinsic' and 'extrinsic' religious attitudes. 'The distinction' he tells us (Allport 1966: 454), 'helps . . . to separate churchgoers whose communal type of membership supports and serves other (non-religious) ends from those for whom religion is an end in itself – a final, not instrumental good'. A number of other researchers have built upon this suggestion and devised scales to identify and measure these two orientations. Results gathered seem to suggest that the distinction is illuminative of religious attitudes and behaviour, and to confirm Allport's conclusions (see Gorsuch and Aleshire 1974). On the basis of this it could be maintained that prejudice would be reduced if 'extrinsically' orientated religious people were encouraged to become more religious and come to appreciate the value of religion for its own sake.

A different perspective on religious intolerance is provided by empirical research showing that exclusive truth claims and strong emotional attachment to a group can create hostility towards those who do not share in the group's beliefs (see Freud 1922: 51; Glock and Stark 1966). Strong group attachment fosters religious intolerance. It is strong group attachment that is the crucial factor, not religion. Some writers have extended this line of enquiry and concluded that strong religious commitment correlates to authoritarianism, and it is the latter which is the crucial determining factor: people with authoritarian personality traits are naturally attracted to conventional forms of religion which maintain clear and rigid distinctions between right and wrong (Adorno *et al.* 1950).

Religion is not the cause of intolerance, *per se*, rather it provides an occasion for the manifestation of religious intolerance.

On the basis of this brief overview of empirical research, which is necessarily selective, there is justification in concluding that there is *no clear causal* connection between religion and intolerance; at least in the case of Christianity. The situation of other religions or some other religion may be different (and if so, some account needs to be taken of this in education). Hull's third premise that religious uniqueness *causes* religious intolerance is unwarranted either as necessarily or as contingently true, or at least as contingently true in any sense that legitimately justifies moving from the proposition 'This religion is true' to the conclusion that religious intolerance is appropriately shown to those who reject it. It may be that some religions do justify intolerance towards non-adherents, but this is on the basis of other specific beliefs and not on the basis that the religion is alone true. Therefore, there is no good reason why religions should renounce their claims to uniqueness (conclusion 4) or why the full weight of the educational process and its institutions should be thrown behind attempts to deconstruct religious superiority (conclusion 6).

Further objections to the liberal model of religious education

There are a number of other considerations that challenge the central commitments of the liberal model of religious education, which may be illustrated by reference to the position of Professor Hull.

Hull acknowledges that religion can be criticised in an educational context and that good and baleful features of religion can be identified and discussed. At one point he even admits that it is compatible with an even-handed approach to the representation of religion in the classroom for criticism to be made of elements of a religion which is not one's own. He gives the example of a Christian who prefers Christianity over Buddhism because the former is more 'world-affirming'. What is not permissible, according to him, however, is to conclude on the basis of this, that Christianity is true and Buddhism less true (Hull 1998: 340–341). A personal preference in religion is permissible but such preferences must not take the form of denying the religious (salvific) validity of any other religion. To endorse Christianity and some particular spiritual value in it does not entitle one to claim that other religions are less true or authentic because they lack that value; they have other values to which people are properly attracted. This move by Hull to include a place for criticism of religion within his anti-religionist approach to the teaching of religion is clearly necessary, because otherwise the position would be manifestly self-contradictory. It is on the basis of identifying and criticising the baleful elements of religion that he proposes his anti-religionist approach to the teaching of religion. It would be straightforwardly self-contradictory for him to exclude criticism of religion. But has he really escaped contradicting himself? There are reasons for concluding that his position remains self-referentially incoherent.

Religionism, for Hull, includes the judgement that one religion is true and valid and that other religions are false. At the heart of his position here, and the point at which he believes religionism follows with all its attendant social evils, is the judgement of wrongness on the deeply felt and important issue of religious truth. Let us consider an individual who believes Islam to be God's final revelation to humankind, a revelation in the light of which all other (supposed or acknowledged) revelations have to be judged and corrected. Hull believes this to be a mistaken judgement; he believes that such a judgement sanctions religious intolerance and prejudice. But surely Hull has also expressed a judgement on the truth of religion: he has expressed the negative judgement that someone who believes only in the truth of his or her own religion is wrong. Hull regards his particular religious judgement as true and the Muslim who believes that the Qur'an provides the *final* revelation of God as false. Within the terms of his own argument, Hull is also guilty of religionism: he is making the same judgement that he regards as giving support to religious intolerance and prejudice. He is right; the Muslim (who believes that Islam is the only true religion) is wrong!

A further difficulty in Hull's position at this point is that his strategy of allowing only *internal* criticism of religion exposes him to the objection that his anti-religionist programme is a covert form of religious confessionalism (not the traditional Christian form but liberal religious confessionalism) similar to that which is implicit in phenomenological and experiential versions of religious education. If anti-religionist teaching requires that criticism of religion can only go so far in the classroom, in that it must stop short of questioning the ultimate truth of any religion, then it follows that the ultimate truth of religion *per se* cannot be challenged or questioned in an educational context, because it is itself an inviolate educational principle. But if this is the case then schools are effectively being charged with inculcating the truth of religion in young people. If teachers and pupils in education cannot question the assumption that religion is true, then education is serving a religious purpose. This is an unacceptable implication for a educational programme that purports to further religious tolerance in schools within a pluralist, democratic society.

Traditionally and historically, adherents of the different religions have regarded themselves as advancing contrasting and opposing religious identities. One normally contrasts Christian religious identity with Muslim religious identity; one does not think of an individual as a Muslim and a Christian, a Jew and a Buddhist. Religious identities (for followers of the main world religions) can be and tend to be exclusive in a way other forms of identity are not. The fact that religious identities are exclusive means that individuals convert from one to the other and often such conversions are on the basis that the new religion is believed to be true or true to a degree denied to the old religion, though no doubt there are social factors involved as well. Religions' adherents often represent the religions as being in competition with each other – it is this competitive element that has made 'proselytism' such a charged religious and political issue in some places, particularly in those Islamic states that forbid conversion from Islam to a different religion or to atheism. That religions are in competition with each other (which presupposes that they are divided over the issues of religious truth and of salvation) is denied by some modern Western academics, for one reason or another, and presumably the cause of social harmony is one such reason. This does not change either official or popular perceptions of competition between religions. To present the different religions in the classroom as not in competition with each other, as Hull recommends, is to falsify the self-understanding of many religious adherents, and though such self-understanding should not prevent educators raising and debating critical questions in relation to religion and to particular beliefs and practices, the religions should be presented, in the first instance, in ways that reflect faithfully the self-understanding of those who are committed followers. Representation of religions in education should reflect religions as they are for their followers and not what Western liberal theologians would like them to become. Certainly religious education should take account of modern re-readings and interpretations of traditional religious beliefs but only after the meaning and the continuing significance of traditional beliefs is appreciated and understood.

While it is important to focus on the self-identity of religious believers and their perceptions of identity at a particular point in time and space, it is also important to appreciate that the identity of believers is typically regarded by them as reflecting the commitments and values of the teachings of their sacred scriptures. Religious identity, while no doubt a composite creation resulting from a variety of sources, is often chiefly indebted to what is believed to have been revealed to special individuals and subsequently recorded in sacred scriptures. Muslims, for example, believe in the teachings of the Qur'an and take those and the example of Muhammad as their guide to how they should act in the world. Religious attitudes towards adherents of 'other' religions and those who profess no religion are determined by the beliefs and values of their sacred scriptures and what is regarded as conveying divine revelation; and, as is well known, the sacred scriptures of most religions (particularly the theistic religions) make claims to exclusive truth or at least claim to possess and convey religious truth to a degree denied to other religions (see Christian 1972 and 1987). Hull is aware of such claims but dismisses them as religionist, and as not an authentic aspect of religious identity.

There are good reasons for believing that Hull has misinterpreted the nature of religion at this point, not only with regard to the way in which the beliefs of one religion disagree with the beliefs of another but also with regard to the way in which beliefs within a religion are interrelated and mutually dependent on each other. Hull holds that belief in the exclusive truth of one's own religion causes religious intolerance of others. His solution is for the religions to relinquish claims to uniqueness and superiority. The link Hull identifies between superiority and intolerance, however, actually finds its origins further back in the distinctive beliefs of a religion. For example, belief in the 'supremacy' of Christianity by Christians is advanced on the basis of other beliefs and is regarded by them as entailed by, say, commitment to the doctrine of the deity of Christ or to the doctrine of the atonement: it is the doctrines that characterise Christianity and distinguish it (propositionally) from other religions that provide the basis and foundation for assertions of Christian uniqueness. In relation to Christianity, Hull speaks as if belief in Christian uniqueness is external to the system of Christian belief, as if this one doctrine is optional and detachable from the rest. He fails to appreciate the interconnected and mutually supportive character of Christian doctrine (or Muslim doctrine, for that matter). Religious beliefs are not independent of each other in the way he imagines. A shift of Christian perspective at one point requires a corresponding shift somewhere else within the web of Christian beliefs: accommodation occurs elsewhere (see Quine and Ullian 1978). More systematic theological critics of the superiority of Christianity, such as John Hick (1973), recognise this, and acknowledge that a fairly radical revision of Christian belief and doctrine is required to effect a new and more liberal understanding of its relation to other religions.

Hull's proposals commit him to a similar revisionist policy towards Christian belief and doctrine, though he is hesitant to admit it. This is because one of the strengths of his position, as he presents it, is its (purported) neutral character. In truth, however, his position contains a particular theological commitment to the idea that all religions are equal. On this basis he would require religious believers to revise and even relinquish orthodox religious beliefs. What presents itself as a neutral educational programme for the advancement of tolerance in schools on closer inspection reveals itself as having radical implication for the presentation of the nature and 'truth' of Christianity (and other religions) in schools.

Hull believes that if religious adherents could be 'educated' into believing that there is soteriological value in every religion, this would undermine what he judges to be the chief cause of religious intolerance, namely, the notion of superiority that judges a religion other than one's own as less true and less capable of realising certain essential religious ends. He contends that if religious adherents could be convinced that there is no competition between religions then religious intolerance would be considerably lessened, if not eliminated. This solution is of course hopelessly unrealistic. It is unrealistic because it is unlikely that all religious adherents will renounce claims to superiority for their particular religious commitments; it is also based on a misinterpretation, for it fails to recognise that the existence of difference, however and wherever conceived, provides the potential for intolerance and unjust discrimination. Hull's solution does not actually address the challenge of religious diversity in society and of developing respectful attitudes to those who are religiously different. Religious diversity is explained away as not ultimately significant, for all religions are in fundamental agreement. Hull's strategy does not encourage or help people to become more tolerant or respectful of difference. In fact by encouraging religious believers to view their commitments as complementary and relative, within the terms of his argument, he is effectively denying that there are situations where religious tolerance and its converse, religious intolerance, can arise: if people agree over religion, there is no need for religious toleration, for one religion does not affirm what any other needs to deny; tolerance has an application only where people disagree, only where there is difference and diversity. The virtue of tolerance, in its traditional sense of putting up with opinions and behaviour of which one disapproves, however, will always be relevant to a world which is genuinely plural and where real differences exist, including religious differences.

The fundamental problem with Hull's anti-religionist programme and that of the liberal model of religious education generally is that religious difference is not taken seriously. Difference is explained away as unimportant and secondary to a more fundamental unity. One consequence of this is that traditional religious believers will recognise that their cherished religious values and convictions are being misrepresented in education (in order to square them with the equal truth of other religions). They will then conclude that their views and beliefs are not truly respected, that there is no real respect for difference. If there were such respect then the differences between the religions would be faithfully acknowledged and not ignored or reinterpreted to fit liberal theological convictions.

The educational strategy of convincing pupils that the religions are in essential agreement actually undermines respect for difference in a further sense. Consider the logic of the strategy. One is encouraged to accept adherents of other religions and to relinquish intolerance of them on the ground that their ultimate convictions are in agreement with your own. One adopts a positive attitude to 'the other' because the other shares a similar and complementary commitment to the divine. Acceptance of the religious other is predicated on essential religious agreement (say in religious experience). But this carries the implication that no such respect for difference may be forthcoming in those cases where there is genuine disagreement – no respect for those who resist the liberal temptation to view all religions as true (or indeed for the atheist or the agnostic who resists a religious interpretation of life). If there were true respect for religious difference there would be no need to attempt to convince pupils of the essential agreement between the religions or the use of methodologies that assume this. This liberal strategy has the capacity to 'demonise' 'the other' just as effectively as strategies that acknowledge the exclusive nature of particular religious commitments. The line between insiders and outsiders is drawn in a different place, this time between inclusivists and exclusivists rather than, say, between Muslims and others or Hindus and others, but the same binary distinction is employed. Respect for religious difference (and respect for others) is compromised when those who are to be accepted and affirmed must first relinquish any claim to religious distinctiveness. True respect for religious difference is not shown when respect is predicated on prior acceptance of a 'pluralist' theology that effectively denies any real substance to religious disagreement and presumes essential agreement. The religious 'other' should be respected whatever his or her religious theological commitments.

By attempting to impose on pupils the theological principle that all religions are equal, the liberal model of religious education has engaged in a form of confessionalism (albeit with the best of intentions), believing that religious intolerance and discrimination are the inevitable accompaniments of belief in the uniqueness or superiority of any one religion over others. It has been argued that such an understanding of the relationship of religious superiority to prejudice and intolerance is simplistic and woefully inadequate. There is no direct connection between belief in the truth of one's own commitments and intolerance of those who hold contrary commitments. Belief in the superiority of humanism over Christianity, for example, does not (logically) sanction humanists to be intolerant of Christians. Superiority of belief need not issue in an attitude of superiority! The two are quite distinct. In addition, by devoting its educational energies to the pursuit of this principle, religious education has both misrepresented the nature of religion, as interpreted by most religious believers, and failed to engage fully with the complex web of interrelationships between beliefs, attitudes and feelings that combine on occasions to encourage religious intolerance and discrimination.

Note

1   There are legitimate limits to tolerance, in the sense that certain forms of behaviour should not tolerated, for example the sacrifice of infants or the sexual exploitation of children. In other words, we should properly be intolerant of certain forms of behaviour. However, for the purposes of this chapter I shall assume that tolerance is always a virtue and intolerance is always a vice. Thus I am omitting any reference to circumstances or situations where intolerance is the appropriate moral stance to take.

11

POSTMODERN THOUGHT

At a number of points it has already been stated that, following the demise of confessionalism, the modern model of religious education enjoyed unrivalled influence in Britain until the 1990s. That decade, however, was a period of transition, and in retrospect it can be seen that a new postmodern model began to emerge and vie with modern conceptions of religious education for influence and support. Something of the nature of this transition is captured by Terence Copley (2008) in his history of religious education in England and Wales. In the chapter devoted to developments in the 1990s, Copley refers to a range of issues and debates, including the work of Robert Jackson and the interpretive approach to religious education which was emerging under Jackson's leadership of the Warwick RE Project. He writes (2008: 169):

> Changing paradigms about the nature of religion itself were reflected in the Warwick RE Project . . . The Warwick group were concerned about the problems of locking young people into stereotypical religious and cultural identities. They argued that the current concepts of religions and religion were modern, post-Enlightenment constructions.

Copley comes close to identifying the emergence of a new postmodern model of religious education in the work of Jackson and his associates. He recognises that the interpretive approach to religious education draws upon 'changing paradigms about the nature of religion', though he does not explore either the nature of these paradigms or the extent to which the interpretive approach may represent the emergence of a new paradigm of religious education. It is also noteworthy that Copley does not refer to *postmodern* paradigms, either in relation to religion or to religious education. What he does say is that these new paradigms (models) are critical of modern, post-Enlightenment constructions of the nature of religion. Yet it is precisely the questioning and rejection of modern, post-Enlightenment beliefs and commitments that is the point of departure of postmodernism as a broad critical movement and of postmodern treatments of religion in particular.

Moving beyond a negative characterisation of postmodern thought is difficult. In fact the wide range of positions that are designated as postmodern serves to some extent to undermine use of the term, because it is impossible to know, without careful attention to detail, what exactly is denoted. Furthermore, postmodern ideas are sometimes characterised as unclear, unsystematic, ambiguous and obscure, a characterisation that undoubtedly lies behind Ernst Gellner's (1992: 41) assessment of postmodernism as 'metatwaddle'. When described in this way it is entirely understandable why some in the field of religious education (Robert Jackson, for example; see Chapter 12) do not choose to identify themselves and their commitments as postmodern. None of this means that distinctions between modern and postmodern ideas cannot be made, when suitably contextualised and qualified, and when such an exercise is undertaken, particular positions and commitments in religious education may be appropriately identified as postmodern. On this understanding, use of the term postmodern is descriptive and critical, not pejorative and negative. This descriptive usage is intended in what follows; it does not mean that postmodern commitments escape criticism, rather that the identification of a belief or commitment with postmodernism tells us nothing about its validity or its value – criticisms need to be justified and substantiated, not simply assumed on the basis of their identification.

Postmodernism and its cognates are used to designate a range of commitments with distinctive emphases and accents, and, correspondingly, postmodern religious education exhibits these same commitments and their associated emphases and accents. Simply put, postmodern religious education is the application of postmodern ideas, beliefs and commitments to the subject. It follows from this that an outline of the beliefs and values of postmodern thought provides both the necessary means of identifying postmodern accents and commitments in religious education and a useful orientation to the underlying beliefs and commitments of postmodern approaches in religious education.

The contours of postmodernity

Characterising postmodern thought is anything but straightforward, for the simple reason that the recognition of difference and diversity is central to it. In fact some contend that attention to diversity is its defining feature – postmodernity is a protest against uniformity and attempts to reduce human and social reality to a set of bounded rational principles that enjoy universal application. In addition, the meaning of postmodernity varies according to particular disciplines – art, architecture, cultural studies, human geography, philosophy, public policy, sociology, and so on. Obviously a movement that accentuates the importance of difference and incorporates a range of viewpoints and disciplines is not easy to categorise and conceptualise. Some commentators distinguish between *postmodernity* as it relates to society, culture and history (Archetti 1996) and *postmodernism* as it relates to philosophy, particularly philosophy inspired by French post-structuralist thought. This distinction will not be followed, chiefly because it is not universally observed and also because some of the ideas discussed (in connection with Foucault in particular) do not fit neatly into either category; nevertheless, the emphasis here will be chiefly on philosophical matters.[1]

One helpful way to provide an orientation to postmodern thought is to contrast it with 'modernity', or 'the Enlightenment Project' as it is often glossed. Such a strategy is not uncommon among postmodern thinkers themselves; in fact some way of distinguishing postmodern from modern thought is a requirement for those who self-consciously describe themselves as postmodern. The following set of oppositions will provide a basis for a provisional orientation to the nature of postmodern thought.

Modernity	*Postmodernity*
universal rationality	contextual wisdom and historical 'truths'
impartiality	partiality
foundationalism	anti-foundationalism
truth as correspondence	truth as socially constructed
referential theory of language	meaning as used in social contexts
determinate reference	indeterminate reference
'grand narratives' (Lyotard)	local narratives
scientific knowledge	'subjugated knowledges' (Foucault)
uniformity	difference/pluralism/fragmentation
universalism	particularism
knowledge	power

This list could be further extended, but an understanding of the nature of the contrast between modernity and postmodernity should be beginning to emerge.

Postmodernity challenges Enlightenment ideas such as the omnicompetence of human reason; the inevitability of scientific progress as a necessary good for humanity; the limitation of knowledge to what can be proved to the satisfaction of the 'disinterested', critical and enquiring mind; the unitary nature of truth and the idea that the nature of reality is explicable in terms of all-encompassing theories that reduce human and social differences to deeper more fundamental laws or principles that are revealed to reason. Criticism of the Enlightenment concept of autonomous reason has taken various forms. Critics have pointed out that the interpretation and use of reason always presupposes a set of principles and convictions, which as background beliefs cannot themselves be proven (see Wolterstorff 1984, for example). Others have pointed out that the Enlightenment concept of reason is just as historically conditioned and partisan (see Foucault 1984) as alternative accounts of rationality, which Enlightenment thinkers and their contemporary followers dismiss as irrational and unwarranted (see Lyotard 1984). Finally, a range of criticisms have focused on the social consequences of modernity and the ways in which disinterested reason lent its support to colonialism, imperialism (Hulme 1990), racism (Eze 1997) and sexism (see Foucault 1979). Scientific rationality and objectivity became the tools by which the West and the intellectual elite exerted their influence and perpetuated their privilege (see Horkheimer and Adorno 2002; and in relation to religion, Chidester 1996).

A different line of criticism has been to identify the ways in which modern rational thought has increasingly become suspicious of its own foundations and as a consequence become divorced from life, commitment and action. In a sense the circle of justified beliefs sanctioned by 'universal reason' has become ever smaller, too small in fact to warrant much of the traditional content of philosophy and about how to live morally and act responsibly in the world: philosophy on this epistemological footing is irrelevant to questions of meaning and purpose, social policy, religion, and so on. One thinks immediately here of the emergence of Logical Positivism in the 1930s. Its commitment to the principle that words have a (determinate) meaning only when that meaning can be specified in terms of sense experience and subject to empirical verification represents, in many respects, the apogee of Enlightenment's valorisations both of method and of science (and of course these come together in the idea of a distinctive scientific methodology). According to A. J. Ayer (1946: 9), who popularised Logical Positivism in the English-speaking world, 'a statement is held to be literally meaningful if and only if it is either analytic or empirically verifiable'. As is well known, this and further revised empiricist criteria (the principle of falsification, for example, popularised by Flew, 1971) were used to conclude that religious, moral and aesthetic statements were factually empty, literally 'without sense'. The inspiration for much of this kind of thinking came from the conviction that empiricism and an empiricist criterion of meaning reflected the methodology of science and the way in which it distinguished justified from unjustified beliefs. Ironically, it soon became apparent that much of the body of scientific truth cannot be established on either an empiricist or a verificationist basis (it may be noted that not all empiricist criteria of meaning need be verificationist). More widely, the failure of Logical Positivism pointed to problems with foundationalist epistemologies (both rationalist and empiricist) and the notion that (non-basic) justified beliefs can be traced back to a set of basic foundational beliefs that in incorrigible or indubitable form serve as a secure foundation for all other beliefs. The details of this need not detain us (see Plantinga 1983). As a consequence, among analytic philosophers there has been a movement away from foundationalist epistemologies to 'coherentist' or holistic conceptions of knowledge that interpret beliefs as mutually supportive and interconnected with each other: propositional beliefs are more in the metaphorical shape of a web than a house with foundations (see Quine and Ullian 1978).

Typically, however, there remains a commitment to some form of realism and the conviction that the nature of the world and reality can be reflected and captured in language, and that knowledge and objective truth are attainable. Among a small number of British and American philosophers schooled in the analytic tradition, however, the demise of foundationalism has signalled a shift either to pragmatism and the conviction that beliefs should be assessed on the basis of their practical consequences, with Richard Rorty (1989) as a clear example, or to some form of social constructionism that stresses the necessarily limiting contribution of human societies/human subjects to conceptions of knowledge and of reality (see Berger and Luckmann 1966).

Among Continental philosophers, particularly those schooled in the phenomenological tradition, the demise of foundationalism has clearly signalled a new focus on the social and institutional conditions of knowledge and on the ideological commitments of belief systems. These different groups tend to eschew broad theories or accounts of knowledge and instead limit themselves self-consciously to local and cultural forms of 'knowledge', and by implication to a relativist view of knowledge and truth. In the case of some Continental philosophers, a commitment to relativism about knowledge and ontology is quite explicit and is regarded as a bulwark against oppressive and enslaving Enlightenment rationalities. At the very least all parties have concluded that the Enlightenment notion of the disinterested self, which in splendid isolation sits in judgement over reality and in 'objective' fashion distinguishes truth from error according to an infallible method, is mistaken.

Criticism of foundationalist approaches to knowledge has been accompanied by questioning of a referential theory of meaning. For many modern philosophers language mirrors ('pictures' for Wittgenstein in the *Tractatus* 1963) states of affairs (and correspondingly, for Wittgenstein, 'facts') in the world. Nouns and substantives ideally have a one-to one correspondence with objects in the world; other linguistic forms either describe the attributes of objects or describe the relationship between objects. A true statement is when the linguistic statement accurately mirrors the actual state of affairs in the world. What could be simpler!

Much of the philosophy of the later Wittgenstein (1958 and 1976) is devoted to showing the inadequacies of a referential theory of meaning (at least as a comprehensive theory), of the kind that he espoused in his earlier *Tractatus*. He drew attention to the different ways in which words are used and how words convey meaning without the necessity of possessing a determinate or essential sense, and also to the ways in which linguistic meaning is embedded in specific forms of life and, by extension (according to some interpreters), in specific communities. The implications of Wittgenstein's critique are variously assessed and remain controversial philosophically (for discussion, see Hacker 1996: 240–253). He is often interpreted as undermining a referential theory of meaning (and by implication, for some, a correspondence theory of truth), though this is a simplification that does not do justice to his position. First, Wittgenstein was more concerned with meaning than with truth, and even with regard to meaning it should be acknowledged that he would not have conceived his work as constituting a *theory* of it. Second, while allowing that Wittgenstein raises critical points against a correspondence theory of truth, it is debatable whether his position excludes the view that certain uses of language (as propositions) are more successful in describing reality than others, and that some descriptions deserve the status of knowledge or warrant. In short (and it is the interpretation I espouse), the position of the later Wittgenstein may be compatible with certain forms of philosophical realism (see Blackburn 1998, McCutcheon 2001). Much of course turns here on what is meant by 'realism'; and in some respects the issue is not whether the later philosophy of Wittgenstein supports realism or not but whether there is philosophical support for some form of realism (say, critical realism) of the kind advocated by Roy Bhaskar (2008 and 2011).

More typically, postmodern thinkers and philosophers interpret Wittgenstein as supportive of the view that linguistic meaning and truth are solely social constructions (conventions even) that do not accurately describe the nature of reality or 'the order of things' but provide, given the variety of different social conditions and communities, alternative accounts of making sense of the world and interacting with it. Jacques Derrida is often interpreted in this way.

Derrida, logocentrism and deconstruction

In one of his most influential early books, *Of Grammatology* (1976) Derrida complains that Western intellectual culture and history have been obsessed with speech rather than writing. On this account truth emerges from face to face dialogue, whereas writing is one step removed from the original act of speaking. There is a binary opposition between speech and writing, and, according to Derrida, writing has been the repressed side of this opposition ever since Plato. The privileging of speech over writing, with the idea of the speaker being present in person, Derrida equates with 'logocentrism' (*logos* is the Greek term for 'speech, word, law, or reason'). Moreover, the priority of speech over writing creates the illusion that words (signs) refer to concrete objects that are directly present to speakers who enjoy privileged access to them. Derrida (1976: 50) calls this 'the metaphysics of presence': the belief that we can gain direct access to the world independently of the different ways in which we talk about and act on it. This, in turn, is motivated by a desire for 'transcendental signification' (1976: 49), for a meaning that exists outside language and transcends what he believes to be the constant process of subversion inherent in all linguistic signification. Terry Eagleton (2008: 113) describes logocentrism as commitment 'to a belief in some ultimate "word", presence, essence, truth or reality which will act as the foundation for all our thought, language and experience'. Western thought generally has expended its energy in trying to penetrate beyond the written word to the original mind and intention of the speaking subject, with the assumption that there is always an original 'transcendental' signifier, referent and significance to be identified behind the original linguistic speech act. Logocentrism, and the prioritising of the role of human consciousness and intention in the construction of meaning, fails, according to Derrida, for two main reasons. First, it fails because it overlooks the autonomy of the system of signs. For Derrida (1976: 160) 'the person writing is inscribed in a determined textual system':

> The writer writes *in* a language and *in* a logic whose proper systems, laws and life[,] his discourse by definition cannot dominate absolutely. He uses them by only letting himself, after a fashion and up to a point, be governed by the system.
>
> *Derrida 1976: 158; author's emphasis*

Language is a structure that determines what is thinkable and therefore what is expressible —what can be experienced. Such a manner of speaking reveals the influence on Derrida of the semiotic theory of Ferdinand Saussure ([1916] 1995), according to which language is a self-contained system, independent of any given author or speaker. For Saussure, we do not express ourselves in words: words provide us with the means to express ourselves; thus the linguistic system determines what can and cannot be said. Derrida also follows Saussure in accepting that signs have meaning not in relation to the world but in relation to other signs within the overall system of signs, for all signifying systems are purely relational. Signs have meaning because they 'stand' in relation to other signs and contrast with other signs which on occasions are assumed and implied yet absent. Meaning is always differential, never referential.

The second reason logocentrism fails is because it assumes that meaning is fixed and determinate, whereas the meaning of any sign is always open, plural and indeterminate (in this he departs from the position of Saussure). It is in this context that Derrida (1978: 279–294; the essay was first published in French in 1967) coined the term 'différance' to underline the fact that every sign gains meaning in relation to what it is not, that is, from other terms or signs with which it contrasts; and the line of contrasts between signs can continue indefinitely.[2] Meaning is not 'present' within the sign but is gained in relation to other signs. The continual deferral of meaning from one signifier to another is part of a linguistic structure that is open-ended, and thus a structure that has no centre, only a 'series of substitutions of centre for centre' (Derrida 1978: 279). Every sign is ambiguous and open to different meanings. Signs always bear within themselves 'the trace' (another semi-technical term for him, see 1976: 9–10, for example) of other excluded items in a way that undermines the ideal of self-sufficient units of meaning. The same ambiguity and indeterminacy applies to configurations of signs in texts (see below).

A particular focus of Derrida's criticism is the role of binary oppositions in language (see 1976 and 1978), which are used (or implied) to reinforce, 'privilege' and accentuate one pole of the opposition over the other: presence/absence; good/evil; male/female; light/darkness; white/black; civilised/uncivilised; citizen/immigrant; heterosexual/homosexual. In each case it is the first term that is accorded precedence and normative status. On this basis, social reality (and material reality on occasions) is divided into distinct and discrete binary categories. One does not need a vivid imagination or a particularly deep knowledge of nineteenth-and twentieth-century history to appreciate the use to which some of these oppositions have been put. Derrida's constructive point is that although it is the symbolic system that structures, enforces and forces such oppositions, this same system provides the means to undermine and challenge the oppositions. First, the polarity can be reversed and the second term accorded precedence: accepted norms are challenged and 'turned on their head'. Second, language provides the means of 'deconstructing' constructed oppositions. For example, daylight changes to night, but the transition is not immediate – the process is gradual and consequently there are times when it is appropriate to say, 'it is more night than day', 'more day than night', 'it is twilight', and so on.

The same kind of analysis can be applied to oppositions with controversial social and political implications. In fact it is central to Derrida's deconstructive analysis to draw attention to the social and political consequences of endorsing binary oppositions. Take the binary opposition of heterosexual and homosexual, which posits an either/or opposition and which until recent times has favoured heterosexual identity – socially, culturally and politically. Derrida's intention is to question and challenge simplistic and empirically dubious dichotomies. Human sexuality can take diverse forms: fetishism, heterosexual, gay, lesbian, transgender and bisexual relationships and voyeurism (and these do not exhaust the categories). In addition there are different taxonomies of human sexuality that could be constructed; we could, for example, frame a binary opposition between a man who has sex with a woman who is younger and a man who has sex with a woman who is older, or we could construct a category to privilege sexual relationships with a member of one's socio-economic group over sexual relationships with someone who is not. Derrida explores binary categories of thought in order to uncover their ideological function and to undermine their presupposed essential nature and cultural permanence. Language itself provides the resources for challenging binary oppositions, for it provides the potential not only to construct different, more inclusive, categories but to show that these categories already exist and are latent within the existing semiotic system.

The weakness in Derrida's analysis, in this case as in others, however, is that binary oppositions may also express moral commitments, which in turn reflect objective moral judgements. Another problem is that, apart from exposing the degree to which 'essentialised' oppositions may legitimise discrimination and intolerance, Derrida has not addressed the underlying moral issue. Whether certain practices or behaviour are morally appropriate or not does not depend upon whether local constituencies of language users employ binary oppositions in relation to them: the moral legitimacy of human acts is determined by uniquely moral considerations, though this does not exclude the possibility that moral properties supervene on non-moral properties. Derrida could retort, of course, that moral valuations are entirely internal to language and that different communities of language users may *legitimately* express different moral valuations – say, that torture is morally appropriate for the community of criminals but not for some other communities. Those who are moral realists may be unimpressed by this response, and may well conclude that it reveals inherent weaknesses in Derrida's position rather than tell against the objective nature of moral judgements.

Once the self-conscious Enlightenment quest for transcendental signification is relinquished, and the idea that true meaning is found only in the 'presence' of the original speaker or of an immutable independent, external reality, then any 'text' becomes open to multiple readings. Meaning becomes exclusively contextual and one of the most important (if not the most important) determinants of context is the human subject that interprets from his or her own unique perspective. The diversity of human interests, commitments, expectations, and so on, ensures that meanings proliferate. The same text can be read in different ways. Derrida does not mean by this that people as a matter of fact pursue different interpretations of the same text, rather he means that the same text is open to and is *properly* interpreted in different ways; moreover, the same text can be interpreted in ways that may conflict with each other. There is no transcendental meaning behind the text in the mind of the original author, and no extra-linguistic reality which acts as a normative rule to limit what can or cannot *rightfully* be said about the text. This is the point of his remark (1976: 158 and 163) that 'there is nothing outside the text' (*Il n'y a pas de hors-texte*).

It follows from what has been said that, for Derrida, interpretation is not about reproducing what the writer or speaker thought and expressed 'in a text', for this suggests that there is a non-textual reality that governs the meaning of the text (1976: 163), it is about appropriating the text to expose and undermine the oppositions, hierarchies and paradoxes that are implicit in it. Derrida equates this with a deconstructive reading (21 and *passim*). Deconstruction aims to analyse the text to uncover the contradictions that are implicit in it and that challenge the unity of purpose, signification and meaning that texts are presumed to possess; such a reading 'attempts to make the not-seen accessible to sight' (163). According to J. A. Cuddon (2000: 210), in a deconstructive reading

> a text can be read as saying something quite different from what it appears to be saying . . . it may be read as carrying a plurality of significance or as saying many different things which are fundamentally at variance with, contradictory to and subversive of what may be seen by criticism as a single 'stable' reading. Thus a text may betray itself.

The application of deconstruction to texts yields different results in the hands of different practitioners (in this sense at least consistent with its underlying philosophical commitments). Texts are explored for their hidden meanings, often drawing on Freudian or etymological insights, insights which are overlooked and even unappreciated by the original authors. Shifts or breaks in continuity of meaning are mined for their underlying significance – shifts in tone, in point of view, in tense, the transition from first person to third person, are identified as illustrative of the inherent contradictions within language and by extension within life. According to Peter Barry (1995: 77), '[t]he deconstructive reading [of texts]. . . aims to produce *dis*unity, to show that what looked like unity and coherence actually contains contradictions and conflicts which the text cannot stabilise and control'.

Certainly Derrida is right to draw attention to the role of ideology in discourse and to the way in which language is used, often in the form of binary oppositions, to privilege one pole of a constructed dichotomy and to give an impression of 'naturalness' or universality to particular judgements and evaluations. Through such uses of language, beliefs and values are transmitted unconsciously. Derrida reminds us that language is not a neutral medium and that its partisan nature is inherent in the structure of language itself. For him, it is precisely because the nature of language is essentially contradictory and linguistic meaning is deferred, indeterminate and ambiguous that the application of a deconstructive analysis is required; in this way notions of univocal meaning and purpose and of internal textual consistency are undermined – 'deconstructed' and 'decentered'. Yet critical questions intrude. Can the meaning of a text be divorced from the intention and purpose of the author? Is there not a responsibility on the interpreter to reflect what the author says and intends?

There is also the issue of the permissive character of a deconstructive reading of a text: the reader and the interpreter can assign any meaning or lack of meaning to it. The text becomes a hook on which any idea of the reader can be hung; and ironically this reinstates and legitimises a role for ideology. If there are no rules to govern the interpretation of a text, and no need to be accountable to the original author and his or her intended meaning, then, through an ideological reading of what has been written, it becomes possible to advance the prejudices and commitments of the reader. But surely a written text cannot legitimately be interpreted in any way that happens to be conceivable, just as an action is not subject to any conceivable interpretation: some interpretations are more credible and more convincing than others.

Some of Derrida's valuable insights can be appropriated, however, while avoiding many of his overstatements and errors, by distinguishing between the meaning of a text and its significance, and allowing that 'significance' can be understood in different ways and on different levels. For example, the original meaning of a text can be distinguished from its significance; consequently significance may be tied closely to the original meaning, or significance can be understood more loosely to allow for new applications of the original meaning and even for personal appropriations of the original meaning. At a deeper level still, the commitment of Derrida to the contradictory nature of language and of the world of experience determined by language is finally a metaphysical position, whether Derrida wants to admit this or not. The view that there is no 'order of things' to identify – not even a naturalistic order, never mind a supernatural order – is a controversial ontological commitment, and one that needs more sustained philosophical support and argument than is found in Derrida's penetrating but unsystematic and 'playful' insights and remarks.

Lyotard, metanarratives and local knowledge

The point of departure for a discussion about Derrida was the support both Wittgenstein and he are sometimes regarded as giving to relativism about ultimate beliefs and values, while acknowledging that there is little evidence that Wittgenstein directly influenced Derrida at this point (or at any other). The same cannot be said of Jean-François Lyotard, who was much influenced by Wittgenstein and the notion of language games, particularly in his highly influential formulation of postmodernism in *The Postmodern Condition: A Report on Knowledge*, commissioned by the government of Quebec and first published in French in 1979. For many commentators this book is one of the foundational texts of postmodern thought.

Lyotard takes the view that the theory of language games means that each of the various categories of utterance can be defined in terms of rules specifying their properties and the uses to which they can be put. Language games are heterogeneous and incommensurable – denotative utterances, promises, questions, narrations – the meanings of which depend on context; and moves in one language game cannot be translated into moves in another language game (Lyotard 1984: xxiv). For example, a prescriptive statement cannot be derived from a descriptive statement: scientific statements are not moral statements and neither can be reduced to or derived from the other. More controversially, Lyotard underlines the point that knowledge has become fragmented in modern society, not simply in the sense that there are different disciplines with their own individual perspectives on knowledge but in the stronger sense that there is no (and in his view there can be no) all-encompassing framework in which knowledge within different language games comes together in one consistent whole. In his words, 'the speculative unity' of knowledge is 'broken' (1984: 35).

Society is composed of different and incompatible language games, and it is these that determine the moves which can be made within them by reference to 'narratives of legitimation', which are deemed appropriate by their respective social constituencies and institutions. In his consideration of the legitimation of knowledge, Lyotard (1984: 8–9) makes the provocative statement that '[w]hen we examine the current status of scientific knowledge . . . knowledge and power are simply two sides of the same question: who decides what knowledge is, and who knows what needs to be decided? In the computer age the question of knowledge is now more than ever a question of government'. As Andrew Wright (2004: 25) remarks: 'knowledge has been transformed into just another commodity to be bought and sold in the open market'. Lyotard (1984: 51) had already written that '[t]he question (overt or implied) now asked by the professional student, the State, or institutions of higher education is no longer "Is it true?" but "What use is it?"'. In this way Lyotard connects scientific knowledge with social and political reality and the nature of this connection suggests to him that scientific knowledge is both determined by ideology and limited in its scope to denotative (factual) statements. Scientific knowledge, which for twentieth-century heirs of the Enlightenment represented the apogee of critical reason and 'which instantiated itself as the ruler over life' (Peukert 1999: 119), can no longer provide a foundation for philosophical or social critique or hold out any prospect for political and social emancipation. The story of modern science is that as it presumed to determine truth from falsehood in all aspects of human experience, and consistent with its increasingly empiricist positivist orientation, it came to lose faith in its own foundations and science simply became a servant to the ruling ideologies in society. As Lyotard notes (1984: 34): 'The humanist principle that humanity rises up in dignity and freedom through knowledge is left by the wayside'.

Lyotard extends his critique of scientific knowledge to include what he calls the rejection of metanarratives, by which he means 'totalising stories' about history and the goals of the human race that ground and legitimise knowledge and cultural practices (the French original *grands récits* is variously translated as 'grand narratives', 'master narratives', 'metanarratives' or 'metadiscourse'). He associates metanarratives with the Enlightenment and modernity: 'I [i.e. Lyotard] will use the term modern to designate any science that legitimates itself with reference to a metadiscourse of this kind making an explicit appeal to some grand narrative, such as the dialectics of Spirit, the hermeneutics of meaning, the emancipation of the rational or working subject, or the creation of wealth' (1984: xxiii). These grand narratives, which once functioned under modernity to legitimise knowledge have been replaced with a narration of efficiency. For Lyotard (xxiv), the collapse of metanarratives as a legitimising or unifying force marks the end of the modern era. One of his most quoted phrases is the definition of the postmodern as 'incredulity towards metanarratives' (xxiv). Metanarratives ignore the diversity and variety of human existence; they also embody pretentious views of historical development, in terms of progress towards a specific goal (*telos*).

Over against (discredited) scientific knowledge and its legitimising metanarratives, which have now lost their cultural power to substantiate their claims to objective truth, Lyotard sets 'narrative' knowledge. Narrative knowledge is 'local', the knowledge of custom and tradition that is based on storytelling, myth, dramatic narration, music and dance; the kind of knowledge associated with and prevalent in 'primitive' or 'traditional' societies. Narrative knowledge does not seek to justify itself, rather in its retelling it establishes its own credibility, which comes from the proof of authenticated tradition within an on-going community:

> . . . narrative knowledge does not give priority to the question of its own legitimation . . . it certifies itself in the pragmatics of its own transmission without having recourse to argumentation and proof. This is why its incomprehension of the problem of scientific discourse is accompanied by a certain tolerance: it approaches such discourse primarily as a variant in the family of narrative cultures.
>
> *Lyotard 1984: 27*

Narrative knowledge traces its origins to 'small narratives' (*petits récits*), stories that are hallowed by tradition within a community, particularly stories that are

> told by a community, about that community, and to the people in that community, [such stories] give meaning to the culture of that specific society by uncovering and disclosing any transformations or disputes in their history. All voices of the community contribute to the little narrative. None are privileged over any other voice.
>
> *Bevel 2004: 15*

This summary of Lyotard's understanding of small narratives, when read in conjunction with our discussion above, illustrates the way in which 'totalising discourses', that is, forms of discourse that claim universal application and validity, are regarded as inherently intolerant of difference and diversity. The universal pretensions of scientific knowledge have to be resisted in the name of respect for difference and in the creation of an inclusive community. Scientific knowledge is exclusive, while narrative knowledge sees itself as one version among equals, and it is this 'epistemic humility' that creates the conditions for a truly civil society. According to Lyotard there should be a multiplicity of theoretical and practical standpoints in a society rather than grand, all-encompassing theories. In the final few pages (of the English edition) of *The Postmodern Condition*, after aligning the work of the philosopher with that of the novelist and the poet, Lyotard (1984: 82) concludes that it is the work of the philosopher 'not to supply reality but to invent illusions to the conceivable which cannot be presented'. The answer to the terror of metanarratives, he tells us in his concluding sentence, is to 'wage war on totality; let us witness to the unpresentable; let us activate the differences and save the honour of the name'.

It may be acknowledged that scientific knowledge is a mixed blessing: along with resources to alleviate suffering and disease and the invention and application of technologies that have cut the production costs of food and created life-enhancing products, science has lent its support to eugenics, racism, sexism, and so on. Scientific knowledge can be directed to a variety of goals, some moral, some less moral, some immoral and some without moral import; but given that science and technology are chiefly modern, Western creations it was not entirely unpredictable that it has been employed in the service of military aggression, colonialism, imperialism and much else that is unworthy. This employment is by one group of persons against others. Nevertheless, it would be naive to think that the pursuit of wealth and power and the desire to dominate and oppress are peculiarly local traits confined to one section of humanity, say the Western world, and that human subjects had to await the invention of scientific knowledge to advance their self-centred interests. Certainly what the twentieth century should have taught us is that scientific knowledge, when harnessed to grand political schemes, invariably becomes party to the exploitation and subjugation of those who are perceived as 'other'. In fact if the analysis of the philosopher

John Gray (1995 and 2000) is correct, all utopian political visions, which of necessity harbour a universal application – not just fascism (*national* socialism), communism and Islamic fundamentalism but free-market capitalism, Blairite socialism and liberal democracy as well – end in violence and oppression, for there will always be those who resist their own 'best interests' and the 'common good' (as defined by others of course).

And yet, one cannot help concluding that Lyotard's preference for local knowledge and tradition, which he believes are supportive of positive social relationships and of 'open community' (Lyotard 1984: 64), is an overly romanticised vision. Local communities can be intrusive, exploitative, intolerant of difference, dominated by local elites, divided by sectional and class interests, and oppressive. It is just as likely that one species of local knowledge will clash with another as it is that grand narratives will clash with it. Similarly, if local knowledge is confined to one geographical location and is unchallenged, then to all effects it enjoys the monopoly to which grand narratives aspire, and consequently local knowledge may exhibit the same oppressive features.

What Lyotard fails to recognise is that it is the bare existence of difference that creates the potential for intolerance and division; and while he is right to identify the dangers of grand political and socio-economic schemes, he is mistaken to think that a retreat to local knowledge is sufficient to thwart human capacities for resentment, intolerance, discrimination and victimisation.

The problem that arises in almost all varieties of postmodern thought, and it is one already identified in our preceding discussion, is that of relativism as it relates to truth and to morality. Lyotard contrasts small stories and local knowledge with grand narratives and universal claims to truth; the aim of this comparison is not just to legitimise local knowledge but to delegitimise universal knowledge. The critical questions are whether knowledge can be local in any sense that distinguishes it from superstition, opinion or belief and whether knowledge can by its nature be exclusively local. Certainly, knowledge can be local if myths and stories are interpreted as incorporating existential truths about particular communities or if the propositions concerned relate only to the local area, local events and local history. However, one difficulty with such a circumscribed understanding of the nature of knowledge is that it excludes the possibility of learning from other communities and cultures: nothing can be learnt from elsewhere because that would transgress the limits of local knowledge. In addition, implicit in many claims to knowledge is a presumption to truth that extends beyond the confines of some particular locality or community.

Is there a line on a geographical map that marks the physical boundary where one variety of local knowledge gives way to another, where one epistemology and ontology yields to another? One community may believe that human disease is caused by the actions of the gods and that human intervention is useless; another community believes that diseases have natural explanations in terms of diet, one's genetic inheritance and exposure to infection and that there are treatments and drugs that can cure certain diseases. Can both explanations be true? Presumably for Lyotard both can be true for their respective communities. Truth is what one's community believes to be true. But is the assertion that diseases have natural explanations a purely local form of knowledge: is such knowledge true in one locality but not in another? Can some particular disease be cured by the appropriate drug in one locality but not in another?

It may even be asked whether Lyotard's 'incredulity towards metanarratives' is intended to apply to *all* metanarratives. If it does apply to all then this is a universal statement that extends beyond local knowledge, and consequently contradicts his own ban on universal knowledge; if it is not a universal statement then there are metanarratives which are credible and which do embody universal knowledge. The charge of inconsistency in his understanding of the nature of knowledge and truth may be a criticism that Lyotard anticipated, even though his response is anything but convincing. In *The Postmodern Condition* he opines that his portrayal of the state of knowledge 'makes no claims to being original *or even true*', and that his hypotheses 'should not be accorded predictive value in relation to reality, but strategic value in relation to the questions raised' (Lyotard 1984: 7, my emphasis). When no truth claims are advanced, there is nothing to refute! Perhaps Lyotard was merely engaging in a language game to entertain but not to convince, or if to convince others to embrace his prejudices then only to do so by the use of rhetoric, not argument. But if to convince, and he does not believe that the propositions in which he wants his hearers or readers to believe are true, then his aim is exclusively ideological and his position is properly interpreted as an attempt to exert power and influence over people and manipulate them to his advantage.

Lyotard clearly wants to legitimise diversity: he wants to validate local diversity over against appeals to universal autonomous reason that historically have been used to marginalise and oppress individuals and communities. What he fails to recognise is that it is often universal traditions that challenge and overcome local knowledge which is oppressive of others within the same community. One thinks here of Christian opposition to infanticide in the early centuries of the Common Era and appeals to human rights in modern times both to prosecute those who committed 'crimes' during World War II (which were legal in the eyes of the state of which they were citizens) and to criticise and challenge a range of local customs and traditions, such as the practices of clitoridectomy, 'honour' killings and human slavery. It may be that a principled distinction can be drawn between philosophies of autonomous reason, truly grand narratives, and other narratives, which, while making universal claims about human nature, do not claim legitimacy by reference to supposed universal truths of reason or scientific knowledge. Such a view finds support in the examples of metanarratives that Lyotard cites – the dialectics of Spirit (Hegel), the hermeneutics of meaning (Schleiermacher), the emancipation of the rational (Kant) or the working subject (Marx), or the creation of wealth (Smith). These are the grand narratives of the Enlightenment.

Metanarratives, according to Lyotard, are distinctively modern phenomena; they are stories that not only express a grand narrative but profess to be justified by reference to autonomous human reason. On these two criteria, a distinctively modern narrative of universal scope, which appeals to autonomous, scientific reason, most religious narratives do not qualify as metanarratives. Religious narratives may claim universal scope but their origins are not modern and they typically do not legitimise themselves on the basis of exclusively rational appeals. Some religious narratives, however, do fulfil the criteria, for example, Enlightenment accounts of rational religion, and, more controversially, post-Enlightenment interpretations of religion that postulate religious unity behind religious difference and diversity. On the basis of this analysis, it could be argued that the modern paradigm of religious education in Britain represents an educational metanarrative, one which marginalises and stigmatises difference by reinterpreting the religions to conform to an Enlightenment vision: religious believers are to be convinced by teachers that beneath religious difference lies essential religious unity.

Foucault, knowledge and power

'[K]nowledge and power are simply two sides of the same question'. Although this statement is Lyotard's (and already quoted above), one might be forgiven for attributing it to the French philosopher Michel Foucault, as he is often portrayed as equating knowledge with power; and while such a reading may ultimately be unsustainable, it does give an indication of the focus and broad orientation of his thought. Although interpreters have identified different stages in the development of his ideas, no attention will be given to this in what follows. The aim is to provide a basic orientation to his position that identifies the main themes but not to trace their emergence and development in his writings. The exploration of the relationship of knowledge to power is central to all of Foucault's writings. For him, systems of knowledge serve and are served by systems of power. The two, while distinguishable, are intimately connected:

> Power and knowledge directly imply one another . . . there is no power relation without the correlative constitution of a field of knowledge . . . the subject who knows, the objects to be known and the modalities of knowledge must be regarded as so many effects of the fundamental implications of power/knowledge and their historical transformations.
>
> *Foucault 1991: 27–28*

What counts as knowledge is constituted within 'technologies of power' – political, social, and economic structures that possess and mediate power to the wider society. Knowledge is not neutral, it is always socially conditioned, correlated to systems of power and authoritarian social institutions. This means that, for Foucault, knowledge is historical in the sense that it reflects and is conditioned not just by the prevailing historical values and norms within society but also by society's ruling power structures; these two influences collectively constitute what can be known and what can be practised in the name of knowledge. Knowledge, so determined, falsifies Enlightenment visions of the 'rational progress of society' and the 'perfectibility of man' (see Passmore 1979 for discussion). Foucault rejects modern notions of progress and the idea that truth necessarily increases with the passage of time. History is not a coherent narrative of 'causes and effects that produce human events, and are thus traceable, in a linear and logically satisfying fashion, backward to origins' (Deal and Beal 2004: 93). The narrative of history is the product of textual revisions, embellishments, deletions and additions, with no means now of recovering the original meaning, uncorrupted and uncontaminated by the ruling structures of belief and power. Knowledge has a history but does not progressively unfold through history: knowledge simply assumes different forms in history, forms that are reflective of and determined by social conditions and the on-going interactions of social groups and of human institutions as they vie for power and influence:

> Humanity does not gradually progress from combat to combat until it arrives at universal reciprocity, where the rule of law finally replaces warfare; humanity installs each of its violences in a system of rules and thus proceeds from domination to domination.
>
> *Foucault 1977: 151*

Yet, for Foucault history is not entirely mute, for we as interpreters of the past can discern some modest meaning in it. That the narrative of history is fragmented, contested, ambiguous and subject to different interpretations *are* lessons to be learned; and this negative view of historical enquiry also provides the resources to identify the ways in which social conditions shape ideas, and thus shape knowledge. The term *genealogy* is used by Foucault to refer to a mode of historical enquiry that eschews any ultimate meaning or purpose in history ('theological or rationalistic', Foucault 1977: 154) and attends to the different ways in which events are interpreted and reinterpreted in relation to technologies of power. The history that the genealogist finds is that 'there is "something altogether different" behind things: not a timeless and essential secret, but the secret that they have no essence or that their essence was fabricated in a piecemeal fashion from alien forms' (Foucault 1977: 142). History is not the gradual unfolding of the essence of things, say along Hegelian lines through the manifestation of Spirit (*Geist*; Hegel 1956) or along empiricist lines that view science as revealing an increasingly determinate view of the world. That things have no essence for Foucault means that our concepts about things have no essence either. Concepts like events 'engage in different roles' and there is no grand scheme or essential meaning that encompasses the uses to which they are put. Words and concepts are used 'to do' different things and at different times the same word may be used to do different things: the meaning of words changes in relation to changing beliefs and changing structures of power.

Foucault develops his genealogical understanding of the relationship of knowledge and power through case studies of the role of institutions, such as hospitals and prisons, in constructing systems of meaning, which he calls discourses, that create, propagate and enforce ways of thinking and acting. A discourse is a system of describing, defining, labelling and thinking about people and things within an institutional context in a particular cultural setting. Discourses are diverse fields of constructed knowledge, or in his distinctive terminology, 'regimes of truth', that invariably serve the interests in society of a few while controlling and 'disciplining' the behaviour of many.[3] Foucault accepts that power is unequally distributed in society and that different discourses privilege different groups, and in this sense there are 'winners' and 'losers', yet he also stresses that often those who benefit believe themselves to do so by virtue of obedience to commonly accepted rules of belief, management and practice, whose rational character should be (and is) accepted by all. In fact those who benefit may do so precisely on the basis of their obedience to commonly accepted *rational* rules, for such rules are constitutive of the discourse. Different discourses and the rules they embody and instantiate cultivate their own legitimacy; and legitimacy is chiefly conferred through 'ownership' of that portion of knowledge that is relevant to the discourse.

In *Madness and Civilization* (1988), *The Birth of the Clinic* (2003) and *Discipline and Punish* (1991), Foucault illustrates the ways in which experts like doctors, psychiatrists and criminologists, historically increased their authority and status on the basis of their development of new discourses. These modern discourses did not simply reinforce and extend claims to professional expertise, they also 'constituted or invented deviant groups as objects worthy of study, containment, and reform and the experts who were entitled to control them' (Smith 2001: 123). Institutions are governed according to rules that are ostensibly rational, intuitive and compelling, yet in reality the rules serve sectional interests and provide the means of reinforcing community prejudices against certain constituencies of individuals and particular forms of behaviour: the former criminalising of homosexuality in society is a case in point; in addition, this example shows the way in which different discourses work in society to reinforce each other – the medical discourse of disease or mental instability reinforcing the legal and moral discourse of homosexuality as undermining morality. Institutions, particularly public institutions, *police* society not with threats or acts of physical force but with appeals to rationality that are enshrined in publicly sanctioned forms of discourse. This picture of reality ordered by objectivity and scientific knowledge, and directed by accountable professionals, is, according to Foucault, entirely false. For him (as quoted above), 'humanity installs each of its violences in a system of rules and thus proceeds from domination to domination'. People perpetrate 'violences' against other people in the name of knowledge: the disappearance of one discourse and the emergence of a new one does not represent a move in the direction of liberation but the succession of one means of domination by another.

Foucault's ideas have understandably stimulated debate and controversy, and there are fruitful and defensible applications of some of his ideas to modern religious education, which are briefly considered below. There are also powerful criticisms. Some writers maintain that he overestimates the ability of discourses to control the individual and minimises human capacities for resistance, independent thought and self-directed agency. Analytic philosophers find flaws in his understanding of the nature of knowledge and his idea that technologies of power thwart all efforts to constitute knowledge on an objective basis. Social historians question his narrative reconstructions of history that identify rupture and inconsistency while affirming a series of non-rational developments that create successive discourses of control and privilege (for some). The most telling criticism, to my mind, is that if knowledge is compromised by technologies of power to the extent that Foucault believes, what significance should be given to his exposure of the primacy of power over knowledge? Is his narrative one more example of a 'will to power' (Nietzsche 1967)? If so, his ideas constitute one more discourse to add to the unending succession of overarching systems of 'power/ knowledge' (Foucault 1980). The problem is that if Foucault offers his analysis as a *true* description of social reality then power and knowledge are not as intimately connected as he believes: the 'false consciousness' of discourses can be identified and truth and knowledge are possible.

Finally, one cannot read Foucault without gaining a sense of his moral earnestness, passion and outrage: injustice, prejudice and inequality are exposed by his genealogical analyses. Yet implicit in their recognition and exposure by Foucault is the conviction that such characteristics are wrong and that such wrongs call for correction: Foucault himself participated in political demonstrations for gay rights. This suggests that he possesses some form of moral knowledge, a knowledge of what is morally right and what is morally wrong. From where does this knowledge come and what is its justification? Presumably, if Foucault does possess moral knowledge, he has shown that it is possible to overcome the distorting effect of discourse and what he has done is possible for others to do.

British religious education after Foucault

Of all the ideas considered in this chapter it is the ideas of Foucault that offer the greatest potential for illuminating the commitments and practices that are constitutive of post-confessional religious education in Britain. In fact a complementary study can be envisaged, which pursues a genealogical reading that identifies the influence of ideology. This would expose the ways in which rival groups and individuals have competed to exert influence over policy developments and pedagogy in religious education, achieving this not on the basis of the rational force of their arguments but by gaining political control over the key institutions and bodies concerned with it. This 'alternative' history could consider the work of non-statutory bodies, such as the Qualifications and Curriculum Development Agency (QCDA), in its various forms and names, up to March 2012 when it was abolished; 'representative' groups such as the

Religious Education Council of England and Wales; and key organisations, such as the National Association of Standing Advisory Councils for Religious Education and the Association of University Lecturers in Religious Education. Attention could be given to public statements and pronouncements, representations to government, publicity campaigns, and the role of individuals who have held positions in these organisations and campaigned to have their own ideas implemented in schools and even translated into legislation. Some of the material to which reference is made in Chapter 1 clearly belongs in this alternative history, though there is no shortage of new material. Here are some examples: efforts by the National Association of Teachers of Religious Education and the QCDA to have the non-statutory Religious Education Framework made statutory before the general election in 2010 and continued efforts by different bodies and organisations to centralise religious education and reduce the democratic influence and role of locally constituted Standing Advisory Councils for Religious Education. Many of the organisations and groups claim to be representative of professional opinion and expertise, yet there is ample evidence of efforts to circumvent democratic processes and to profess views of professional unanimity when no such unanimity exists.

A (Foucaultian) genealogical history of post-confessional religious education would undoubtedly reveal the ways in which the modern paradigm of liberal religious education came to attain, and continues to enjoy, a privileged institutional position and how much political effort is expended in extolling its virtues and ignoring and undermining criticism. In the Introduction to this book it was noted how the Religious Education Council of England and Wales (RE Council) accredits identified weakness in religious education to inadequate funding: no need for a reassessment of theory or practice in the face of mounting criticism and evidence (which is increasingly difficult to explain away), only the need for more money to further entrench and extend existing policies.

A similar response was made even more recently in response to research conducted by a team of researchers from the University of Oxford, led by Nigel Farncourt, which concluded that the teaching of Christianity in English schools was 'too stereotypical', on occasions actually 'incoherent', and that lessons lacked 'intellectual development'. John Keast, the new chairperson of the RE Council, actually welcomed the project findings with this comment: 'With almost total withdrawal of government support for RE, it is good to see a major university project, sponsored by charitable trusts, providing a positive way forward.' For him, even bad news is good! No need for self-reflection and to entertain the thought that the current teaching of Christianity, which the interim report criticises, reflects commitments and practices that the RE Council has commended and supported politically for years. Furthermore, the cause of failure is predictable – 'almost total withdrawal of government support for religious education'. It is difficult to know what Keast means by this, given that the current government, through official spokespersons, has expressed its commitment to religious education in schools and spoken of the positive contribution it makes to education and to society. There have been no legislative changes in relation to religious education, and funding continues for the subject to be taught in schools, for RE teachers to be trained, for the statutory work of local councils in relation to it, and so on. Perhaps what Keast says is best interpreted as a veiled way of requesting more funding for religious education (and for his own organisation), with the implicit message that spending more money will necessarily improve the quality of teaching and learning. Seldom is the will to power and influence so undisguised!

Some of the best examples of the role and influence of ideology in British religious education are documented in Penny Thompson's neglected study, *Whatever Happened to Religious Education?* (2004). Thompson's research also provides numerous first-hand examples of the construction and use of binary oppositions to support and commend the liberal, non-confessional model of religious education to teachers: the distinction between the non-confessional and confessional models is expressed as that between education and indoctrination and as between open education and closed education. To this may be added the further example of the way in which teachers who practise a non-confessional form of religious education are described as professional, whereas those who do not are never described thus – thereby constructing a binary opposition between professional, non-confessional religious educators and, by implication, non-professional confessional teachers. The pursuit of a Foucaultian reading of post-confessional religious education in Britain is incidental to my main argument. The remarks here are intended to illustrate its potential and to suggest that such an approach offers insights and vistas that are complementary and confirming of my own more intellectually focused reading of the 'progress' of religious education, which attends to the beliefs and commitments that characterise different models of religious education.

Notes

1 The distinctions and their connotations noted here do not exhaust the possibilities; for example, Marshall (1994) regards post-structuralism primarily as a theory of knowledge and language, and postmodernism as primarily a theory of culture, society and history.

2 *Différance* is a deliberate misspelling by Derrida of *difference*, which picks up the etymology of the latter: it is derived from both *defer*, 'to put off', which for him, is what happens to meaning in language in a relational system where signs do not have essential meanings, and from *differ*, 'to be unlike, not identical'; this second meaning (sometimes referred to as *espacement* or 'spacing') concerns the way that signs are differentiated from one another and, in so doing, engenders binary oppositions and hierarchies that underpin meaning itself.

3 'Discipline' is a technical term for Foucault that refers to a mechanism of power that regulates the behaviour of individuals in the social body; he also refers to prisons, hospitals, asylums, schools and army barracks as examples of disciplinary institutions.

12

POSTMODERN RELIGIOUS EDUCATION

At the beginning of the last chapter it was noted that the 1990s were a period of transition that saw the emergence of a new postmodern model of religious education in Britain. It was admitted that identifying the model as 'postmodern' is controversial, chiefly for the reason that the term is rarely used as a self-designation, and in some cases is deliberately rejected by those religious educators whose accounts of religious education reflect postmodern beliefs and commitments. Clive Erricker (2007) is a notable exception. He openly acknowledges his commitment to postmodern philosophy, an acquaintance with which, he believes, should have the effect of moving religious educators 'to embrace relativism' (Erricker and Erricker 2000: 58). It may be that Erricker's acceptance of relativism, and his association of this with postmodern thought, illustrates why many religious educators are reluctant to claim the title as their own and to designate their approaches as postmodern. Historically, relativism sits uncomfortably with traditional interpretations of religion that claim universality; in addition, advocacy of relativism in education will quickly attract attention from conservative religious and political critics.

Part of the nature of postmodernism is to embrace diversity and to incorporate different viewpoints, and, as such, it resists precise definition. Yet in saying this, a clue is given that helps to characterise and capture something important about it, namely postmodernism sets itself over against modern thought and the idea of individual essences and determinate meanings. This negative characterisation sits comfortably with the discussion in the previous chapter that highlighted the different points at which postmodern thought self-consciously opposes modernity and post-Enlightenment ideas and commitments: the idea of the universal scope of reason, the unity of knowledge, grand metaphysical narratives, and so on. Obviously, there is a sliding scale in relation to opposition to modern beliefs and commitments. For example, one may be sceptical about Enlightenment metanarratives while believing that some religions, in a formal sense, escape such scepticism. Ironically, the distinctively postmodern point is that in many cases modern and postmodern thought cannot be distinguished in absolute either/or terms. This is the precise reason why it is both difficult and controversial to distinguish modern from postmodern religious educators: an educator may reflect modern beliefs and commitments at one point and espouse postmodern beliefs and commitments at another, and there are shades of opinion and tendencies of thought between any two constructed oppositions. Recognition of this creates the possibility of mediating positions between modern and postmodern models of religious education; it is one such mediating position, designated as post-liberal, which has already been identified as the model best suited to religious education and to securing the social aims appropriate to education in a religiously and ethnically diverse society, though this model still awaits more systematic exposition (see Chapter 15).

The issue remains how to characterise postmodern religious education. The straightforward answer is to augment the negative stance towards modern ideas about religion with support for postmodern ideas and beliefs: postmodern religious education:

- accentuates local traditions of religion over universal expressions;
- focuses on issues of interpretation and representation;
- views claims to religious knowledge and truth with suspicion and looks to identify the influence of technologies and hierarchies of power in any claim to knowledge;
- rejects binary oppositions;
- privileges individual expressions of belief over communal beliefs;
- is sceptical of essential definitions of religious beliefs and practices;
- identifies the way in which human language is used to reinforce and perpetuate religious structures of power; and
- draws attention to internal diversity and the contested nature of religious traditions.

On the basis of this characterisation, which religious educators exhibit these commitments? (Although not all commitments need be present, a sufficient number do if the designation postmodern is appropriate.) Clive Erricker has already been identified as a self-confessed postmodern religious educator, but who else? Other examples are Mark Chater (2001), Denise Cush (1999),[1] Robert Jackson (see below for references) and Dan Moulin (2009); of these Robert Jackson has been by far the most influential, and because of this, discussion will focus exclusively on his work and writings.

To consider the position of Jackson as representative of postmodern religious education is not uncontroversial; it is a designation and identification he rejects, and for this reason the matter is further considered at the end of the chapter, where the reasons for this identification are summarised. The main focus of the chapter, however, is on providing an accurate and reliable overview of Jackson's understanding of an interpretive approach to religious education; the following chapter will seek to identify its strengths and weaknesses.

Robert Jackson and interpretive religious education

Of contemporary British religious educators Robert (Bob) Jackson is probably the most influential and renowned. In 2012 he retired from the University of Warwick, where he was Professor of Education and Director of Graduate Studies, and Director of the Warwick Religions and Education Research Unit (WRERU). He is a well-established author and authority, whose writings have attracted international interest and acclaim. Until recently he was editor of the *British Journal of Religious Education*, one of the leading international peer reviewed journals in the field, and in 2004 a 'panel discussion' was devoted to his book *Rethinking Religious Education and Plurality: Issues in Diversity and Pedagogy* (2004) at the annual meeting of the American Academy of Religion in San Antonio, Texas, an event that illustrates his international reputation and importance. His name is particularly associated with an 'interpretive approach' to religious education, which he has developed in numerous books, essay contributions and articles over a period of 25 years. At a conservative estimate, he and his colleagues (within WRERU) and collaborators from elsewhere have published somewhere in the region of 10 books (some edited collections, others single authored monographs) and over 100 academic articles that relate in one way or another to this interpretive approach to RE in schools. To this can be added curriculum texts and classroom materials that translate the theory into practice (see Jackson 2000: 147–148).[2] Although the interpretive approach was originally developed for use in publicly funded community schools in England and Wales, it has subsequently been applied and developed further in Norway, Germany, Canada and Japan, among other places. The approach has also provided the theoretical framework both for a Council of Europe project on integrating the dimension of religious diversity into intercultural education across its 46 members states and for a series of pedagogical studies conducted as part of a European Commission Framework Programme 6 research project on religious education by a consortium of nine European universities (Jackson 2008; 2011).

How can one summarise the interpretive approach in a way that is faithful to its range and complexity? One possibility would be to focus on recent publications, on the grounds that they provide a mature and considered expression of Jackson's understanding of interpretive religious education, an understanding that incorporates the adjustments and revisions that he has made in dialogue with other writers and positions over the years. The obvious weakness in this approach, however, is that it overlooks the actual line of development in his ideas and commitments over time and fails to engage with the historical sources and debates that contributed to and shaped his present position. This observation suggests that the best (or at least an intellectually defensible) way to do justice to his oeuvre is to identify the main themes that characterise interpretive religious education in his early writings and trace their trajectory, in terms of reaffirmation, reinterpretation and development, through subsequent writings. This might initially seem a daunting task, given the volume of his work, but thankfully Jackson has always been self-critical and reflective, and this means that a number of publications at different stages of his academic career can be identified as significant in terms of expressing and summarising his position in relation to the inner logic of his own developing commitments and to contemporary debates, both in education generally and in religious education. Consequently attention will focus on a small number of temporally successive publications that are representative of Jackson's position as it has developed and evolved from the early 1990s until the present.[3] These are his programmatic article, 'Religious Education's representations of "religions" and "cultures" ' (1995); his fullest book-length exposition of interpretive religious education in *Religious Education: An Interpretive Approach* (1997); and finally his book on the interpretive approach in relation to diversity and its challenges to education in a democratic society, *Rethinking Religious Education and Plurality* (2004). Reference will also be made to more recent publications, though the position taken here is that his later writings do not greatly revise or modify his earlier commitments.

Interpreting Jackson and interpretive religious education

Jackson writes clearly and is careful in his choice and use of words, which means that, for the most part, his position is readily accessible and comprehensible. That said, the straightforward nature of his writings disguises a number of challenges for interpreters, especially for critics. First, Jackson is a wide-ranging thinker who draws on various disciplines in developing and expressing his position. His work reveals fluency in philosophy, ethnography (particularly ethnographic anthropology), critical theory and religious studies, as well as educational theory and practice, and of course theory and practice in religious education. Moreover, he also seems to track recent trends in these disciplines while combining them in novel and distinctive ways. There is a sense in which it requires a considerable degree of competence and confidence across a range of disciples to interpret his work correctly; obviously this is also the case if criticisms are to be made and substantiated. Second, Jackson is an 'inclusive' writer in the sense that he refers frequently and positively both to the work of other members of the WRERU and to other European researchers who acknowledge their indebtedness to his influence. The effect of this, which no doubt is unintentional, is that it is not always easy to identify the commitments and practices that are *distinctive* of an interpretive approach or which fit naturally within this framework.

'Religious education's representation of "religions" and "cultures" '

One of the earliest and clearest expressions of the central themes and distinctive emphases of interpretive religious education is in an article entitled 'Religious education's representation of "religions" and "cultures" ', which was published in the *British Journal of Educational Studies* in 1995.[4] In many respects the position Jackson sets out and develops in this publication provides the essential foundation for all his subsequent writings; and for this reason it will be reviewed in detail.

The opening section of the article begins with a personal observation by Jackson about the efficacy of religious education in 'countering racism' (1995: 272): 'I do not think any approach [in religious education]', he tells us, 'can solve the problem of deep seated racism'; more positively, however, he goes on immediately to say 'that having an understanding of the religious culture of people in our societies might be a necessary, though not a sufficient, condition for reducing racial and cultural prejudice' (273). Apart from the tentative nature of this comment, which is characteristic of the way in which Jackson often presents his own positive proposals, there are a number of points that are interesting and noteworthy in this the preamble to his argument. First, the social challenge to religious education is conceived in terms of countering racism and reducing racial and cultural prejudice; it is not conceived in terms of countering *religious* prejudice and discrimination. Is the omission of reference to religion deliberate or is this reading too much into a solitary case of usage? In fact at no point in the article does Jackson refer to prejudice or discrimination that is essentially religious or religious in origin. He does, however, refer to 'the *religious cultures* of people' (quoted above) as in some sense related to racism and prejudice. There are different ways of interpreting this reference to religious cultures. It may be read as apologetic, for example, in that religion *per se* is not the cause of prejudice, but rather cultural interpretations of religion; in this way authentic religion may be exonerated from criticism. This is a not unfamiliar tactic among liberal religious apologists, see Kimball (2003) for example. Within the context of Jackson's writing as a whole (see below), however, an apologetic reading is unlikely – he may simply be assigning priority to culture over religion in a way that views religion chiefly as an expression of culture. What precisely is meant by this, and the implications that follow from it for education, take us to the heart of an interpretive approach and consequently is a subject that will be central to our analysis and review.

The second point to consider is that Jackson conceives much of the role of religious education in the curriculum as focused on the social and moral aims of education, more specifically on 'reducing racial and cultural prejudice'. This, he believes, is to be achieved through pupils gaining 'an understanding of the religious culture of people in our societies' (273). For Jackson, gaining a proper understanding of the (religious) culture of others, which in later writings he glosses as gaining an understanding of the nature of plurality, can challenge racial and cultural prejudice: gaining an understanding of pluralism is a necessary component of any educationally appropriate strategy for lessening racial and cultural prejudice.

The next two sections of the article, in which Jackson considers representations of cultures in education and representations of the different religions in Western academic literature education, respectively, introduce themes and commitments that are central to interpretive religious education.

The point of departure for Jackson's account of the nature of culture is perceptions of a growth in racism across Europe in the early 1990s, which in Britain aggravated inherited colonial attitudes that assumed the 'incompatibility of cultural traditions' and regarded British culture as superior to others (273). Recognition of the significance of a wider understanding of racism, which takes account of the causes and consequences of ideas of cultural superiority, however, was not entirely new to British educators. During the 1980s, multicultural education and multicultural policies in education had become the focus of criticism from a group that identified themselves as 'antiracists' (e.g. Mullard 1984; see Chapter 2 for discussion). This group combined liberal educational ideals with Marxist ideology and identified group conflict as central to forms of association and relationships between communities in the modern nation state. Jackson provides a numbered summary of the key criticisms of multicultural education from the standpoint of anti-racist educators and social critics (1995: 274–275; the following is my shortened account of his summary).

1. Culture is perceived by multiculturalists in terms of a closed system, with a fixed understanding of ethnicity.
2. Treatment of culture is superficial, which reinforces 'platitudes and stereo-types' and helps to 'maintain racism intact'.
3. The exotic, the other, is emphasised.
4. Lack of attention is given to 'hierarchies of power'. 'Cultural and religious groups . . . [are] perceived in simplistic terms as holistic and unified communities'.
5. Racism is perceived psychologically in terms of personal attitudes that can be changed through knowledge and learning the value of tolerance. Structure of power – institutions and social practices – are ignored.
6. There is emphasis on discrete cultures and this allows them to be perceived as rivals to the national culture, which, through its tolerance, allows them to express themselves.

Jackson notes that 'with the benefit of hindsight. . . many of these criticisms hold true of RE, especially with regard to some of its teaching materials and sometimes to its delivery in the classroom' (1995: 275). While Jackson believes that anti-racists are on the right track in their strictures of 'superficial and closed accounts of culture and ethnicity' (275), he also thinks that such strictures need to be further developed and also extended to incorporate superficial and closed ideas about religion as well. Anti-racists may have identified the importance of representations of culture, ethnicity and, in a more limited way, religion in education, but they 'have been short of ideas for dealing with the complex issues of culture, ethnicity and religion' (275). This Jackson aims to correct by looking 'for new ways of representing and interpreting religious and cultural material which takes on board key elements of the antiracist critique' (275).

In the next section he addresses the issue of 'the representation of religions in Western academic literature' (276), chiefly to note 'that the concepts of "religion" and "religions" that are generally accepted uncritically by recent and contemporary religious educators . . . are relatively modern and are contestable' (276) and, in addition, that their application to complex phenomena in different cultural contexts is 'largely a construction by more powerful outsiders' (276). In other words, 'religion' and 'religions' are not 'native' categories. These observations draw on the work of Wilfred Cantwell Smith (1978) and others and will be familiar to those who are acquainted with recent debates and controversies in religious studies. The focus of Jackson's interest is on the issue of how religion is defined and interpreted, and builds on recent research that attends to the connotations and denotations of religion and its cognates as these have evolved and changed over time. Jackson points out that at the period of the Protestant Reformation the Latin term *religio* largely referred to personal piety, but in the next two centuries this usage was 'largely displaced by a concept of religion as schematic, intellectualist and "exterior", and which portrayed religions as belief systems' (276). 'This concept,' he tells us, 'reflected and stimulated religious conflict, and was used to delineate groups within Christianity and to classify and encompass what was perceived to be equivalent material in non-Christian cultures encountered by the West' (276).

Further shifts of meaning subsequently occurred. At the end of the eighteenth century Friedrich Schleiermacher revived the 'inward and non-intellectual meaning of religion' (276), and during the nineteenth century the terms 'religion' and 'religions' came to be used more widely, along with the emergence of most of the modern names by which the religions are distinguished and denominated. Religion is the genus of which there are different species; or in philosophical terms, religion is a type with many tokens – Buddhism, Christianity, Islam, Judaism, and so on. Jackson also traces the emergence, under Hegelian influence, both of the idea of the essence of religion in general and of the distinctive essence of different religions. This form of (what he calls) 'reification' also underlies, he believes, later twentieth-century phenomenological interpretations, which went further still and (controversially) identified the essence of different types of religious experience.

The next step in his argument is to identify the influence of these characteristically modern understandings of religion on British religious education. He provides three different illustrations to show that religious educators 'have not been critical of the notion of a "religion" ' (1995: 278). The first example he cites is that of the post-war agreed syllabuses which interpreted the religions as 'essentialised', 'separate systems or "wholes"', with similar structures and in competition with each other' (278). The second example is the 'world religions' movement in British religious education, associated with Ninian Smart. The final example focuses on an attempt by 'right-wing' Christian exclusivists in the 1980s to turn back the clock and revert to post-war religious education and educational efforts to institutionalise the superiority of Christianity in schools. According to Jackson, what these different examples have in common is 'an uncriticized assumption of separate, distinct "religions" having similar structures and types of content' (278).

In the next two sections Jackson focuses more closely on representations of culture, first in religious education and then in social anthropology. He interacts with two contrasting but not, he contends, fundamentally different interpretations of culture in the religious education literature, that of John McIntyre (1978) and that of Edward Hulmes (1989). His basic criticism is that 'both perceive cultures as wholes, constantly shifting but essentially distinct from each other' (282), though he acknowledges that for Hulmes different cultures may hold certain values in common. In contrast to the idea of cultures as discrete wholes, Jackson finds more open and flexible views of the nature of culture in the work of recent anthropologists, such as Clifford Geertz (1973; 1983) and James Clifford (1986), and in the work of cultural critics, such as Edward Said (1989). These writers appreciate the dynamic, internally diverse and contested nature of cultures.

The relevance of these explorations of the nature of cultures and of religions for religious education is then considered in a separate section. The conclusion that Jackson reaches is that attention needs to be given to 'the deeper issues of how religious traditions and cultures are represented as well as to techniques of interpretation' (284). He then provides an outline of one curriculum development project, with which he is associated, that attempts to incorporate the necessary theoretical insights and the degree of sophistication in representing and interpreting religion that he believes is required in religious education: 'The Project regards the concepts of religions and religion as modern post-Enlightenment constructions and acknowledges the role of colonial power in defining the 'other' in terms of discrete religions and cultures' (284). These theoretical insights, supplemented by ethnographic studies of religious communities in Britain (which focus on the issue of the transmission of religious culture to the young, using Geertz's concepts of 'experience near' and 'experience distant') and the work of anthropologists and social psychologists are used to produce a matrix to show the interrelationships between the religious tradition, membership groups and individuals. Jackson records that '[i]n each "tradition" we [the team of researchers] found a body of symbols that exhibited detailed difference but a close family resemblance across different membership groups, sufficient to argue that it makes sense to speak in a qualified way of "religions" ' (285).

The concluding short section reiterates the need for religious educators to attend to the fundamental issues of representation and interpretation of cultures and of religions and to develop new pedagogical models 'which avoid the simplistic portrayal of religions as discrete systems of belief and which also accommodate internal diversity and change' (287).

Religious Education: An Interpretive Approach

The next publication to be considered is Jackson's first book-length exposition of interpretive religious education, appropriately entitled, *Religious Education: An Interpretive Approach* (1997). In most respects it is a straightforward expansion of the themes and commitments we have already considered. In fact there is an almost perfect correspondence between sections of the article and the chapters in the book.

In the 'Introduction' Jackson describes his work as 'both a *development* and a *sympathetic critique* of [Ninian] Smart's work in religious education' (1997: 2; my emphasis) and in Chapter 1 he gives substance to this comment by providing a detailed account of the origins and commitments of the phenomenological approach to religious education and an assessment of its strengths and weakness. Clearly Jackson wishes to situate his work within the on-going tradition of mainstream British religious education and for his work to be perceived as in continuity with what has gone before. No doubt such a perception of his work by others in this tradition brings advantages to the propagation and reception of his own work. The *sympathetic* aspect of Jackson's critique is that he is supportive of Smart's commitment to non-confessional, multi-faith religious education and to the educational aim of 'attempting to grasp the religious outlook of others in their own terms' (7). The *critical* aspect of his support for the work of Smart is that he concludes that 'classical' phenomenological methodologies (of which he considers a number) 'could not provide the basis for an approach to religious education which considered material from different cultural contexts authentically in its own terms' (27). His route to this conclusion is interesting in that he first defends the phenomenological approach in religious education from the standard, but serious, criticisms made against it by educators (e.g. that it leads to superficial learning or that the coverage of so many religions tends to confuse pupils), and then develops a number of criticisms, some familiar and some novel, that strike at the heart of the central assumptions and commitments of religious phenomenology. These are that its understanding of religion and its appeal to *epoché*, which he glosses as a form of intuition, are too subjective, 'with no reference to historical or cultural context' (21); that to posit an 'essence' for religious concepts such as 'religion', the 'numinous' and the 'soul' is to make 'a category mistake' (23, using the terminology of Gilbert Ryle) and that its methodology conceals 'a Christian theological agenda' (21). This prepares the way for the constructive part of his programme and the case for interpretive religious education.

Chapter 2 sets out the positive case for religious educators to draw on the intellectual resources of social anthropology and on the 'interpretive' anthropology of Clifford Geertz in particular. According to Geertz (1973), in order to understand another person's or society's way of life it is important to identify and interpret the central symbols of the particular culture that shapes what is believed and practised; these symbols and local categories of thought will often be religious or relate to religion in some significant way. The challenge is how to identify the central symbols of a culture, and for this Geertz advocates an ethnographic approach, in the form of field work, with direct observation and recording of the way individuals and societies behave and give meaning to their actions. This is followed by the production of a critical written description and analysis of the subject and culture under study.

A focus on the meaning of behaviour, as interpreted by the 'actors' themselves, and on the wider form of life, of which specific beliefs and actions are a part, are central to Geertz's (1973, 1983) understanding of ethnography – these commitments betray the influence on him of Wittgenstein and his insight that human meaning is symbolic and contextual. The relationship between individual aspects (or beliefs) of culture and the wider form of life is dialectical: actions gain their meaning within a wider form of life, with its associated symbolic systems and meanings, yet the wider form of life, as a distinctive culture, is an expression of the sum total of individual meanings. This alerts Geertz to the need to interpret particular symbols (e.g. stories, narratives and actions) and particular parts of cultures (e.g. institutions) in relation to the wider cultural 'whole' and then to interpret the latter in relation to its constituent parts. This insight goes back to Schleiermacher and Dilthey in the nineteenth century and is often referred to as 'the hermeneutical circle', though the hermeneutical task is, to change the metaphor, more that of a spiral (where understanding of both part and whole develops progressively in tandem) than of a circle with its potential for understanding to be arrested by a static and fixed interpretation of both the part and the whole. The task of interpretation is, however, not confined to the issue of describing events and symbols within the context of the wider culture – what Geertz refers to as 'thick description' (again following Ryle) – there is also the challenge of *translating* the concepts, symbols and institutions of 'insiders' into the language and vocabulary of the ethnographer for the purposes of analysis and understanding, which often means translating the concepts of one culture into the language and vocabulary of another. Translation is a technical term for Geertz (1983: 10) with a specific meaning:

> Translation . . . is not a simple recasting of others' ways of putting things in terms of our way of putting them (that is the kind in which things get lost), but displaying the logic of their ways of putting them in locutions of ours, a conception which again brings it rather closer to what a critic does to illuminate a poem than what an astronomer does to account for a star.

Again the influence of the later Wittgenstein of the *Investigations* (1958) and *On Certainty* (1976) can be identified in Geertz's reference to the aim of translation as 'displaying the logic of their ways', that is, to understand the rules or 'grammar' (Wittgenstein) that govern how concepts can be used and related to one another; translation 'shows' these connections. Clearly what Geertz is cautioning against is the idea that words and concepts in one language can simply be translated into another using 'equivalent' dictionary terms, or the idea that the meaning of concepts and terms from one form of life can simply be read off uncritically without attention to context and translation: Wittgenstein distinguished between 'surface grammar' and 'depth grammar' in order to make this point.

The above account of interpretive anthropology represents my own summary rather than that of Jackson's, though it is not unfaithful to the broad contours of his account (he adds an evaluative section, the relevant conclusions of which are summarised below). The reason for this is that Geertz's focus on thick description and on the significance he attaches to religion as a symbolic system of meaning are important insights into the nature of religion, which responsible representations of the religions in education need to incorporate and reflect. What Geertz also alerts us to is the need for self-criticism and reflexivity in relation to 'second order' descriptions and interpretations of religious life and practice, though as Jackson notes, recognition of this is insufficiently emphasised and Geertz has been criticised at this point. The critical question is, whether sufficiently emphasised by Geertz or not, do the terms and categories of (what Geertz calls) 'the specialist', that is, the person who interprets religious culture, capture the true meaning of the first order ('insider') beliefs, practices, customs and institutions? The warning here is, *inter alia*, against facile comparisons that assume that 'similar' practices possess identical meanings, for example, that the 'sacred text' of the Qur'an corresponds in meaning and significance to the 'sacred text' of the Christian Bible, or that Muhammad as 'sacred founder' occupies the same role in Islam as Jesus occupies in Christianity.

Jackson is positively disposed toward Geertz's interpretive anthropology and he believes that 'techniques from interpretive anthropology have a great deal to commend them', though he identifies potential weaknesses, which include 'the tendency to suppress individual voices of insiders; [and] the possibility of constructing artificial wholes from the experiences of individuals . . .' (45). This last potential weakness in Geertz's interpretive anthropology is, for Jackson, fully realised in British religious education (47): '. . . "religions" and "cultures" are rarely presented in a vibrant, flexible and organic way. RE tends to treat "religions" as discrete belief systems, and "cultures" . . . as separate bounded entities'.

Chapters 3 and 4 of *Religious Education: An Interpretive Approach* are extended discussions of the ways in which the religions and cultures are represented in academic literature and in education. While fuller and more detailed lines of argumentation are pursued, the dialogue partners and the list of references are chiefly confined to those discussed and the literature cited in the central sections of his earlier article, 'Religious Education's representation of "religions" and "cultures" ', summarised above: essentially, these two chapters are expansions of the parallel sections of the article. The advantage of this is that it is not necessary to repeat what has already been said. Jackson's own summary of Chapter 3 and attention to some of the things he says in both chapters are sufficient for our purposes.

Critical to the discussion [in Chapter 3] is a consideration of the emergence of the modern concepts of religion and of religions in the West, especially the view of religions as schematic systems of belief, the establishment of the names of the religions, the emergence in the nineteenth century of 'religion' as a generic category, and the appearance in the twentieth century of the term 'world religions'. The political dimension of this, in terms of power relations, is also discussed. A model for analyzing religious data which treats religious traditions as organic, internally diverse and more complex than 'belief systems' is suggested . . . (50)

Whereas Chapter 3 focuses on religion, Chapter 4 focuses on culture. Attention is given (as in the article already considered) to multicultural and anti-racist forms of education and of religious education: fixed and 'static' interpretations of culture along with the idea of an unchanging national culture, which is identified in ethnic or religious (Christian) terms, are strongly criticised; both personal and group identity are interpreted as fluid and shifting and this Jackson believes challenges the accuracy and propriety of religious, cultural and ethnic stereotypes. Finally, in his view 'more flexible models of the multicultural society need to be developed [in religious education], emphasizing communication and the exploration of "overlapping values" ' (91).

Chapter 5 provides both a summary of ethnographic studies of children from different religious communities in Britain, conducted by Jackson and his team, and a description of the application of their findings to religious education, with the development of curriculum material to illustrate the potential of an interpretive approach to enable 'communication across cultural, religious and ethnic boundaries' (95). The ethnographic studies focus on 'religious socialization' and 'the transmission of religious culture' to young children in different religious communities. The research material is structured around 'examining the relationship between individuals, relevant groups to which the individual belongs, and the wider religious traditions' (66). The curriculum material produced on the basis of the research, we are told, 'plays down' usage of the modern names for religions, with emphasis placed upon people rather than systems, and caution is expressed about using concepts like 'the numinous' or the 'spiritual' and in subsuming the content of religion under common themes, such as festivals, worship, etc. The forms of representation and interpretation of religious material used in the curriculum project are seen as

central to a religious education that seeks as a basic aim to develop an understanding of the religious worldviews of others, their religious language and symbols, and their feelings and attitudes. Through this it is hoped, *additionally*, that good relationships between those from different religious and cultural backgrounds will be promoted (111–112; Jackson's emphasis).

In the final chapter, Chapter 6, Jackson explores the implications of an interpretive approach for religious education. The chapter begins by defending multi-faith religious education against the charges of relativism and reductionism and then considers a range of other issues, such as the aims of religious education in publicly funded schools and the (then) contemporary political context of religious education. For the most part, however, the positions advocated in these other matters neither follow from the beliefs and commitments of interpretive religious education nor bear directly on it. Consequently they can be overlooked, with one important exception – the introduction and treatment of the theme of 'edification' by Jackson. But first, attention will be given, albeit briefly, to his rebuttal of the charges of relativism and reductionism.

The consideration of relativism by Jackson focuses exclusively on the claim by the sociologist Kieran Flanagan that '[t]he desire for racial pluralism and tolerance has the effect of forcing Christianity to muffle its exclusive claims in the interests of securing cultural and political harmony' (quoted by Jackson, p. 122). Jackson does not address the criticism that Christianity has had to 'muffle its claims' in religious education head on and he does not acknowledge its relevance to post-confessional religious education in England and Wales, as, for example, in the work of John Hull and others; instead he accuses Flanagan of 'reifying Christianity, rather than speaking of Christians or even institutional groups of Christians' (123), and of overlooking the diversity among Christians with regard to its central claims and its relationship to other religions. In response to the charge of reductionism, interpreted as the charge that 'the internal diversity of religious traditions challenges the existence of religions as coherent wholes' (126), Jackson affirms that there is some provisional sense (for hermeneutical purposes) in talking about a religion in general terms, yet 'the wholes should be recognized as abstractions or reification' (127). He then refers negatively to post-war agreed syllabuses where '"other" religions are considered as separate systems, with similar structures and in competition with each other'; such a representation, he suggests, is (following Edward Said 1978) 'Orientalist in character' (127).

The theme of edification is introduced by Jackson in the context of a further elaboration of the idea of the hermeneutical circle (or what has here been called the hermeneutical *spiral*): 'The interpretive process starts from the insider's language and experience, moves to that of the student, and then oscillates between the two' (130). For the student this activity of interacting with and 'grasping another's way of life', Jackson tells us, 'is inseparable . . . from that of pondering on the issues and questions raised by it' (130). In addition, religious education needs to provide 'structured opportunities for [personal] reflection', so that students can make connections between different worldviews and identify 'points of contact . . . and points of commonality' that always exist between different ways of life, however culturally or religious distinguished they might appear to be (130). Interestingly, in this context Jackson does not refer to the need for pupils to reflect on the nature and implications of difference and diversity between worldviews. This process of reflection and of making connections between worldviews can, according to Jackson, lead to edification, a term he takes over from the philosopher Richard Rorty. He shares the idea with Rorty (2009: 357–394) that edification is a 'transformative concept' and that '[t]hrough the challenge of "unpacking" another worldview one can, in a sense, become a new person' (Jackson 1997: 130–131).[5] Those familiar with the history and terminology of recent British religious education will recognise that Jackson's idea of edification, as it is developed, is closely related to what Michael Grimmitt refers to as 'learning from religion'. Jackson acknowledges the ideas are related, though this is immediately qualified by the assertion that 'there are some significant differences' (131). Somewhat predictably, Grimmitt's understanding of learning from religion is accused of reifying religions and cultures.

One particular criticism of Grimmitt by Jackson is worth mentioning. Jackson points out that not all learners endorse the liberal educational aim that they should become 'fully autonomous individuals': 'they may not share the same views of the nature of knowledge or views on the role of authority in their lives' (132). This criticism seems to be directed to Grimmitt's idea that learning from religion should include the critical evaluation of truth claims. Jackson's point is that *formal* consideration of religious truth claims *may not* be appropriate in religious education because all learners (and note it is in terms of *learners* that Jackson frames his argument, not educators) do not accept that identifying truth is an aim for religious education in schools. This needs careful exposition, and given that Jackson chooses not to develop the point, a certain degree of caution is required. It may be that Jackson thinks of religious truth as a purely personal affair upon which religious education, for a variety of reasons, has nothing *important* to contribute or any significant skills to impart in terms of enabling pupils to make their own judgements. In any case a *formal* consideration of religious truth may be inappropriate for religious educators; and this is consistent with his earlier comment in the same chapter that '[t]ruth claims [in religious education] are *perhaps* better discussed spontaneously on the basis of pupils' questions' (125; my emphasis). There is some ambiguity that surrounds use of the word 'perhaps' in this quotation: perhaps should or perhaps should not! Such usage does not make the challenges of interpretation and ultimately of evaluation easy.

Rethinking Religious Education and Plurality

In all probability, *Rethinking Religious Education and Plurality* (2004) is one of the most important books on religious education to be published in recent years and it consolidated Robert Jackson's reputation as one of the leading international authorities on the subject. It covers a range of topics, summarises a wide body of work and interacts both with other religious educators and with international research in the field of religious education. There are interesting and important discussions, such as: whether there should be state funding for religious schools;

religious education in relation to citizenship; intercultural and values education; and a masterly overview of the role of research in religious education. There are also discussions of Clive Erricker's form of 'postmodernist' religious education, of which he is almost entirely critical, and of Andrew Wright's advocacy of religious literacy as the goal of religious education; among other things, Wright is criticised for 'his tendency to reify religion' (86). The dangers of reification for educators are also emphasised by Jackson in a chapter entitled 'Interpretive approaches to religious education' (note the plural 'approaches'). The discussion here is wide ranging, with inclusion of such subjects as religious education in South Africa, representing African religion, school based research on values, and the issue of involving pupils in planning religious education.

The weakness in this presentation of the interpretive approach, which continues in a second chapter entitled 'Dialogical approaches in religious education', is that the concept of interpretive religious education is extended to include insights and ideas that can just as readily be appropriated by other approaches. Positively, perhaps Jackson is drawing attention to the compatibility of interpretive religious education with other methodologies, a point he often makes, and how it can be complemented by other insights and strategies. However, the effect, for those unacquainted with his earlier more sharply focused writings on interpretive religious education (in 1995 and 1997), is arguably to make it difficult to identify the distinctive features of interpretive religious education and to know where it differs from other approaches. A Saussurean (1995) perspective suggests that if an interpretive approach does not differ from other approaches and has no distinctive elements, then in a strict sense it is unnecessary, for what it denotes overlaps with other existing approaches.

While the familiar accents of interpretive religious education are rehearsed (the need for reflexivity, the importance of ethnographic research, etc.), on this occasion Jackson (89–92) presents the interpretive approach as a middle way between two extremes, between that of viewing 'religions and cultures as "organic entities" ', which while changing, maintain a bedrock of core values and beliefs, and viewing them, on a deconstructing reading, as empty of public content and simply expressions of creative on-going 'personal narratives'.[6] Negatively, this middle way entails that the 'European Enlightenment view of the "religions" as clearly distinct and internally consistent belief systems should be abandoned in favour of a much looser portrayal of religious traditions and groupings . . .' (90). What does emerge in this particular account of interpretive religious education is a much clearer focus on the issue of personal identity (88 and 91) and that one of the purposes of religious education is 'to help them [pupils] to clarify their own sense of identity' (94). This is an important point, although my own opinion is that religious education has the potential to, and is required to do more than, clarify for pupils their sense of identity, understood as uncovering their preconceptions and commitments (what Gadamer called our 'prejudices' and 'horizon of understanding'). Religious education as a *critical* discipline needs to provide pupils with the skills and intellectual resources to evaluate and assess religious claims to knowledge and truth and to revise their religious identity, should they so wish. 'Clarity', in other words 'is not enough', to use the title of a celebrated collection of essays, edited by H.D. Lewis (1963), which argues that (then) current interpretations of linguistic philosophy were too preoccupied with analysis and description and overlooked the substantive matters of ultimate reference and truth.

Robert Jackson, an interpretive approach and a postmodern model of religious education

Earlier it was noted that Jackson does not identify interpretive religious education with postmodernism and he expressly rejects the description of his work as postmodern. Moreover, he consistently criticises the work of Clive Erricker and those religious educators who openly acknowledge postmodern commitments. These considerations, while naturally urging caution, do not establish the conclusion that Jackson's interpretive approach is not best interpreted as representative of a postmodern model of religious education, while recognising that other approaches may equally be classified as postmodern and be susceptible to more serious criticisms. Certainly his emphasis upon the relationship of power to knowledge betrays the influence of Foucault, though this influence is mediated chiefly by the work and writings of Edward Said (1978). Jackson also draws upon Rorty's idea of edification (Rorty 2009) and distinguishes it from Michael Grimmitt's notion of 'learning from religion' (Grimmitt 1987) in ways that are consistent with Rorty's own postmodern commitments. For example, while Jackson allows that the idea of edification may include some element of transformation, it is clearly not a transformation that he believes should be occasioned by either a comparison between religions or a consideration of religious beliefs and their truth claims, elements that are included in Grimmitt's account of learning from religion. Even Jackson's use of interpretive anthropology, which is central to his overall understanding of interpretive religious education, is qualified by the inclusion of criticisms and insights drawn from other ethnographers, who, he acknowledges, 'are influenced by "deconstructive" literary theory, and who are sometimes described as postmodernists . . .' (1997: 38) – James Clifford, Vincent Crapanzano and Paul Rabinow. These critics, according to Jackson, are 'applying ideas and using terminology derived from such writers as Derrida, Lyotard or Foucault' (1997: 38), ideas to which Jackson is indebted.

The identification of specific instances where Jackson draws upon writers who are commonly identified as postmodern does not exhaust the case for regarding his account of interpretive religious education as an example of a postmodern approach. Further evidence is provided by the broad orientation of his thought, which clearly reflects commitments that are characteristic of postmodern philosophy. For example, Jackson privileges individual expressions of belief over communal beliefs; he questions 'essentialised' and determinate definitions both of religion and of religious terms, drawing attention to their etymological origins and ideological functions; he accentuates internal diversity, cautions against thinking of a religion as a coherent and consistent set of beliefs and practices and gives attention to the way in which human language is used to reinforce and perpetuate structures of power and privilege. All of these betray postmodern accents and commitments. Perhaps the reluctance of Jackson to identify his position with postmodernism is because he associates the latter with (what he calls) a 'strong' form of relativism (Jackson 2004: 67) and a commitment to 'anti-realism' in epistemology, both of which he identifies in Erricker and both of which he rejects. The critical issue is whether a strong form of relativism and anti-realism are co-jointly necessary features of postmodern thought. May postmodern thought not also embrace weak forms of relativism and/or some attenuated form of realism? Attention to philosophical interpretations of postmodern thought indicates that the issue of whether postmodern thinkers necessarily embrace relativism and anti-realism is controversial, and although some postmodern thinkers openly embrace relativism in conjunction with anti-realism, not all do. The charge of relativism in conjunction with anti-realism is most frequently raised by critics of postmodernism and resisted by some of those so accused: Richard Rorty (1991), for example, questions the appropriateness and validity of any 'constructed' dichotomy between realism and anti-realism, and positively describes himself as a 'pragmatic realist'. This suggests that a more neutral, broad-ranging definition of postmodern thought is appropriate, for hermeneutical reasons, to gaining an orientation to its features and characteristic commitments. Such a definition is attempted by Janet Flax (1987: 624):

> Postmodern discourses are all 'deconstructive' in that they seek to distance us from and make us sceptical about beliefs concerning truth, knowledge, power, the self, and language that are often taken for granted within and serve as legitimation for contemporary Western culture.

Flax is quite careful in the construction of this definition and in her choice of words: postmodern discourse is not identified with relativism, nor with scepticism, *per se*, but with scepticism about beliefs concerned with 'truth, knowledge, power, the self, and language *that are often taken for granted within and serve as legitimation for contemporary Western culture*' [my emphasis]. Postmodern discourse, on this understanding, is not necessarily sceptical about truth, knowledge, power, the self, and language, but sceptical about certain interpretations of these beliefs that are and have been influential in contemporary Western culture and which serve to reproduce and perpetuate Western culture and (in the spirit of the definition, it may be added) the forms of exploitation and dominance that accompany it. A plausible case can be made that Jackson's version of interpretive religious education is appropriately defined as 'postmodern' on this understanding. Interpretive religious education questions inherited ideas of truth and knowledge, such as the notion of a universal religious consciousness that is revealed through a range of religions. It also draws attention to the role of powerful elites and groups in constructing religion and in defining and legislating for the use of religious terms. In any case the matter of definition, as also noted in the last chapter, is not the crucial issue. The real challenge is to assess the extent to which an interpretive approach faithfully reflects the nature of religion and contributes to the personal development of pupils and the social development of communities.

Notes

1   I include Denise Cush in this list on the basis of her influential article on pluralism (1999) in which she employs the heading, 'There is no such thing as religion, culture, race, ethnicity, or nationality', and states that '[n]o such entity "exists" as self, religion, culture, race, ethnicity, or nationality' (1999: 4). In her final paragraph she says that her form of 'positive pluralism' in religious education 'takes seriously the . . . incommensurability of truth claims' (11). Modern talk of incommensurability goes back to Thomas Kuhn (1970), who argued that competing paradigms of science lack any means of common adjudication because they use different concepts and methods to address different problems: scientific paradigms cannot be compared and there is no rational way of deciding between them. Certainly Cush's commitment to the incommensurability of religious truth claims takes pluralism seriously, but only by espousing religious relativism and effectively banishing the issue of religious truth from consideration by pupils. After all, if the religions are incommensurable they are simply different ways of being and relating; one cannot even say they are different ways of interpreting the world or reality, for then they would have a common orientation and purpose: that is interpreting the *same* world – and if interpreting the same world, then one is entitled to ask which interpretation best fits the world.

2   A full list of publications by Jackson is available online:: http://bit.ly/169V10q (accessed 13 October 2013).

3   Attention will focus exclusively on the work and writings of Jackson and will not include reference to the publications of the wider research community with which he is connected; this is because he is both the originator of an interpretive approach and, to my mind, its most able exponent.

4   References in this section and in subsequent sections that refer to and discuss one particular publication by Jackson will after the first full reference cite only the relevant page or pages.

5   At the end of this quoted sentence, Jackson includes the reference 'Rorty 1980', but unfortunately this reference is not included in the bibliography of the book. In my opinion the reference is to the 2nd corrected 1980 printing (1st edition 1979) and the first paperback version of Rorty's *Philosophy and the Mirror of Nature*; the page reference to Rorty in my text refers to the 2009 anniversary edition.

6   In my view Jackson has insufficiently extended one of the (what he calls 'extreme') poles of his continuum: it should properly run from those who view religions and cultures as *unchanging* over time, maintaining the same values and beliefs, and viewing them, on a deconstructive reading, as empty of public content and simply expressions of creative on-going personal narratives; on this broader continuum, those who view religions and cultures as organic entities, which while changing, maintain a bedrock of core values and beliefs represent 'a middle way'. Objectively, Jackson's interpretive approach to religion should be situated towards the personal narrative 'extreme' pole of this continuum.

13

INTERPRETIVE RELIGIOUS EDUCATION, REPRESENTING RELIGIONS AND CHALLENGING PREJUDICE

The aim of this chapter is to complement the account of interpretive religious education that was developed in Chapter 12 with an assessment of its strengths and weakness, particularly in relation to whether it faithfully captures the nature of religion and how successful it is in challenging prejudice and contributing to the moral and social aims of education. This is supplemented by the identification of a range of issues to which further attention needs to be given by its proponents.

The strengths of an interpretive approach to religious education

It is easy to appreciate why the interpretive approach has gained the attention of religious educators and why it has been used to provide the theoretical framework for a number of important European projects that are concerned not just with religious education but with citizenship and intercultural education. In some respects it is suited to the increasingly secular nature of many Western societies, and (certainly in Britain) to the increasingly secular nature of education and of the teaching profession. It represents a decisive break with the modern model of religious education – the phenomenological approach and experiential religious education, for example, which found its educational rationale and unity in a commitment to the spiritual validity of different religions and religious traditions. The modern model of religious education is inherently theological, whereas a postmodern model of religious education is non-theological; an interpretive approach falls on the postmodern side of this distinction.

One of the most important insights of interpretive religious education is the recognition (derived from the later philosophy of Wittgenstein) that 'people from different cultural settings or ways of life use language and other symbols in particular ways which expose the meaning of words and practices within them' (Jackson 1997: 23). Meaning is contextual and any particular symbol, linguistic or otherwise, gains its meaning in relation to the wider symbolic whole and the broader form of life of which it is a part. As Jackson notes (again echoing Wittgenstein), '[t]he "grammar" of language use has to be grasped before the meaning of the terms or actions becomes evident' (1997: 23). The meaning of a belief or practice is gained by understanding its role within the wider framework of beliefs and actions.

Although Jackson endorses the contextual nature of religious symbols and Geertz's notion of thick description, he does not fully exploit their potential in his account of interpretive religious education. His discussion of Wittgenstein and the need to understand the grammar of religious and cultural utterances and actions is chiefly directed to criticising the positing of 'universal religious essences' by phenomenologists of religion who abstract ideas from their original context and then identify essential agreement across religious and cultural boundaries. What Jackson fails to appreciate fully is that 'grasping the grammar' of religion involves exploring religious beliefs and doctrines and recognising the way in which they shape and facilitate religious experience and give meaning to it. Religious meaning is determined by what one believes; consequently the propositional side of religion should be an important focus in education (this is part of the argument of Chapter 8). The positive point is that Jackson is aware of the role of beliefs in religion, even if he does not draw out the full implications of this awareness because it challenges some of his other more controversial commitments (see below).

A further strength of an interpretive approach to religious education is its appreciation of the hermeneutical challenge of interpreting the beliefs, values and practices of others. In fact the issue of interpretation is implicit in what has already been said about the need to explore the grammar of religious and cultural beliefs and practices. For the most part, phenomenologists of religion were untroubled by the historical and cultural distance that separated them from religious phenomena. Once the mind was focused on some particular practice or experience, a description of it was believed to be relatively straightforward. The issue of the language used to describe religious phenomena was regarded as unproblematic and uncontroversial, as were the categories that were used to classify what were presumed to be cross-cultural, cross-religious experiences.

The challenge, as perceived by phenomenologists, comes at the level of 're-experiencing' the event and intuiting its inner or existential meaning. One's personal capacity to recreate religious experience is essential to gaining an understanding of religion. An interpretive approach shifts the hermeneutical focus to that of engaging with the public world of religious symbols and ritual actions (which are, by contrast, regarded as constitutive of religious meaning) and to the subjects of experience as they interact with their local cultural and religious communities and with the wider religious tradition. An interpretive approach, as developed by Jackson, is also attentive to the particular situation of the contemporary observer or student of religion, who brings his or her commitments to the task of describing and interpreting the ideas and practices of others. Consequently Jackson explores the notion of reflexivity, which includes looking critically at one's own stance and presuppositions, and at the categories of interpretation that are used to understand the commitments and practices of others. There is no need to repeat what was summarised in the previous chapter about the nature of the hermeneutical task (see pp. 188–190). Jackson has clearly identified the issues and provided the resources for gaining a sophisticated and intellectually respectable account of the form interpretations and representations of religion in education should take.

Positively, an interpretive approach also emphasises the personal element in religion and the role of the individual in appropriating, constructing and reshaping religious traditions to produce both new connections with different aspects of culture and new religious meanings. At some stage in their educational careers pupils need to become acquainted with the diversity of beliefs and practices within religions. They need to be aware, first, of the diversity that correlates to the major doctrinal and institutional divisions within the religions and, second, of what may be termed personally chosen diversity, whereby individuals affirm some elements of their religious background and upbringing while rejecting other elements. At the level of the individual it should not be assumed (if it ever could) that those who identify with a religion necessarily endorse some prescribed set of beliefs that are regarded by the guardians of orthodoxy as constitutive of the tradition. Recognition of this can be a liberating experience for some people who discover that their sensitivities about (or rejection of) certain beliefs or practices that the 'community' expects them to endorse, is shared with others. This is another way of speaking about the contested nature of the boundaries of (a particular) religion.

Consistent with the emphasis of interpretive religious education on the personal element is a focus upon religion as it is lived and experienced by individuals in different cultural contexts. Too many textbooks in religious education present the religions as a set of beliefs and practices that seem remote from and unrelated to the modern, often secular, world of pupils. It is important that pupils have opportunities to see how religion is lived and experienced by people from their own culture and of their own age. This is why religious biographies and stories about contemporary religious adherents are helpful in showing the relevance of religion.

An interpretive approach: issues for reflection

Before considering the main weaknesses of an interpretive approach to religious education, it is useful to identify a number of issues that warrant further attention by its supporters and practitioners.

One of the strengths of Jackson's account of an interpretive approach, noted above, is the attention it gives to hermeneutical issues, particularly the terminology and nomenclature that is used to identify and categorise 'religious' phenomena. Jackson 'problematises' some of the most used and familiar terms in the study of religion, such as the term 'religion' itself, 'culture', 'religions' and 'Hinduism'. He considers the modern historical development of these terms and the ideological purposes that (he suggests) have frequently accompanied their use. The implications of this for the study of religion may be disputed (see below), though there is little doubt that it is a profitable exercise to subject the central terms of any discipline or field of study to critical analysis and examination.

What Jackson fails to do, however, is to subject other terms that are relevant to his exposition and understanding of interpretive religious education, and to his application of an interpretive approach to other aspects of the curriculum, to the same close analysis and scrutiny – terms such as 'citizenship', '*democratic citizenship*', 'intercultural education' and 'rights'. A focus on the use of these terms by educators and politicians should raise critical questions about the role of religious education in advancing the interests and aims of the nation state (and centralised European institutions) and of the emergence, some suggest, of new forms of civil religion in European Union funded projects on the role of religion in education (see Gearon 2012 for a powerful statement of this view).

Reservations about use of the discourse of citizenship and rights in religious education are expressed in the next chapter. More broadly, there is a need for both a genealogical analysis and an exposé of the ideological commitments implicit in the use by religious educators of such terms as progress, justice, inclusion and fairness.

The next issue is similar in form to the last, in that what is a strength of an interpretive approach is not fully exploited. Although Jackson extols the value of empirical research in religious education, his use of research in developing an interpretive approach is narrowly drawn and confined to small-scale ethnographic studies, to the complete neglect of broadly based quantitative research. There may be a conceptual issue here that unnecessarily limits his use of empirical research to ethnographic studies, which by their nature provide an incomplete picture of the reality of religion and the religious life.

Jackson derives his *interpretive* approach to religious education in conscious dependence on the interpretive anthropology of Clifford Geertz and the latter's (exclusive) use of ethnography to gain a detailed and nuanced understanding of the nature and meaning of cultural systems. Consistent with this interpretation, Jackson confines his attention to ethnographic studies of contemporary expressions of religious behaviour and practice.

Unfortunately this orientation overlooks both other forms of empirical studies of religion and other aspects of religion, for example the historical dimension (though see Jackson 2004: 92–94); it also minimises the significance of doctrine in religion, the content of sacred scripture, creation myths, and so on. Only those parts of religion that are 'revealed' in the lives of ordinary believers today are open to observation and thus illuminated by an ethnographic approach; and even here Jackson's use of the interpretive approach is restrictive, for the studies carried out by him and his team of researchers have been confined to children and young people and the processes of religious nurture. Such research will reveal only a small portion of the character and form of lived religion, for children are not adults and their expressed understanding of religion and religious rites and practices is necessarily limited.

One of the important aims of religious nurture is to instruct young people in the nature of their religious commitment, precisely because such an understanding is not innate and some form of induction, training and education is necessary. A full understanding of religion needs to interact with the beliefs and practices of adults as well as children: attending exclusively to the religious nurture of children does not provide a balanced or accurate account of the beliefs, practices and behaviour of religious communities and traditions. In addition, a focus on children almost entirely fails to consider the moral dimension of religion, for children have limited moral responsibility and therefore it is only in emergent adulthood and in adulthood proper that moral principles, values and beliefs come to full expression and require full implementation in the lives of adherents.

Discussion of the moral dimension of religion is almost entirely absent from Jackson's account of interpretive religious education. Recognition of these limitations may lie behind his frequent admission that his approach is just one among others and that it should be complemented by other approaches. This is fine in itself, but it raises the critical question why Jackson confines himself to qualitative ethnographic studies of the religion of children and adolescents and never engages with the full range of empirical research about religious beliefs and practices.

In fact the findings of the ethnographic research summarised in *Religious Education: An Interpretive Approach* (1997) seem to question Jackson's view that religions are *highly* variegated internally. The studies of his research group on 'the transmission of religious culture to children' (1997: 96) reveal, with regard to Christians, that in '[a]ll cases, the Bible and life of Jesus were of central importance', and the diversity that is reported reflects denominational distinctions (see 1997: 98–100; and noted in the last chapter). The ethnographic research on Muslim children also shows little internal diversity.

The element that Jackson neglects in his discussion and analysis of these findings on religious nurture is the normative role played by sacred scriptures in determining the content and nature of religious identity. For example, different groups within Christianity assent to the normative authority of the Bible, and in many respects the Bible is a focus of unity for Christians. What many Christians believe is determined by what they take to be the teachings of the Bible. This means that any serious study of Christians and of Christianity needs to attend to the literature of the Bible and to its content; it also means attending to biblical criticism and to hermeneutical issues about the original meaning of biblical passages and to their contemporary meaning and significance. Naturally, such study will consider the ways in which the Bible is subject to diverse interpretations and how the various denominations emphasise particular doctrines and derive different practices from the Bible. Similar points can be made in relation to other religions – Islam, for example.

There is a compelling case for extending Jackson's (exclusive) reliance on small-scale ethnographic studies of children to embrace a broader empirical perspective on religion and to use the findings in framing, developing and even testing different approaches and methodologies in religious education. What might this broader empirical perspective reveal that is relevant to assessments of the central commitments and assumptions of an interpretive approach? Certainly empirical studies of religion show that there is internal diversity within religions, but also show that followers of different religions possess distinctive commitments across a range of religious dimensions and in relation to religious and moral issues.

There are broad commonalities of attitude, belief and practice among adherents of a particular religion. For example, recent research by Gallup (2009: 30–35) revealed a remarkable degree of agreement among British Muslims about personal morality: fewer than 1% believe that homosexual acts are acceptable (compared with 58% of the general British public); 95% believe that abortion is morally unacceptable (compared with 45%); 97% believe that sex outside marriage is morally wrong (compared with 18%); and finally 99% of Muslims believe that viewing pornography is morally wrong (compared with 65%). In relation to Christianity it is a well-established fact among empirical researchers that there are striking levels of agreement in belief and moral valuation among regular churchgoers: 89% of such believe in heaven; 62% believe in hell; 83% believe in life after death; and 81% believe in miracles (see Gill 1999, for example).

Over the last two decades Professor Leslie Francis has identified a range of correlations between Christian commitment among young people and particular beliefs, attitudes and practices. What his research shows is that commitment to Christianity is a significant predictor of attitudes, beliefs, practices and moral valuations (see Kay and Francis 1996; Francis 2001b, for summaries of his extensive body of empirical research findings). Empirical studies support the view that distinctive patterns of beliefs and practices are correlated to membership of different religions and religious communities. This suggests that Jackson's interpretation of religion, which questions the importance of the religions as distinctive or schematic systems of belief (Jackson 2004: 90), is derived from (what is here regarded as controversial) theoretical and philosophical assumptions rather than from empirical research. Interestingly, in an essay published in 2000, Jackson (131) admits this:

> . . . the main pedagogical methods and principles associated with the project [i.e. the Warwick RE project and the interpretive approach to religious education] are not inextricably bound up with ethnography; they are associated with theory from an eclectic range of sources in the humanities . . . social sciences . . ., and with methodology from the social sciences that is influenced by hermeneutics . . .

The critical question is the extent to which these eclectic sources capture the nature of religion; if they do not then Jackson's interpretive approach is flawed.

The weaknesses of an interpretive approach to religious education

The chief weaknesses of an interpretive approach relate to four main areas: its understanding of the relationship of religion to culture; the extent to which interpretive religious education faithfully represents the nature of religion; its treatment of the truth claims of the religions; and, finally, its contribution to challenging intolerance and to developing responsible and respectful relationships between different individuals and communities.

There is a notable similarity between Jackson's interpretation of cultures and his interpretation of religions: both for him are internally diverse, contested, organic and flexible; both lack coherence in terms of beliefs and values; and no one internal form of religion or culture can legitimately claim authenticity over any other form. For him, a religious way of life is an example of a different cultural way of life; and the tools required to study culture, such as Geertz's interpretive ethnographic approach, are equally suited to studying religion. There are no important differences. Religion is a manifestation of culture.

But is religion best interpreted as solely a manifestation of culture and are the categories for interpreting culture equally appropriate to interpreting religion and capturing its different dimensions and diversity (as Jackson presupposes by his exclusive reliance on ethnography)? If religion and religions can be distinguished conceptually and empirically from culture (part of the argument of Chapter 8 is relevant to this), then there is the possibility of identifying and conceptualising different relationships that exist between them. The weakness in Jackson's understanding of religion is that he does not fully attend to or take sufficiently seriously the diversity of relationships that may exist between religion (or religions) and culture. Certainly, for him, aspects of religious tradition may interact in different ways with cultural values and beliefs, but what is lacking in this perspective, and what causes him to underestimate the significance of the encounter between religions and cultures, is the normative quality that often attends religious beliefs, for these are regarded by many adherents as having been revealed by God and therefore possess for them an epistemic status that is denied to cultural beliefs. For example, Muslims believe that the teachings of the Qur'an constitute a revelation from God, in the light of which cultural practices in any particular society can be condemned, corrected, endorsed or regarded as irrelevant to the practice of religion.

None of this suggests that distinguishing religious from cultural beliefs and practices is always straightforward and easy, and in particular instances in historically religious societies the two may be conjoined in such a way as to render the distinction otiose, from the perspective of those who belong to the society. Recognition of this, however, does not undermine the appropriateness of the distinction and its applicability. By ignoring the normative element in religion, which derives from its appeal to the divine, Jackson effectively overlooks the perspective of religious believers and their understanding of the creative and diverse ways in which *they believe* religion relates to culture.

If the divine does not exist and we live in a naturalistic world, then any distinction between religious and cultural beliefs that acknowledges the explanatory role of religion in society and in culture may ultimately be redundant and inappropriate, and on this understanding all religious beliefs can without remainder be reduced to cultural beliefs that are appropriately explained and accounted for naturalistically. But if the perspective of the religious believer is taken seriously in education, as acknowledged by most religious educators, then opportunities exist for identifying and reflecting on different cultural encounters and responses to religion. One naturally thinks here of the potential of H. Richard Niebuhr's (1951) typology of the relationship between Christ and culture, which can be reframed in terms of religion (or of a particular religion or religious tradition or sub-group): religion against culture; a religion of culture; religion above culture; religion and culture in a paradoxical relationship; and finally, religion as the transformer of culture.

Jackson's interpretive approach to religious education overlooks some of the possibilities that exist for learning about religions and reflecting on their influence on culture. Ironically, what the interpretive approach overlooks is the diversity of relationships that exist between religions and culture, particularly at the point where religious claims to revelation and the beliefs established on the basis of such claims impact on and interact with culture.

The second chief weakness of an interpretive approach focuses on a cluster of difficulties that surround Jackson's interpretation and representation of religion. These difficulties relate, in part, to philosophical matters concerned with his understanding of the use and employment of words: he embraces a mistaken theory of reference and meaning. His discussion of 'the establishment of the names of religions, [and] the emergence in the nineteenth century of "religion" as a generic category' (Jackson 1997: 50) provides a convenient starting point. Jackson finds general terms such as 'religion' and the names of the different religions – Christianity, Hinduism and Islam, for example – problematic. He believes that use of the term religion to cover different historical-cultural traditions gives an artificial impression of sameness and therefore imposes a false unity on heterogeneous material. Use of the names of individual religions suggests 'bounded and incontestable systems', each with its own internal 'constructed' essential features, which marks it off from other religions, while simultaneously sharing other essential features with all religions. Jackson acknowledges that there is some provisional sense (for hermeneutical purposes) in talking about a religion in general terms, yet 'the wholes should be recognized as abstractions or reification' (1997: 127).

There are a number of confusions here. Jackson misunderstands the nature of general terms. What makes a term general is that the same word is used to apply to more than one thing, even though no two of these may be identical. We can point to four different chairs; they all differ in greater or lesser degrees from each other (even the same chair made on the same day to the same style by the same manufacturer), yet we can helpfully describe and name them as chairs.

They are chairs. By calling them such does not mean all chairs are identical or that there is some essential form of 'chairness' that all must possess to be designated as a chair. The fact that all chairs are not the same at every point does not mean that we can speak of chairs only in a provisional or qualified way. What is true of the use of the term 'chair' is also true of 'religion'.

In places, Jackson expresses himself in a way which suggests that those who use general terms either assume, naively, that there exists a Platonic form that fixes the reference of a term or are beguiled into thinking (because the same word is used) that each use of the term must denote either a common 'object' or different objects with identical attributes. This is not the case. To return to the example of the chair, all the difficulties that surround use of the term 'religion' could equally apply to use of the term 'chair' – there could be debate over the characteristics of a chair, some particular instance of a chair could be disputed: 'This is not a chair, it is a stool', 'How could one sit on this?', which draws the response, 'You do not sit, it is ornamental', and so on. The point that religions do not all share the same features does not detract from the descriptive value of the term. Jackson espouses the paradoxical position that expects words to have a determinate reference and then, after showing that they do not have a determinate reference, concludes that their usage must be provisional and qualified. But words can be meaningful and descriptive anyway: the fact that they do not have a determinate reference does not entail that we should be suspicious of their usage or use them only in a qualified way.

Why should general terms have precise rules for their application? Ambiguities and latitude of usage are characteristic of many terms, yet we do not caution against use of these terms or think that to use them immediately necessitates some kind of qualification. Take the terms liberalism, citizenship, values, politics or love: these are general terms, moreover they are abstract terms, like religion. Can we use these terms only in a provisional and qualified way? When one person says 'I love you', must it immediately be added that 'love' is being used in a qualified (or reified) way, because the sentiments and practices associated with love differ from person to person? Does everyone love in this *qualified* way?

Many of Jackson's reservations regarding the use of general terms to categorise and distinguish religions from each other reduce to his fear that general terms impose a false uniformity upon the beliefs and practices of religious believers. Thus to speak of 'Christianity' (as a general term) is to suggest and impose a uniformity of belief and practice upon 'Christians' that does not exist in reality. But, again, this reveals a failure to understand the way words and language are used.

Jackson mistakenly believes that a word is a self-contained unit of meaning; moreover, a unit of meaning that is unchanging in different contexts and over time. But the meaning of a word may change depending upon the context in which it is used. The meaning of Christianity in some particular context may be given not in a single isolated sentence but in the wider linguistic and conceptual context in which the word is used. Furthermore, we can use other words to clarify, to revise, and to interrogate what is meant.

It may be said that 'Christianity is a body of beliefs and practices that gain their meaning and justification by reference to God's revelation in the history of Israel and in his incarnation in the person of Christ, as these are authoritatively witnessed to in the Bible'. It can then be added that 'Christians are divided on certain matters', that 'not all Christians believe the same things' and then specify the matters on which there is disagreement and discuss the nature of this and its relevance to the identity of Christianity. In other contexts Christianity may be used to denote a form of spirituality that takes inspiration from the life and ministry of Jesus of Nazareth; it may be used to refer to certain political commitments, certain forms of worship, and so on. Jackson thinks that a word has the same determinate meaning in all the different contexts in which it is used and he wants to counteract this viewpoint by expressing reservations about the use of the word. This is unnecessary.

What Jackson fails to appreciate is that the same (imagined or constructed) 'problems' attach to the use of any abstract or general term – institution, education, ideology, friendship, sexuality, for example. The use of religious terms is not necessarily different from the use of other abstract terms or subject to greater ambiguity or confusion. Why would it follow, for example, that to speak of '*British* religious education' necessarily suggests to readers that there is unanimity of belief and uniformity of practice among British religious educators? Who thinks this? In any case, the wider context will make clear what degree of agreement actually exists among British religious educators and whether there is a distinctive set of beliefs and commitments shared by them.

Similarly, why would one think that to speak of Christianity presupposes that all Christians believe the same things? The meaning attached to Christianity is given in the way the term is used in particular contexts. None of this discussion means that the term Christianity may not properly denote a particular set of beliefs and values or describe the fact that most Christians agree on certain beliefs or that there is a set of beliefs and practices that characterise adherents of Christianity.

A further difficulty with Jackson's (implied) philosophy of language is that he views the emergence of vocabulary for the study of the religions as often betraying ideological motives and as attempts to impose uniformity on disparate collections of phenomena. This is the view he takes with regard to the emergence of the term 'religion', the names of the different religions and, more broadly, much of the vocabulary of religious studies. The irony is that the evolution of language and the emergence of new words is, in no insignificant part, a response to the awareness and recognition of difference and diversity. Words distinguish between objects and concepts and the emergence of new words and the use of new terms and vocabulary are directly intended to identify and denote difference: the wider the vocabulary of a society, the wider the range of difference and diversity that is recognised within it. Recognition of difference and diversity lies behind our ever expanding vocabulary. This is not something to bemoan, for the creation of new words and terms gives recognition to diversity.

The emergence of new terms and distinctions is a direct human response to our expanding understanding of diversity and our efforts to understand physical and social reality. In relation to religion, for example, we employ terms to distinguish between religious and cultural ideas, religions and ideologies, religious and secular activities; new terms and distinctions can denote new realities or bring fresh perspectives to bear on our understanding of reality. In fact the increasing expansion of vocabulary and creation of new classificatory systems in any discipline or field of study is frequently indicative of a deeper understanding of the nature of the subject, and increasingly 'fine grained' descriptions and interpretations accompany this.

Even our use of comparative and inclusive terms, upon examination, presupposes diversity and difference: to designate a set of beliefs and practices as a religion entails a distinction between religion and non-religion, out of which a concept of the secular and secularity emerges. It assumes a range of other differences between diverse cultural practices and phenomena that are 'sanctioned by the gods' – those that are forbidden and those that are religiously neutral; and it assumes a difference between natural and supernatural events. Further distinctions could be enumerated, but they all presuppose difference and diversity.

The individuating of different religions and their designation by different names draws attention to similarities and differences across cultures and across historical periods. The religions are, in part, individuated because they enshrine *different* beliefs about the divine, the nature and means of salvation, the after-life, the human condition and the nature of the good life. It is the diversity of religion that justifies speaking of different religions. If there were uniformity of religious belief and practice, there would be no need to distinguish beliefs and practices into separate categories; and of course one of the most important reasons for individuating religions is because their beliefs are incompatible with each other: if God is triune, he is not the *Sunyata* ('emptiness' or 'great void') of Mahayana Buddhism.

In addition, knowledge of religious diversity and its implications are historically conditioned. There was no Western name for Hinduism until Westerners came into cultural contact with Indians who held beliefs about the divine that differed from their own. These beliefs existed before Westerners arrived but it was only in the Western encounter with them that their difference (to Westerners) was known and appreciated, and consequently the term Hinduism began to be used as a category to identify and conceptualise these differences. The identification of different religions through the use of different names is rooted in diversity and difference.

Even the fact that particular words were first used by 'more powerful outsiders' (Jackson 1997: 276) tells us nothing about the appropriateness or the descriptive value of terms.[1] The term 'Christian', for example, was first used, as Jackson himself notes, by outsiders in Antioch to denote those who professed 'Jesus as

Lord' and regarded Jesus as God's agent of salvation, in fulfilment of Hebrew prophecy. Those who were not followers of Christ recognised the distinctive commitments of those who were followers of Christ and consequently coined a new descriptive term: a difference in belief, practice and worship was denoted by the use of a new word, 'Christian'. Most likely this new term was initially used in a pejorative way; nevertheless, it did identify and denote a new social grouping with distinctive 'religious' commitments.

In any case, words change in their use and reception: what was originally coined as a pejorative term may lose those connotations, while retaining other descriptive ones. It is also the case that originally neutral words may be applied in new ways and acquire pejorative connotations with some users but positive ones with others – the term *gay* as applied to 'a homosexual person', for example.

We now turn explicitly to Jackson's etymological survey of religious terms (appropriated from Smith 1978), which he uses to caution against 'uncritical' interpretations of religion that 'imagine' religions to be distinct 'wholes'(Jackson 1995: 276).[2] Incidentally, what neither Jackson nor Smith seems to appreciate is that shifts of meaning and usage of a term do not preclude continuity of reference. Religion may mean different things in different historical epochs while maintaining the same referent. Both seem to assume that a difference of meaning necessarily indicates a change of reference; hence for them 'conceptual ambiguity and confusion' attaches to the term 'religion'. From a philosophical viewpoint this is a highly controversial thesis that requires justification.

The problem with etymological reviews of the use of particular words and terms is that every word has a history and the meaning of most words changes over time. For example, the term *theology* is not found in the New Testament, and the Early Fathers used the term solely in a negative way because of its associations with non-Christian, mythical cults. It was the third century before the term was adopted and used positively by Christians to denote their own commitments and beliefs (see Bayer and Peters 1998). Theology has carried different connotations over the centuries. Equally, as Jackson notes, the term religion has had different historical connotations: personal piety, an overt system of beliefs, an empirical phenomenon, a set of ritual practices, and so on. None of this entails that current usage is confused or ambiguous.

To show how words acquire their original meaning, from whom, and how meanings change over time, tell us nothing about the validity of their contemporary application and their descriptive or interpretive value. The theory of evolution would still be true if it had originated as Nazi propaganda, and its distinctive terminology would still retain its explanatory role! Recognition of this has relevance to Jackson's observation that the names of some of the different religions were originally given by 'more powerful' outsiders. Nothing interesting philosophically follows from this. It may be that the name of a religion was usefully applied, then and now, to conceptualise and systematise certain aspects of social reality and to denote something distinctive. It may be that it was not usefully applied, then or now. But this is a different matter and requires justification and argument; it does not follow from recitation of the history of usage.

The concept of religion as denoting a set of beliefs and practices is effectively denied by Jackson's emphasis on internal diversity. He acknowledges, for example, that the term Christianity can be used, though in a provisional way only, for Christians espouse and construct different interpretations of life. In relation to 'Christian groups' (he deliberately does not use the word Christianity in this context), he tells us, there are 'shifting and contesting interpretations of key symbols *within* each' group (1997: 79). To which Christian groups is he referring? Are there 'Christian groups' that deny the existence of God or the role of Jesus in mediating salvation? To speak of key symbols in this context undermines his own argument, for to admit that there are 'key symbols' is precisely to concede the point that there are certain beliefs that are central to the identity of Christians, even though there may be some latitude of interpretation of these symbols.

Jackson seeks to support his denial of the existence of 'religious wholes' by maintaining that religions such as Christianity are more than 'schemes of belief'. Of course religions are more than schemes of belief; they are ways of life that embody beliefs, practices, attitudes and emotions. But religions are, at least, schemes of belief; and in certain contexts are appropriately described as such. If the argument of earlier chapters is convincing then beliefs are constitutive not only of a religious way of life but of all ways of life; what we think, say, do, and experience follows from what we believe. For example, it makes no sense to describe Christian worship in church without an appreciation that worship centres on God and certain beliefs about God and his revelation, his relationship to humankind, and so on.

There are key beliefs in each religion. It is these key beliefs and the differences between them that justify distinguishing between the different religions. One should not describe someone who does not believe in the central beliefs of a religion as an adherent of that religion. Saying this opens up educational and classroom opportunities for exploring the nature of religious commitment and for recognising the distinctions that can be drawn between forms of commitment and their relationship to religious identity; for example, the distinction between full commitment and nominal commitment, or the issue of individuals who identify with a religion for cultural, economic or political reasons but who do not share the beliefs that their outward behaviour or profession suggests, and so on.

Jackson excoriates 'essentialised' views of religion in education. Presumably such a view of a religion is one that regards certain beliefs as central or essential to it. At no point does he expand upon this criticism and illustrate what an essentialised view of any particular religion, religious tradition or religious community looks like. Is the following an essentialised view of Islam: 'There is no God but Allah and Muhammad is his prophet'? Can one be a Muslim and deny that Muhammad is the final prophet of God, implicit in which is the view that Muhammad received revelations from God that are now contained in the

Qur'an? Christians confess that 'Jesus is Lord': is this belief essential to Christianity? Certainly the early Christians regarded this confession and the beliefs and commitments that follow from it as distinctive of their identity and community.

What Jackson needs to do, if he rejects the idea of 'essentialised' versions of religions, is to tell us what one of these looks like, in respect to a particular religion, and then contrast this with a 'non-essentialised' version of the kind he thinks should be conveyed through religious education. The critical question that follows is whether his non-essentialised versions are representative of how adherents view their religious commitments or carefully crafted versions that reflect Jackson's own interpretation of the different religions.

What about Jackson's strictures (1997: 126) against viewing religions as distinct or 'coherent wholes'? If by denying that religions are distinct wholes he wants to draw attention to the fact that religions are historically and theologically related, the point is well taken, though uncontroversial. Almost all students of religion are aware of the different ways religions have influenced each other, sometimes directly, sometimes indirectly, sometimes obviously, sometimes less obviously, and so on. This is not, however, Jackson's central contention, which is that religious wholes are 'artificial constructions from the experiences of individuals' (1997: 45). What would be a *natural* construction of the experiences of individuals? At this point Jackson is getting very close to endorsing a Cartesian inspired account of the relationship between mind, language and reality that is the target of Wittgenstein's 'private language' argument in the *Investigations* (1958). Each individual espouses a personal interpretation of a religious tradition but there is no collective public form of interpretation – though a collective term can be used provisionally before advancing to an appreciation of the deep diversity that falsifies all statements of a general nature.

If there are, properly speaking, no such things as religious wholes, then presumably there are also no such things as non-religious wholes: there is no Marxism, no liberalism, no humanism, no conservatism, and no fundamentalism; no set of ideas and beliefs that are central to these ideologies or that are usefully categorised under these conventional names. Presumably, there are just Marxists, liberals, humanists: but how are they identified? The irony is that on a number of occasions Jackson refers confidently to different worldviews and to overlapping worldviews (1997: 91). Clearly people do not overlap in any kind of literal sense – when he speaks of overlapping worldviews he means that they share certain beliefs, and, it should be added, while disagreeing over other beliefs. At no point does he state that worldviews are 'provisional', 'abstractions or reifications'.

If there is such a thing as a worldview, which Jackson admits, it makes sense to enquire about its distinctive beliefs, for without those there is no way of distinguishing one worldview from another. If Marxists believed in a free competitive market, in private ownership, in the pursuit of profit, and so on, there would be no need to distinguish between Marxism and capitalism as economic ideologies. It makes sense to ask about the nature and content of worldviews. If they exist, why do religions not exist? A religion can be conceptualised as a worldview that includes some reference to the divine.

The denial by Jackson that religions are 'coherent wholes' divorces the study of religion, at any level of education, from critical issues and questions about the coherence of religious systems of belief that have been and are central to philosophical approaches to religion. There should be a place within religious education for critical philosophical study of the different religions and this necessarily includes the extent to which their beliefs are internally coherent (and one may add, consistent with what we know about these and other matters from diverse sources). The problem of suffering, for example, essentially focuses on the coherence of certain theistic beliefs – that God is all-good, all-powerful, and all-knowing – and their compatibility with the existence of evil and suffering in the world.

Coherence between a set of propositions is typically regarded as a precondition of their collective truth, and for this reason is regarded as a principle of rationality. If religions are not coherent wholes, and should not be regarded as coherent wholes, then much of the enterprise of the philosophy of religion as historically practised rests on a mistake. It is possible that religious people hold inconsistent beliefs or that all religious beliefs systems are internally incoherent at some point, though this is not what Jackson is claiming: his is the equally controversial assertion that there is no set of beliefs *shared* by adherents of the same religious worldview that can be assessed for their coherence; as he says, 'the internal diversity of religious traditions challenges the existence of religions as coherent wholes' (126).

What is missing in Jackson's representation of religion in an interpretive approach, and a matter already touched on, is any appreciation of the role and significance of sacred wrings in the religions and the authority accorded to claims to divine revelation. Religious beliefs, attitudes, practices and behaviour are often grounded in claims to revelation from God, appeals to the Qur'an, the Hebrew Bible and the New Testament, for example. Religious believers regulate their lives on the basis of what they believe to be revealed in their scriptures.

However, the role of revelation, creeds and confessions of faith in determining religious identity and fostering a sense of community is effectively denied by Jackson's account of an interpretative approach. There is a normative and prescriptive element in all religions and religious traditions and this element is omitted from Jackson's approach to religious education. Moreover, it is this prescriptive element that determines the boundaries both of religious identity and of religious diversity within particular religions. The religions are fluid and flexible, but within limits, for not every belief is compatible with the key beliefs that are regarded as derived from revelation by adherents. Religions have boundaries; and while these may shift and be contested, this does not mean that boundaries are infinitely extendible or contractible. The beliefs of Christianity, established by reference to the Christian scriptures, restrict and constrain Christian identity. The beliefs and practices of Islam, established by reference to the Qur'an, restrict and constrain Muslim identity. Jackson needs to represent the religions as they are actually believed and practised and not as he wants them to be – sets of variation on a cultural theme.

The critical question to ask is: why does Jackson fail to appreciate the constitutive role of belief in religion and why does he espouse such anti-intuitive positions that the names of the different religions should not be regarded as connoting certain beliefs or practices and that religions are not (minimally) coherent belief systems? The answer is given in a few isolated passages scattered throughout his writings, but some of the remarks he makes in *Religious Education: An Interpretative Approach* (1997) are more explicit. In the context of criticising the concept of individuating religions on the basis of their beliefs and regarding religions as 'systems of belief' that emerged historically in the seventeenth and eighteenth centuries, Jackson identifies the social consequences that followed. 'This concept', he tells us, '*reflected* and *stimulated religious conflict* and was used both to delineate groups within Christianity and to classify and encompass what was perceived to be equivalent material in non-Christian cultures encountered by the West' (1997: 60; my emphasis). (What this historical aside fails to note is that religious division and conflict in many cases emerges within a group and only afterwards are labels assigned to distinguish the opponents into rival camps.) Some pages earlier he expresses dissatisfaction with using the term '*world religions*', for it conveys the view that religions have a 'universal message' and consequently 'a universal mission' (1997: 53): different *universal* missions obviously accentuate the difference between religions and throw their competitive nature into sharp relief.

In the final chapter, Jackson returns directly to the theme of competition in religion, in the context of a defence of interpretive religious education against the charge of reductionism: after quoting from the 1947 West Riding Agreed Syllabus, he adds that '[t]he key [negative] point here is that other "religions" are considered as separate systems, with similar structures and *in competition with each other*' (1997: 127; my emphasis). To regard the religions as species of a single genus, according to Jackson, raises the issue of competition between them, for, as individually distinguished within a wider essential definition, it becomes possible to compare religions and for adherents of one religion to regard themselves as superior to others (see 1997: 127). This, in turn, provides fertile ground for intolerance to become a feature of the relationship between adherents of different religions or of different branches of religions.

With this understanding in mind we are now in a position to appreciate more fully Jackson's reluctance to assign any real significance to the belief systems of the religions: a focus on contrasting sets of beliefs (which purport to 'reveal' the same divine being and mediate salvation) highlights differences and draws attention to the fact that these may be intractable, and consequently one or other may be true and others false, or perhaps one more true and others less true in certain respects. In an important sense the religions are in competition with one another over the nature of reality (they enshrine and express different truth claims), just as they are in competition with secular worldviews (there either is a God or there is no God; both claims cannot be true). Jackson's interpretation of the religions minimises this aspect of religious reality because he fears the strife and division that occurs as a result of religious competition. What he has failed to appreciate, and what our analysis in Chapter 2 shows about the nature of diversity in relation to possible conflict, is that any perceived difference can be used as a justification for prejudice and violence. Jackson, like Hull, bases his recommendations for religious education on too narrow an understanding of the nature of diversity and difference and of the potential ways perceived differences can give rise to prejudice and intolerance.

It is the failure to identify and address the contrary teachings of the different religions, and therefore the competitive element between religions, that vitiates Jackson's treatment of the issue of truth in religion. He refers to truth claims in religion but what he says, within the context of his work as a whole, is best construed as referring to claims that individuals advance about their own interpretation of religion and not to truth claims that enshrine and express the set of beliefs of some particular religion or religious tradition. His denial of the religions as coherent schemes of belief leaves no place for a consideration of the truth of the different religions, and the reason for this neglect is, as argued above, that he seems to regards the idea of religions competing against each other as likely to create tension and strife, even conflict, in society.

The final criticism focuses on the contribution of interpretive religious education to the moral and social aims of education. Jackson conceives the role of religious education in the curriculum, and of interpretive religious education in particular, as contributing significantly to 'reducing racial and cultural prejudice' (1995: 273). He is not concerned with representing the moral teaching of the different religions in education or with imparting moral beliefs and values, at least as this has traditionally been understood as conveying definite moral commitments across the range of personal and social issues. He is concerned with the need for pupils to respect the rights and viewpoints of others. The contribution of religious education to moral education is procedural, not substantive; this is a position that reflects much post-confessional religious education in Britain. (A full discussion of the relationship of religious education to moral education follows in the next chapter.)

One of the attractions of an interpretive approach, and the reason why it has been applied to citizenship education and to intercultural education, is precisely its claim to remove the barriers to positive personal and social relationships. The obvious question to begin with is to ask if there is any empirical evidence that confirms that an interpretive approach is more successful than other pedagogies in enabling pupils to live respectfully and responsibly in pluralist societies. This is not meant as a criticism as such, for an appeal for empirical evidence in this case obviously raises a number of challenges for researchers; and to some extent it may even be conceded that interpretative and critical issues may enter into the assessment of any evidence produced. A pertinent question focuses on whether the aim of enabling pupils to gain an *understanding* of diversity exhausts the contribution of religious education to the social aims of education in general. Is understanding diversity enough or should religious education be more direct in challenging prejudice in society? The view, which is advanced in the final chapter, is that religious education can and should be more direct and pro-active in challenging prejudice, intolerance and discrimination; this presumes that there are reasons for thinking that an understanding of the nature of diversity along the lines that Jackson pursues is incapable of achieving the results he expects.

What is it about Jackson's interpretive approach that enables it, he believes, to serve the educational needs of pupils in multicultural societies and to achieve the moral and social aims of education more effectively than other pedagogies of religious education? He does not explain exactly how this approach works to lessen prejudice, though what he does say in different places can be pieced together and extrapolated in a way that reflects its natural logic to provide an overview of how and why he believes an interpretive approach facilitates good personal and social relationships.

The place to begin is with his (now familiar) interpretation of religion and his repeatedly expressed reservations about 'individuating religions' and distinguishing them from each other (1997: 60). Religions, for him, are not coherent wholes or schemes of belief or separate and distinctive; for given the pervasiveness and depth of diversity there are no formal schemes of belief to oppose each other. There are only personal interpretations of 'religious traditions' and these lack sufficient agreement with other personal interpretations to allow anyone to speak confidently of public interpretations of religions that are widely shared and coherent, though there may be some degree of family resemblances between interpretations. Note again, his denial that religions are 'coherent wholes'. The implication is that religions do not *formally* contradict each other because, under his analysis, they are deconstructed into personal interpretations with different commitments, beliefs, emphases and values. These interpretations may overlap, connect and even contradict each other, but they lack substantive form. For example, there is no Christian religion or set of beliefs constitutive of Christian identity, rather there are Christians who share some ideas and beliefs with others Christians, disagree in other respects, share ideas with adherents of some other religion or worldview, disagree at points, and so on.

Jackson can happily acknowledge that some people view their personal interpretation of religion as true and exclusive, and it is this acknowledgement that allows him to profess that an interpretive approach takes account of the concept of truth in religion. What he does not countenance is that the different religions doctrinally oppose each other in a direct way and this is because, as he tells us, there are no coherent religious schemes of belief, or alternatively, and more modestly, in line with his implicit nominalism, there are some individuals within a tradition who claim coherence for their set of beliefs but their particular claim enjoys no more authority or degree of support than other interpretations. In a sense, the contrary teachings of the different religions and any competition between them (and also the competition with non-religious worldviews) 'die the death of a thousand interpretations': diversity is everywhere. Each individual has his or her own personal perspective on religion but, because these personal perspectives lack consistency of belief and commitment, there are no proper public religions to which people owe their allegiance and around which people can construct identities that formally challenge other identities. The degree of diversity within traditions ensures that there are no religions or religious wholes to disagree and therefore the possibility of community division over religion dissolves. There is a certain irony in this position: diversity gives rise to the 'construction' of separate identities, which can view each other competitively; and diversity, in turn, deconstructs the idea of separate identities, for identities are contested, fluid, shifting, impermanent, and relative.

For Jackson, religious diversity is similar in form to cultural diversity. Historically, people from one culture looked disapprovingly on people from other cultures: one's own culture was regarded as superior. Implicit in this judgement was the idea that cultures are separate, unchanging and coherent wholes. It is now realised, after reflection, bitter disputes and conflicts, that cultures are interconnected, interdependent, fluid and fragmented. Realisation of this undermines ('deconstructs') imperial and colonial ideas of cultural superiority. Jackson views religious superiority in a similar light. Historically, people from one religion looked disapprovingly on people from other religions; one's own religion was, and still is by some, regarded as superior. Implicit in this judgement is the idea that religions are separate, unchanging and coherent wholes. It is now realised, after reflection, bitter disputes and conflicts, that religions are interconnected, interdependent, fluid and fragmented. . . and that religions, like cultures, are patchwork affairs, with no overall, fixed patterns (which in the past were used to compare religions and create a simple binary distinction between one true religion and all the other false ones). But if religions are not like cultures in all important respects, as has been argued here, then he has provided neither a fully convincing interpretation of the nature of diversity nor a fully convincing strategy for challenging prejudice and intolerance.

The final irony in Jackson's account of an interpretive approach is that he does not take sufficient account of diversity: all forms of diversity are accommodated but not the (religious) form that traces its teachings to revelation and inspires followers of religions to seek to build a community in faithfulness to these teachings. The normative quality of the religious life is not sufficiently acknowledged by Jackson. At this important point his interpretive approach has failed to capture the nature of religion, and failure at this point, all other strengths apart, seriously undermines the effectiveness of an interpretive approach to realise the moral and social aims of liberal education.

Notes

1 The binary distinction between 'insiders'/'outsiders' needs to be questioned in this context.
2 In contrast to Smith, who uses his etymological survey of religious terms to identify the generic element of faith in all religious traditions.

14

RELIGIOUS EDUCATION AND MORAL EDUCATION

In a recent study of curriculum development in English religious education, which adopts a case study approach, Stephen Parker and Rob Freathy (2011) traced the changing nature and content of religious education through a close analysis of successive Birmingham Agreed Syllabuses from the 1970s until the present. In the context of their discussion they noted that a linkage between religious education and moral education has 'often been deliberately disassociated [by religious educators and others] from the 1960s onwards' (2011: 258). This is a perceptive observation by two highly respected historians of religious education in England and Wales. Unfortunately the context militated against any further discussion or illustration of the way in which British religious education became detached from moral education. Nevertheless, their comment alerts us to an inherent weakness in post-confessional religious education in Britain; namely, it fails to justify an essential role for religious education in the moral education of pupils.

The chief aim of this chapter is to reconnect religious education with moral education and to provide a principled justification for the inclusion of moral content in religious education. The reason for this is not simply to make the point that moral practice is central to religion (and that for religious believers morality is essentially related to religion) but also to illustrate the potential contribution of religious moralities to both personal development and the social development of communities. Naturally, an argument along these lines relates to and expresses the wider case for the adoption of a new post-liberal model of religious education, as well as giving specific direction and content to such a model.

In straightforward terms, a model of religious education that provides the educational and intellectual resources to support and reaffirm the important role of moral education within religious education has an advantage over current models that (as Parker and Freathy note above) disassociate them. Within this general orientation, a number of subsidiary aims are also pursued. Attention is given to showing how the disassociation of religious and moral education came about. The focus here is not chiefly historical, if by this is meant assembling the facts and identifying the historical steps whereby religious education and moral education, for the most part, went their separate ways, rather it is genealogical – in this instance to uncover the beliefs and commitments that initiated and consolidated the separation, albeit through their historical manifestation and sequence. A further aim is to explain why the disassociation of religious education from moral education is a necessary outcome and feature of successive models, both liberal and postmodern, of post-confessional British religious education.

The argument of this chapter is structured in the following way. First, attention is given to the 'modern' narrative of English religious education and the different ways in which the contribution of non-confessional religious education to moral education has been conceptualised and practised. What this genealogical review reveals is that the role of moral education in religious education, as envisaged by educators from the 1970s until the present, has been largely procedural and formal, and overlooks not only the moral content of the different religions but much of the potential that religion brings to the enterprise of moral education. In a second section, the negative thesis that post-confessional religious education is largely disassociated from moral education is further developed, qualified and defended. Third, the case is made for the role and importance of religious education in the moral development and moral education of pupils; it is argued that the notion that morality and religion are discrete domains of human experience, which has provided the intellectual framework for diminishing the moral content and ambitions of religious education, is controversial philosophically and contrasts with the way many religious believers construe the relationship between morality and religion. Finally, there is a short exploration of the ways in which the religious and moral content of the different religions can contribute to the personal and moral development of pupils and to the social development of communities. This last section takes advantage of the 2007 Birmingham Agreed Syllabus for Religious Education and its attempt to reconnect religious with moral education.

A genealogical account of the contribution of post-confessional religious education to moral education

How did the discourse of autonomous moral 'knowledge' come to displace and supplant religious interpretations of morality and religious morality in religious education? The crucial document in this regard is *Working Paper 36* (Schools Council 1971), the position of which on this matter was discussed in Chapter 5. It was concluded there that the combined effect of the phenomenology of religion's identification of religious experience with the essence of religion and uncritical endorsement of analytical philosophy's divorce of morality from religion was to re-orientate religious education around exclusively religious content and to diminish the role of religious education in the provision of moral education.

If religion cannot provide a foundation for morality, contrary to what most religious educators had formerly assumed, what contribution could religious education make to the moral and social aims of education? The answer (given the logical independence of morality from religion thesis) is that religious education may provide and encourage religious motivation for attitudes and actions that express values and beliefs that can claim an exclusively moral justification. On this understanding, religious education can support secular norms of behaviour in a variety of ways, say by reinforcing the point that secular norms of behaviour are also demanded by God, or by noting that morally good behaviour is pleasing to God or that God will reward good behaviour, and so on. On this understanding the role of moral education within religious education is reconceived as endorsing those moral beliefs and values that are enjoined by secular approaches to moral education.

In the post-confessional history of religious education in Britain three basic interpretations or accounts of the contribution of religious education to moral education can be distinguished. Consistent with the commitments of phenomenological religious education and of secular moral philosophy, all assign a diminished role to the moral content of religion and to the moral ambitions of religious education when compared with confessional religious education. Each, in part, represents a distinctive conception of morality and of the needs of society in relation to moral education in schools. The three accounts are historically successive in influence, though later accounts do not entirely eclipse the influence of earlier accounts.

The first form of moral education in religious education that succeeded confessional religious education can be characterised as the *multicultural account*. While admitting greater internal diversity than the Christian-cultural account that it superseded, it broadly viewed acquaintance with the diversity of religions as a means to develop tolerance, understanding and mutual respect among Britain's increasingly diverse cultural and religious population. One of the reasons given by *Working Paper 36* in favour of the adoption of a phenomenological approach by religious educators was the potential it was believed to hold for challenging discrimination and fostering positive relations between different individuals and communities. We are told that the phenomenological approach enables pupils to gain a 'sympathetic understanding of the inner life' of others (Schools Council 1971: 23), which in turn fosters an appreciation of religious difference. Accordingly, religious educators believed themselves to be contributing significantly to the creation of an inclusive society. In this form of moral education, religious education moves away from prescribing specific forms of morality and advocating certain life-styles to commending acceptance of 'the religious other'.

That the multicultural account was less effective in combating religious intolerance than was anticipated was beginning to be recognised by the late

1970s, and this, in part, along with increasing political and social awareness of the growing challenge of criminal and anti-social behaviour by young people, underlined the need for a more effective and significant role for education in the provision of moral education. Identified associations between spirituality and certain attitudes and dispositions that are regarded as conducive to positive conduct gave impetus to the emergence of what can be called a *spirituality account* of the contribution of religious education to moral education.

The concept of spirituality was perceived as providing a number of advantages over the traditional emphasis upon the different world religions in religious education. First, the language of spirituality, with its inherent ambiguity, is more inclusive in range than the term religion and its cognates. This means both that non-religious forms of spirituality can be incorporated into religious education, and hence conceivably contribute to the moral education of non-religious pupils, and that religious education cannot be accused of favouring one religion over another, or indeed favouring religion over non-religious beliefs and values.

Second, the concept and language of spirituality is thought by many religious educators to draw attention to non-dogmatic, experiential forms of religion (as in Hay 1998), which are viewed as inherently more tolerant and conducive to social harmony than doctrinal (dogmatic) forms of religion. Such an opinion reflects the liberal theological commitments that undergird much post-confessional religious education in Britain; it also, unfortunately, in part, helps to perpetuate the tradition in modern English religious education of ignoring the controversial issue of competing religious truth claims in the classroom (a feature which has already been the subject of criticism in earlier chapters). In addition, it raises the critical question about whether such a strategy is appropriate in a cultural context where many people disagree fundamentally about religion: is ignoring this issue the best strategy? According to its supporters, spirituality contributes to moral development by seeking to enhance the dispositions of love, sympathy and responsibility that they believe provide the mainspring for moral action, while simultaneously refusing to elevate any particular morality or any particular moral stance over others. Critics, by contrast, point out that, by favouring and perpetuating liberal forms of religion, spiritual development effectively overlooks the moral content of the different religions and concedes priority to secular morality in both the personal and public realms.

The third and final form of the relationship of moral education to religious education is the *civic account*. This emerged in the first years of the twenty-first century, subsequent to the introduction of citizenship as a school subject by the then Labour Government (the Citizenship Order of 2000). According to this understanding, public education should be concerned with the creation of good citizens and not with the private lives and behaviour of individuals. What matters is adherence to the law. The law, *per se*, is not concerned with personal morality (often disparagingly referred to as 'private' morality) but with social morality. A 'good' citizen obeys the laws of the land and respects the rights of others. A number of religious educators, Mark Chater (2000), for example, have claimed that religious education provides an ideal vehicle for furthering the citizenship agenda.

The civic account, however, has a number of serious weaknesses (in this context problems relating to the epistemological and ontological status of rights will be overlooked; see Warnock 1998: 54–74.) The first weakness questions the assumption that a focus within religious education upon social responsibility and citizenship, without attention to issues of personal morality and 'private' virtue, is likely to yield the desired improvements in public morality (construed as obedience to the law) and political participation. A plausible empirical case can be made for the view that those who are socially responsible are precisely the same people who adhere to high standards of personal morality. Personal behaviour and social responsibility are related, for morality is of a piece. Furthermore, it is the personal aspects of morality that provide the foundation for social morality: it is the commitments, values, beliefs and positive emotions that are cultivated and educated in the immediate and wider family, and subsequently reinforced in social situations and social institutions, that for the most part determine the character and practice of social responsibility. To ask schools to attend to social responsibility and to overlook its foundation in personal morality is to misconceive the nature of morality; and consequently to risk disappointment when the focus in schools on social morality alone fails to translate into increasing levels of social responsibility.

The second weakness relates to the observation that a rights-based approach to moral education provides only a minimum level of moral commitment, and that this level of moral commitment falls short of what is required for a stable, cohesive and respectful society. There is a clear distinction between what is good for individuals and for society and the legal and moral rights that individuals enjoy. For example, a society in which both parents take long-term responsibility for the well-being of their children would be a better society (overall) than one in which many children are born into single-parent households or households where the mother has serial, short-term (personally irresponsible) partners, given that statistics show the devastating effects on children of being brought up in such contexts (see Social Justice Policy Group 2006). Furthermore, not all immoral acts and instances of bad or irresponsible behaviour are regarded as criminal offences (or matters of public morality in the strict sense of attracting formal disadvantage or punishment).

As a society we choose to enshrine some 'goods' in legislation, say protection against unfair dismissal from work or a right to education, and allow individuals to choose other goods for themselves, say the viewing of pornography or the right to smoke in one's own home. In Britain we criminalise some activities (such as prostitution, which some other societies legalise and regulate), but allow married individuals to divorce or pursue extra-marital sexual liaisons if they so choose. The simple point is that the existence of a right may not necessarily mean that the right ought (morally) to be exercised, because it does not guarantee the morality of its exercise. To have a right to divorce does not mean that divorce is a good thing or that it yields positive effects for children or for society at large, though on occasions it may be the lesser of two evils. The realm of rights is not identical with the realm of morality and moral goodness (though there is overlap). The rights you enjoy as a citizen should not all be exercised and some certainly may be exercised in pursuits of dubious moral worth that are detrimental to society at large. If this is the case then citizenship education with its orientation to rights is necessarily inadequate as a vehicle for creating a good society for all. A society in which everyone was extended courtesy and respect by others would be a better society than one in which this does not occur, yet the kind of courtesy and respect that most people would like to receive cannot be legally required.

Basically, a good society, where individuals and communities are valued and respected, is a society that requires the practice of a much 'thicker' conception of morality (see Williams 1985: 140–143) than that required by adherence to and observance of human rights. If religious education is to contribute to the creation of a good society, where communities live harmoniously with each other, it needs to attend to the development of personal and social virtues in pupils that extend beyond the realm of legally mandated morality of the form consistent with the observance of human rights. In other words, if religious education is serious about its commitment to the development of toleration and respect for others, it must extend its moral and social aspirations beyond the narrow realm of rights and their observance. To recast the social aims of religious education in terms of 'respect' for human rights alone is effectively to overlook much of the potential religious education brings to moral education.

Refining and defending the argument

Part of the legacy of non-confessional religious education in England is ambiguity about the role of religion (and of course religious education) in moral education. On the one hand, under phenomenology, religious education was relieved of the 'burden' of moral education, whereas on the other, the focus on explicitly religious phenomena, to the exclusion of a consideration of moral issues and the moral content of religion, led to disinterest among many older pupils. Under phenomenology, religious educators gained confidence in the belief that their subject demarcated a distinctive area of content in the curriculum, yet this confidence was eroded by recognition that in an increasingly secular and multicultural society the worth of religious education in schools is often judged by its contribution to the wider moral and social aims of education and the needs of the community. As phenomenological religious education was refined and complemented by other methodologies, so the sharp distinction (maintained by *Working Paper 36*) that divorced religious education from moral education came to be qualified and blurred. Theoretically, religious education was distinct from moral education; practically, it committed itself to the shifting moral and social agenda of the liberal nation state in efforts to ensure its educational relevance and continuing compulsory status in the curriculum. This contradiction lies at the heart of English religious education in its relationship to moral education and explains why we have the 'anomalous' situation where religious education, despite its theoretical stance, purports to contribute to the moral aims of education, while overlooking the moral content and teachings of the different religions.

Any argument that identifies a schizophrenic attitude towards moral education at the heart of religious education in England will obviously attract criticism from religious educators. Objections will naturally focus on questioning the contention that post-confessional religious education largely relinquished its responsibility for the moral education and moral development of pupils. A number of objections along these lines will be considered, and in the process of responding, the argument will be further clarified and refined.

Some critics of the view that the moral contribution of the different religions to moral education has largely been overlooked may point out that Ninian Smart combined his support of phenomenological religious education with a dimensional account of the nature of religion that identified an ethical (or moral) dimension alongside other dimensions. Furthermore, in the curricular materials produced by the Schools Council Project on Religious Education in the Secondary School, which Smart directed, some attention is given to both moral issues and the moral dimension of religion. These observations, however, are not particularly telling. The point is that the disassociation of religious education from moral education *is* consistent with the assumptions and commitments of the phenomenological approach to religious education, as has already been noted. In keeping with this, as the phenomenological approach gained ascendancy in schools during the 1970s, so the focus of religious education increasingly came to be upon explicitly religious material, with little attention or seriousness attached to the moral teachings of the different religions. This judgement is confirmed by reference to the locally produced agreed syllabuses of religious education that were produced in the 1970s and 1980s, most of which adopted and commended a phenomenological methodology.

If the contribution of religious education to moral education is defined in traditional terms of acquainting pupils with the moral teaching of the different religions and in exploring the moral beliefs and values of religion as they relate to contemporary moral and social issues, or in presenting to pupils a vision of the form a moral life might take when religiously sanctioned and inspired, then clearly judged in these terms religious education has disassociated itself from moral education. One further piece of evidence that supports this view is that by the 1980s some religious educators were already beginning to question the appropriateness of the phenomenological approach on the grounds that it neglected the personal and *moral* dimensions of education, as well as ignoring the pupil's quest for meaning and significance (see Cox 1983: 131–135; Slee 1989: 130–131).

A more serious challenge to the contention that non-confessional religious education largely renounced its role in moral education is that it not so much renounced its role as redefined and reconceptualised it. Moreover, is this not the true position of Smart? Although he argued that moral education should be a separate school subject from religious education (because morality is independent of religion), he also believed that multi-faith phenomenological religious education challenged religious intolerance and fostered positive attitudes to religious diversity. According to this narrative, religious education has been in the forefront of championing moral issues in education. Is this not what our genealogical review of the relationship of religious education to moral education reveals? There are two issues here: one empirical, the other conceptual and interpretative.

Is there any evidence to show that religious education has been successful in achieving the moral and social aims of education? Unfortunately, we do not have any direct evidence, chiefly because the relevant research has not been undertaken and because there are conceptual matters relating to such research that are not easily resolved. There is some evidence, however, that is relevant, though difficult to access. We have already referred to Penny Jennings's large-scale questionnaire survey in 2004 of pupils' attitudes towards RE (see Chapter 1, Table 1.1); at this point our interest is confined to her findings with regard to pupils' attitudes toward the moral aspects of the subject. In response to the statement 'RE helps me to find rules to live by', 14% responded positively, 60% negatively and 26% of pupils were unsure; in response to the statement 'RE helps me to sort out my problems', the respective responses were 8%, 73% and 19%; and finally, to the statement 'RE helps me to lead a better life', 9% only responded positively (68% negatively and 23% unsure).

What is the most reasonable explanation of these findings? There are two possibilities, both of which can be regarded as lending support to the thesis that post-confessional religious education is *disassociated* from moral education and the moral development of pupils: either religious education aims to contribute significantly to the moral development of pupils, but for the most part fails, or religious education does not aim (or at least is not perceived by pupils) to contribute to their moral development. To this may be added statistics that show that there are high levels of drug and alcohol abuse and criminal and anti-social behaviour (at least high compared with statistics for the 1960s) among young adults (see Social Justice Policy Group 2006). We also know that mental health problems, depression and suicide among the young remain at stubbornly high levels (Scowcrof 2012). How such statistics can be related to education and the influence or otherwise of moral education in schools is another matter. What can be said is that the moral influence on pupils of religious education is not all that obvious, and what evidence there is does not inspire confidence. In one sense this should not surprise us, given our genealogical review of the different understandings of the specific role and contribution of religious education to moral education and the range of weaknesses there identified. Post-confessional religious education, in all probability, contributes little to the moral development of pupils because it pursues largely ineffective policies and construes the relationship in ways that at best minimise the contribution of religion to moral education and at worst undermine the contribution of religion and religious education to moral education.

Attention to our genealogical review of the different post-confessional forms of moral education in religious education also reveals a further disquieting feature that reinforces the earlier observation that the moral teaching and traditions of the different religions are largely overlooked in schools. Attention to the aims of the different accounts of moral education in religious education shows there is no intrinsic connection between the content of religious education and the moral aims educators seek to realise. The religion of Christianity may be used to illustrate this.

The moral and spiritual aims of Christianity do not centre on producing good citizens or on encouraging reflection on spiritual matters; instead they focus on the need for Christians to emulate the character of Christ and to practise justice and righteousness. Christian spirituality begins with recognition that individuals become acceptable to God by virtue of his grace and that moral obedience without faith in God is, in religious terms, not efficacious. Christian spirituality and morality are concerned with inspiring and encouraging those who trust in Christ for their salvation to obey the moral precepts of the New Testament. It is not that Christians are unspiritual or make poor citizens; it is that Christian spirituality and morality centre on loyalty to God, not on loyalty to the nation state and its evolving legal norms.

The wider point is that when religious education pursues moral aims and seeks to contribute to the moral development of pupils, it fails to connect with the actual beliefs and values of the different religions that are the proper subject matter of religious education. More critically, when religious education pursues moral education, religion is reduced to a set of formal moral principles that mirror secular morality (as in the Chichester project on teaching Christianity; see Minton 1987). Religious beliefs and values are instrumental to the aims of secular moral education. Basically, religious morality is not allowed to speak its own voice in education but is required to mirror the truncated 'moral' aims of the secular state.

The reappropriation of moral education by religious education

How can the schizophrenic stance towards moral education at the heart of religious education in Britain be overcome? The first step is to reconnect the two in a fully principled and educationally justified way. Two possibilities suggest themselves.

The first strategy is to take up the point that one of the central aims of religious education is to understand the nature of religion. What it is to understand a religion is not uncontroversial, but whatever form a broad-ranging form of understanding takes, it must include an appreciation of the way (or ways) that religious adherents interpret their respective traditions and beliefs – and clearly, they connect their beliefs and values to practices and behaviour that embrace and express moral commitments. Each of the religions has a vision of the good both for the individual and for society; each of the religions has a historically evolving body of moral teachings; and each of the religions has made important responses to contemporary moral issues.

The critical question is, why should those who hold to the independence of morality from religion have the right to conform representations of religion in religious education to their particular beliefs, as historically has been the case? The view that religion and morality are intimately connected in some substantive philosophical sense is one shared by many Christians, Jews and Muslims, and this 'democratic' mandate is the crucial point for educational purposes. There may even be a case for concluding that because secular commitments enjoy unopposed dominance in all other aspects of the curriculum, in religious education the primacy of the believer's perspective in the study of the subject should be privileged (though not in such a way as to exclude critical engagement and evaluation of religious truth claims).

The second strategy is to note that the view that morality and religion are ontologically separate no longer commands the same degree of philosophical support as it once did. Is the independence of morality from religion one of the assured results of (analytic) philosophy? Certainly, at the level of practice morality and religion are linked. Religions, for the most part, enjoin moral behaviour. A positive connection between religion and moral practice, however, is not relevant to the sense in which philosophers maintain that the two are independent; their point is epistemological or logical. They contend that religion cannot provide a justification for morality but that it may provide additional motivations to be moral. The fear of eternal punishment, for example, may account for religious people (i.e. those swayed by such motivations), being in some cases more moral than their secular counterparts.

The philosophical reasons for asserting the logical independence of morality and religion (or God) are typically derived from a dilemma posed by Plato (1981: 10a) in a particular exchange between Socrates and Euthyphro:

> Is the pious loved by the gods because it is pious, or is it pious because it is loved by the gods?

There are different ways of expressing this dilemma for the theist, and much turns philosophically on how it is expressed (see below). Here is one form: does God approve of something because it is good, or is something good because God approves it? A different form is: does God command something because it is right, or is something right because God commands it? Basically (in the latter form of the dilemma): if an action is right because it is commanded by God, then it seems that his commands are arbitrary and what he commands could be immoral; rightness depends on the whim of God. Alternatively, if God commands an action because it is right then what is right is independent of God. Consequently, morality cannot be dependent on God and religion (and hence the thesis that morality is independent of God). This is a false dilemma for the theist, even if the philosophical reasons for this conclusion cannot be fully explored in this context.

In the first instance, theists believe God is not an arbitrary power: the God who commands is a loving God, who commands in accordance with his nature. An action commanded by God is right because his will (and hence his commanding) is determined by his loving nature; the commands of God are not arbitrary. God (and the righteous in heaven) 'cannot worketh abomination, or maketh a lie' (Revelation 21.27), as the King James Version of the Bible expresses it. Equally, the challenge of the second horn of the dilemma does not require theists to conclude that morality is independent of God. An action is right because God commands it; his commanding, because it is the command of a loving God (who has fashioned human nature to know and reflect the nature of God), gives an action the quality of rightness.

It might be contended that as human beings we have to judge whether an action, purporting to come from God or not, is right. Does this not show that morality (here entirely construed as concerned with *rightness*, i.e. obligatory actions) is in fact independent of religion? *We* have to judge what is right, so consequently morality is independent of God. We possess a standard of goodness by which the rightness or wrongness of actions is determined. This is to confuse an epistemological with an ontological point. For theists the fact that individuals may have to decide whether an action is right or wrong, despite its ontological status as commanded or forbidden by God, does not entail that God is not the *ultimate* standard of ethical rightness.

An action is right because it is commanded by God, but our recognition of rightness may be made on the basis of its rightness and not on the basis that we know it is commanded by God. Nevertheless, our moral judgements need not be regarded as independent of God (in any sense that would exclude God as the ultimate foundation of morality), in that we are God's creatures and he has created us in such a way that 'there is a congruence between divine notions of truth, beauty and goodness and proper human notions of the same' (McGrath 2008: 312). We are created by God in his image (*imago dei*) and through the proper use of our created faculties individuals have the aptitude (and freedom) to recognise (and to engage in) actions and behaviour that reflect his nature. Individuals are created by God to recognise what is right and in recognising the objective quality of what is right individuals (on a theistic understanding) bring their judgement into conformity with the command of God and affirm the rightness that reflects the rightness (righteousness) of God.

This is a preliminary sketch of a theistic account of the dependence of morality upon God. Much more is required by theists to counter the Euthyphro dilemma and the objections implicit in it. In my view, for a defence to be plausible, some kind of distinction needs to be drawn between the axiological issue of the goodness of God and the (deontic) issue of moral rightness and moral obligation (note that the focus of what is said above is on the deontic issue). This distinction allows, even requires, theists to defend voluntarism (and reliance upon God's will) with regard to moral rightness, and hence to affirm that it is the commands of God that constitute what is right for humans, while at the same time defending non-voluntarism in axiological matters, such as goodness and badness. This means that goodness can be given a broader reference, both a broader *moral* reference than rightness and a broader aesthetic and non-moral reference, perhaps expressed in terms of excellences. The next step is to argue that axiological goodness can depend ultimately on God even if it does not depend on the commands of God. This account grounds only deontological properties in God's commands (an argument of this broad form is developed by Adams 1999).

At the very least, the revival of a divine command theory of ethics among analytical philosophers (and the outline above is only one such expression of a family of meta-ethical divine command theories) illustrates that theists need not necessarily accept (and probably have some reasons for rejecting) the secular thesis that religion and morality are ontologically independent. If the reasons in favour of the independence of morality from religion are not philosophically compelling, in a way that those who reject them are patently obscurantist or obviously contradicting relevant epistemic norms, then it is inappropriate to conform representations of religion in education on the basis of a controversial and contested (and predominantly secular) philosophical conclusion.

The second step in overcoming the schizophrenic stance of religious education towards moral education is to recognise the educational advantages that may result from a rediscovered focus in schools on religious morality and religious responses to moral issues. It is widely appreciated that by neglecting moral issues, under the influence of the phenomenology of religion, the subject lost much of its relevance to young people; though subsequently, to some extent, a number of religious educators have made efforts to reinstate the moral content of religion in lessons. The weakness in much of this, as we have already noted, is that this content is viewed as instrumental to secular moral aims and thus there is often a failure to engage fully and constructively with the moral traditions and visions of the different religions. The problem is that there is no model of religious education currently available that fully justifies the inclusion of moral content. The proposals that are developed here are intended to contribute to such a framework by providing a basis for the reconnection of religious education with moral education. The chief educational advantage of such a reconnection is the potential that the reconfigured subject of religious education brings to the moral development of pupils and to the social development of communities.

The 2007 Birmingham Agreed Syllabus of Religious Education

It is part of the nature of different models of religious education to accommodate some degree of diversity. A model provides the framework within which learning and teaching occurs, yet within a particular framework there is room for innovation and 'progress': different content, pedagogical methodologies, classroom practices and attitudes to specific educational policies may all be equally consistent with the beliefs, values and commitments of a particular framework. Consequently, a model of religious education, while prescriptive and exclusive in certain respects, is also non-prescriptive and accommodating in others. For example, it has been argued in earlier chapters that both the phenomenological and experiential approaches can properly be interpreted as different expressions of the same liberal model of religious education. The purpose of drawing attention to the capacity of different educational models to accommodate some degree of latitude of belief and practice is to show the relevance of a consideration of the 2007 Birmingham Agreed Syllabus of Religious Education and the supporting curriculum resources. These provide one example of material that is both consistent with a post-liberal model that reintegrates moral education into religious education and shows something of the potential that such a reintegration brings.

The Syllabus, written under the direction of Marius Felderhof (as Conference Drafting Secretary) and expressing positions on a range of issues that he has supported and defended elsewhere (see Felderhof 2005 and 2010), provides an interesting and stimulating example of what religious education could look like when it explores and exploits the content of religion for moral purposes in a way that is faithful both to the nature of religion and to the intentions of religious adherents. The Syllabus is a unique attempt in recent religious education to justify and reinstate the importance of moral education within religious education and to exploit the contribution of the different religions to the personal development of pupils and the well-being of society. Two attainment targets are specified: Learning from Faith and Learning about Religious Traditions. These mirror the attainment targets of the National Framework but reverse their order 'to put greater emphasis on the development of pupils in community and making religious traditions subordinate to that task'.[1] What is distinctive, however, is that the syllabus goes on to specify twenty-four different qualities or 'dispositions' that children should develop in religious education. These include being: thankful; fair and just, sharing and generous; open, honest and truthful; and courageous and confident. The real strength of this focus upon the precise dispositions that are to be developed in pupils is that each one is linked to religious content from different traditions, as appropriate to the four school key stages. This overcomes the objection that the content of religion is extrinsic to the moral aims of education. Furthermore, by focusing on the qualities and dispositions of character, that is, by showing how religions can contribute to the human virtues of honesty, truthfulness, justice and so on, pupils will have the opportunity to engage with the moral claims of religion and the challenge of becoming 'a religious person'.

The 2007 Syllabus provides one interesting and stimulating example of the way in which religious education can contribute to the moral education and moral development of pupils. Within the parameters of a post-liberal model there are other possible ways in which religious education can reconnect with moral education; for example, attention can be given to the nature and character of religious versions of morality and to religious responses to contemporary moral and social issues. While much of what is said in this chapter has been critical of existing theory and practice, the overall aim has been the positive one of reaffirming the role of religious education in moral education and of providing an account of the kind of intellectual framework and some of the content that religious education needs to espouse if it is to reaffirm its role and contribution to moral education.

Note

1   This reference is taken from the official Birmingham City Council Website, Faith makes a Difference www.faithmakesadifference.co.uk/landing, where the syllabus material is available (accessed 15 October 2013).

15

A POST-LIBERAL MODEL OF RELIGIOUS EDUCATION

The two-fold purpose of this final chapter is to draw the threads of the argument together and to set out the central beliefs and commitments of a new post-liberal model of religious education.

Models of religious education

The inspiration for thinking about the nature of religious education in terms of different models or paradigms comes from Thomas Kuhn's *The Structure of Scientific Revolutions* (1970). Kuhn used the term *paradigm* to refer to the common assumptions, beliefs and commitments that unite a particular group of scientists and regulate their experiments; and in a similar way the term paradigm or model has been used here to refer to the common assumptions and commitments that unite *a particular group of religious educators* and regulate their practice. Two contrasting models of post-confessional religious education have been identified as influential in Britain: a liberal model and a postmodern model. The nature and role of models in religious education provide a number of parallels with Kuhn's understanding of the role of paradigms in science, some of which have already been noted in earlier chapters. These parallels are worth exploring further, for a consideration of them provides a focus around which to summarise much of the preceding argument and to distinguish between what is new in a post-liberal model of religious education and what it takes over and accommodates from other models.

Before considering specific parallels, however, it is useful to compare and contrast the aim of science with the aims of religious education. One may ask, 'What is the aim of natural science?' The most common answer is 'to explain natural phenomena' – to provide scientific explanations. There are philosophical debates about the character of scientific explanations and what it means for an explanation to be scientific rather than some other kind of explanation. Some suggest that scientific explanation centres on the identification of causal laws; yet since Hume the idea of causation has been controversial philosophically. In addition, although causal laws are important, not all examples of scientific explanation involve citing causes, at least not in an obvious way. The ideal gas law, for example, explains the temperature of gas at equilibrium by reference to its simultaneous pressure and the volume it takes up. But these cannot be causes, since all three – the temperature, the volume and the pressure, obtain at the same time. The nature of scientific explanation need not detain us. The success of different scientific models is measured in terms of their capacity to *explain* nature, however explanation is construed; the success of religious education is measured in terms of its capacity to achieve the aims appropriate to it.

Almost fifty years ago, the influential religious educator Edwin Cox addressed the issue of aims in a book entitled *Changing Aims in Religious Education* (1966). Cox began his discussion by considering 'The legal position and its assumptions' (1966: 7–20). This orientation makes sense, for clearly the aims of religious education are often conditioned, perhaps in some contexts determined, by legislation. However, whether they are conditioned by legislation or not, it is important to consider these aims as a separate subject in their own right, that is, in a strictly educational or normative way. We need to ask, what *should* the aims of religious education be? There would seem to be a number of concerns central to religious education, from which its aims must be derived and to which they must relate. Clearly, religious education must relate to religion, for it is this that justifies the subject as *religious* education. The most convincing answer to the question of *how* education relates to religion is that it should reflect the nature of religion. In the language of Ninian Smart, religious education should reflect 'the logic of religion'. The controversial issue is not that religious education should aim to reflect the nature of religion and enable pupils to gain an understanding of it on this basis but how the nature of religion is construed and represented in different pedagogies and methodologies in religious education. Much of the preceding argument has focused on this and it has been concluded that the two educationally dominant models of post-confessional religious education in Britain, the modern and the postmodern, fail to provide fully convincing interpretations and representations of the nature of religion.

To identify and represent the true nature of religion in education (in its different dimensions and in its diversity) is the ideal to which religious educators should aspire. Religious education needs to represent religion as it is and not as some interpreters would like it to be or to become. This comment is, as has been shown, particularly relevant to representations of religious diversity in education, where aspects of the nature of diversity in religion are misinterpreted or ignored in order to facilitate or exaggerate (what is thought to be) the positive contribution of religious education to education. A number of religious educators, John Hull, for example, deliberately attempt to conform the self-understanding of religious believers to their own liberal views about the nature of religion and of religious truth. The irony is that inadequate and flawed interpretations of the nature of religious diversity, as has been shown, reduce the ability of religious education to challenge prejudice and intolerance and to contribute positively to the moral and social aims of education.

This reference to the moral and social aims of education conveniently identifies two other concerns relevant to the aims of education – that of the human subjects of education and that of the communities (and the wider society) to which they belong. Again much could be said on these issues, for clearly the aims of education relate to individuals and to communities in deliberate and intentional ways; for example, to provide individuals with the knowledge, skills and abilities to contribute economically and socially to society and to enable them to realise their potential as persons with the capacity to follow purposes and projects of their own rational choosing. Religious education has obvious relevance to the moral and spiritual development of individuals and to the social development of communities. The two are not unrelated, part of the argument of Chapter 14 is that moral development and moral commitments are linked to positive social attitudes and behaviour. It may be acknowledged that in different societies at different times the moral and social aims of education may reflect distinctive needs and be required to respond to different challenges; yet there are few who would question that the challenge of enabling people and communities with diverse identities and commitments to live responsibly and respectfully together is one of the most pressing faced by educators in most late-modern democratic societies. Religious education has an important role to play in meeting this challenge, and if the argument of preceding chapters is convincing, current models of religious education lack the necessary intellectual resources to contribute to a successful educational response.

Against this background, parallels between the nature and role of models in science and the nature and the role of models in religious education can be properly considered. One of the points that Kuhn (1970) makes in relation to paradigms is that they are often exemplified in particular books and in the position of certain individuals. He refers to Nicholas Copernicus' *On the Revolution of Celestial Bodies* (1543) as exemplifying a heliocentric model of the solar system and as providing the framework for subsequent scientific research and practice. Analogously, *Working Paper 36: Religious education in the secondary school* (Schools Council 1971) and the post-1968 writings of Ninian Smart exemplify the modern paradigm of religious education, as does the work and writings of John Hull. In fact, in some respects Hull's work illustrates even more clearly than Smart's (for what is implicit in Smart is explicit in Hull), the defining assumption of the modern model that the different religions mediate salvation and the presence of the divine. Postmodern religious education is not as easily exemplified, as the term postmodern covers a variety of positions, with no defining belief. Nevertheless, a case was made for regarding Robert Jackson's interpretive approach as illustrating many of the features associated with postmodern thought; accordingly, *Religious Education: An Interpretive Approach*

(1997), and his subsequent writings, may be regarded as exemplifying *one* particularly influential postmodern model of religious education.

Kuhn's account of 'normal science', understood by him as science carried out within the parameters of an accepted paradigm, also has parallels with the work of religious educators. Teachers of religious education are inducted into a set of beliefs, commitments and practices that gives a sense of overarching unity and coherence to the subject and provides a rationale for its practice and the theoretical resources to achieve its aims. Induction takes place in different ways: through explicit teaching; through textbooks and the writings of prominent religious educators; through political efforts to have a particular model endorsed in policy documents; through research projects and their dissemination, and so on.

Hans Küng (1989: 11) has stated, self-consciously paraphrasing Kuhn, that 'in practice, students accept certain models of understanding less as a result of proofs than because of the authority of the textbook they study and of the teacher to whom they listen'. Each model is presented by its proponents as 'natural', 'rational' and 'compelling'; and challenges to it are robustly rebutted. Take the example of Hull's response to those who accused thematic teaching of confusing pupils: a strong defence of the modern model of religious education was needed because thematic teaching was an ideal vehicle for inducting pupils into the belief that similarities between religions (which 'justified' thematic teaching) pointed to the deeper spiritual unity among the religions, which, in turn provided the subject with an effective means of undermining and challenging prejudice.

Kuhn points out that 'normal science', conducted on the basis of a particular framework, is not interested in falsification as this would jeopardise the paradigm. Normal science is wholly concerned with confirming its foundational model, to make it more precise, to apply it in different ways, to broaden its scope, influence and 'success'; 'it is interested in development by aggregation, accumulation, a slow process of growth in knowledge' (Küng 1989: 13). Implicit in this is the point made in the last chapter – that paradigms are broadly based frameworks that allow for innovation (within limits) and accommodate a degree of flexibility. Thus models of religious education can accommodate a variety of methodologies (e.g. a modern model can accommodate both the phenomenological and experiential approaches). In addition, different models do not contradict each other at every point, and in religious education, as in science, can accommodate different beliefs, emphases and practices, provided these do not contradict the central beliefs and commitments of the model.

Another point already made, which reflects Kuhn's understanding of normal science, is that normal religious education may be conducted on the basis of a model that is largely implicit and often unselfconsciously espoused. Practitioners may be unaware of the unstated assumptions and commitments that are embedded in particular forms of religious education and their associated practices and procedures, a point borne out by attention to the argument and analysis of earlier chapters. Teachers may operate on the basis of a modern or a postmodern model, or even on the basis of a combination of commitments and beliefs derived from different paradigms, without consciously subscribing to any particular one or appreciating the contradictions that lie behind their practice. One must beware of attributing a degree of conceptual clarity and theoretical self-awareness to classroom practice that is not reflective of reality and what actually happens.

Kuhn also noted that the expectations of scientists, which are determined by the ruling scientific paradigm, are not always fulfilled – observations and results accrue that seem anomalous: experience in places may not fit what is hypothesised and experiments yield unanticipated results. Anomalies can lead to refinements of the initial paradigm or, if they are of a sufficient seriousness or number, they can challenge the coherence and credibility of the ruling paradigm. This brings about what Kuhn refers to as a 'crisis-state', that is, a situation where there is widespread appreciation by scientists that the ruling model is increasingly becoming incapable of accommodating anomalous research data or experience. A 'paradigm shift' occurs when a new theory or disciplinary matrix is proposed that explains the data that was formerly explained by the original paradigm but in addition resolves the anomalies that attach to the original. One paradigm is superseded by another.

The preceding argument has been mainly concerned with identifying weakness and 'anomalies' in post-confessional religious education in Britain: accusations of secularism and the alienation of religious minorities; superficial and truncated pupil learning; the negative attitudes of pupils to the subject and their perception that religious education has little or no relevance to their concerns, sense of identity or spiritual development; the disassociation of religious education from moral education; misrepresentations of the nature of religion; the failure to develop strategies that effectively challenge prejudice and intolerance, and so on. It has been maintained that these weaknesses are symptomatic of deeper issues that find their origin in one or other of two models of religious education that have provided, and still provide, the beliefs, commitments and axioms that determine classroom pedagogy and practice in much post-confessional religious education in Britain.

The interpretation and representation of diversity, particularly religious diversity, was used as a focus both to identify the nature and commitments of these two contrasting models and to test their capacity to realise the aims of religious education. By 'aims' is not meant only the social and moral aims of education, as one might imagine, given that these aims relate most directly to diversity (e.g. in challenging prejudice), but the full range of aims appropriate to religious education. This is because diversity raises a number of issues: about the nature of religion and what it is to represent religion in education; about the nature of religious understanding and the knowledge and skills necessary to interpret religious phenomena; and also about the skills needed for pupils to respond individually to religion and to assess and evaluate contrasting religious beliefs and values. A focus on diversity facilitates an overall grasp of the character and form of the different models of religious education that lie behind a range of methodologies and classroom practices, just as it relates in one way or another to the different aims of religious education.

It was the challenge of diversity to society in the late 1960s and early 1970s that provided the original stimulus for the emergence of post-confessional forms of religious education. Both the modern and the postmodern models justify the place and statutory role of religious education in the curriculum on the basis that it provides effective strategies for challenging and overcoming prejudice, albeit both attempt this in different ways. After a thorough analysis, it has been concluded that both models are inadequate for this task, and that inadequacy at this point compromises their overall credibility and ability to realise the range of aims appropriate to religious education.

Kuhn noted that the shift from one scientific paradigm to another leaves much of the practice of science unaffected. In fact, one of the chief reasons he cites for the acceptance of a new paradigm within the scientific community is that it preserves the explanatory powers of the old paradigm while fitting them into a more comprehensive framework that resolves, or has the potential to resolve, the anomalies associated with the model it succeeds. Certainly, the new model does not 'leave everything as it is', to use Wittgenstein's phrase (1958, paragraph 124), but it does not mean that everything changes. These observations have strong parallels with the role of models in religious education. Although there are serious weaknesses with both the modern and postmodern models, this does not entail a complete rejection of every commitment and practice associated with them. Much of the argument in succeeding chapters has been negative and this may have given the impression that there is nothing in either model that should be retained. A careful reading of what has been said, however, reveals that positive features have been identified in both the modern and postmodern models and that any new model needs to acknowledge this and accommodate them. What are these features?

In Chapter 4 it was argued that confessional religious education is inappropriate for state schools that aim to be inclusive of the community; though it was also argued that the confessional model is appropriate in some contexts (and, consequently, one of the advantages of a post-liberal model of religious education is that it can accommodate both confessional and non-confessional forms, unlike either the modern or postmodern model).

A positive case was made in Chapter 5 for the educational relevance and appropriateness of multi-faith religious education in state schools, thus endorsing the argument of *Working Paper 36* (Schools Council 1971). Support was also given in that chapter to both systematic and (with reservations) thematic presentations of the different religions in religious education, as was support for the principle that the content of religious education should reflect its historical and religious context. In the case of Britain, this means that the subject of Christianity should predominate at the different educational and developmental stages of the formal school careers of pupils; in other contexts this may be different. The final point at which the position of *Working Paper 36* was endorsed (and defended against later practice) was in relation to the need for a balance to be struck between providing pupils with knowledge and understanding of religion and addressing their existential concerns as they search for meaning in experience. Too much religious education in Britain neglects the interests and concerns of pupils (see below).

Much of value was identified in Robert Jackson's interpretive approach to religious education, and Chapter 13 acknowledges this while also identifying weaknesses. Attention is given by Jackson to the role of individuals in appropriating and reinterpreting religious traditions and to the way religion is 'lived out' in the life and experience of religious believers. Particularly valuable is his account of the hermeneutical challenge of interpreting religion and his positive proposals for portraying religions and religious phenomena to pupils in the classroom. Jackson also looked positively upon and took advantage of empirical studies, and while in his case there is a certain narrowness of vision and application (see Chapter 13), his work does illustrate the relevance and fruitfulness of the use of empirical research in religious education.

These elements from both the modern and postmodern models of religious education need to be appropriated by any new model. Chapter 9 introduced Lakatos' distinction between the 'hard core' or essential commitments of a research programme (or model) and auxiliary commitments and hypotheses that flesh it out and enable it to be explicated and applied in different contexts. This distinction is vital in the development of a post-liberal model of religious education for it provides the means for the new model to appropriate and incorporate valuable secondary commitments and insights from both the modern and the postmodern models while rejecting their controversial philosophical and theological central commitments.

A post-liberal model of religious education

In Chapter 11 it was noted that Derrida follows Saussure in accepting that signs have meaning not in relation to the world but in relation to other signs within the overall system of signs; both denied any referential role in meaning. It is not necessary, however, to exclude a referential component in all instances of linguistic meaning in order to recognise that meaning can be contextual and on occasions (chiefly or exclusively) internal to the system of signs. What this means in relation to explaining the commitments and beliefs of a post-liberal model of religious education is that criticism of both the liberal and postmodern models provides an invaluable orientation to what it means and entails. To state what something is not is to provide an orientation to what it is. The greater the number and range of negative points, the clearer becomes any alternative that is proposed. Such is the case with a post-liberal model of religious education. It should be clear, by now, what it is not, and the negative connotations point in the direction of its positive content. It is now appropriate to speak plainly of this positive content.

A commitment to the importance and reality of diversity is fundamental to a post-liberal model of religious education. This is why Chapters 2 and 3 analysed the concept of diversity in society and attempted to gain an understanding of its nature and implications for education. Part of the overall argument has been that the 'solutions' of religious education to the challenge of diversity, both modern and postmodern, have failed, precisely because they are based on a mistaken diagnosis of the challenge of diversity and the ways in which differences, real or imagined, can give rise to prejudice, intolerance, civil strife and violence. The totalising discourse of essential agreement or the deconstructive discourse of insubstantial (or incommensurable) disagreement needs to give way to an appreciation of the distinctiveness and uniqueness of the different religions alongside the diversity within them. Recognition needs to be given to all aspects of religious diversity: to highly eclectic versions of spirituality, to personal appropriations of particular religions and to traditional forms of the different religions. Just how distinctive and different the religions are has been underlined by Stephen Prothero in *God is Not One: The Eight Rival Religions That Run the World – and Why Their Differences Matter* (2010). Prothero writes from the perspective of religious studies (he is professor of religion at Boston University). In response to the idea that '[t]he fundamentals or essentials of all religions are the same. There is difference only in non-essentials', he writes (2010: 2–3):

> This is a lovely sentiment, but it is dangerous, disrespectful, and untrue. For more than a generation we have followed scholars and sages down the rabbit hole in a fantasy world in which all gods are one. This wishful thinking is motivated in part by an understandable rejection of the exclusivist missionary view that only you and your kind will make it to heaven or Paradise. For most of world history, human beings have seen religious rivals as inferior to themselves . . . [T]he idea of religious unity is wishful thinking . . . and it has not made the world a safer place.

In a later section in the same chapter, as has been quoted from above, called 'Pretend Pluralism' (2010: 5–7), Prothero (6) accuses those who profess essential agreement between religions as 'not describing the world but reimagining it': 'differences. . . matter to ordinary religious people' (3). As has been shown, even those religious educators who deny that there is essential agreement between religions do not necessarily recognise or take cognisance of the range of religious positions encompassed by diversity. What is often overlooked, which is surprising as it is one of the most obvious aspects of religious diversity, is the diversity between religions that traces its origins to different sources of (claimed) revelation. Religions make different normative claims and it is these that account for and justify (to their respective followers) religious diversity and the 'intractable' nature of religious divisions. Any model of religious education that does not take account of this will necessarily fail to frame and implement policies and methodologies that are effective in challenging religious prejudice and intolerance. Points of similarity should be noted between religions, but the exaggeration of similarity in the service of liberal theology or of 'good community relations' has no role to play in state education in a pluralist democracy. A post-liberal model aims to reflect accurately and faithfully the nature of religion in all its aspects and in all its diversity.

Of central relevance to a post-liberal model of religious education is the importance of beliefs and doctrines. Beliefs are constitutive of religion and of religious experience. This understanding of the nature of religion and religious ways of life, which is indebted to Wittgenstein's later philosophy, has been advanced at various points in earlier chapters and defended most fully in Chapter 8. This does not entail, as some detractors might suggest, the transformation of religious education into theology. As has already been stated, a concern with religious beliefs extends to include the different ways in which beliefs are expressed in rituals, art, music and drama, in history and in the lives of famous religious believers. Religions are more than schemes of belief and this 'more than' is important educationally, but to deny that religions are schemes of belief is to misrepresent the nature of religion and to falsify the self-understanding of many religious people. Prothero (2010: 337) calls for 'religious literacy', which he equates with knowledge 'about the basic *beliefs* and practices of the world's religions'. In an earlier publication (2007: 13) he defines religious literacy as 'the ability to understand and use religious terms, symbols, images, practices, scriptures, heroes, themes and stories', so, clearly, it includes both knowledge and understanding of the different aspects and dimensions of religion. Like other forms of literacy, religious literacy is not a fixed accomplishment but one that is fluid and shifting in relation to culture and context. Religious literacy enables one to talk about religion and its role in private and public life; as Prothero (2007: 14) says, '[i]t is the ability to participate in our ongoing conversation about the private and public powers of religion'. The only word of caution that needs to be sounded about Prothero's ambitious aim of knowing about the beliefs and practices of the world's religions is the educationally relevant point that not every religion can be studied in schools: issues of relevance and importance have to be addressed. To consider a number of religious at greater depth is preferable to providing a superficial knowledge of a wide range. This means that the recommendation of the national framework for religious education (QCA 2004) that over ten different religious traditions be studied should be rejected; it is a recipe for superficiality and confusion and detracts from the overall credibility of the document. What is needed is for religious educators to take the concept of transferable skills seriously and for pupils to be equipped to be able to extend and enlarge their knowledge and understanding of religion on the basis of the knowledge and skills they acquire in religious education.

A focus on the doctrinal (and cognitive) dimension of religion naturally raises the issue of religious truth, for the different religions teach different things and prescribe different activities. Pupils need to be equipped with the skills to reflect upon and to evaluate religious phenomena and to engage in public debates about the truth of the different religions. Our society confronts young people with a rich kaleidoscope of religious ideas and practices, yet post-confessional British religious education has resolutely failed to help them to develop a critical perspective that can identify the appeals that are used by religions to authenticate their beliefs and practices and the considerations that are relevant to their assessment. At one level British religious education has paid lip service to religious truth: the modern model by insisting that truth inheres in all religions; a postmodern model by identifying a diversity of views about the nature of religious truth and then concluding that all such claims lack public, substantive form. Both models fail to engage critically with the issue of truth in religion and to equip pupils with the knowledge and skills to enable them to choose responsibly from the rich variety of religious options that are culturally available.

Support is not given here to the view that state schools should endorse the truth of any one particular religion or even the truth of religion in general; what is required in education is for the truth claims of religion (and of particular religions) to be presented to pupils and for attention to be given to the forms of evidence to which religions appeal and to the kinds of assessment that are relevant to the consideration of this evidence. Furthermore, any appreciation by pupils of the contested nature of religious truth must also necessarily take account of religious scepticism, which in the form of atheism can act as a cultural substitute for religion. Religious scepticism frequently provides the horizon of meaning against which religious phenomena are interpreted and assessed. Pupils need to be familiar both with secular challenges to religion and with religious challenges to secularism. There must be an open, dialectical and critical enquiry into religious truth, an enquiry that interprets and evaluates not only religious beliefs and practices but also secular ones.

A post-liberal model of religious education reaffirms the importance and role of moral education in religious education and self-consciously rejects the disassociation of latter from the former that is a feature of much post-confessional religious education in Britain. Chapter 14 provided a principled justification for the inclusion of moral content in religious education, which is something that both the modern and postmodern models of religious education are incapable of doing, if they remain faithful to their underlying commitments and beliefs. A focus on contemporary moral issues and religious responses to these issues offers a way of reconnecting the subject with the interests and concerns of pupils and of overcoming the negative attitudes that are characteristic of pupils towards religious education. Uninvolved and uninterested pupils make poor learners. Religious education has a positive and substantive role to play in the moral development of pupils. It can also make pupils aware of religious moral alternatives to secular, procedural forms of morality that dominate mainstream culture and public life.

It is clear that the study of religion in education needs to be balanced with attention to the interests and concerns of pupils. Certainly one of the reasons why post-confessional religious education often fails to capture the imagination and interest of pupils is because it neglects to address their moral concerns and the moral issues of the day. Yet religion is broader than morality and not all the teachings of the religions are focused on moral issues. This means that there needs to be an engagement between the interests and concerns of pupils and the wider beliefs and values of religion. Pupils can 'learn from religion' only if appropriate attention is given to showing its relevance to their particular experience and to human experience more broadly. Attention has already been drawn to this in Chapter 5, but it is worth reiterating, not because the need to relate religious content to the concerns of pupils is a need that can be fulfilled only by a post-liberal model of religious education but because it is a necessary component on any credible model of education. It is worth briefly considering the 'concept cracking' methodology of Trevor Cooling in this connection; an added advantage of this is that it underlines again the way in which a post-liberal model can accommodate different insights, methodologies and approaches.

Trevor Cooling's methodology gives explicit attention to the challenge of relating religious content to the 'lifeworld' of pupils. He speaks of the need to build conceptual bridges between the world of religious belief (and this world often traces its origins to ancient texts and remote cultures) and the contemporary experiences of young people. The challenge for teachers is to make religious beliefs and practices accessible to pupils by drawing on universal aspects of human experience that are analogous to religious concepts, emotions and attitudes; this, he believes, may be achieved by the use of stories, illustrations, art and poetry, for example. Cooling's point is that secular, non-religious analogues to Christian experience can be developed to show that distinctively religious concepts are not entirely unrelated to the contemporary experience of young people. Cooling (1994: 12) gives the example of falling out with someone and then restoring the relationship through forgiveness as an experiential analogue of receiving religious forgiveness from God. Such analogues provide an insight into the world of religion and are suggestive of the ways in which religious concepts might relate to the lives of young people. The advantage of this way of relating religious content to pupils' experience is that it attempts to show the specifically *religious* relevance of material, unlike the 'exemplars of good practice' provided by the Qualifications and Curriculum Authority in 2000. In teaching pupils about the Five Pillars of Islam under 'learning about', it is stated: 'All the time Muslims believe . . . [followed by a list of the things Muslims believe]' and 'Five times a day Muslims pray'; the 'learning from' objective that is correlated to these propositions are 'All the time, I believe . . .' and 'Every day I intend to . . .' (this example and others like it are discussed in Thompson 2004: 124–130). These are not the kind of extrinsic connections that responsible religious education should aim to make between the experience of pupils and religious content. In the QCA cases the connections are exclusively external; what is learnt from the Five Pillars has nothing whatsoever to do with religion or the Five Pillars. One possible defensive response might be to say that for some pupils the 'learning from' component will not connect to religion. This is an entirely inadequate response: the criticism is that the 'learning from' component in each case does not even aim to relate the content of religion to the experience of pupils: it is not that the pupils are unable to make the connection between religion and their experience – it is that there is no educational attempt to make a connection.

A post-liberal model of British multi-faith religious education must also engage fully in challenging religious intolerance and religious prejudice. The respect that is shown to religious believers by taking seriously their beliefs and practices needs to be complemented by explicit challenges to religious and secular sources of intolerance. A range of arguments and considerations can be employed: philosophical, moral and religious. Use needs to be made of tradition-specific arguments, alongside arguments of a more general and accessible nature; and attention needs to be given to the relationship of religion to culture, the legacy of colonialism and both religious and secular affirmations of human dignity and human freedom.

Each of the religions has resources within their sacred scriptures and their historical traditions that endorse freedom of religion and condemn religious prejudice and intolerance. For example, there are Christian imperatives to 'love your neighbour', 'do good to those who persecute you', 'go the extra mile', 'turn the other cheek' and 'love your enemies', and there are stories in the Christian scriptures that give narrative force to such injunctions, the Parable of the Good Samaritan being an obvious example. Alongside specifically religious con-siderations there are non-religious and secular arguments to which appeal can be made. It would be naive to believe that even direct challenges to prejudice and intolerance will always be successful. This is because such negative attitudes and dispositions are often encouraged within the context of close relationships, such as families and peer groups, and these relationships convey a sense of belonging in the context of personal acceptance. That rational or religious arguments and considerations may not succeed does not mean that the aim of challenging prejudice should be abandoned, only that religious education should redouble its efforts and use all the available resources it can identify and employ.

It would be partisan to refer to the power and transformative quality of religion for good, while overlooking its negative influence. Unfortunately the negative aspect of religion receives little attention in religious education, even though it should. One of the reasons for this is that post-confessional religious education in Britain typically speaks of the need to respect *beliefs* and *religions*, as in the national framework document (QCA 2004: 22), which speaks of pupils 'developing respect for their own cultures and beliefs and those of other People' and of treating 'beliefs with respect'. Such a manner of speaking gives credence to the view that criticism of religion and religious ways of life is disrespectful, and as a consequence pupils are not encouraged to voice their criticisms. This association has also contributed to the reluctance of teachers to engage with religious truth claims – for fear that criticism of these will be interpreted as evidence of disrespect.

Post-confessional religious education misplaces its emphasis with regard to the concept of respectfulness. Respect for persons has primacy over respect for beliefs. In fact, there are good philosophical reasons for thinking that respect for the beliefs and values of others is secondary and derived from respect for persons. In normal English usage it is more natural to affirm that we respect others than to say that we respect their values and beliefs. We respect persons, which, in part, means that we acknowledge their worth. That persons have value, that they have an inherent dignity, is not a belief confined to those who are religious; it is a principle affirmed by different philosophies of life and religions. We respect the values and beliefs of others because we respect them as persons. Respect for what people believe and the actions and attitudes that express respect are derived from this basic consideration. There is a certain 'unnaturalness' of usage when we state that we respect someone's beliefs or, more pertinently, require pupils to respect someone's beliefs; more properly we think that beliefs are true or false, important or trivial, interesting or uninteresting, relevant or irrelevant, appropriate or inappropriate. British religious education has failed to appreciate that one can respect adherents of the different religions and those who profess no religious beliefs, while equipping pupils with the skills and abilities to make a reasoned choice about religion and even criticise religion or aspects of particular religions.

The thrust of the overall argument of this book is that current models of religious education in Britain are limited in their capacity to challenge prejudice and religious intolerance. Religious education, as currently practised, misrepresents the nature of religion and is conceptually ill-equipped to develop respect for persons because it lacks the theoretical resources to affirm respect for others alongside recognition of the intractable nature of religious difference. A new theoretical model of religious education is required to enable the subject to fulfil its educational potential and to achieve its aims. Attention has been given to this and the commitments and beliefs of a new *post-liberal* model of religious education have been identified and discussed. The creation of such a post-liberal model, however, needs the co-operation and the support of other religious educators. A beginning has been made. Religious education may still make some significant contribution to the creation of a more humane, tolerant and inclusive society.

REFERENCES

Acland, R. (1966) *We Teach them Wrong*. London: Gollancz.

Acton, H. B. (1970) *Kant's Moral Philosophy*. London: Macmillan.

Adams, R. M. (1999) *Finite and Infinite Goods*. Oxford: Oxford University Press.

Adorno, T. W., Frenkel-Brunswik, E., Levinson, D. J. and Sanford, R. N. (1950) *The Authoritarian Personality*. New York: Harper and Row.

Allport, G. (1966) 'The religious context of prejudice'. *Journal for the Scientific Study of Religion* 5(3): 447–457.

Alves, C. (1991) 'Just a matter of words? The religious debate in the House of Lords'. *British Journal of Religious Education* 13(3): 168–174.

Ammerman, N. T. (ed.) (2006) *Everyday Religion: Observing modern religious lives*. New York: Oxford University Press.

Anderson, W. T. (1999) *The Future of the Self: Inventing the postmodern person*. New York: Tarcher.

Ansari, H. (2004) *'The Infidel Within': Muslims in Britain since 1800*. London: Hurst.

Araújo, M. and Santos, H. '"Race", culture . . . and what about religion? A postcolonialist contribution to education in multicultural societies', Paper presented to the Centre for Research on the European Matrix Conference, Multicultural Britain: from antiracism to identity politics to . . .? Roehampton University, 14–15 June 2006.

Archetti, E. (1996) 'Post-modernity', in A. Kuper and J. Kuper (eds) *The Social Science Encyclopedia*. London: Routledge.

Ashworth, J. and Farthing, I. (2007) *Churchgoing in the UK*. Middlesex: Tearfund.

Atkinson, W. (2010) *Class, Individualization and Late Modernity: In search of the reflexive worker*. Basingstoke, UK: Palgrave Macmillan.

Ayer, A. J. (1946) *Language, Truth, and Logic*. London: Gollancz.

Ayer, A. J. (1967) in Department of Education and Science, *Children and their Primary Schools*. London: HMSO.

Barley, L. (2007) 'Introduction: The context for churches today', in J. Ashworth, and I. Farthing, *Churchgoing in the UK*. Teddington, Middlesex: Tearfund.

Barnes, L. P. (1987) 'Light from the East? Ninian Smart and the Christian-Buddhist Encounter'. *Scottish Journal of Theology* 40(4): 67–83.

Barnes, L. P. (2000) 'Ninian Smart and the phenomenological approach to religious education'. *Religion* 30(4): 315–332.

Barnes, L. P. (2008) 'The 2007 Birmingham Agreed Syllabus for religious education: A new direction for statutory religious education in England and Wales'. *Journal of Beliefs and Values* 29(1): 73–81.

Barnes, L. P. (2010) 'Enlightenment's wake: Religion and education at the close of the modern age', in G. Durka, E. Engebretson and L. Gearon (eds) *International Handbook of Inter-religious Education: International Handbooks of Religion and Education, Vol. 4.* Philadelphia: Springer.

Barnes, L. P. (2012) (ed) *Debates in Religious Education.* Abingdon: Routledge.

Barnes, L. P. and Wright, A. (2006) 'Romanticism, representations of religion and critical religious education'. *British Journal of Religious Education* 28(1): 65–77.

Barry, B. (2002) *Culture and Equality: An egalitarian critique of multiculturalism.* Cambridge, MA: Harvard University Press.

Barry, P. (1995) *Beginning Theory.* Manchester: Manchester University Press.

Barth, K. (1959) *God, Gospel and Grace.* Edinburgh: Oliver and Boyd.

Bartley, W. W. III (1984) *The Retreat to Commitment.* Chicago: Open Court Publishing Company.

Bates, D. (1992) 'Religious Education in England 1953–1992'. *Word in Life* 40: 5–15.

Bates, D. (1994) 'Christianity, culture and other religions (Part 1)'. *British Journal of Religious Education* 17(1): 5–18.

Bates, D. (2006) 'John Hull: A critical appreciation', in D. Bates, G. Durka and F. Schweitzer (eds) *Education, Religion and Society: Essays in honour of John M. Hull.* London: Routledge.

Baumfield, V. (2004) 'Editorial: The place of religious education in the school curriculum'. *British Journal of Religious Education* 26(2): 115–117.

Bayer, O. and Peters, A. (1998) 'Theologie', in J. Rittter and K Gründer (eds) *Historisches Wörterbuch der Philosophie.* Bd.10, Basle: Schwabe.

Beck, U. (1992) *Risk Society: Towards a new modernity.* London: Sage Publications.

Beck, U. (1997) *The Reinvention of Politics: Rethinking modernity in the global social order.* Oxford: Polity Press.

Bellah, R. N., Madsen, R., Sullivan, W. M., Swidler, A. and Tipton, S. M. (1996) *Habits of the Heart: Individualism and commitment in American life.* Berkeley, CA: University of California Press.

Berger, P. (1968) 'A bleak outlook is seen for religion'. *New York Times*, 25 April: p. 3.

Berger, P. (1981) 'The pluralistic situation and the coming dialogue between the world religions'. *Buddhist-Christian Studies* 1(1): 31–41.

Berger, P. (1985) 'Western individuality: Liberation and loneliness'. *Partisan Review* 52: 323–336.

Berger, P. (1997) 'Epistemological modesty: An interview with Peter Berger'. *Christian Century* 114: 29 October: 972–978.

Berger, P. (ed) (1999) *The Desecularization of the World: The resurgence of religion in world politics.* Grand Rapids, MI: Eerdmans.

Berger, P. (2001) 'Reflections on the sociology of religion today'. *Sociology of Religion* 62(4): 443–454.

Berger, P. and Luckmann, T. (1966) *The Social Construction of Reality: A treatise in the sociology of knowledge.* Harmondsworth: Penguin Books.

Berger, P., Berger, B. and Kellner, H. (1974) *The Homeless Mind: Modernization and consciousness.* Harmondsworth, UK: Penguin Books.

Bernhardt, R. (1994) *Christianity Without Absolutes.* London: SCM Press.

Bertram-Troost, G. (2008) 'Learning to live together? The impact of religious diversity or homogeneity in Dutch schools for secondary education', unpublished paper from International Seminar on Religious Education and Values. Ankara, July 2008.

Bevel, M. W. (2004) 'Mystery, magic, and myth: The power of narrative'. *Journal of Philosophy and History of Education* 54: 15–18.

Bhaskar, R. (2008) *A Realist Theory of Science*. Abingdon, UK: Routledge.

Bhaskar, R. (2011) *Reclaiming Reality: A critical introduction to contemporary philosophy*. Abingdon, UK: Routledge.

Birmingham City Council (2013) *Faith Makes a Difference: RE in Birmingham*. Online. Available <www.faithmakesadifference.co.uk/landing (accessed 22 April 2013).

Blackburn, S. (1998) 'Realism and Truth: Wittgenstein, Wright, Rorty and Minimalism'. *Mind* 107(425): 157–181.

Blaylock, L. (2004) 'A professional RE bookshelf'. *Resource* 26(3): 18–20.

Bolton, P. and Gillie, C. (2009) *Faith Schools: Admissions and performance*. Standard Note SN/SG/4405, London: House of Commons Library.

Brandt, G. (1986) *The Realization of Anti-Racist Teaching*. Lewes, UK: Falmer Press.

Brophy, B. (1967) *Religious Education in State Schools*. London: Fabian Society.

Brown, A. (1995) 'Changing the agenda: Whose agenda?' *British Journal of Religious Education* 17(3):148–156.

Brown, C. G. (2001) *The Death of Christian Britain: Understanding secularisation 1800–2000*. London: Routledge.

Brown, G. (2007) 'Statement on National Security', 14 November. Online. Available http://bbc.in/1d1hLas (accessed 17 October 2013).

Browning, D. (1983) *Practical Theology*. San Francisco: Harper & Row.

Bruce, S. (1988) *The Rise and Fall of the New Christian Right: Conservative Protestant politics in America, 1978–88*. Oxford: Clarendon Press.

Bruce, S. (1995) *Religion in Modern Britain*. Oxford: Oxford University Press.

Bruce, S. (1998) *Conservative Protestant Politics*. Oxford: Oxford University Press.

Budd, S. (1977) *Varieties of Unbelief: Atheists and agnostics in English society, 1850–1960*. London: Heinemann.

Burn, J. and Hart, C. (1988) *The Crisis in Religious Education*. Harrow, UK: Educational Research Trust.

Butler, R. A. (1971) *The Art of the Possible: The memoirs of Lord Butler*. London: Hamish Hamilton.

Capek, M. E. S., and Mead, M. (2006) *Effective Philanthropy: Organization success through deep diversity and gender equality*. Cambridge, MA: MIT Press.

Casanova, J. (1994) *Public Religions in the Modern World*. Chicago: Chicago University Press.

Cavanaugh, W. T. (2009) *The Myth of Religious Violence: Secular ideology and the roots of modern conflict*. New York: Oxford University Press.

Chalmers, A. F. (1982) *What is this thing called Science?* Milton Keynes: Open University Press.

Chantepie de la Saussaye, P. D. (1887) *Lehrbuch der religionsgeschichte*. Tübingen: Mohr.

Chater, M. (2000) 'To teach is to set free: Liberation theology and the democratisation of the citizenship agenda'. *British Journal of Religious Education* 23(1): 5–14.

Chater, M. (2001) 'Children, doorposts and hearts: How can and should the religious traditions respond to spirituality in a postmodern setting?, in J. Erricker, C. Ota, and C. Erricker (eds) *Spiritual Education: Cultural, religious and social differences*. Brighton: Sussex University Press.

Chidester, D. (1996) *Savage Systems: Colonialism and comparative religion in Southern Africa*. Charlottesville, VA: University Press of Virginia.

Christian, W. (1972) *Oppositions of Religious Doctrines: A study in the logic of dialogue between religions*. London: Macmillan.

Christian, W. (1987) *Doctrines of Religious Communities: A philosophical study*. New Haven, CT: Yale University Press.

Clark, E. (1962) *The Song of Roland. Legacy Library No. 7*. London: Frederick Muller.

Cliff, P. (1968) 'The significance of Goldman's research for curriculum materials'. *Religious Education* 63(6): 435–439.

Clifford, J. (1986) 'Introduction: Partial truths', in J. Clifford and G. Marcus, (eds) *Writing Culture: The poetics and politics of ethnography*. Berkeley, University of California Press.

Cohen, P. (1988) 'The perversions of inheritance: studies in the making of multiracist Britain', in P. Cohen and H. Bains (eds) *Multi-racist Britain*. London: Macmillan.

Cole, W. O. (1984) *Six Religions in the Twentieth Century*. Cheltenham, UK: Stanley Thornes.

Committee on Tolerance and Understanding (1984) *Final report of the Committee on Tolerance and Understanding*. Edmonton: Government of Alberta, Department of Education.

Conroy, J. C., Lundie, D., Davis, R. A., Baumfield, V., Barnes, L. P., Gallagher, T., Lowden, K., Bourque, N. and Wenell, K. (2013) *Does Religious Education Work? A multi-dimensional investigation*, London: Bloomsbury.

Cooling, T. (1994) *Concept Cracking: Exploring Christian beliefs in school*. Nottingham, UK: Stapleford Centre.

Copley, T. (2005) *Indoctrination, Education and God*. London: SPCK.

Copley, T. (2008) *Teaching Religion: Sixty years of religious education in England and Wales*, 2nd edn. Exeter, UK: University of Exeter Press.

Côté, J. E. and Schwartz S. J. (2002) 'Comparing psychological and sociological approaches to identity: Identity status, identity capital, and the individualization process'. *Journal of Adolescence* 25(6): 571–586.

Cox, E. (1956) 'The strategy of Bible teaching'. *Religion in Education* 23(3): 96–100.

Cox, E. (1966) *Changing Aims in Religious Education*. London: Routledge & Kegan Paul.

Cox, E. (1983) *Problems and Possibilities for Religious Education*. London: Hodder & Stoughton.

Cox, H. (1966) *The Secular City*. London: SCM Press.

Cox, J. (2006) *A Guide to the Phenomenology of Religion: Key figures, formative influences and subsequent debates*. London: T & T Clark.

Crawley, A. E. (1905) *The Tree of Life*. London: Hutchinson.

Cuddon, J. A. and Preston, C. E. (2000) *The Penguin Dictionary of Literary Terms and Literary Theory*. Harmondsworth, UK: Penguin Books.

Cush, D. (1999) 'Potential pioneers of pluralism: The contribution of religious education to intercultural education in multicultural societies'. Diskus, 5. Online. Available http://bit.ly/17Q3ZzJ (accessed 17 October 2013).

Davie, G. (1994) *Religion in Britain since 1945: Believing without belonging*. Oxford: Blackwell.

Davie, G. (2002) *Europe: the Exceptional Case. Parameters of faith in the modern world*. London: Darton, Longman & Todd.

Day, D (1985) 'Religious Education Forty Years on: A permanent identity crisis?' *British Journal of Religious Education* 7(2): 55–63.

Deal, W. E. and Beal, T. K. (2004) *Theory for Religious Studies*. New York: Routledge.

Dearden, R. F. (1968) *The Philosophy of Primary Education*. London: Routledge.

Derrida, J. (1976) *Of Grammatology*. Baltimore, MD: Johns Hopkins University Press.

Derrida, J. (1978) 'Structure, Sign and Play in the Discourse of the Human Sciences', in *Writing and Difference*. Chicago, IL: University of Chicago Press.

Dunn, J. (1982) *The Political Thought of John Locke: An historical account of the argument of the 'Two Treatises of Government'.* Cambridge: Cambridge University Press.

Durkheim, É. ([1912] 2008) *The Elementary Forms of Religious Life.* Oxford: Oxford University Press.

Eagleton, T. (2008) *Literary Theory: An introduction.* Minneapolis: University of Minnesota Press.

Edwards, R. (1972) *Reason and Religion: An introduction to the philosophy of religion.* New York: Harcourt Brace Jovanovich.

Edwards, T. (2000) *Contradictions of Consumption: Concepts, practices and politics in consumer society.* Buckingham, UK: Open University Press.

Eliade, M. (1958) *Patterns in Comparative Religion.* London: Sheed and Ward.

Erricker, C. (2007) 'Children's spirituality and postmodern faith'. *International Journal of Children's Spirituality* 12(1): 51–60.

Erricker, C. and Erricker, J. (2000) *Reconstructing Religious, Spiritual and Moral Education.* London: Routledge.

Eze, E. C. (1997) *Race and the Enlightenment: A reader.* Oxford: Blackwell.

Felderhof, M. (2005) 'RE: Religions, equality and curriculum time'. *Journal of Beliefs and Values* 26(2): 201–214.

Felderhof, M. (2010) 'Degeneracy and English religious education'. *Journal of Beliefs and Values* 31(2): 155–164.

Fitzgerald, T. (2000) *The Ideology of Religious Studies.* New York: Oxford University Press.

Flax, J. (1987) 'Postmodernism and gender relations in feminist theory'. *Signs* 12(4): 621–643.

Flew, A. (1971) 'Theology and Falsification: A symposium', in B. Mitchell (ed) *The Philosophy of Religion.* London: Oxford University Press.

Foucault, M. (1977) 'Nietzsche, Genealogy, History', in *Language, Counter-Memory, Practice: Selected essays and interviews.* Ithaca, NY: Cornell University Press.

Foucault, M. (1979) *The History of Sexuality – Volume 1: An introduction.* Harmondsworth, UK: Allen Lane.

Foucault, M. (1980). 'Two lectures', in Colin Gordon, (ed) *Power/Knowledge: Selected interviews.* New York: Pantheon.

Foucault, M. (1984) 'What is Enlightenment?', in P. Rabinow (ed.), *The Foucault Reader.* New York: Pantheon Books.

Foucault, M. (1988) *Madness and Civilization: A history of insanity in the age of reason.* New York: Random House.

Foucault, M. (1991) *Discipline and Punish.* Harmondsworth, UK: Penguin Books.

Foucault, M. (2001) *The Order of Things: Archaeology of the human sciences.* London: Routledge.

Foucault, M. (2003) *The Birth of the Clinic.* Abingdon, UK: Routledge.

Francis, L. J. (2001a) 'Christianity and dogmatism revisited: A study among fifteen and sixteen year olds in the United Kingdom'. *Religious Education* 96(2): 211–226.

Francis, L. J. (2001b) *The Values Debate: A voice from the pupils.* London: Woburn.

Francis, L. J. and Robbins, M. (2003) 'Christianity and dogmatism among undergraduate students'. *Journal of Beliefs and Values* 24(1): 89–95.

Freeman, D. (2012) *Muslim Independent Schools: A qualitative study concerning faith-based education.* Unpublished M.Phil dissertation, Glyndŵr University.

Freud, S. (1922) *Group Psychology and the Analysis of the Ego.* London: Hogarth Press.

Gadamer, H.-G. (1975) *Truth and Method.* New York: Seabury Press.

Gallup (2009) *The Gallup Coexist Index 2009: A global study of interfaith relations,* Washington, D.C.: Gallup Poll Consulting University Press.

Gardner, M. and Engler, S. (2012) 'Semantic holism and the insider–outsider problem'. *Religious Studies* 48(2): 239–255.

Gaskin, J. C. A. (1984) *The Quest for Eternity: An outline of the philosophy of religion*. Harmondsworth: Penguin Books.

Gaskin, J. C. A. (1987) *Hume's Philosophy of Religion*. London: Macmillan.

Gates, B. (2007) 'Religious education and change'. *Resource* 29(3): 4–8.

Gearon, L. (2012) 'European religious education and European civil religion'. *British Journal of Educational Studies* 60(2): 151–169.

Geertz, C. (1973) *The Interpretation of Cultures*. New York: Basic Books.

Geertz, C. (1983) *Local Knowledge*. New York: Basic Books.

Geertz, C. (1985) 'Religion as a cultural system,' in M. Banton (ed) *Anthropological Approaches to the Study of Religion*. London: Tavistock Publishers.

Gellner, E. (1992) *Postmodernism, Reason and Religion*. London: Routledge.

Gent, B. (2009) 'Editorial'. *Resource* 31(2): 3.

Gereluk, D. (2008) *Symbolic Clothing in Schools: What should be worn and why*. London: Continuum.

Gerrish, B. A. (1984) *A Prince of the Church: Schleiermacher and the beginnings of modern theology*. London: SCM Press.

Giddens, A. (1984) *The Constitution of Society: Outline of the theory of structuration*. Oxford: Polity.

Gill, R. (1999) *Churchgoing and Christian Ethics*. Cambridge: Cambridge University Press.

Girard, R. (1986) *The Scapegoat*. Baltimore: Johns Hopkins University Press.

Glock, C. Y. and Stark, R. (1966) *Christian Belief and Anti-Semitism*. New York: Harper & Row.

Goldman, R. J. (1964) *Religious Thinking from Childhood to Adolescence*. London: Routledge & Kegan Paul.

Goldman, R. J. (1965) *Readiness for Religion*. London: Routledge & Kegan Paul.

Gorsuch, R. L. (1988) 'Psychology of religion'. *Annual Review of Psychology* 39: 201–222.

Gorsuch, R. L. and Aleshire, D. (1974) 'Christian faith and ethnic prejudice: A review and interpretation of research. *Journal for the Scientific Study of Religion* 13(3): 281–307.

Grace, G. (2004) 'Making connections for future directions: taking religion seriously in the sociology of education'. *International Studies in Sociology of Education* 14(1): 47–56.

Graham, E. (2004) 'Public theology in an age of voter apathy', in William F. Storrar and Andrew R. Morton (eds) *Public Theology for the 21st Century*. London: T. & T. Clark.

Graham, G. (2004) *Eight Theories of Ethics*. London: Routledge.

Gray, J. (1995) *Enlightenment's Wake: Politics and culture at the close of the modern age*. London: Routledge.

Gray, J. (2000). *Two Faces of Liberalism*. New York: The New Press.

Greer, J. (1985) 'Viewing "the other side" in Northern Ireland'. *Journal for the Scientific Study of Religion*. 24(3): 275–292.

Grimmitt, M. (1978) *What can I do in RE?* 2nd edn. Great Wakering, UK: Mayhew-McCrimmon.

Grimmitt, M. (1987) *Religious Education and Human Development*. Great Wakering, UK: McCrimmons.

Hacker, P. M. S. (1996) *Wittgenstein's Place in Twentieth-Century Philosophy*. Oxford: Blackwell.

Halman, L. (2001) *The European Values Study: A third wave*. Tilburg, NL: EVS: Tilburg University.

Hanson, S. (1997) 'The secularization thesis: Talking at cross purposes'. *Journal of Contemporary Religion* 12(2): 159–180.

Hardy, A. (1966) *The Divine Flame: An essay towards a natural history of religion.* London: Collins.

Hargreaves, D. (1994) *The Mosaic of Learning: Schools and teachers for the new century.* Demos Paper 8. London: Demos.

Hart, C. J. (1993) *RE Changing the Agenda.* Newcastle-upon-Tyne, UK: Christian Institute.

Harte, J. D. C. (1989) 'The religious dimension of the Education Reform Act 1988'. *Ecclesiastical Law Journal* 5 (July): 32–52.

Hay, D. (1977) 'Religious experience and education'. *Learning for Living* 16(4): 156–161.

Hay, D. (1998) *The Spirit of the Child* (with Nye, R.). London: Fount.

Hay, D., Hammond, J., Moxon, J. Netto, B., Robson, K. and Straughier, G. (1990) *New Methods in Religious Education Teaching: An experimental approach.* Harlow, UK: Oliver & Boyd.

Heaphy, B. (2007) *Late Modernity and Social Change: Reconstructing social and personal life.* London: Routledge.

Heelas, P. and Woodhead, L. (eds) (2004). *The Spiritual Revolution: Why religion is giving way to spirituality.* Oxford: Blackwell.

Hegel, G. W. F. (1956) *Lectures on the Philosophy of History.* New York: Dover.

Heiler, F. (1961) *Erscheinungsformen und Wesen der Religion.* Stuttgart: Kohlhammer.

Hempel, C. G. (1965) *Aspects of Scientific Explanation.* New York: Free Press.

Hervieu-Léger, D. (1999) *Le Pèlerin et le converti. La religion en movement.* Paris, Flammarion.

Hick, J. (1973). *God and the Universe of Faiths.* London: Macmillan.

Hirst, P. (1972) 'Christian education – A contradiction in terms'. *Learning for Living* 11(4): 6–11.

Hirst, P. (1974) *Knowledge and the Curriculum.* London: Routledge & KeganPaul.

Hobbes, T. [1651] (1998) *Leviathan.* Oxford: Oxford University Press.

Hocking, W. (1932) *Re-Thinking Missions.* New York: Harper & Brothers.

Home Office (1978) *The West Indian Community: Observations on the Report of the Select Committee on Race Relations and Immigration.* London: Home Office.

Horder, D. (1971) 'Religious education in secondary schools'. *Learning for Living* 10(4): 10–14.

Horkheimer, M. and Adorno, T. W. [1947] (2002) *Dialectic of Enlightenment: Philosophical fragments.* Palo Alto, CA: Stanford University Press.

Hubrey, D. (1960) *The Experiential Approach to Christian Education.* London: National Sunday School Union.

Hughes, F. (1998) 'Serving many masters: the place and nature of Christian nurture', paper presented at International Seminar on Religious Education and Values, Carmarthen, Wales [unpublished].

Hull, J. M. (1982) *New Directions in Religious Education.* Lewes, UK: Falmer Press.

Hull, J. M. (1991) *Mishmash: Religious Education in Multi-Cultural Britain: A study in metaphor.* Derby: Christian Education Movement.

Hull, J. M. (1992). 'The transmission of religious prejudice'. *British Journal of Religious Education* 14(2): 69–72.

Hull, J. M. (1993) *The Place of Christianity in the Curriculum: The theology of the Department for Education.* Frinton-on-Sea, UK: Hockerill Education Foundation.

Hull, J. M. (1995) *The Holy Trinity and Christian Education in a Pluralist World.* London: National Society.

Hull, J. M. (1996) 'A critique of Christian religionism in recent British education', in J. Astley and L. J. Francis (eds) *Christian Theology and Religious Education: Connections and contradictions*. London: SPCK.

Hull, J. M. (1998) 'Religion, religionism and religious education', in J. Lähnemann (ed) *Interreligiöse Erziehung 2000. Die Zukunft der Religions und Kulturbegegnung*. Hamburg: EBV-Rissen.

Hull, J. M. (1999) 'Christian boundaries, Christian identities and the local church'. *International Journal of Practical Theology* 1(1): 1–13.

Hull, J. M. (2000) 'Religionism and religious education', in M. Leicester and S. Modgil (eds) *Spirit and Religious Education*. London: Falmer Press.

Hull, J. M. (2003) 'The blessings of secularity: Religious education in England and Wales'. *Journal of Religious Education* 51(3): 51–58.

Hull, J. (2005). 'Religious education in Germany and England: The recent work of Hans-Georg Ziebertz'. *British Journal of Religious Education* 27(1): 5–17.

Hulme, P. (1990) 'The spontaneous hand of nature: Savagery, colonialism and the Enlightenment', in P. Hulme and L. J. Jordanova (eds) *The Enlightenment and its Shadows*. London: Routledge.

Hulmes, E. (1989) *Education and Cultural Diversity*. London: Longman.

Husserl, E. (1931) *Ideas: General introduction to pure phenomenology*. London: Allen & Unwin.

Institute for the Study of Islam and Christianity (2005) *Islam in Britain: The British Muslim community in February 2005*. McLean, VA: Isaac Publishing.

Institute of Christian Education (1957) *Religious Education in Schools*. London: SPCK.

Jackson, R. (1995) 'Religious education's representation of "religions" and "cultures"'. *British Journal of Educational Studies* 43(3): 272–289.

Jackson, R. (1997) *Religious Education: An interpretive approach*. London: Hodder & Stoughton.

Jackson, R. (2000) 'The Warwick Religious Education Project: The interpretive approach to religious education' in M. H. Grimmitt (ed) *Pedagogies of Religious Education: Case studies in the research and development of good pedogogic practice in RE*. Great Wakering, UK: McCrimmons.

Jackson, R. (2004) *Rethinking Religious Education and Plurality: Issues in diversity and pedagogy*. London, RoutledgeFalmer.

Jackson, R. (2008) 'Teaching about Religions in the Public Sphere: European policy initiatives and the interpretive approach.' *Numen: International Review for the History of Religions* 55(2/3): 151–182.

Jackson, R. (2011) 'The interpretive approach as a research tool: Inside the REDCo project'. *British Journal of Religious Education* 33(2): 189–208.

Jackson, R. (2012) 'European developments', in L. P. Barnes (ed) *Debates in Religious Education*. Abingdon, UK: Routledge.

Jarvis, P. (2008) 'Religious experience and experiential learning'. *Religious Education* 103(5): 553–567.

Jennings, P. (2004) *Cornwall Religious Education Survey 2004: Final Report*. Online. Available http://bit.ly/1i12gND (accessed 18 October 2013).

Johnston, C. (1996). *Christian Teachers and World Faiths*. Derby, UK: Christian Education Movement.

Jones, K. (2003) *Education in Britain: 1944 to the Present*. Oxford: Polity Press.

Kant, I. [1781](1991a) *Critique of Pure Reason*. London: Macmillan.

Kant, I. [1784] (1991b) 'What is Enlightenment?", in H. S. Reiss (ed) *Kant: Political Writings*. Cambridge: Cambridge University Press.

Kant, I. [1793] (1998) *Religion within the Boundaries of Mere Reason*. Cambridge: Cambridge University Press.

Kay, W. K. (1997) 'Phenomenology, religious education, and Piaget'. *Religion* 27(3): 275–283.

Kay, W. K. and Francis, L. J. (1996) *Drift from the Churches: Attitude toward Christianity during childhood and adolescence*. Cardiff: University of Wales Press.

Kay, W. K. and Smith, L. D. (2000) 'Religious terms and attitudes in the classroom (Part 1)'. *British Journal of Religious Education* 22(2): 81–90.

Keast, J. (2006). 'An RE for Europe'. *Resource* 28(3): 13–15.

Kepel, G. (1993) *The Revenge of God: Resurgence of Islam, Christianity and Judaism in the modern world*. Oxford: Polity Press.

Kimball, C. (2003). *When Religion Becomes Evil*. San Francisco: HarperCollins.

King, P. (1976) *Toleration*. London: George Allen & Unwin.

Knitter, P. F (1985) *No Other Name?: Critical survey of Christian attitudes towards the world religions*. London: SCM Press.

Knitter, P. F. (1995) *One Earth Many Religions: Multifaith dialogue and global responsibility*. Maryknoll, NY: Orbis Books.

Knott, K. (1986) *Hinduism in Leeds*. Community Religions Project, Leeds, UK: University of Leeds.

Kristensen, W. B. (1960) *The Meaning of Religion*. The Hague: Nijhoff.

Kuhn, T. (1970) *The Structure of Scientific Revolution*, 2nd edn. Chicago, IL: University of Chicago Press.

Kuhn, T. (1977) *The Essential Tension: Selected studies in scientific tradition and change*. Chicago, IL: University of Chicago Press.

Küng, H. (1989) 'Paradigm change in theology', in H. Küng and D. Tracy (eds) *Paradigm Change in Theology*. New York: Crossway.

Kymlicka, W. (2009) 'Categorizing groups, categorizing states: Theorizing minority rights in a world of deep diversity'. *Ethics & International Affairs* 23(4): 371–388.

Lakatos, I. (1970) 'Falsification and the methodology of scientific research programmes', in I. Lakatos and A. Musgrave (eds) *Criticism and the Growth of Knowledge*. London: Cambridge University Press.

Laplante, R. L. (1989) 'Religious education au Canada or Catholic Religious Education in Canada'. *British Journal of Religious Education* 11(3): 144–153.

Larvor, B. (1998) *Lakatos: An introduction*. London: Routledge.

Laura, R. S. and Leahy, M. (1989) 'Religious upbringing and rational autonomy'. *Journal of Philosophy of Education* 23(2): 253–265.

Leech, A. J. H. (1989) 'Another look at phenomenology and religious education'. *British Journal of Religious Education* 11(2): 70–75.

Leeson, S. (1947) *Christian Education*. London: Longmans Green

Leeuw, G. van der [1933] (1964) *Religion in Essence and Manifestation*, translated by J. E. Turner, with appendices incorporating the additions of the second German edition by Hans H. Penner. London: Allen & Unwin.

Lessing, G. E. (1957) 'The education of the human race', in *Lessing's Theological Writings*: Selections in translation. Stanford, CA: Stanford University Press.

Lewis, H. D. (1963) *Clarity is Not Enough: Essays in criticism of linguistic philosophy*. London: Allen & Unwin.

Lienesch, M. (2006) *Redeeming America: Piety and politics in the new Christian Right*. Chapel Hill, NC: University of North Carolina Press.

Lindbeck, G. A. (1984) *The Nature of Doctrine: Religion and theology in a postliberal age*. London: SPCK.

Locke, John [1689] (1955) *A Letter Concerning Toleration*. New York: Liberal Arts Press.

Loosemore, A. (1993) 'Agreed syllabuses of religious education: Past and present in England'. *Panorama* 5: 79–95.

Louden, R. B. (2007) *The World We Want: How and why the ideals of the Enlightenment still elude us*. New York: Oxford University Press.

Loukes, H. (1961) *Teenage Religion*. London: SCM Press.

Loukes, H. (1965) *New Ground in Christian Education*. London: SCM Press.

Lyotard, J.-F. (1984) *The Postmodern Condition: A report on knowledge*. Minneapolis: University of Minnesota Press.

MacIntyre (1985) *After Virtue: A study in moral theory*. London: Duckworth.

MacIntyre (1988) *Whose Justice? Which rationality?* London: Duckworth.

Madge, V. (1965) *Children in Search of Meaning*. London: SCM Press.

Marshall, B. (1994) *Engendering Modernity: Feminism, Social Theory and Social Change*. Cambridge: Polity.

Martin, D. (1993) *Tongues of Fire: Explosion of Protestantism in Latin America*. Oxford: Blackwell.

Martin, W. (2005) *With God on Our Side: The rise of the Religious Right in America*. New York: Broadway Books.

Marvell, J. (1976) 'Phenomenology and the future of religious education'. *Learning for Living* 16(1): 4–8.

Marvell, J. (1982) 'Phenomenology and the future of religious education', in J. Hull (ed) *New Directions in Religious Education*. Lewes, UK: Falmer Press.

Masterman, M. (1970) 'The nature of a paradigm', in I. Lakatos and A. Musgrave (eds) *Criticism and the Growth of Knowledge*. London: Cambridge University Press.

Matheson, J. M. (2010) *The UK population: how does it compare?: Population Trends*, No. 142, Winter. London: Office for National Statistics.

Matthews, H. F. (1966) *Revolution in Religious Education*. Oxford: Religious Education Press.

McCutcheon, F. (2001) *Religion within the Limits of Language Alone: Wittgenstein on philosophy and religion*. Aldershot, UK: Ashgate Publishing.

McGrath, A. (2008) *The Open Secret: A New Vision for Natural Theology*. Oxford: Wiley-Blackwell.

McIntyre, J. (1978) *Multi-Culture and Multifaith Societies: Some examinable assumptions*. Occasional Papers. Oxford: Farmington Institute for Christian Studies.

McKelway, A. J. (1964) *The Systematic Theology of Paul Tillich*. Richmond, UK: Lutterworth Press.

McKenzie, P. (1998) *The Christians*. London: SPCK.

McLeod, H. (2000) *Secularisation in Western Europe 1848–1914*. London: Macmillan.

Micklethwait, J. and Wooldridge, A. (2010) *God is Back: How the global rise of faith is changing the world*. London: Penguin Books.

Mill, J. S. [1859] (1972) 'On Liberty', in *Utilitarianism, On Liberty, and Considerations on Representative Government*. London: J. M. Dent & Sons.

Miller, J (2009) 'So, what do the Toledo Guiding Principles have to do with me?' *Resource* 31(2): 6–9.

Minney, R. (1975) *Of Many Mouths and Eyes*. London: Hodder & Stoughton.

Minton, D. (1987) 'Mottoes and morality: Christian ethics in the classroom', in C. Erricker (ed) *Teaching Christianity: A world religions approach*. Cambridge: Lutterworth Press.

Mitchell, C. (1984) 'Some Themes in Christian Education c.1935–60'. *British Journal of Religious Education* 6(2): 82–87.

Moran, D. (2000) *Introduction to Phenomenology*. London: Routledge.

Moulin, D. (2009) 'Challenging Christianity: Leo Tolstoy and religious education'. *Journal of Beliefs & Values* 30(2): 183–191.

Mullard, C. (1984) *Anti-Racist Education: The three O's*. Cardiff: National Association for Multiracial Education.

Nagel, T. (2012) *Mind and Cosmos: Why the materialist neo-Darwinian conception of nature is almost certainly false*. New York: Oxford University Press.

Newman, J. (1978) 'The idea of religious tolerance'. *American Philosophical Quarterly* 15(3): 187–195.

Niebuhr, H. R. (1951) *Christ and Culture*. New York: Harper & Row.

Nietzsche, F. (1967) *The Will to Power*. New York: Random House.

Northcott, M. S. (2004) *An Angel Directs the Storm: Apocalyptic religion and American empire*. London: I. B. Tauris.

ODIHR (Office for Democratic Institutions and Human Rights) (2007) *Toledo Guiding Principles about Religions and Beliefs in Public Schools*. Warsaw: ODIHR.

Office for National Statistics (2013) *Religion*. Online. Available http://bit.ly/16fpGih (accessed 17 October 2013).

Ofsted (2007) *Making Sense of Religion*. London: Ofsted.

O'Grady, K. (2005) 'Professor Ninian Smart, phenomenology and religious education'. *British Journal of Religious Education* 27(3): 227–238.

O'Grady, K. (2009) 'Honesty in religious education: Some further remarks on the legacy of Ninian Smart and related issues, in reply to L. Philip Barnes'. *British Journal of Religious Education* 31(1): 65–68.

O'Keeffe, B. (1988) 'The churches and educational provision in England and Wales', in V. Alan McClelland (ed) *Christian Education in a Pluralist Society*. London: Routledge.

Orteza y Miranda, E. (1994) 'Religious pluralism and tolerance'. *British Journal of Religious Education* 17(1): 19–34.

Osmer, R. R. and Schweitzer, F. (2003) *Religious Education in Context: New perspectives on the United States and Germany*. Grand Rapids, MI: Eerdmans.

Otto, R. (1931). *Religious Essays: A supplement to 'The Idea of the Holy'*. London: Oxford University Press.

Otto, R. [1917] (1950). *The Idea of the Holy*, London: Oxford University Press.

Parker, S. and Freathy, R. (2011) 'Context, complexity and contestation: Birmingham's Agreed Syllabuses for Religious Education since the 1970s'. *Journal of Beliefs & Values* 32(2): 247–263.

Parrinder, G. (1973) *Man and God*; *Goal of Life*; *Right and Wrong*. London: Hulton Educational.

Passmore, J. (1979) *The Perfectibility of Man*. London: Duckworth.

Peukert, D. J. K. (1999) *Max Webers Diagnose der Moderne*. Göttingen, DE: Vandenhoeck & Ruprecht.

Plantinga, A. (1983) 'Reason and belief in God', in A. Plantinga and N. Wolterstorff (eds) *Faith and Rationality*. Notre Dame, IN: University of Notre Dame.

Plato (1981) *Plato: Five Dialogues*. Indianapolis, IN: Hackett Publishing.

Poulter, S. (1990) 'The religious education provisions of the Education Reform Act'. *Education and the Law* 2(1):1–11.

Priestley, J. G. (1981) 'Religious story and the literary imagination'. *British Journal of Religious Education* 4(1): 17–24.

Prothero, S. (2007) *Religious Literacy*. San Francisco: Harper.

Prothero, S. (2010) *God is Not One: The eight rival religions that run the world – and why their differences matter*. New York: HarperOne.

Putnam, R. (2000) *Bowling Alone: The collapse and revival of community in America*. New York: Simon & Schuster.

(QCA) Qualifications and Curriculum Authority (2000) *Religious Education*. London: QCA.

(QCA) Qualifications and Curriculum Authority (2004) *Religious Education: The non-statutory national framework*. London: QCA.

Quine, W. V. O. and Ullian, J. S. (1978) *The Web of Belief*. New York: Random House.

Race, A. (1983) *Christians and Religious Pluralism: Patterns in the Christian theology of religions*. London: SCM Press.

Radford, M. (1999) 'Religious education, spiritual experience and truth,' *British Journal of Religious Education*. 21(3): 166–174.

Rawls, J. (1988) 'The priority of rights and ideas of the good'. *Philosophy and Public Affairs* 17(4): 251–276.

Reardon, B. M. G. (1988) *Kant as Philosophical Theologian*. London: Macmillan.

(RE Council) Religious Education Council of England and Wales (2005) *Towards a National Strategy for Religious Education*. London: RE Council.

(RE Council) Religious Education Council of England and Wales (2007) *A National Strategy for Religious Education*. London: RE Council.

Robinson, J. (1963) *Honest to God*. London: SCM Press.

Robson, G. (1996) 'Religious education, government policy and professional practice 1985–1995'. *British Journal of Religious Education* 19(1):13–23.

Roebben, B. (2007) 'School, religion and diversity: a West-European perspective on religious identity formation'. *Journal of Religious Education* 55(3): 39–45.

Roof, W. C. and McKinney, W. (1987) *American Mainline Religion: Its changing shape and future*. New Brunswick, NJ: Rutgers University Press.

Rorty, R. (1989) *Contingency, Irony, and Solidarity*. Cambridge: Cambridge University Press.

Rorty, R. (1991). *Objectivity, Relativism, and Truth: Philosophical Papers, Volume 1*. Cambridge: Cambridge University Press

Rorty, R. (2009) *Philosophy and the Mirror of Nature*. Princeton, NJ: Princeton University Press.

Said, E (1978) *Orientalism*. London: Routledge & Kegan Paul.

Said, E. (1989) 'Representing the colonized: Anthropology's interlocutors'. *Critical Inquiry* 15(2): 205–225.

Saussure, F. ([1916] 1995) *Course in General Linguistics*. New York: Columbia University Press.

Schlamm, L. (1992) 'Numinous experience and religious language'. *Religious Studies* 28(4): 533–551.

Schleiermacher, F. (1928) *The Christian Faith*. Edinburgh: T & T Clark.

Schleiermacher, F. (1958) *On Religion: Speeches to its Cultural Despisers*. New York: Harper & Row.

Schools Council (1971) *Working Paper 36: Religious Education in Secondary Schools*. London: Evans/Methuen.

Schweitzer, F. (2006). 'Let the captives speak for themselves! More dialogue between religious education in England and Germany'. *British Journal of Religious Education* 28(2):141–151.

Scowcroft, E. (2012) *Samaritans: Suicide Statistics Report*. Online. Available www.samaritans.org.

Scruton, R. (1981) *A Short History of Modern Philosophy: From Descartes to Wittgenstein*. London: Routledge & Kegan Paul.

Shani, G. (2007) *Sikh Nationalism and Identity in a Global Age*. London: Routledge.

Sharpe, E. F. (1975a) 'The phenomenology of religion'. *Learning for Living* 15(1): 4–9.

Sharpe, E. F. (1975b) 'The one and the many', in N. Smart and D. Horder (eds), *New Movements in Religious Education*. London: Temple Smith, pp. 191–203.

Sharpe, E. F. (1975c) *Comparative Religion: A history*. London: Duckworth.

Sharpe, E. F. (1983) *Understanding Religion*. London: Duckworth.

Sheffield Institute of Education (1961) *Religious Education in Secondary Schools: A survey and a syllabus*. London: Nelson.

Shortt, J. (1986) 'A Critical Problem for Rational Autonomy?' *Spectrum* 18(2): 107–121.

Simmonds, D. (1984) *Believers All: Book of six world religions*. Glasgow: Blackie Schools.

Slee, N. (1989) 'Conflict and reconciliation between competing models of religious education: Some reflections on the British scene'. *British Journal of Religious Education* 11(3): 126–135.

Social Justice Policy Group (2006) *Fractured Families*. Online. Available http://bit. ly/1cAUauI (accessed 17 October 2013).

Smart, N. (1958) *Reasons and Faiths*, London: Routledge & Kegan Paul.

Smart, N. (1964) *Doctrine and Argument in Indian Philosophy*. London: Allen & Unwin.

Smart, N. (1966) *The Teacher and Christian Belief*. London: James Clarke.

Smart, N. (1968) *Secular Education and the Logic of Religion*. London: Faber.

Smart, N. (1971) *The Religious Experience of Mankind*. London: Collins.

Smart, N. (1973) *The Phenomenon of Religion*. London: Mowbrays.

Smart, N. (1981) *Beyond Ideology: Religion and the Future of Western Civilisation*. London: Collins.

Smart, N. (1989) *The World's Religions*. Cambridge: Cambridge University Press.

Smart, N. (1996) *Dimensions of the Sacred: An anatomy of the world's beliefs*. Berkeley: University of California Press.

Smith, D. L. and Kay, W. K. (2000) 'Religious terms and attitudes in the classroom (Part 2)'. *British Journal of Religious Education* 22(3): 181–191.

Smith, J. W. D. (1969) *Religious Education in a Secular Setting*. London: SCM Press.

Smith, P. (2001) *Cultural Theory: An introduction*. Oxford: Blackwell.

Smith, W. C. (1978) *The Meaning and End of Religion*. London: SPCK.

Snook, I. A. (1972) *Indoctrination and Education*. London: Routledge & Kegan Paul.

Stark, R. and Finke, R. (2000) *Acts of Faith: Explaining the human side of religion*. Berkeley: University of California Press.

Stern, J. (2006) *Teaching Religious Education*. London: Continuum.

Stoll, D. (1990) *Is Latin America Turning Protestant? The politics of evangelical growth*. Berkeley: University of California Press.

Street, R. (2007) *Religious Education in Anglican Voluntary Aided Secondary Schools: moving from transmission to transformation*, unpublished PhD thesis. King's College London.

Strenski, I (2006) *Thinking About Religion: An historical introduction to theories of religion*. Oxford: Blackwell.

Swann, Lord/Department for Education and Science (1985) *Education for All: Final Report of the Committee of Enquiry into the Education of Children from Ethnic Minority Groups, under the chairmanship of Lord Swann*. London: HMSO.

Tamney, J. B. (1994) 'Conservative government and support for the religious institution: Religious education in English schools'. *British Journal of Sociology* 45(2): 195–210.

Taylor, C. (1992) *The Ethics of Authenticity*. Cambridge, MA: Harvard University Press.

Taylor, C. (2007) *A Secular Age.* Cambridge, MA: Harvard University Press.

Teece, G. (2005) 'Traversing the gap: Andrew Wright, John Hick and critical religious education'. *British Journal of Religious Education* 27 (1): 29–40.

Thiessen, E. J. (1993) *Teaching for Commitment.* Leominster, UK: Gracewing.

Thiessen, E. (2011) *The Ethics of Evangelism.* Milton Keynes, UK: Paternoster.

Thompson, P. (2004) *Whatever Happened to Religious Education?,* London: Lutterworth Press.

Tillich, P. (1948) *The Shaking of the Foundation.* New York: Charles Scribner's Sons.

Toynbee, A. (1957) *Christianity Among the Religions of the World.* New York: Charles Scribner's Sons.

Trigg, R. (1973) *Reason and Commitment.* Cambridge: Cambridge University Press.

Trigg, R. (2007) *Religion in Public Life: Must faith be privatized?* Oxford: Oxford University Press.

Troyna, B. (1987) 'Beyond multiculturalism: towards the enactment of anti-racist education in policy, provision and pedagogy'. *Oxford Review of Education* 13(3): 307–320.

Troyna, B. (1993) *Racism and Education.* Buckingham: Open University Press.

Vertovec, S. (2006) *The Emergence of Super-diversity in Britain.* Oxford: Centre on Migration, Policy and Society.

Vidler, A. R. (1966) *Soundings: Essays concerning Christian understanding.* Cambridge: Cambridge University Press.

Voas, D. (2009) 'The rise and fall of fuzzy fidelity in Europe'. *European Sociological Review* 25(2): 155–168.

Waardenburg, J. (1973) *Classical Approaches to the Study of Religion. 1: Introduction and anthology.* The Hague: Mouton.

Waldron, J. (2002) *God, Locke, and Equality: Christian foundations in Locke's political thought.* Cambridge: Cambridge University Press.

Wallace, C. (1995). 'How old is young and young is old? The restructuring of age and the life-course in Europe', Paper presented at Youth 2000: An International Conference. Middlesbrough, UK.

Warnock, M. (1998) *An Intelligent Person's Guide to Ethics.* London: Duckworth.

Watson, B. (1993) *The Effective Teaching of Religious Education.* London: Longman.

Watt, W. M. (1963) *Muslim Intellectual: A study of Al-Ghazali.* Edinburgh: Edinburgh University Press.

Westmeier, K.-W. (2000) *Protestant Pentecostalism in Latin America: A study in the dynamics of missions.* Madison, NJ: Fairleigh Dickinson University Press.

White, J. (2004) 'Should religious education be a compulsory school subject?' *British Journal of Religious Education.* 26(2): 152–164.

Whiting, J. R. S. (1983) *Religions of Man.* Cheltenham: Stanley Thornes.

Wiebe, D. (2000) *The Politics of Religious Studies.* London: Macmillan.

Williams, B. (1985) *Ethics and the Limits of Philosophy.* London: Fontana.

Wittgenstein, L. (1958) *Philosophical Investigations.* Oxford: Basil Blackwell.

Wittgenstein, L. (1963) *Tractatus Logico-Philosophicus.* London: Routledge & Kegan Paul.

Wittgenstein, L. (1976) *On Certainty.* Oxford: Clarendon Press.

Wolterstorff, N. (1984) *Reason within the Bounds of Religion.* Grand Rapids, MI: Eerdmans,

Wright, A. (2004) *Religion, Education and Post-Modernity.* London: RoutledgeFalmer.

Wuthnow, R. (2002) *Loose Connections: Joining together in America's fragmented communities.* Cambridge, MA: Harvard University Press.

Yandell, K. (1984) *Christianity and Philosophy.* Grand Rapids, MI: Eerdmans.

Yasukata, T. (2002) *Lessing's Philosophy of Religion and the German Enlightenment*. Oxford: Oxford University Press.

Young, I. M. (1990) *Justice and the Politics of Difference*. Princeton, NJ: Princeton University Press.

Ziebertz, H-G. (2003). *Religious Education in a Plural Western Society: Problems and challenges*. Münster, DE: LIT Verlag.

Zweig, C. (1995) 'The death of self in the postmodern world', in W. T. Anderson (ed) *The Truth about the Truth: Deconfusing and re-constructing the postmodern world*. New York: Tarcher/Putnam.

INDEX